Mercy and British Culture, 1760–1960

Mercy and British Culture, 1760–1960

James Gregory

BLOOMSBURY ACADEMIC
LONDON · NEW YORK · OXFORD · NEW DELHI · SYDNEY

BLOOMSBURY ACADEMIC
Bloomsbury Publishing Plc
50 Bedford Square, London, WC1B 3DP, UK
1385 Broadway, New York, NY 10018, USA
29 Earlsfort Terrace, Dublin 2, Ireland

BLOOMSBURY, BLOOMSBURY ACADEMIC and the Diana logo
are trademarks of Bloomsbury Publishing Plc

First published in Great Britain 2022
This paperback edition published 2023

Copyright © James Gregory, 2022

James Gregory has asserted his right under the Copyright, Designs and
Patents Act, 1988, to be identified as Author of this work.

For legal purposes the Acknowledgements on pp. xi–xii constitute an
extension of this copyright page.

Cover design: Terry Woodley
Cover image: *The Return of the Prodigal*, an engraving after the painting by
Alfred Rankley (1819–72). Look and Learn/Illustrated Papers Collection/
Bridgeman Images. Coloured by Rebecca Heselton.

All rights reserved. No part of this publication may be reproduced or
transmitted in any form or by any means, electronic or mechanical, including
photocopying, recording, or any information storage or retrieval system,
without prior permission in writing from the publishers.

Bloomsbury Publishing Plc does not have any control over, or responsibility for,
any third-party websites referred to or in this book. All internet addresses given
in this book were correct at the time of going to press. The author and publisher
regret any inconvenience caused if addresses have changed or sites have
ceased to exist, but can accept no responsibility for any such changes.

A catalogue record for this book is available from the British Library.

Library of Congress Cataloging-in-Publication Data
Names: Gregory, James (Historian), author.
Title: Mercy and British culture : c.1760–1960 / James Gregory.
Description: London ; New York : Bloomsbury Academic, 2021. |
Includes bibliographical references and index.
Identifiers: LCCN 2021023776 (print) | LCCN 2021023777 (ebook) |
ISBN 9781350142589 (hardback) | ISBN 9781350142596 (ebook) |
ISBN 9781350142602 (epub)
Subjects: LCSH: Mercy. | Great Britain–Civilization.
Classification: LCC BV4647.M4 G737 2021 (print) | LCC BV4647.M4 (ebook) |
DDC 241/.4–dc23
LC record available at https://lccn.loc.gov/2021023776
LC ebook record available at https://lccn.loc.gov/2021023777

ISBN:	HB:	978-1-3501-4258-9
	PB:	978-1-3502-3004-0
	ePDF:	978-1-3501-4259-6
	eBook:	978-1-3501-4260-2

Typeset by Integra Software Services Pvt. Ltd.

To find out more about our authors and books visit www.bloomsbury.com
and sign up for our newsletters.

To DECG

Contents

List of Illustrations	viii
Acknowledgements	xi
Introduction	1

Part 1 Religion, culture and embodiment

1	Mercy: Religious and philosophical dimensions	13
2	The culture of mercy in the long nineteenth century	37
3	Merciful agents and subjects	57

Part 2 Mercy challenged

4	Mercy for Ireland	77
5	British mercy and the French Revolution	95
6	Empire of mercy	105
7	The mercy of war	119
	Conclusion: Modern mercy	135

Notes	155
Select bibliography	257
Index	269

Illustrations

1.1 'St Luke Chap. X. The merciful Samaritan'. Early-eighteenth-century engraving. Author's collection. — 14

1.2 Title page of R. Cocks, *The Great Importance of a Meek and Merciful Spirit. A Sermon Preached At The Temple-Church, July 4. 1714* (London: Browne, 1714). Author's collection. — 15

1.3 First page of R. Cocks, *The Great Importance of A Meek and Merciful Spirit. A Sermon Preached At The Temple-Church, July 4. 1714* (London: Browne, 1714). Author's collection. — 16

1.4 Engraving by Charles Taylor after *Mercy and Truth* by Angelica Kaufmann, reprinted as frontispiece to A. Calmet, *Fragments Illustrative of the Manners, Incidents and Phraseology of The Holy Scriptures* (London: Charles Taylor, 1798). Author's collection. — 19

1.5 Detail of steel engraving, 'A Suttee. From a Drawing in the Possession of the Hon: E.I.Cy.' from E.H. Nolan, *The Illustrated History of the British Empire in India and the East, from the Earliest Times to the Suppression of the Sepoy Mutiny in 1859* (2 vols, London: James S. Virtue, 1858), vol.1, p.37. Author's collection. — 24

1.6 Wood engraving of 'The Car of Juggernaut', *The Mirror of Literature, Amusement and Instruction*, 24 April 1824, p.257. Author's collection. — 25

1.7 Japanese print of Kwanon reproduced in P-André Lemosine, 'Les Primitifs de l'estampe japonaise', *Gazette des Beaux Arts*, April 1909, pp.334–52 [p.337]. Author's collection. — 27

2.1 'Act of Mercy Window'. Designed by Heaton, Butler and Bayne for St Nicholas Church, Harpenden. Engraving. Author's collection. — 50

2.2 After William Etty, 'The Combat: Woman Pleading for the Vanquished'. Wood engraving *c.* 1880. Author's collection. — 51

2.3 'An Act of Mercy', after J.A. Vinter, *Illustrated London News*, 29 December 1849. Author's collection. — 52

2.4 'An Act of Mercy', engraving after Jessie Macgregor, *The Graphic*, 20 January 1872, p. 45. Author's collection. — 53

2.5 E.J. Poynter, 'Mercy. The prodigal son', colour print from L. Valentine, *The Nobility of Life, its Graces and Virtues* (London: Warne, 1869), after p.60. Author's collection. — 55

2.6	'Angels of Mercy', *The Graphic*, 3 September 1870, p.217. Author's collection.	56
3.1	'Rescue of Captain Smith by Pocahontas'. wood engraving, *Pictorial Times*, 1846, p.340. Author's collection.	58
3.2	Frank Mundell, *Heroines of Mercy* (London: Sunday School Union, 1896). Author's collection.	62
3.3	First page of *Our Merciful Brigade* no.2, June 1883. Author's collection.	65
3.4	Front cover illustration, *Band of Mercy*, December 1891. Author's collection.	68
4.1	'The Massacre of the Irish Loyalists on Wexford Bridge', engraving by Ambrose William Warren after Woodruffe, from G.C. Lyttlelton, *The History of England, from The Earliest Dawn of Authentic Record, to The Commencement of Hostilities in the Year 1803* (1804). Author's collection.	81
4.2	The Earl of Mulgrave. Portrait by H.P. Briggs, engraved by H. Robinson. (London: Fisher, Son, 1838). Author's collection.	85
4.3	'Dublin Castle as Hospital for Casualties in the Rebellion', *Illustrated War News*, 10 May 1916, p.41. Author's collection.	92
5.1	Jacques Necker (1732–1804), stipple engraving *c.* 1800. Author's collection.	97
5.2	Lithograph, *c.* 1840s. *L'enfant de Giberne. Clémence de Napoléon no.4* (Paris: A. Bes and Dubreuil). Author's collection.	101
5.3	*An Appeal for Mercy, 1798*. Engraving of the picture by Marcus Stone painted in 1876. Author's collection.	104
6.1	White metal medal of William Frederick, Duke of Gloucester as Chancellor of Cambridge University, 1811. Author's collection.	113
6.2	Benjamin Constant, '*Mercy!*' 'A Bulgarian village retaken – the Inhabitants brought before the Turkish commander', *The Graphic*, war number, 29 September 1877, pp 10–11. Author's collection.	116
7.1	Detail from steel engraving by J.C. Armytage after John Trumbull, *Death of General Warren at the Battle of Bunker's Hill, June 17, 1775* (1786), from *The History of England. With a Continuation to the Year 1859 (Present Time). From the Invasion of Julius Caesar to the End of the Reign of James II*, by David Hume; *Continued from the Reign of William and Mary to the Death of George II* by Tobias Smollett; *and from the Accession of George III to the Twenty-third Year of the Reign of Queen Victoria* by E. Farr and E.H. Nolan (3 vols; London: Virtue, 1859), vol.3, p.79. Author's collection.	123
7.2	*The Death Warrant of Major John Andre*. Steel engraving by G.R. Hall after the painting by Alonzo Chappel *c.* 1855 (New York: Martin & Johnson). Author's collection.	124

7.3 'Holy Father in Thy Mercy', postcards in a wartime series by Bamforth and Co. of Holmfirth. Author's collection. Reproduced with permission of Bamforth & Company. 128

7.4 '"Kamerad!" Bewildered Huns come out of their dugouts at Thjepval in answer to our bombs'. Realistic Travels Publishers. Author's collection. 129

7.5 'The Angel of Mercy'. One side of a stereoscopic card image. Author's collection. 131

C1 E.H. Shepard, 'The Highest Cause', *Punch*, 22 February 1939, p.211. Reproduced under licence from Punch Cartoon Library / Topfoto. 141

C2 E.H. Shepard, 'The Neglected Child', *Punch*, 21 February 1945, p.153. Reproduced under licence from Punch Cartoon Library / Topfoto. 151

Acknowledgements

This study of British culture through the perspective of mercy began by exploring the monarchy's exercise of acts of mercy over the long nineteenth century, in *The Throne of Mercy*. Here mercy is examined more widely in the British world in the last two and half centuries.

It is a pleasure to thank my colleagues at the University of Plymouth (which granted me a semester's sabbatical during which the project was formed) including Darren Aoki, Harry Bennett, James Daybell, Claire Fitzpatrick, Daniel Grey, Elaine Murphy, Angela Smith and Nick Barnett, who listened to, challenged and responded to my musings on mercy over the years. Richard Huzzey gave invaluable advice on an early draft of a section on mercy and slavery, Xavier Guégan offered telling comments on a paper exploring mercy and empire, and Sam Brewitt-Taylor shared his post-war expertise on British religion. They bear no responsibility for the final work.

Bloomsbury's anonymous reader gave me much food for thought at a late stage about the possibility that there *was* a discernible transition in the story of British mercy towards derision and irony. If I do not agree with this, I recognize the possibility that readers may also see this development in the unfolding chapters. The research was impossible without the digital cornucopias of google.books and archive.org. Apart from collections available through my university, including JISC *Historical Texts*, British Online Archives and *Mass Observation Online*, I used specialist archives such as ProQuest's *Literature Online* and *British Periodicals Collections III*; Gale's *Nineteenth Century Collections Online*, Bloomsbury's *Churchill Archives*, margaretthatcher.org, the digitized records of the Bureau of Military History (Republic of Ireland), *Old Bailey Proceedings Online* and catalogues and digitized images on the National Archives, Imperial War Museum and National Maritime Museum Collection websites. I am indebted to many other websites for access to: twentieth-century British political speeches, newsreel and film, and projects dedicated to figures such as Charles Darwin (Dr John van Wyhe's Darwin Online) and Algernon Charles Swinburne (Indiana University's Swinburne Project). Newspaper research depended on British Newspapers Archive, UKPressOnline and the National Library of Australia's Trove portal.

I am thankful to all those providers of images and books via eBay or antiquarian bookshops, who made the finding of mercy-related imagery such a pleasure. The two cartoons by Ernest Shepard from *Punch* are reproduced under licence from Punch Cartoon Library/Topfoto; and I gratefully acknowledge the permission of Ian Wallace to reproduce the two postcards produced by Bamforth of Holmfirth.

For permission to quote from Max Aitken's *Success* (1921), I am grateful to the Beaverbrook Canadian Foundation. Quotations from Vera Brittain are by permission of Mark Bostridge and T.J. Brittain-Catlin, Literary Executors for the Estate of Vera Brittain 1970. For permission to quote from Arthur Bryant's *Pageant of England 1840–1940*, published by Harper & Brothers, New York, Arthur Bryant's *Unfinished Victory*, published by Macmillan, and Arthur Bryant's 'Our NoteBook', published in the *Illustrated London News*, 27 January 1968, I am grateful to David Higham Associates. Quotation from Aldous Huxley's *Jesting Pilate* is by permission of the Aldous Huxley estate, with thanks to Cora Markowitz at the Georges Borchardt Literary Agency. Extracts are used, with permission, from *The Problem of Pain* by © C.S. Lewis Pte Ltd 1940, and 'The Humanitarian Theory of Punishment' by © C.S. Lewis Pte Ltd 1949. Quotations from Mass Observation are reproduced with permission of Curtis Brown, London on behalf of The Trustees of the Mass Observation Archive © The Trustees of the Mass Observation Archive. For permission to quote from John Cowper Powys's essay (in *The Pleasures of Literature*, 1938), I am grateful for the advice from Michael Kowalewski and the Powys Society. Quotations from the speeches of Margaret Thatcher are with the permission of the Margaret Thatcher Foundation. For permission to quote from Rex Warner's 'The Cult of Power' (1941), I am grateful to Curtis Brown. For permission to quote from Frances Brett Young, *Portrait of Clare*, published by Heinemann and *The Island*, published by Heinemann, I am grateful to David Higham Associates. For permission to quote from Lin Yutang's *Between Tears and Laughter* (1943) I am also grateful to Curtis Brown. This book, with *The Royal Throne of Mercy* in 2020, depended on the support given by Abigail Lane and her colleagues at Bloomsbury Academic and the meticulous attentions of Aarthi Babu, Shanmathi Priya Sampath, and their colleagues at Integra Software Services in Pondicherry.

I have left out of the final book for reasons of space, sections such as an exploration of mercy's handling in post-war British fiction with the notable examples of its chilling extirpation in George Orwell's *1984*, Graham Greene's dramatization of the strangeness of divine mercy in *Brighton Rock*, and J.R.R. Tolkien's *The Lord of the Rings* on the fateful mercy – or pity – of hobbits, but also taking in musings such as Arthur C. Clarke's powerful short story, 'The Star'. The book essentially ends in the 1960s. By doing so, much that might demonstrate mercy's presence in recent British popular culture, whether in television or the newspaper press, has been left for others to examine.

James Gregory, Plymouth, 2021

Introduction

The rationale and scope for a history of mercy

This book studies British culture over two centuries through the perspective of the virtue of mercy. The study is grounded in an examination of mercy's religious and philosophical treatment from the mid-eighteenth century. As an exercise in cultural history I consider mercy's artistic representations which were shaped by, and expressed, ideas about gender, race, and human and non-human nature. Mercy is a political virtue and the book examines its place in Anglo-Irish relations, in responses to the first French Revolution, during colonial rebellion in North America and in the campaign for the abolition of slavery. It explores the roles that mercy played during the Great War, and ends by outlining the varied ways it was invoked in twentieth-century Britain before and after the Second World War.

Why should a historian study mercy and why in this period? After all, while justice has attracted more scholarly attention, there are studies reflecting mercy's place in Western culture from the classical age onwards.[1] Mercy is examined in classical texts although the title of Grace Macurdy's 1940 study of Greek literature employs a phrase from *The Merchant of Venice* central to Anglophonic treatment.[2] Clemency was extolled by Seneca – as classically educated Britons of the early modern and modern periods knew.[3] Students of medieval literature and art explore mercy's representation in texts such as the fourteenth-century *Piers the Plowman* and 'acts of mercy' in Italian art.[4] Mercy figured in post-Reformation polemic: an English Protestant pamphlet ironized Popish 'mercy' and 'justice', for example. Later polemicists invoked God's mercy against the doctrines of election and predestination, while accounts of prodigies of mercy and judgement offered Christian edification.[5] Mercy was debated by Renaissance figures like Montaigne, Shakespeare and Francis Bacon, and Enlightenment thinkers.[6] Countless disquisitions and manuals for government, including the seventeenth-century Sir Edward Coke's, touch on clemency.[7] Jumbled with leniency, compassion and meekness, mercifulness was extolled in mid-eighteenth-century English guides for the fair sex.[8]

Eminent modern thinkers have considered mercy, from the eighteenth-century philosopher Immanuel Kant to the twentieth-century theologian Reinhold Niebuhr, and their thoughts on the topic are debated.[9] Mercy interests theologians, moralists, philosophers, literary experts and jurists. Mercy is brought up in responses to contemporary problems but has a word associated with Christianity lost currency in favour of more secular terms such as humanitarianism? My study ends in the 1960s, yet the word 'mercy' features in texts on legal and criminal justice themes, theology and philanthropy after this period. Figuring in modern discourse on responses to natural and man-made disasters, mercy appears in studies of hospitals and battlefield nurses, and in representing humanitarianism (United Nations or NGOs) against force or destructive conservatism.[10] Modern mercy has its squads, corps, missions and conferences.

Scholarly interest in mercy is widespread but a detailed history transcending a particular discipline (such as jurisprudence and penology) is needed. Focused on the British world, this book considers mercy's treatment in diverse forms and sites. The breadth may be foolhardy. It is banal to observe that this era was constituted by striking intellectual, artistic, political and geopolitical changes. Following a route determined by mercy-discourse offers an unfamiliar yet important focus in British culture. How did conceptions and estimations of one of the gentler virtues respond to sensibility, politeness, Evangelicalism, the Gothic Revival, and the dissolution of atonement theology?[11] How did mercy relate to empire and the ideology of domestic patriarchy? How did it appear in an era of total war and in response to fascist and Communist totalitarianism?

Defining mercy

Although dictionaries and encyclopaedias make the attempt, Nietzsche tells us: only that which has no history has definition.[12] Applying the word to certain acts is seemingly unproblematic – on the battlefield, in law courts and the reprieve and pardon of the capitally convicted – the sword's actual and metaphoric sheathing. But mercy was also due to the children of the poor according to the eighteenth-century philanthropist Jonas Hanway. There was also a growing call for mercy to animals.[13] These might be classed as 'corporal' acts, reflecting the Christian 'six acts of mercy' linked to salvation after the Last Judgement: visiting the sick, feeding the hungry, housing strangers, giving drink to the thirsty, clothing the naked and looking after prisoners (Matt. 25. 35-36). In England and Scotland after the Reformation such acts were recast as fruits of faith.[14] The consequence of this wider usage means that this study includes activities now described as humanitarian or philanthropic.

The etymology is unclear, as nineteenth-century dictionaries acknowledged, for if the accepted origin is from *misericordia*, another, found in *merx* ('a price'), linked the word through the Norman French *amerce* to remittance of punishment (in law and on the battlefield) through fine or ransom.[15] Derrida's work on the death penalty plays with the language of gratitude, forgiveness and pardoning associated with mercy / *merci* in French and English.[16] Politics and compassion combined in the pre-Christian classical understanding of mercy, where mercy figures as a 'pragmatic' political virtue. Tacitus observed that 'in the Beginning of a Reign the Reputation of Clemency is serviceable'.[17] For the classical scholar mercy was olive-garlanded with a crow – apparently the most compassionate of all birds – at her feet or perched on a staff. Drawing on Renaissance

Iconologia classicists knew the shared etymology of the Greek for charity and olive trees (*elaia / elain*).[18]

The obvious places to consider problems of definition and meaning in the eighteenth and nineteenth centuries are dictionaries (general and theological), encyclopaedias and guides to synonyms. Eighteenth-century attempts to define linked it to *sympathy*, thus with typographic nicety a definition of 1737, 'MERCY is that Affection of *Charity*, which creates in us Pain at the Miseries of others, and whereby we are inclin'd to succour and relieve them. It ariseth from *Sympathy*, or a *Fellow-feeling* of each other's Evils, naturally implanted in our Frame.'[19] In 1779 Robert Robinson wrote:

> Our best dictionaries are necessarily vague. 'Mercy,' says Dr Johnson, 'tenderness; goodness; pity; willingness to spare and save; clemency; mildness; unwillingness to punish; pardon; discretion.' Here this laborious and accurate compiler is obliged to leave the word in a general meaning, illustrated by a few pertinent examples.[20]

The *Encyclopaedia Britannica* from 1797 glossed a virtue that 'inspires us with compassion for our brethren, and which inclines us to give them assistance in their necessities'. It also meant 'those favours and benefits that we receive either from God or man, particularly in the way of forgiveness of injuries or of debts'.[21] George Crabb's expansive *English Synonymes Explained* of 1824 said the word derived from *misericordia*, 'pain of the heart' (from *miseria* and *cordis*). Mercy was applicable to all, Crabb argued, whereas leniency or clemency were directed to offenders.[22] Crabb explained 'clemency' was 'arbitrary on the part of the dispenser' and 'defeats its ends by forbearing to punish where it is needful'. *Lenity* might be glossed as the discretionary act. Mercy was also located with *humane* feeling and *compassion* and related to *grace* and *graciousness* (limited by some lexicographers to the Almighty rather than earthly rulers).[23] There was a natural 'temper' to be merciful and in Christian discourse the ideal of a disposition shaped by God's grace.[24]

The sceptical author of *The Art of Knowing Mankind* in 1766 thought mercy one of the 'glittering virtues', not to be judged from a showy presence in histories of rulers as clemency from a Caesar or Augustus did not entail being 'merciful with perseverance'. Mercy was policy to keep power or emanated from good humour, 'from the position of their body, or the good news they have heard, or some secret satisfaction of their desires and passions'; or was 'a vain ostentation of their sovereign power'. Clemency resulted from favouritism and importunity.[25] Critics of particular acts or campaigns whether monarchical or a consequence of popular pressure contrasted 'true' with 'misplaced', 'cruel', 'puling' or 'mischievous' mercy.

One of my tasks is to recover mercy in everyday speech and defined in popular or recondite texts. The expostulation 'mercy on me' became unfashionable.[26] The habit of naming females 'Mercy' (one of the characters in Bunyan's *Pilgrim's Progress*) declined. Nevertheless mercy remained in common discourse in the nineteenth century, reflecting Christian theology and scripture: the Bible-fluent spoke of bowels, seats and thrones of mercy.[27] Recovering from serious illness, devout people referenced mercy and justice.[28] The monarchical aspects of mercy's public language are explored in *The*

Royal Throne of Mercy: Britons evoked the virtue through clichés of royal metaphor in prose and poetry.

One obvious debt in this study is to Raymond Williams's idea of 'keywords' – cultural transformation through the perspective of vocabulary – although since I am interested in gesture and visual image I do not limit myself to historical semantics in texts. Williams did not examine mercy but discussed charity.[29] Mark Fortier studies a related keyword in the concept of equity, taking his examination of this important idea into the modern era. Other scholars dissect related themes such as pity and forgiveness, and the Victorian neologism of altruism.[30]

Recognition of the power of culture is central to this study: mercy and justice were performed in the theatre of law, on dramatic stages, through literary plots and painting. Mercy's routinization and bureaucratization in criminal law through the eighteenth and nineteenth centuries did not end hopes of mercy from those in power via personal means. Looking at a wider body of artefacts offers a context for this specific exercise in mercy. Though privileged as a key location for ideological formation or expression, claims on mercy were made far beyond the legal sphere.

Mercy and modern thought

Reflection on modern mercy – also characterized as clemency, parole, amnesty, or pardon – is extensive, as one might expect from a concept (or quality, or virtue) operating in many fields.[31] This is interrogated at the scale of international relations, the modern state or individual action. This section outlines how experts in philosophy, theology, ethics, penology and political thought, discussed mercy in the last half-century, in order to frame British historical discourse.[32] Such examinations often point to or explore foundational historical texts: Greek and Roman philosophers, Judaeo-Christian scripture,[33] the Fathers of the Church such as St Augustine, medieval canonists and theologians like the thirteenth-century Thomas Aquinas in *Summa Theologiae*.[34] So this perspective on modern thinking is contextualized by a brief survey of traditions of mercy.

The pre-Christian 'European' philosophical treatment of mercy saw it as an immature or emotional response. Aristotle discussed the emotion of pity in *Rhetoric*.[35] Cicero treated it as something to be directed only at those suffering unjustly but also saw the disposition as indicating wisdom and morality. The philosopher-statesman Seneca recognized mercy as interfering with justice but was more positive in *De Clementia*.[36] Medieval ideas about the virtues including mercy appeared in many texts, including Thomas Aquinas's *Summa Theologiae*, which drew upon Fathers of the Church such as Augustine, classical texts by Aristotle and Roman Stoics such as Seneca and Cicero. There was a rich theological discourse in early and medieval Christianity on the nature of divine mercy, how it related to God's essential attributes, to divine justice, and its expression in the incarnation and atonement. Moral theology examined the relationship of God's mercy to human mercy; mercy, penance and forgiveness shaped canon law. Mercy was expressed in individual and organized charity. The liturgy invoked God's or Christ's mercy; and moments for receiving God's mercy included days of penitence and jubilee years. It was also commemorated and extolled in medieval, Renaissance and Counter-Reformation Catholic art depicting the saints, Christ as lord of mercy, and *misericordia* as a crowned female.

Philosophical essays by Alwynne Smart and Claudia Card in the 1960s and 1970s explored mercy in relation to punishment. Smart was disturbed by the idea of mercy towards those committing no wrong.[37] She noted 'very little' was said about mercy in theories of punishment. This stimulated interesting debate about whether her definition was narrower than general usage, with Harry Roberts seeing a better one in 'sacrificing a personal entitlement' and emphasizing the 'gift-like' quality.[38] In 1988 Jeffrie Murphy and Jean Hampton explored mercy in criminal justice: treating it as private rather than autonomous public virtue in criminal justice. A sceptic about mercy's claims, Murphy subsequently published essays reconsidering it, and related ideas.[39] The philosopher Martha Nussbaum sought to reconcile mercy and justice through the Graeco-Roman concept of *epieikeia* or equity.[40] More recently essays by Nigel Walker and John Tasioulas examined mercy towards wrongdoers (i.e. in criminal punishment); others address the twelfth-century theologian St Anselm's well-known paradox of justice and mercy in *Proslogium* IX and XI (Ned Markosian, Bruce Marshall).[41] Tasioulas succinctly defines mercy as 'the putative ethical value that justifies leniency in the infliction of punishment that is due in accordance with justice,' and 'charitable considerations that constitute reasons for *moderating* punishment relative to what justice alone would exact'.[42] But as Markosian shows, when philosophers discuss examples they 'have such wildly divergent intuitions' about whether these exemplify mercy or non-mercy. Trying to avoid a depressing conclusion that people have no common concept, Markosian seeks a 'single, communal concept of mercy, but one that is flexible in an important way'. Earlier efforts to deal with the problem of mercy in criminal law include H. Scott Hestevold's idea of a *superogatory* moral virtue, one not obligatory but possible in the administering of justice through the concept of a 'disjunction' of just punishments from which milder punishment might be selected.[43]

Critics stress a broader application beyond the legal sphere.[44] Merciful agents, including those exercising executive power, relieve suffering or refrain from inflicting punishment and pain.[45] The religious aspect is studied by the Protestant philosopher Thomas Tallbott, whose claims for the identity of justice and mercy in God are part of an effort to argue for universalist salvation.[46] A critic, Robert Hollyer, argues against justice and mercy as synonymous, 'while we may seek to draw the two into a close relationship or claim that one is a part of the other, to equate them … only muddies the waters'.[47] Work in religious ethics has explored clemency in criminal justice.[48] Political studies include analyses of compassion (and mercy and pity) as a 'political virtue'.[49] New perspectives on the Western use of mercy come from the position of Islam.[50]

In an attempt to determine where all this research leaves us, one point to begin with is the perception of modern unfamiliarity with the religious idea. For Michael Welker, the language of 'justice and mercy' of bible and theology is outdated in secular European modernity, belonging to 'a group of religious words that sound increasingly strange to many in contemporary society'.[51] Justice is far more discussed and invoked, theologians claim.[52] In response Catholic theology reasserts the importance of mercy: Gilman, following papal re-emphasis, argues for its priority in establishing a just society.[53]

A contrasting modern approach is to reject mercy's virtuous status. Critical views of mercy's claims appear in this historical study: traceable to Aristotle, Plato and Stoic philosophers. For Enlightenment jurists such as Cesare Beccaria, reform entailed mercy's inherence in penal codes rather than by magistrates' fiat.[54] To cite Welker, 'Is this not a surplus, a luxury in well-ordered and well-functioning societies?'[55] Mercy in this critical view is in tension with justice and with laws, reflecting whim or sentiment rather than reason's application.[56] If it appears to follow rules in a legal context then mercy is a part of justice, we are told – though Nigel Walker's 'taxonomy of leniency' elegantly and succinctly examined this problem in penal justice, suggesting mercy operates as new precedents for leniency and in circumstances where discretionary decisions are needed.[57] It can be seen as the essential basis, through a long history of individual and discretionary acts, 'in the evolution of systems which ultimately make its bestowal irrelevant'. Mercy needed to exist for systems of justice to evolve.[58] Mercy may also be criticized outside criminal justice as a faulty response to social inequalities: 'associated with haughtiness, false pity or camouflage of neglected structural reforms'.[59] Its relationship to 'generalized charitable concern', in any case, means mercy cannot simply be discussed as if limited to wrongdoers whose punishment is merited.[60]

Another approach draws on evolutionary anthropology to locate compassion and empathy in 'deep human history'.[61] Anthropologists see the force of 'prosocial emotion' and 'empathy-produced altruism' in mercy in war.[62] Straight's research asserts that humans' merciful propensity 'consistently destabilizes group organized aggression'. There has also been interest in psychological aspects to forgiveness and mercy.[63]

The organization of the book

This study is organized to explore, through Part I, mercy's theological and philosophical dimensions, wider cultural representation and embodiment; as the foundations for more focused thematic treatment in the rest of the book. The first chapter surveys treatment in religious texts and, employing the term to cover both modern use and the older sense of 'scientific' inquiry, in *philosophical* texts. These range from sermonic and theological texts and keywords of religious mercy, to the response of British freethinkers, the interplay of Christian mercy discourses with the non-Christian, and Enlightenment and nineteenth-century writers on ethics and human nature. The second chapter studies treatment in imaginative and dramatic literature (stage plays, poetry and novels), and the arts of sculpture, fresco and stained glass in parliament, judicial edifices and churches. The third chapter in Part I moves from the philosophical, ideal and abstract to animate beings: studying mercy-objects like animals, children and the imperial or racial other, considering the gendering which associated mercy especially with womankind, and turning to mercy as gesture and expression.

Particular moments and sites reveal British mercy attaining heightened discursive prominence and political importance. Part II explores these, considering first in Chapter 4 its complexities in British imperialism close by, in Ireland. Chapter 5 examines mercy as something to withhold, suspend or protect during the French Revolutionary era. The tendency to present the British Empire as one of mercy (and justice) is interrogated in Chapter 6, which inevitably looks at such large-scale acts of unmercy and mercy as slavery and its abolition. Chapter 7 follows on from the global imperial and ideological conflict of the Revolution and Napoleonic era by surveying mercy in warfare in the century and a half to 1918. It does this by studying mercy's discursive use in the American War of Independence, the imperial warfare of the Victorian era and the Great War. As this penultimate chapter demonstrates, British mercy (and its absence) mattered as rhetoric and propaganda into the twentieth century, and as a lens for viewing acts of philanthropy and humanitarianism.

The conclusion to this study offers an overview from c. 1918 to the 1960s. Mercy's cultural history was not dramatically altered by the slaughter of 1914–18. Exploring discursive uses in the interwar period, wartime and beyond, makes one appreciate its remaining force as moral ideal and practice against enemies revelling in mercilessness and pitilessness; through attempts to restore its operation in post-war European and global settlement; and in discourse of Britain's own unmercy offered by critics of imperialism. Instabilities, in the gendering of mercy allegedly brought about by female emancipation or through eugenicist debate on 'mercy killing' are noted, alongside an exploratory treatment of mercy's presence in art and literature of the first half of the twentieth century.

A historiography of mercy

Since this study explores mercy in the context of such subjects as capital punishment, the anti-slavery campaign, British rule in Ireland and its place in histories of warfare, it will be appreciated that a brief essay in historiography is selective. The historiography of royal mercy is explored in more detail in *The Royal Throne of Mercy* but it is important to note here the studies of medieval and early modern monarchy focused on the politics of mercy by Helen Lacey on fourteenth-century England; Krista Kesselring on the Tudors and Kevin Sharpe on the Stuarts.[64] For the eighteenth century there is Douglas Hay's famous essay in *Albion's Fatal Tree* in 1975.[65] 'Men were merciful and merciless … the historian's task is to answer the questions when, and why,' Hay wrote.[66] He argued that the paternal king who tempered justice with mercy was a distinctive element of criminal law as 'ideological system' before nineteenth-century reform. It 'encouraged loyalty to the king and the state.'[67] Essays in Carolyn Strange's edited collection look at the politics of mercy through British, Australian and Canadian histories. For Strange, since the decline of monarchy, the concept 'acquired an increasingly old-fashioned ring' yet was linked to democratic rule as a popular 'right' exercised by the Crown.[68]

The scholarship on British ideas about mercy looks at cultural artefacts from the theatre (text and performance) and non-dramatic literature, such as religious poetry or novels.[69] Public acts of mercy, real or dramatized, figure largely in this study; I am also interested in human emotion, as well as Christian virtue and divine attribute. What could be more political than the 'emotional politics' of mercy in the eighteenth-century State? The historiography of collective emotions was encouraged by Lucien Febvre's call to create a history of pity beside other 'fundamental sentiments of man and the forms they take'.[70] Histories of the sentiments subsume mercy in related virtues like pity, compassion, benevolence and associated 'humanity'.[71] The rich scholarship developed by literary scholars concerned with understanding changing sensibility and feeling is obviously relevant when charting changes in mercy discourse. Works on eighteenth-century philosophy discuss ideas about pity in human nature.[72] Where did mercy figure in an age of sentiment that witnessed the Terror and transatlantic slavery?[73] How mercy related more broadly to histories of civility and the 'civilizing process' might also be explored: scholars of capital punishment relate this (linked to state exercise of mercy and amelioration of punishment potentially framed as reform in mercy's direction) to the work of Norbert Elias.[74]

Nicole Eustace's work on emotion in eighteenth-century Pennsylvania views mercy from politics, political philosophy and everyday emotional exchanges. In the 'rising tempest of emotion', during the Age of Reason, mercy was a benevolent shared feeling by contrast to 'judgemental' pity.[75] Words for these feelings (mercy, pity, compassion and sympathy) seem synonymous but 'differed subtly but significantly one from another' and in their prominence, over time.[76] Usage reflected 'hierarchical relationships' with 'mercy' unambiguously expressing a clear and immediate relationship to power: bestowed by God, by earthly governor or judge, or simply by those who seized power.[77] For Eustace, its verbal appearance was 'in very particular situations'. 'Sympathy', by contrast, was a shared feeling among peers, its rise in print culture a reflection of an egalitarian ethos as cultural ideal.[78]

Mercy in the archives and historical record

The sources mined for mercy references were largely studied through digitized collections of books, newspapers, periodicals and pamphlets, mostly of the eighteenth and nineteenth centuries. Novels, plays, poetry and song collections were turned to, for significant or representative treatment. Monographs on theology, philosophy, anthropology and ethnography were looked at. I studied periodicals associated with Christian missionaries, animal-welfare bodies, freethinkers, radicals, socialists and the right wing. Speech referring to mercy, including sermons and debates, are preserved as texts. The modern genres of detective, fantasy and science fiction were surveyed although a brief analysis of post-war fiction has had to be excised for reasons of space: scholars have begun exploring speculative fiction's role in forming new and complex understandings of justice.[79]

To turn to another source type – life-writing – the record and judgement on merciful disposition includes biography and historiography. Where character was exposed or extolled, a capacity for the 'crowning grace' of mercy might be referenced.[80] Especially when there was a reputation for cruelty to combat, biography is a rich seam of discourse (e.g. regarding Oliver Cromwell or Napoleon Bonaparte).[81] It was also esteemed in lesser subjects, in the words of one Scottish Episcopalian, 'gentler traits of nature ... what so interesting as the most powerful intellect in its moments of pity, and when softened into a tender compassion'.[82] Pious biography and autobiography frequently mention mercy: to quote Barbara Burn of Hull's eulogy in 1812, 'she would often look back, and help them to record many a past mercy; for *mercy* was her delightful and darling theme.'[83] Studying such works moves us from public acts, those themes explored in the second part of the book, to those 'small mercies' which the pious were asked to be thankful for in their lives.[84]

I am interested in visual and three-dimensional rendering of acts of mercy and attempts to express the virtue in art. Periodicals reviewing long-forgotten artworks offer access to reception of sculpture, history painting, stained-glass memorial and allegorical fresco. Image digitization allows one to see some of the representations confronting worshippers, attendees at courts of justice and recipients of improving religious prize books. Mercy is rarely alone here, as elsewhere, she partners justice, or other virtues, attributes and qualities. The study of these cultural productions indicates the conventional or original in artistic presentation. In the final two chapters, through newsreel and celluloid dramatizations of acts of mercy during the Great War and interwar era, cinematic representation is considered.

As this overview of sources suggests, the archive is appallingly large. My earlier study of royal mercy brought in private and official correspondence in the royal archives and to a lesser extent, the criminal justice records of government. The word 'mercy' may appear in family correspondence, in notes and manuscript essays on religious, ethical or historical topics debated or rehearsed in such places as school, university and mutual improvement clubs in the nineteenth century. Private thoughts on mercy are accessible in some cases through published diaries and letters.[85] A survey of county record office and other archival catalogues does not suggest mercy discourse is picked up in the process of describing archival collections. Time, funds and books having their limits, for this study I preferred printed discourse to manuscript archives.

In tracing discursive histories, I am aware that mercy as an abstract quality is frequently cited alongside or contrasted with other concepts (e.g. cruelty). The word's frequency and lexical associations need to be considered in particular corpora: for discursive patterns of association and appreciation of the dominant, conventional and unusual ways of handling it. A model for this methodology in Anglo-American discourse is Eustace's *Passion Is the Gale*. Alongside 'relational' emotional history through family papers, she charts the fortunes of terms like 'pity', 'compassion', 'sympathy' and 'mercy' in the *Pennsylvanian Gazette* from 1728 to 1800. Mercy was the most frequent synonym for shared feeling (though in decline; while 'sympathy' increased in usage), and reflected dominance and dependence.[86] On a smaller scale Esme Cleall indicates the language of justice's complexity in the imperial context of nineteenth-century Indian missionary discourse.[87] I studied clusters of words around mercy through various databases: these clusters reflect the type of material curated, such as *Nineteenth Century Collections Online*'s collection on 'religion, society, spirituality and reform', and poets' treatment via *Literature Online*.[88]

I study in detail the relationship of the monarchy to British cultures of mercy in *The Royal Throne of Mercy*, which covers the period c. 1700–1910 but has its focus in the Victorian era. The gendered associations made between mercy and a female monarch whose long reign coincided with the unprecedented physical might and cultural force of the British Empire, offered a new way of thinking about the much-examined matriarch. The role of monarchs in appeals to and performance of mercy does figure in the present study: whether it be appeals made to the king during rebellion in the

American colonies and characterization of George III as unmerciful tyrant; in anti-slavery agitation; and Victoria's rhetorical place in Irish nationalist demands for the release of Fenian prisoners, though I have had to curtail a more extensive treatment of the queen's actual interventions (as documented in the Royal Archives) in this particular episode in Anglo-Irish relations. The two books were written together, but whereas the first reflects my interest in the monarch's global reach (noting, for example, the Antipodean circulation of myths of the young queen's merciful proclivities), it is this second book which provides the wider thematic, geographical and chronological focus to interrogate mercy in the British world. Nevertheless, in the course of reading this book it should be remembered how useful was the figure of the earthly ruler for conveying theology in simple terms. Mercy was a central attribute of monarchs, and yet, as one sermonist argued, 'in loving mercy all may cultivate a royal spirit'.[89] The chapters in Part I provide the context in a broader cultural history, for our understanding of the embodiment of mercy by Britons and for that exercise in monarchical mercy. Through religion and moral philosophy, and expressed in diverse artistic forms, mercy was a theme to console, disturb or entertain Britons.

Part One

Religion, culture and embodiment

1

Mercy: Religious and philosophical dimensions

Mercy is a religious word. This chapter establishes its religious and philosophical foundations in our period, beginning with the central theme of Christian mercy, its appearance in confessional polemics and responsiveness to changes in religious thought (and feeling) during the Victorian period. The chapter then shows the ways mercy was defined against the non-Christian other and how religions were reported by British writers as answering the challenge from missionary efforts presenting Christianity as *the* religion of mercy. In this aspect mercy is viewed within imperial and orientalizing contexts returned to in a later chapter focused on anti-slavery. The final chapter in Part I also considers racial, ethnic or national framings through subjection to British mercy. It follows from Christian prosleytism abroad and at home that nineteenth-century free-thought was interested in debating the faith's 'mercy claims'. There is another dimension to thinking about mercy in a profound way, a philosophical dimension owing something to Christian traditions (as 'moral philosophy') or seeking classical and non-religious bases. So this chapter ends by considering Enlightenment examination of mercy as virtue and emotion, and nineteenth-century 'scientific' commentary upon, or use of mercy.

Mercy and British Christianity

The new Dispensation under which we live, left the old Infinite Anger where it was, and brought forward an Infinite mercy, for ever to neutralise it. And now does not something like a climax stand out clear before us? For how could this great belief in Mercy, which is subduing the human heart to an unutterable tenderness – how could it have appeared in the world but for its antecedents, the reign of Divine Anger and of Judgment? The three great ideas of Anger, Judgment, and Mercy are blended together most conspicuously in our own faith.[1]

So asserted the scripturally minded Alexander Alison in an ambitious (reviewers said presumptuous and pretentious) history of civilization in 1860.[2] Human mercy was the mundane version of a divine attribute and imagined as fundamental to Christian faith (see Figure 1.1). It might be maintained that the 'natural man [was] insensible of mercy': though I discuss shortly how British writers imagined it in a non-Christian state.[3] The *Evangelical Magazine and Missionary Chronicle* told readers in 1799 'no

Figure 1.1 'St Luke Chap. X. The merciful Samaritan'. Early-eighteenth-century engraving. Author's collection.

perfection of Deity [was] more celebrated in scripture than that of Mercy' but other evangelicals stressed judgement too.[4] The Wesleyan John Leifchild, lecturing on the Beatitudes in the early 1820s, contrasted the disposition in human nature (and the 'very dictates of humanity ... the voice of nature in our bosom') with its superior form as Christian mercy.[5] To an audience of philosophers, the Anglican clergyman William Irons stated in 1869 that there was 'no known law' of mercy in nature and that a 'fitting Mercy' depended on faith in a 'true' revelation.[6]

Thinking about the nature of God involved contemplating the nature of mercy and justice at the Last Judgement and before. Could God be described as merciful without objects to be merciful to (so 'A.B.' inquired of the *London Magazine* in 1768)?[7] How were cruelty and injustice explicable?[8] Was divine mercy general or particular? As an attribute of divinity, mercy was much debated in Christian literature. It figured in religious encyclopaedias and dictionaries, such as John Fleetwood's *Christian Dictionary* of 1775.[9] A religious dictionary of the 1820s described mercy as 'affectionate pity to such as are in misery and distress and readiness to do them good' and 'kind acts

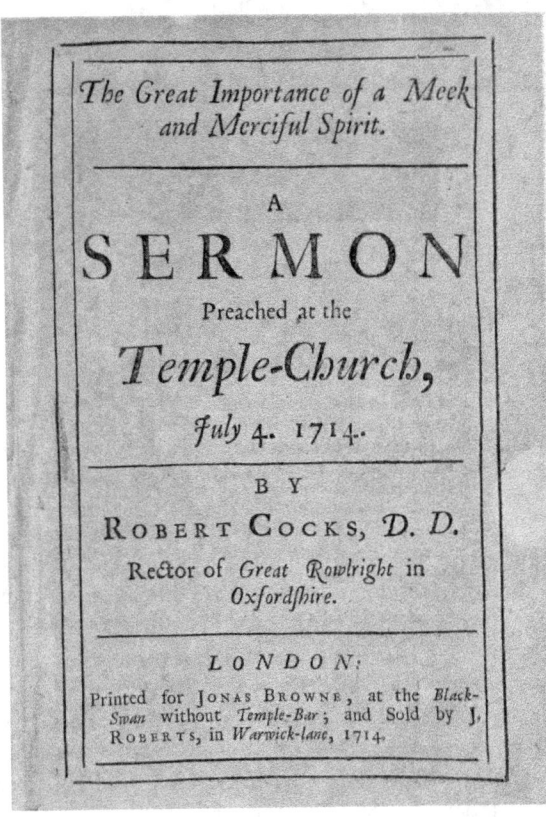

Figure 1.2 Title page of R. Cocks, *The Great Importance of a Meek and Merciful Spirit. A Sermon Preached at the Temple-Church, July 4. 1714* (London: Browne, 1714). Author's collection.

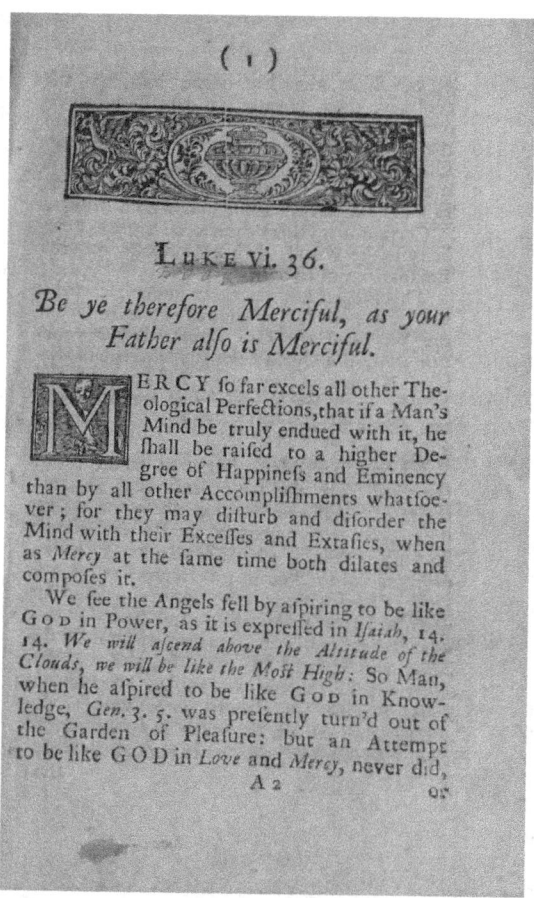

Figure 1.3 First page of R. Cocks, *The Great Importance of a Meek and Merciful Spirit. A Sermon Preached at the Temple-Church, July 4. 1714* (London: Browne, 1714). Author's collection.

proceeding from inward compassion and desire to relieve such as are in pity and want'.[10] The reference to affection reminds us God's mercy might be an emotion – Eustace describes it as God's 'most salient emotional attribute (apart from anger)'.[11] Works of moral exemplification contained models of mercy or clemency.[12] The burgeoning denominational periodicals reprinted discussion.[13] Sermons were important vehicles: printed for readers to have detailed discussion of texts like Matthew v.7, 'Blessed are the merciful,' or Luke 6. 36 (see Figure 1.3).[14] A character in a novel published in 1920 asserted that 'the English nation's character has been very largely created merely by hearing in church, Sunday after Sunday, from childhood to old age, such words as grace, mercy, pity, loving kindness, and humility'.[15]

There were providential acts of mercy and justice. Natural calamities like famines and shipwreck were balanced by humanity's preservation from merited retribution.[16] People even argued that infant death was a mercy ('to prevent the accumulations of crimes'), which the eighteenth-century poet Anna Seward thought 'not entirely reconcilable to God's justice'.[17] The habit of seeing 'divine mercies', associated in the nineteenth century with evangelical Protestants, has a longer history. There were compilations by seventeenth-century clergymen, and hack writers such as Robert Burton, author of *Wonderful Prodigies of Judgment and Mercy* (reaching an eighth edition in 1729), and J.S.'s *Divine Judgment and Mercy Exemplified* (reprinted in 1746). Burton said he published 'in this Age, wherein Atheism and Impiety so much abound', and in J.S.'s case, he meant to *'startle some that are* Atheistically Inclin'd'.[18]

Poetry and prose expressed gratitude for divine mercy after natural disasters.[19] One might see God's mercy operating across nature, as John Grose argued in 1783, when asking for mercy 'so obscure in a private sphere, and so superlatively excellent in an exalted station', to be contemplated not only in 'civil or political procedure', but in 'astonishing display ... through universal nature'.[20] Writers who discussed mercy for the laity included Jean-Joseph Languet de Gergy (1677–1753), a French Catholic whose work, translated, was praised into the Victorian era.[21] The non-conformist minister John Hayter Cox's 'well known and extensively circulated' *Jesus shewing Mercy* (1814) addressed those objections which 'gloomy minds, that love to contemplate judgment rather than mercy, are apt to throw in the way of their own hope'. Later works of religious instruction on the theme included James Culross's *Divine Compassion; or, Jesus Shewing Mercy*.[22]

Christians believed all were guilty and needed God's mercy. In the words of a hymn by the pious Sandemanian, cousin to Johnson's biographer, and a writer to the signet in Edinburgh, Robert Boswell, we find: 'Sweet, sweet's the mercy | That doth to guilty mortal flow, | Sweet, sweet is mercy | To the wretched sons of men | When hope was gone, then mercy shone! | God sent His well-beloved Son | Who did at once for sin atone, | And saved the sons of men!'[23] Thomas Watson, rector of St Stephen's Walbrook, in *A Body of Practical Divinity* (1759) argued that 'God's mercy is one of the most orient pearls of his crown, it makes his Godhead appear amiable and lovely'.[24] How divine mercy was imagined in discourse around the capitally convicted and executed is highly significant to my study. Theological texts, hymns and sermons touched on mercy in this context.[25] William Johnson Fox, a prominent Unitarian preacher and writer, in 1813 asserted that theologians, indeed, needed to look to poets' celebration of monarchical mercy for some sense of the divine capacity – 'Is he a governor, and may he not claim that sweet prerogative, the right of showing mercy, which every earthly prince enjoys?'[26] An American journal in 1825 published verse 'On hearing Mr. — preaching the terrors of the law' putting it pithily: 'Jehovah, slandered, looks indignant down, | Mercy, the brightest jewel of his crown'.[27] Abolitionists naturally quoted scripture, thus 'Gamma', in the *Baptist Magazine* in 1839, headed an essay with 'mercy rejoiceth against judgment' from James ii. 13.[28] The sermon of the Newgate gaol clergyman (before the execution of the eighteen-year-old William Marchant for murdering his fellow servant Eliza Paynton in 1839) imagined the penitent convict 'welcomed to the heavenly abode by 10,000 angels, and become a trophy of sovereign grace, and add another jewel to the diadem of mercy'.[29]

In 1775 the Baptist Robert M'Gregor used a familiar situation in the Bloody Code era, to convey divine mercy's operation: 'Suppose that out of twenty found guilty, his Majesty King George should pardon ten, he is not the cause of the other ten being executed. It was his clemency that pardoned any: it was their breaking the laws of the kingdom that condemned them and not his Majesty.'[30] There is the splendid allegory by the leading popular moralist, Hannah More, in the 1790s: 'THE GRAND ASSIZES; OR GENERAL GAOL DELIVERY, AN ALLEGORY'. It concerned a

> great King, who was also a Judge ... His subjects were apt enough, in a general way, to extol his merciful temper, and especially those subjects who were always committing crimes which made them particularly liable to be punished by his justice. This last quality they constantly kept out of sight, till they had cheated themselves into a notion that he was too good to punish at all.[31]

The devotional guide of the dissenting minister Robert Philip of Maberly chapel in London linked earthly and divine rulers in the 1830s: 'If a good king would reckon it his chief glory to have no death-warrants to sign, well may we believe that the God of Love does not seek his glory from "second-death" warrants.'[32] Others used this simile. Assize sermons analogized these warrants to God's mercy.[33]

Victorians inherited the ideas of a mercy seat and heavenly throne of mercy, as I note elsewhere.[34] They were told that God set the rainbow to remind mankind of His mercy though natural philosophy described a natural phenomenon. Those who studied Revelations knew God's perception as a rainbow of jasper green, symbolizing the covenant of mercy.[35] The medieval period popularized the idea of mercy as one of the four daughters of God, debating humanity's fate in a 'parliament of heaven'. In this tradition, Milton's sketches for *Paradise Lost* included a debate between mercy, justice and wisdom.[36] In the early nineteenth century mercy was depicted in a tale of redemption by the Calvinist Christmas Evans cited as an example of 'Welsh eloquence' in periodicals as diverse as the *London Jewish Expositor* and *Methodist Review*.[37] Angelica Kauffman's depiction of mercy and truth was printed in 1780 (see Figure 1.4, note the rainbow). William Blake also limned mercy and truth, and reflected on mercy alongside pity, peace and love, in a verse entitled 'The Divine Image'. For Blake, mercy and other qualities or 'virtues of delight' were part of the 'human form divine' wherein God was dwelling too.

The Scottish Presbyterian and founder of the Catholic Apostolic Church, Edward Irving, who died in 1834, treated mercy in violent and shocking fashion. His lecture on Luke 3, Matthew 14 and Mark 6 (delivered in 1823) disrupted the idea of the preacher as 'all grace and mercy ... masculine truth ... lisp[ing] in accents of courtesy', and imagined mercy 'too soft for this hard and flinty world to have been sent from heaven alone', her bosom pierced and her outstretched arms nailed to an 'accursed tree'. So God sent 'the terrible form of justice, with his arm revealed; and hand in hand they go over the populous earth, from city to city'.[38]

From the British mid-nineteenth century there was a transition from a forensic God of the atonement – judging and imposing everlasting punishment – to a God,

Figure 1.4 Engraving by Charles Taylor after *Mercy and Truth* by Angelica Kaufmann, reprinted as frontispiece to A. Calmet, *Fragments Illustrative of The Manners, Incidents and Phraseology of The Holy Scriptures* (London: Charles Taylor, 1798). Author's collection.

merciful towards the sinner, whose universe excluded an eternal hell.[39] The seventh chapter of that 'epoch in the history of opinion', *Essays and Reviews*, noted in 1860 a shift 'from the justice of God to the mercy of God'.[40] The transition might be understood as a distinction between Old and New Testaments: a contrast made in many places, for instance a sermon by Samuel Maberley in 1876, where Moses in judgement was contrasted with Jesus in mercy. It was not enough for the erring man to *repent*: Christ's mediation was required.[41]

John Seeley's famous *Ecce Homo* (1866) emphasized mercy's role in Christ's 'legislation'.[42] Another important text is the Anglican clergyman Frederic William Farrar's *Mercy and Judgement* (1881) asserting the hopefulness of Christian teaching about God's mercy in the life to come and arguing that the whole drift of Scripture supported his view.[43] 'Preachers', the Positivist critic of orthodoxy James Morison commented in 1887, 'prefer to dwell on the cheerful and bright side of religion'.[44] Newspapers noted the call in 1876 by William Magee, the Anglican Bishop of Peterborough, for a more 'thoughtful' mercy. Despite the appearance of a Christian England 'saturated with this feeling of mercy, and where there appeared to be no lack of merciful help to those who needed it', from social life and politics to modern literature, Magee questioned the reality of this mercy.[45]

In denominational conflict Protestants evoked the fearful Inquisition to deny the characteristic of mercy to Catholics. Take the Religious Tract Society, equating the Inquisition with 'the worship of Moloch ... the ancient sacrifices of savage Druidism', rather than the 'truth which proclaims mercy to all'.[46] The diplomat and Catholic apologist Joseph de Maistre, in letters written *c*. 1815 (translated for a British audience in 1838), presented the Catholic priesthood, preaching mercy and clemency, as untainted by bloodshed, and the Inquisition as a place uniquely of mercy and justice, unlike the judges of civil courts, through the 'priesthood of the true Church', able to exercise a 'sovereign prerogative' apart from monarchs. Despite the 'frightful display of the inquisitorial apparatus' mercy had precedence.[47]

The convert Kenelm Henry Digby's *Mores Catholici* (1831–42) ventured a wider argument about loss of charity, love and mercy in Protestantism: 'The whole form and tone of society was reversed; mercy was stigmatized as prevarication, all pity choked with custom of fell deeds.'[48] A 'supernatural display of mercy' was lost with the departure from faith.[49] The number of merciful people had not increased since then.[50] Yet Catholics and non-Calvinist Protestants shared common ground in rejecting Calvinist predestination.[51] Thomas Chalmers of the Free Kirk criticized Calvin for treating the divine message of mercy 'in the spirit of an incensed polemic ... of severe and relentless dogmatism'.[52]

Unsurprisingly, given its roots in Luther's rejection of salvation through works, Victorian evangelicalism was ambivalent: disputing 'any merit in works of mercy', according to a character in the Anglo-Catholic Charlotte Yonge's *The Three Brides* in 1876.[53] Yet there was a duty to follow the 'path of mercy', to use Henry Manning's phrase – a clergyman who journeyed from evangelicalism through High Church to Catholicism, and who wrote about the 'works of mercy which lie about our homes' in a tract during the Irish famine, *What one work of mercy can I do this Lent?*[54] The claims of the Sabbath also called for 'pleas of mercy' in infringements such as train or postal service.

Protestant evangelicalism saw the church as founded on redeeming mercy through Christ.[55] Saving man from his 'utter worthlessness and sinfulness' was the unmerited goodness of God, yet man was the chosen 'vessel of mercy'.[56] As one historian observes, the evangelicals 'brought to the contemplation of goodness and mercy something warmer than intellectual assent'.[57] Their diaries, memoirs, wills, periodicals, tracts and hymns are fulsome about divine mercy, merciful recoveries or escapes, and the obligation to convey a message of mercy.[58] Sarah Trimmer, a prominent writer, recorded such great mercies as mere bruising after falling down stairs in April 1797. Another, Hannah More, interpreted surviving a fall during a fainting fit as a 'visitation ... in mercy'. The anti-slavery abolitionist Thomas Fowell Buxton recorded in a memorandum the 'great and immediate mercy', during a bilious fever in 1813.[59] 'Ah!' reflected Edward Bickersteth, who became a leading evangelical, to his parents in 1813, 'of how little value is every mercy and blessing, if we do not enjoy God in them, as the Source of, all, and the best mercy of all'.[60] William Wilberforce's highly influential *Practical View of the Prevailing Religious System of Professed Christians* (1797), necessarily said much on mercy, contrasting worldly and complacent hope for the 'clemency of God, and the mercy of our Redeemer' despite our weaknesses and infirmities with a 'true Christian humiliation' and the emotional state in which true Christians would, 'like the apostles', speak fervently about the 'riches of His unutterable mercy' and throw themselves 'with deep prostration of soul at the foot of the cross, there to obtain pardon'.[61]

The nineteenth century witnessed the creation of several organizations and religious serials referencing mercy. Apart from animal welfare Bands of Mercy there were *Heralds* and *Echoes of Mercy* (the periodical established by the Scottish evangelist Duncan Mattheson and a late-nineteenth-century Plymouth Brethren periodical, respectively[62]). There were 'houses of mercy' and from the 1840s there were Anglican Sisters of Mercy, depicted by the 'Young England' aristocrat John Manners in a poem, 'England's Trust,' as 'gliding forms of purest white' who supplied a missing jewel in England's coronet.[63]

A final area to consider in outlining the religious dimension is the claim of British agency for diffusing a religion of mercy and justice through missionaries. Was mercy intrinsic to the Victorian conception of imperial faith – its 'temper and spirit'? Scriptural precepts about peace and goodwill, and 'blessed are the merciful: for they shall obtain mercy' – how often did they figure in defence of empire? I look closer at the relationship between Europeans and non-Christian religious ideas of mercy (and European misconceptions) in the next chapter and return to justifications for empire in Chapter 6. Some initial comments are worthwhile.

The mercy discourse has been little attended to by scholars, although recent work explores varied ways (theological, moral, legal, administratively) in which 'justice' figured in missionary writings and practice, and identifies its associations with concepts of mercy and 'humanity'.[64] The evangelicals' Church Missionary Society in 1812 spoke of establishing an 'empire of mercy'.[65] Elsewhere we hear of bringing converts into the 'precincts of Mercy'.[66] CMS reports, unsurprisingly, are replete with divine mercy and cast the enterprise in this light: contributions creating a 'Fund of Christian mercy' and local associations expressing a 'proper sense of their own infinite obligations to Divine Mercy'.[67] As with other religious texts, it was assumed only Christianity offered mercy that was abundant or 'without caprice'. Practical works of mercy could be presented as activities to be emulated by non-Christians.[68] There were reflections, too, on compassion's role in motivating missionaries.[69] Tracts presented the gospel message as one of mercy: a missionary in the religious novel *Prsanna and Kamini. The History of a Young Hindu* asserted, 'let your conscience and your heart judge in which religion justice and mercy are to be found'.[70] All medical work might be seen as works of Christian mercy, but there were also medical missionary activities.[71] In *Mercy and Truth*, the CMS's medical mission journal, mercy preceded and prepared the way for the truth.[72]

Debating Christian mercy: The arguments from infidelity

Do we want to contemplate his mercy? We see it in his not withholding that abundance even from the unthankful.[73]

If Mr. Paine was able to draw these principles of justice, mercy, and good will to men, from the Deistical Religion, he did more than any man ever did before, or at the time he lived. It seems that the French people failed to draw the same conclusions, at the same time, that he did from this religion. If they had, the world probably would have been spared the pitiable spectacle which it was called upon to behold during the bloodstained scenes of their revolution. Can any man read the accounts of that revolution, and say that Deism teaches justice, mercy, and good will to men?[74]

This merciful God of the Christians has always acted contrary to all our ideas of goodness and mercy.[75]

Unbelievers vainly boast of entertaining higher ideas of GOD's *mercy*, than those whom they oppose.[76]

It follows from the centrality of atonement and satisfaction in Christianity in our period, that mercy was debated in the literature on infidelity. The first quotation in this section is from Thomas Paine's *Age of Reason* (1794–5), followed by the Californian William Wood's response in an essay on infidelity (1862). The third comment is from a speech by the infidel William Reid during a celebration of Paine's birth, published in the infidel Richard Carlile's *The Republican* in 1825.[77] Carlile's periodicals are rich in discussion and allusion to Christian mercy. The nineteenth-century critique of atheism defended orthodox views of divine mercy (the final quotation is from the erstwhile Church of Ireland Reverend John Walker in 1806, who established a Sandemanian chapel in Dublin). 'What better proof can be desired to establish the hypocritical pretensions of its notorious advocates,' wrote Thomas Ryley Perry – martyr in the free-thought cause – in *The Republican* in 1825, 'than their continual preaching, mercy! mercy! and yet exhibiting no signs of it themselves, if called upon to exercise that beautiful and benignant feeling.'[78] Early-nineteenth-century freethinkers discoursed on the extent to which their notion of a supreme being was related to mercy.[79] As atheists they experienced lack of mercy when the state prosecuted blasphemers.[80] They attacked the penal system: 'Humanitas' in Carlile's *The Lion*, on 'The Cruelty and Absurdity of the Criminal Code of Laws in England' in 1829, for example, quoting the seventeenth-century poet John Denham, 'Justice, when equal scales she holds, is blind; | Nor cruelty, nor mercy, change her mind; | When some escape for that which others die, | Mercy to those, to these is cruelty.'[81]

Carlile thought justice a better word and denied that to be merciful was to be Christian or that the merciful obtained mercy: 'I have not found it so, in my dealings with Christians,' he wrote from Dorchester gaol in 1824.[82] His understanding of the imagery of mercy, and esteem for the virtue, appear in the (posthumous) *Manual of Freemasonry*'s recognition of the symbolism of the 'point' of mercy in masonic orders of chivalry.[83] Carlile's prominence led to anti-infidel writers combatting him, including tackling divine justice and mercy. The Irish dissenting minister Alexander Carson's *Letter to Mr Richard Carlile* (1820) discussed the unmixed, free and sovereign nature of God's mercy, and explained why a mercy which saved one and passed by another was so objectionable to men. 'Men will make God as accountable to them for the exercise of his mercy, as they are accountable to him in the exercise of his justice' … 'Now, sir, were the gospel a forgery, would not the mercy of God be represented in it agreeably to the common views of that attribute?'[84] For Carson the problem of mercy even to 'many called Christians', was an argument for gospel truth.

In tract and public debate, the mercy and mildness of Christianity was a central polemical theme. Lloyd Jones, the Owenite missionary, for example, debating with the Methodist Joseph Barker in the late 1830s, denied the gospel system was one of 'love, of mercy, and of gentleness throughout'. Barker asserted religion made men 'valiant in the cause of truth and mercy'.[85] The Congregationalist John Angell James distinguished between mercy, the merciful disposition of deist or atheist, and the effect 'natural loveliness of disposition without religion may have in lessening the torments of hell'.[86]

Deism was perceived by Christian apologists as weak in explaining divine mercy.[87] The Anglican George Faber's *The Difficulties of Infidelity* (1824) examined deism from the position of a logic requiring a belief in a future state of retribution (so he claimed).[88] There also seemed an emotional chill: the Victorian man of letters John Morley, in his study of Voltaire (1872) suggested deism might argue for a God of mercy and justice, but a void created by losing 'god like natures' under the form of 'a tender mother ever interceding' or 'an elder brother laying down his life', meant 'a mere abstract creation of metaphysic, whose mercy is not as our mercy', was unsatisfying.[89]

Mercy was reflected on by those experiencing the Victorian crises of faith. Francis Newman's *Theism* (1858), puzzling over atonement theology in verse, asked, 'never let me stint the mercy | Of that august loveliness', in 'Future of the Wicked', and argued: 'If his judgments are severe, yet he fails not to be gracious: | And those whom we pity, he must pity; for our hearts are narrower than his. | Whosoever can be saved, he will save; for Mercy inheres in Righteousness.'[90] For non-Christians in the new century, mercy remained a problem to ponder as the necessary balance to justice in the universe. In 'The Idea of Justice', in *First and Last Things* (1908), H.G. Wells found terror in the idea of a just God and defined mercy as 'no more than an attempt to equalize things by making the factors of the very defect that is condemned, its condonation'. For Wells, both were extremes of harshness or ineffectualness.[91]

Mercy's absence: Christian perception of other religions

> Nature is a dispensation of goodness, but the gospel is a dispensation of mercy. It is an emanation from a God of mercy, and bears in every line the signatures of that nature from which it flowed. There is no other system of religion in the world that contains a sentiment similar to the one before us; or if they do, it is derived in some way or other from the Holy Scriptures.[92]

> The Heathen have no knowledge of God's pardoning mercy. They worship imaginary tyrants – cruel, bloodthirsty deities.[93]

> This position of ours – forcing clemency upon a Government which hardly knows what it means, forcing mercy, which is a Christian virtue, upon Mahometans – entails its responsibility. If the quality of mercy is in this sense strained from the Khedive, we are responsible for what follows from the exercise of it.[94]

The three assertions quoted above – from Samuel Gilfillan, a Secession minister of Comrie in 1822; the Anglican Hugh M'Neile in a sermon for the CMS in 1845; and a journalist in 1882 commenting on the resignation of the Egyptian minister of the interior Riaz Pasha when the British insisted on clemency for the leaders of a revolt – express assumptions by British Christians that theirs, perhaps uniquely, was a religion of mercy. As if to demonstrate this, the Church of England had a prayer for mercy to Jews, Turks, Infidels and Heretics.[95] A powerful aspect of the 'othering' of non-European societies was to use non-Christian religion to present the *cruelty* of alien culture. Mercy claims were advanced in missionary discourse and accounts of other religions.[96] Mercy was absent from 'the Koran of Mahomet, in the Shasters of Vishnu, or in the laws of Confucius', Gilfillan claimed.[97] The Scottish missionary Robert Caldwell's tract, published in Madras in 1860, made mercy along with other virtues, a mark of true religion against those 'invented by men'.[98] Islam was the 'religion of force' – though there was recognition that polemical contrast obscured instances of mercilessness by Christians and 'exemplary humanity' by Muslims.[99] Perceptions of the prophet's inconsistency over mercy were highlighted in Christian apologetics; missionaries to Islamic countries received notes on the proof of God's mercy to man, and missionary memoirs reported discussions about the Christian idea of mercy with Islamic scholars.[100]

Polytheistic cultures that seemed to offer bloodshed rather than clemency were contrasted with the 'new religion' European contact brought.[101] The Hindu practices of *sati* and infanticide, the figure of Kali and artefact of Juggernaut, demonstrated self-torture, cruelty and imbrued heathenism with blood (see Figures 1.5 and 1.6).[102] It was

Figure 1.5 Detail of steel engraving, 'A Suttee. From a Drawing in the Possession of the Hon: E.I.Cy.' from E.H. Nolan, *The Illustrated History of The British Empire In India and the East, From The Earliest Times to the Suppression of the Sepoy Mutiny in 1859* (2 vols, London: James S. Virtue, 1858), vol.1, p.37. Author's collection.

Figure 1.6 Wood engraving of 'The Car of Juggernaut', *The Mirror of Literature, Amusement and Instruction*, 24 April 1824, p.257. Author's collection.

argued by one essayist in *Friend of India* (published by the Serampore mission press) in 1818 that Hindus lacked belief in divine mercy. A human seemingly had everlasting reincarnation to expiate sins, '*a Hindoo has no hope in Divine mercy as it respects pardon*: that sin will be forgiven, or the punishment remitted, makes no part of Hindoo faith'.[103] Hindu priorities were judged inhumane. 'They lavished their *krores* of rupees on mountain temples; but mercy to man was first sounded in Indian ears by the Saxons from the West,' was the *Bengal Quarterly*'s self-satisfied assessment in 1855. The writer compared a 'true system of mercy' with animal hospitals and 'everlasting jabber about *their* "religion of mercy" ... ' which neglected mercy to humanity.[104] Yet the activity of native Indian Christian women, inspired by missionaries, was identifiable with works of mercy and compassion.[105]

In other cases, the mercy discourse targeted Buddhism or Jainism. The German Protestant Ernest Eitel informed a Hong Kong audience in 1870-1 that ancient Buddhism knew 'no sin-atoning power; it holds out to the troubled guilty conscience no prospect of mercy, no chance of obtaining forgiveness'.[106] This characteristic of Buddhism (to these Europeans) represented a challenge elsewhere. A report by American missionaries in 1848 stated the 'Siamese mind is peculiarly unfitted for understanding and embracing the doctrine of the forgiveness of sin through an atonement', the 'system of merits' meant that the Buddhist system was 'irreconcilably at enmity with the idea of mercy, or gratuitous favor ... In the government, *justice* is almost unknown. How much more, then, *mercy*?'[107]

Yet in Buddhist Burma, readers of Michael Syme's account of his embassy to Ava in 1795 learned, mercy was the 'first attribute of the divinity ... and they worship God by extending mercy unto all his creatures'.[108] The colonial administrator, judge and evangelical Anglican Robert Needham Cust's *Clouds on the Horizon* (1891) acknowledged Buddha brought mercy, pity and universal charity into religion.[109] In the Edwardian period, with translation of works on Japanese culture including the martial *bushido*, came recognition that codes shaped by Buddhism or Confucian ethics enjoined mercy and forbearance.[110] The personification of mercy in the Chinese deity Kwanyin (Japanese Kwanon) was something that scholars (including missionaries) were aware of and efforts to find common ground between Christianity and Buddhism involved an emphasis on Kwanyin (see Figure 1.7).[111]

Mercy claims by another Indian religion were dismissed: the mid-Victorian missionary William Clarkson, active in western India, described the Jains, with their claim to be *the* religion of mercy, as taking a tenet to an absurd and vicious extreme in concern for insect life rather than the human soul.[112] By the time Johnson's *Oriental Religions and their Relation to Universal Religion* appeared in 1873, there could be a sympathetic response to this animal-welfare sentiment: 'The mercy due from man to the brute life dependent on his care, or ministering to his desires, is indeed only to be learned of the East.'[113]

Arguably, when a discourse of mercy appeared in texts focused on the empire, moving the contrast on to a higher plane of religion and morality turned attention from the venality of British rule, where cruelty and lack of mercy was all too apparent to British (and native) critics. On the other hand, critics of British policy pointed to the damage to missionizing, from activities manifestly against the principles of a religion of mercy (as with slavery).[114] Mercy could condemn or legitimize imperialism.

British rule in India brought forth a criticism of cruelty in Parliament and press in the late eighteenth and early nineteenth centuries, touching on ideas about British justice, Christian mercy and Indian character. In the context of this parliamentary opposition, the artist James Forbes, resident in India for almost twenty years, denied in *Oriental Memoirs* (1813) that there was a 'national character of peaceful innocence' among Indians. He cited Brahminical cruelty and asserted from his experience, 'English generosity and clemency stretch forth the hand of mercy and protection, and endeavouring to rescue the peasantry from the oppressions of the zemindars

Mercy: Religious and Philosophical Dimensions 27

Figure 1.7 Japanese print of Kwanon reproduced in P-André Lemosine, 'Les Primitifs de l'estampe japonaise', *Gazette des Beaux Arts*, April 1909, pp.334–52 [p.337]. Author's collection.

[landowners] and merciless officers in the revenue departments.'[115] Eulogies to British imperial rulers, as at home, included the imagery of justice and mercy. A poem on Augustus Clevland of Bengal (a collector of revenues and administrator of justice for the East India Company who died in 1784) in the *Asiatic Annual Register*, for instance, asserted: 'Let hist'ry tell the deeds his wisdom plann'd, | His bloodless triumphs o'er a barb'rous land. | Bright in his hand, the sword of justice gleam'd, | But mercy from his eyes benignant beam'd, | And mercy won the cause; the savage band | Forsook their haunts and bow'd to his command.'[116] Government was associated with the 'practice of Christianity, in deeds of mercy' – demonstrating in taxation of Indian husbandmen (*ryots*), for example, a religion of good will to all men.[117] Mercy was also appealed to in legal cases, such as that following the deposition of the Rajah of Sattara in western India, for treason, where A.J. Lewis, proprietor of East India stock, asked for justice to be mingled with mercy in a debate in East India House in 1840.[118]

The idea of mercy may be approached from an 'oriental' perspective on religion in British discourse. In the 'cry of mercy for India', supposedly raised against *sati* and 'every species of human sacrifice', religion and policy combined.[119] Perhaps we should not separate the two: as Robert Martin argued in 1862, 'there has been much talk of evangelizing India; but the justice, the mercy, the charity, the unselfishness which lies at the base, and is the very core of a Christian government, have until recently been wanting'.[120] Sometimes distinctions were rhetorical. The seventeenth-century vegetarian Thomas Tryon contrasted merciful 'East-Indian Brackmanny' (Brahmin) and internecine European Christendom.[121] A self-critique of 'professors of religion of mercy', was available through the literary trope of a non-Christian commentator on European ways. In Elizabeth Hamilton's satirical 'translation' of letters from 'a Hindoo rajah' in 1811, her Indian writes:

> I had been taught to believe, that the pure doctrine of benevolence, and mercy, was unknown to all but the favoured race of Brahma; that the Christian faith, like that of the Mussulmans, was a narrow system of superstitious adherence to the wildest prejudices, engendering hatred, and encouraging merciless persecution against all who differed from them.[122]

The contrast between a gospel of mercy, meekness and mildness, and force used to proselytize was commonplace.[123] A religion of mercy was preached 'and wafted towards heaven in prayers', the English Quaker William Howitt noted in 1838, while 'despair and death has been going on for three centuries'.[124] Howitt characterized Europeans as the 'most heartless and merciless race that ever inhabited the earth, committing atrocities from the far west in North America, to the coasts of Africa, and 'busy in the South Sea Islands'.[125]

Howitt probably spoke for a minority. It was a matter of great pride that Britain led modern missionary efforts – one eulogy to George III in 1820 referred to Britain becoming the 'metropolis of christendom', sending out 'numerous heralds of mercy' to convert thousands to the 'God of Britain'.[126] For Daniel Wilson (future Bishop of Calcutta) in 1818, 'this great Protestant Empire ... God appears to have aggrandized, at the present momentous period, with the design of employing her as the herald of mercy to mankind'.[127] Missionaries promoted an understanding of European religion as one of mercy: Baptist Noel spoke in 1835 of 'penetrat[ing] every continent with messages of mercy'.[128] The effort was even figured as a response to the 'heathen' imploring mercy and securing Christian pity.[129] Accounts of work in the Indian subcontinent, Pacific islands, New Zealand and elsewhere portray missionaries and converts as beacons of merciful behaviour.[130] Children were presented with this effort in hymns, 'Let the outposts of the nation | Swell the glorious jubilee ... Let the Indian in his wildness, | Let the bondman in his gloom, taste the mercy and the mildness | Of the Lord who left the tomb'.[131]

In India, Bishop Wilson of Calcutta argued in a sermon in 1837, 'Let us endeavour gently to win *over the Heathen and Mohammedans to our reasonable religion*, our merciful, our mild, our compassionate religion, by our characters, families, and worship of God'.[132] Tracts and lectures discoursed on such ideas, converts wrote essays on the theme, and their biographies emphasized the centrality of a message of justice and mercy.[133] Visual argument was employed, thus an engraving created for a British public by the request of a committee member of the C.M.S. about 1816 showed a fakir with withered arms, celebrated in Calcutta, with the legend, 'Go, Christian Missionary! Open the eyes of these infatuated men. Reveal to them the God of Mercy; who delights not in the sufferings of his creatures'.[134]

The Brahmo Samaj provides one moment when Christian ideas interacted with Hindu reform movements.[135] The 'theistic church of India' announced in the *Indian Mirror* in October 1868 offered divine mercy to those worshipping one god: a development that led a British missionary paper to scorn the 'mercy from a God of single personality … mercy without an atonement', in Brahmoism.[136] The freethinker Sophia Collet's review in the *Contemporary Review* was more sympathetic. And as the *Indian Mail* noted, there were echoes of contemporary American and English theism in treatment of atonement and revelation.[137] Orthodox British missionaries and clergy of the early 1860s reported movement in Hindu belief towards an emphasis on justice, according to one British report of the 'Unitarians of Hindostan', as some called them.[138] In a course of lectures for educated natives, this development in Hindu thinking 'by an important section of educated and thoughtful Bengalees' was discussed – the lectures examined Christian belief in God's attributes of justice and mercy, 'these persons have seen the error of sacrificing divine justice to mercy. They contend, that since the Almighty is perfectly just He must and will deal with men according to their deserts,' but this led to a 'rigid justice' which left 'no place for mercy'.[139]

Yet one important figure in the Brahmo Samaj, Keshub Chunder Sen (who visited Britain) emphasized that the religion of the future *would* centre on a theology of 'God's infinite mercy'.[140] Sen's characterization of European and Hindu character – the one perceived by native Indians as a lupine lack of forbearance and mercy, the other characterized by feminine mildness and meekness – was also presented to British readers.[141] Hindu critics studying the Bible and noting practices such as carnivorism concluded Christianity lacked mercy. Swami Dayanand Saraswati asked, 'As the God of the Christians is a flesh-eater, what business has he with mercy?'[142] Other responses of the Bengali renaissance such as Bankim Chandra's study of Krishna (1886), contrasting Christ and Buddha with the Hindu deity, also questioned mercy claims.[143]

Mercy in Enlightenment and nineteenth-century philosophy

How did philosophers understand mercy in the eighteenth and nineteenth centuries?[144] In answering this question, one must appreciate that, as now, their discussions involved legal justice and ethics.[145] Mercy was also related to individual and social emotions (affections, feelings, sympathies, sentiments) which fascinated Enlightenment moral philosophy.

For the Irish philosopher Francis Hutcheson, rejecting the idea that virtuous acts were derived from self-love or interest, mercy was one of the personified 'Qualities of Mind' that sacred poets depicted: before the Almighty's face or looking down from the heavens.[146] Later-eighteenth-century disquisitions on beauty similarly pondered mercy's role.[147] Mercy was classified as one of the 'sympathetic affections' by the English philosopher David Hartley in 1749 as one of 'those by which we grieve at the misery of others' and as opposite to anger and cruelty.[148] Hartley saw it as similar to compassion, but that in mercy and unmercy a demerit checked the object's title to happiness. To be merciful was to curb feelings of resentment through compassion, 'whence it appears, that the Compassion required in Acts of Mercy, is greater than in common Acts of mere Compassion: Agreeably to which, it is observable, that mercy is held in higher Esteem, than mere Compassion.'[149] The Scottish philosopher David Hume's *Enquiry Concerning the Principles of Morals* (1751) stated that the epithet 'merciful' was universally esteemed alongside other 'benevolent or sober affections' as the 'highest merit, which human nature is capable of attaining'.[150] It reflected a change in the 'distribution of excellencies and virtues' through 'nature, or rather education' so that the present day, with its 'degree of humanity, clemency, order, tranquillity, and other social virtues' would seem incredible to one from the era of the ancient philosophers and heroes.[151]

For the natural philosopher Joseph Priestley, 'Sympathy, Compassion, Mercy, and Sociability are early generated by Association; the selfish element is slowly eliminated and we are led on to Theopathy.' He wrote (1787) that 'justice, mercy and veracity, with every thing else that is of a moral nature, are in fact, and philosophically considered, only modifications of benevolence'.[152] For Edward Gibbon, in *Decline and Fall of the Roman Empire* (1776–89), a work with many instances of historic Christian and Islamic mercy and unmercy, 'Ossian' material, if true, suggested that the 'untutored Caledonians, glowing with the warm virtues of nature', were to be contrasted in their clemency with vindictive Romans. When merciful abolition of capital punishment occurred in the twelfth-century Byzantine Empire under John II Komnenos, Gibbon reflected that it was a law 'most delightful to the humane theorist, but of which the practice, in a large and vicious community, is seldom consistent with the public safety'.[153]

The political philosopher and revolutionary Thomas Paine kept a place for mercy in his idea of a god but rejected the divine origin of the Bible because of unmerciful utterances such as Deuteronomy 7:2, denying that 'God ever gave such a *Robesperian precept* as that of shewing *no mercy*'.[154] Paine's radical associate William Godwin discussed mercy and justice in the context of property, criticizing the wealthy for the merit accrued when they acted with clemency and mercy, for 'bestowing the most slender pittance of their enormous wealth in acts of charity'. Elsewhere he saw mercy and gratitude as 'contradistinguished' from justice, and defended Oliver Cromwell's clemency.[155] In an essay unpublished in his lifetime, on the creed of everlasting torment, he defined mercy 'in the most enlarged figure which can be given it,' as 'but a part of justice'.[156] Concerning God, according to Mary Wollstonecraft (Godwin's wife briefly from March 1797), 'Perhaps, no representation of his goodness so strongly fastens on the human affections as those that represent him abundant in mercy, and willing to pardon.'[157] Her comments on the French Revolution rejected an argument from the vice of the *ancien régime* for suspension of morality – the statues of Equity and Mercy were not to be veiled for a moment.

Just as today, philosophers debated mercy's place in a legal system – could it be exercised without wronging the victims or those who suffered the full weight of the law as punishment?[158] Was it not, as the minor poet Edmund Smith phrased it in a play based on Racine's *Phèdre* in 1707, 'a virtue coin'd by villains'?[159] Penal reformers could be presented as enacting Christian mercy: John Howard was depicted in Erasmus Darwin's *The Botanic Garden* (1789) taking 'stern ey'd Justice to the dark domains | If not to sever to relax the chains | Or guides awaken'd Mercy through the gloom.'[160] Discussion of mercy's relationship to justice appears in such diverse texts as the works of Edmund Burke, the writings of Charles James Fox (or Samuel Parr's notes on his notes)[161] and the various writings on the law by Jeremy Bentham. Burke saw mercy as an 'essential part' rather than opposed to justice.[162] His *Remarks on the Policy of the Allies with Respect to France* (c. 1793) suggested, as a necessary aspect of bringing a peaceful settlement, a 'council of mercy … with powers to report on each case, to soften the penalty, or entirely to remit it, according to Circumstances'. We are told he 'did not spare to recount', to those in authority, 'the necessity of that union between Mercy and Justice, without which one degenerates into weakness, and the other into cruelty'.[163] This theme of mercy in the era of the French Revolution from a British perspective is returned to in a later chapter.

In Bentham's device, the 'Divine Eye' was surrounded by Vigilance, Justice and Mercy.[164] But Bentham saw the pardoning power, or prerogative of mercy, as an exercise in tyranny whether it was needed if the law was too harsh, or when the law was mild.[165]

> If a man not guilty has been convicted, – no, not then neither: he is to be saved or not, as he can find favour: the credit of saving him is to be taken out of the hands of open and discerning justice, and made a perquisite of, for the benefit of secret yet ostentatious mercy. As if every praise bestowed on mercy were not purloined from justice; as if the very distinction between justice and mercy had anything but blindness and weakness for its source; as if such mercy were anything better than tyranny, with hypocrisy for a covering to it.[166]

Bentham's *Constitutional Code* describes the tyrant's mercy and more constrained exercise in a limited monarchy, concluding that mercy and justice are incompatible.[167] He argued that 'the praise of mercy may, in proportion as the despotism is pure and complete, be reaped in conjunction with the profit of tyranny'.[168] In his manuscript 'Radicalism not Dangerous', of c. 1819–20 from which I have just quoted, mercy was the mantle that covered vice. He provocatively argued that 'all mercy supposes tyranny – every claim to the praise of mercy is a confession of tyranny: take away tyranny, that which is called mercy, if beneficially exercised, nothing more than justice'.[169] Bentham spoke clearly of the relationship to power, 'for every lot of evil which the monarch abstains from producing, he obtains at the hands of the prostrate multitude the praise of mercy. Monarchy is almost the only soil in which that species of vice which calls itself mercy can make its appearance.' It was 'seldom claimed' under aristocracy, whilst in a democracy, where no single person had the power of doing evil with impunity, 'there is no place for mercy'.

The justice and mercy of kings became a debating point for the critic William Hazlitt's disquisition (1805) on John Locke's essay on the human understanding. Here the essayist quoted at length from an illustration by the French philosopher Helvétius on the mind, which Rousseau had responded to (where three illustrations in the mind – the king orders the execution of criminal, the king releases the criminal and the criminal kills fifty fellow citizens – prove that the judgement that justice in a king is preferable to mercy is based on 'sensation').[170]

For the rest of the nineteenth century, mercy was neither the particular nor extended focus of British philosophy.[171] In 1848 the polymath William Whewell simply described mercy, alongside other 'benevolent affections' or 'virtuous affections' such as compassion, and pity, with mercy as abstinence from adding to pain felt and charity in the removal of pain or want.[172] John Stuart Mill merely used a statement about God being merciful to analyse syllogisms in 1865.[173] The philosopher Henry Sidgwick's *Methods of Ethics* (1874) had a chapter on benevolence which overlooked mercy, despite referring to the duties of pity. The youthful Francis Herbert Bradley's *Ethical Studies* (1876) ignored mercy.[174]

I want to broaden the focus to see how mercy was discussed in works by Victorian scientists and historians. While few may have gone as far as the Flemish poet and playwright (and aspirant scientist) Maurice Maeterlinck in stating that 'all justice, mercy, beauty and truth are so many secretions of human consciousness, as silk is of the silkworm', scientists might be expected to further develop the Enlightenment naturalistic analysis of human values and emotions.[175] How did mercy relate to new evolutionary ideas in natural science? Sympathy and pity were seen as underlying the principle of natural selection, according to both contemporary commentators on Charles Darwin following his publication of *The Descent of Man* (1871), and more recent studies, such as Dixon's exploration of the history of altruism.[176] Darwin disregarded mercy in *Expression of the Emotions in Man and Animals* (1872), although pity was discussed in relation to expression of sympathy and tears. He used the example of Fijian pitilessness, alongside 'North American Indian' cruelty to wounded companions, in discussing pity in animals – which he explained as an instinct to avoid being followed by beasts of prey.[177] His cousin, Francis Galton, considered 'ruth' and 'mercy' lacking in terms of evolution on the earth thus far, as measured by intelligence and mercy.[178] Galtonian eugenics had a particular notion of mercy:

> Helpfulness to the weak, and sympathy with the suffering, is the natural form of outpouring of a merciful and kindly heart ... a practical and effective way in which individuals of feeble constitution can show mercy to their kind is by a celibacy, lest they should bring beings into existence whose race is preordained to destruction by the laws of nature.[179]

Yet eugenicists who believed in spiritual development and mutual help argued for mercy's 'survival value' beside other 'sympathetic virtues'.[180]

Herbert Spencer considered pity and other 'ego-altruistic sentiments' in his evolutionary theory, and although seemingly more intrigued by explaining the 'luxury of pity', offered a brief paragraph on mercy in a textbook on the principles of psychology in 1855, as a state of consciousness in which:

> the execution of an act prompted by the sentiment of justice, is prevented by an out-balancing pity; by a representation of the suffering to be inflicted. Here we have two altruistic sentiments in antagonism; and it is interesting to observe how, occasionally, there arises a painful hesitation between their two dictates, each of which would seem morally imperative in the absence of the other. The anxiety to avoid giving pain prompts one course; and an opposite course is prompted by the sentiment responding to those supreme principles of equity which cannot be relaxed without danger.[181]

By the time of *The Principles of Ethics* (1892–3) he had added mercy to his ethical response to evolution and characterized it as part of the ethics of peace emerging in the era 'appropriate to industrialism'.[182]

By contrast to Spencer, the exiled Russian anarchist Piotr Kropotkin's overview of the 'morality of nature', in the aftermath of Darwinian theory, noting the long tradition of seeing a morality of 'nature' (self-assertion) as softened through recourse to the supernatural and an appeal to benevolence or mercy, argued for the roots of ethics and 'higher conceptions' of morality in primitive community and sociability.[183] For the Irishman William Lecky, writing a history of European morals, benevolence was discernibly a Greek development. The 'increasing prominence of the benevolent or amiable as distinguished from the heroic qualities and of the enlargement of moral sympathies' was signified by the Athenian altar to Pity, 'the first great assertion among mankind of the supreme sanctity of Mercy' and the plays of Euripides, as 'the first great revelation of the supreme beauty of the gentler virtues'.[184] Another commentator, the historian Herbert Fisher, reviewing the pre-eminent historian Lord Acton, queried the unchanging nature of moral standards while agreeing with the Regius Professor of Modern History at Oxford Goldwin Smith's assertion that 'justice has been justice, mercy has been mercy'. Smith believed 'each of these qualities [he cited five] is one and the same in the tent of the Arab and in the senates of civilized nations'.[185]

In exploring the origin of the 'moral sentiments', through what he called the 'ethical process', the scientist Thomas Huxley ignored mercy. The 'evolution of the feelings out of which the primitive bonds of human society' were forged, the 'acquired dialect of morals', the social sympathies creating approbations and disapprobations, the 'sympathetic humanity', no doubt incorporated development of pity, and certainly Huxley referred to the evolution of justice and ideas of 'desert' in 'Evolution and Ethics'.[186] The survival of the 'ethically best' as opposed to 'ruthless self assertion' clearly related to the idea of 'ruth'.[187] For Huxley, humanity constructed an artificial world in the cosmos, changing human nature, 'curbing the instincts of savagery in civilized man' with fear and love checking self-will.[188] On the other hand, Huxley defended the idea of justice and mercy as making up the most beautiful character in humanity, in response to the biologist St George Mivart's critique of Darwin on moral and formal goodness or morality in *The Genesis of Species* in 1871.[189]

Mercy figured in commentary about shifts in sentiment towards capital punishment through ancient, medieval and modern societies, with religion and the 'mere sentiment of mercy' replaced by scientific calculation of the aetiology of crime and impact of punishment, in the liberal Leonard Hobhouse's *Morals in Evolution* (1906). Hobhouse documented cultural moments of mercifulness / mercilessness and identified primitive ethics with the 'free play' of 'movements of pity', for instance towards strangers.[190] More obscure commentators offered interpretations: in the 1820s interesting reflections in the context of 'benevolence' were published by the barrister James Bicheno (future Colonial Secretary in Van Diemen's Land), using the concept of 'instinctive activity', defined as an 'inchoate state' of virtue, a 'mere animal propensity' needing to be developed through education and civilization (instancing the kindnesses shown to Captain Franklin by 'Indians' as 'after all ... but an animal propensity').[191] Others sought to dissect feelings: the neglected English philosopher Shadworth Hodgson analysed equity and mercy as two of the 'reflective emotions' in *The Theory of Practice: An Ethical Enquiry* (1870) which unsatisfactorily described mercy as 'commanded and enforced solely by the moral and spiritual law, the law of conscience'.[192]

What, then, was distinctive about Victorian discussion of mercy outside religious contexts? I have indicated that nineteenth-century British philosophers added nothing to the subject beyond Bentham's dismissiveness. Mercy's place in the behaviour of primitive human societies had fleeting appraisal by historians, sociologists, ethnologists and anthropologists. One apologist for anthropology argued for the need of a higher law, 'call it hope, shame, conscience, confidence', to ensure this 'practical science' was 'at once merciful and just, intelligible and active'. So mercy might, at least for this writer, be part of the new science.[193] But this new study of man expressed in novel vocabulary old chauvinisms about national mercy and (in the form of James Hunt's Anthropological Society) racist beliefs about the incapacity of the 'African race' to comprehend Christian virtues such as mercy.[194] Mercy and the other 'gentler and nobler virtues' were largely absent from primitive man, asserted the Positivist and anthropologist Joseph Kaines.[195] Yet mercy was identified, as I indicated by reference to Herbert Spencer, with the neologism of altruism, a tendency that was the 'result of evolution'.[196] Mercy was a component of the 'social virtues' originating in sympathies derived from man's social instincts, though for critics of the Darwinian interpretation the fact that morality and moral sentiment were earth-born rather than consequential on a divine or special source was shocking.[197] And in the natural environment there was 'no morality, no sympathy. Mercy is unknown'.[198] While it did not figure in any lengthy discussion of the origins and evolution of the moral sense, mercy's necessity was briefly referenced in terms of evolutionary success and racial advancement by evolutionary scientists and eugenicists.[199] Those examining morality, spirituality and religion in the light of evolutionary theory, as I outlined above, might ask how mercy came into being as sentiment or virtue.

The next chapter turns from the grappling with, or glimpsing of, mercy in philosophy and natural philosophy to the dramatizing, philosophizing and material rendering of mercy in works of art and craft. If some of these appearances might seem to be at the level of mere decoration (mercy's conventional coupling with justice in statuary for legal edifices), cumulatively such cultural representation meant something. At its most basic: mercy was accorded a public place and an inevitable presence whether in books of Christian virtues for juvenile instruction or on the stage in plays for adults' entertainment and edification.

2

The culture of mercy in the long nineteenth century

How did British people of the eighteenth and nineteenth centuries discuss and depict mercy, outside works of theology and devotion? How was it performed, embodied and viewed away from religious sites? This chapter begins with the plotting, extolling or debating of the quality of mercy, on stage. Central to these practices was Shakespeare's legacy. His words resonated with later playwrights and were a stock part of public speaking and literary allusion. From the poetry of theatre I survey mercy's representation by major and minor poets through the long nineteenth century. As a theological and philosophical question, mercy was the subject of prose essays in the popular press and figured in prose fictions from short story to three-decker novel. Mercy was present visually through parliamentary, ecclesiastical, municipal and judicial architectural sculpture and interior decoration. Merciful acts were cast or carved into memorials, were common themes for artworks exhibited to the public at a variety of sites, and reproduced in engravings. These representations shaped audiences and readers' understanding of mercy.

Staging mercy in the theatre

Theatre and dramatic criticism provided important locations for representing and discussing virtues. Medieval morality plays featured mercy and justice (as 'daughters of God', representing theological graces or virtues) and traces of this practice are visible in nineteenth-century non-conformist religious activities.[1] Eighteenth-century dramatic theory allowed for the exhibition of 'vicious Character' and the 'Odiousness of some particular Vice' to 'create a Distaste and Aversion in the Minds of the Audience', to quote one critic from 1753. Thus vengeful characters offered instruction in humility or resignation. In the tragedy *Boudicea* by Richard Glover (1753), lessons on mercy are provided through the queen's sister Venusia ('Of all the paths which lead to human bliss, | The most secure and grateful to our steps | With mercy and humanity is mark'd').[2]

The central influence in staging mercy in our period was Shakespeare's comedies of mercy (the *Merchant of Venice, c.* 1596–9; *Measure for Measure c.* 1604). His lines shaped the way mercy was discussed outside the theatre. Portia's speech, beginning 'the quality of mercy is not strain'd', in *Merchant of Venice* (act IV, scene 1) appeared in encyclopaedia definitions of mercy. The *Encyclopaedia Britannica*'s entry, that 'virtue that inspires us with compassion for our brethren and which inclines us to give them assistance in their necessities … those favours and benefits that we receive either from God or man particularly in the way of forgiveness of injuries or of debts', quoted the speech *in extenso*. Other encyclopaedias similarly cited it.[3] Shakespeare's lines, as one modern philosopher notes, are so oft-quoted as to be clichés fit for Hallmark cards.[4] Portia's speech was used in nineteenth-century discourse on capital punishment and in referring to royal mercy, as were Isabella's words in *Measure for Measure* (act II, scene 2, 'Not the king's crown, nor the deputed sword, | The marshal's truncheon, nor the judge's robe, | Become them with one half so good a grace | As mercy does').[5] They were applied in many different contexts where arguments about mercy were relevant – including the Anglo-American freethinker Moncure Conway's contrary assertion that rather than dropping as the gentle rain from heaven, mercy was 'projected into heaven from compassionate human hearts beneath'.[6]

Shakespeare's interest in mercy's exercise was 'a favourite topic', noted an essayist in the *Universal Magazine* in April 1793.[7] This fascination transcended the stage to encompass novels, graphic political satire and political commentary, material artefacts and traces of private reading. For instance, the novel *The Cry, a New Dramatic Fable* (1754), probably largely by Sarah Fielding, had a passage discussing mercy between the allegorical Una (presumably named for Spenser's character) and two central characters, the young women Portia and Cylinda.[8] Shakespeare's lines for Portia figured in a satirical print about attacks on royal power in 1788.[9] Widespread newspaper quotation or allusions to the Portia speech in political commentary include *The Country Constitutional Guardian* (of Bristol) condemning 'effects of over-strained philanthropy in Ireland' in May 1822, and the *Morning Post* in March 1836 reporting Lord John Russell exercising mercy at Marylebone Radical Club's behest.[10] The *Post* linked belated State mercy towards convicted Dorset agricultural labourers, with James Savage's exultant intoning of Portia's speech, at this club.[11]

One late-eighteenth-century Lord Chancellor, Edward Thurlow, reputedly cried after a 'slight tremulousness in his voice' when reading 'that beautiful scene'.[12] The diarist Hester Thrale recorded that when Mansfield occupied the bench (as Lord Chief Justice from 1756 to c. 1788) 'it was usual, whenever the Merchant of Venice was played, for Portia in the celebrated speech about mercy, to mimic the gesture, tone, and manner of his lordship'.[13]

For the nineteenth-century reader, the *Merchant of Venice* passage was familiar from 'gems of Shakespeare' collections and the Lambs' *Tales from Shakespeare* (1807).[14] One allusion in 1875 described it as an 'elegant extract' speech.[15] 'Read in moderate time', the *Manchester Reader* (1871) for elementary school children instructed, 'with feeling and emphatic pauses'.[16] The speech was a text for orthography – H.D. Smith selling an example for penmanship in 1852.[17] In the art historian Anna Brownell Jameson's *Characteristics of Women* (1832), Portia is classified as an 'intellectual women'; an etching by the author heading the opening passage has Portia prominently named. Julia Hankey's study of Victorian treatment of Portia takes Jameson's treatment as a significant intervention.[18] How others responded is suggested by this account from

1839, from an essay arguing for the existence of appropriately religious sentiment on stage or through the theatrical medium:

> This speech is invariably responded to by a burst of applause, arising less from the impressive delivery of the words, than a profound admiration of the solemn truth so beautifully conveyed and which has struck forcibly on the hearts of every auditor. It would be hard to believe that any one can utter or listen to these lines in that situation, with other than reverential feelings, nor can even prejudice itself maintain that this introduction of the sacred name is either 'flippant or profane'.[19]

In the eighteenth and nineteenth centuries Portia's speech had a high status as a set piece for famous actors (and for fiction depicting actors, thus George Reynolds's Ellen Percy triumphs in the part in the eponymous novel published in 1856[20]). Dramatic reviews provided the occasion for writers to comment on the sentiment and actor's delivery. Portraits of the actors in the role were created.[21] The *Companion to the Playhouse* of 1764 judged the speech 'perhaps the finest Piece of Oratory on the Subject (tho' very fully treated on by many other Writers), that has ever appear'd in our or any other Language'.[22] The *Theatrical Review* in 1772 thought it ornamented the stage and honoured the pulpit: 'It has ever been the subject of general approbation amongst the critical Admirers of Beauty and Elegance.'[23] Elizabeth Griffith's *The Morality of Shakespeare's Drama Illustrated* in 1775 thought the character of mercy 'beautifully described' and that the passage could 'never be too often read. There is no danger of its growing seared and tedious as Angelo says of the laws of justice.'[24]

The *Dramatic Censor* in 1770 examined the abilities of several eminent actors in this role, including Peg Woffington, Kitty Clive, Maria Macklin, Mary Ann Yates and Frances Abington. Woffington's effort was 'marked as well as anybody'.[25] Clive's depiction was comic, 'for that clever but not too discriminating actress used throughout that scene to give imitations of the leading pleaders of her time'.[26] The *English Review* of 1783, in a telling comment on Georgian audiences, judged that Mary Bulkley 'when the house has been attentive, deliver[ed] Portia's celebrated speech … with so much propriety and feeling that she has obtained universal applause'.[27] Sometime mistress of the Duke of York, Mary Anne Clarke's performance (c. 1792) showed 'a feeling and taste that would have graced some of our best performers'.[28] In the 1770s and 1780s Sarah Siddons's portrayal of 'sweet Portia' was 'uncommonly fine': she enraptured audiences and 'scarcely ever fails in successful delivery'.[29] Several portraits were made of her in the role.[30] Sarah West was praised in *The Portfolio* in 1826: 'Shakespeare's Portia in you receive new birth | Thy mercy-dealing speech, with soft harmonious tongue | Flies to the heart, like strains by angels sung.'[31] The *Literary Chronicle* thought her recitation of the 'celebrated apostrophe to mercy' was exquisite.[32] Victorian 'improvements' to the play according to *The Spectator*'s review of Ellen Kean in the role in 1858, enhanced the speech. Kean 'earned one of her best laurels by her exquisite delivery of the speech on Mercy, the part is so much elevated by the improved version of the play, that it requires a completely new expenditure of talent'.[33]

For 'Timothy Plain' the role demanded 'superior abilities' which Fanny Kemble displayed in the speech 'where mercy is so beautifully defined and inculcated'.[34]

Critics sometimes identified a 'school boy' style of delivery, unsurprising given the speech's status in elocution and public-speaking texts. Thus the *Edinburgh Dramatic Review*, in 1824 thought that the speech 'should be given with feeling and earnestness but [in Kemble's aunt Sarah Siddon's depiction] it is given in the style of schoolboy recitation'.[35] In New England in 1827, a reviewer of one performance detected a similar tendency in the actress Miss Rivers's performance, noting 'a large portion of the school boy whine and manner'.[36] As a set piece there was anticipation from the audience, as James Boaden's memoirs of Siddons suggested, wondering of such passages as Portia's speech, how much a false stage delivery was owed to 'the particular expectation thus excited'.[37]

An essayist on stage morality in the *London Magazine* in December 1777 contended, taking in the Restoration plays of Dryden, Behn, Farquhar, Congreve, Vanbrugh and Wycherley, 'I am much deceived, if among all the heroes and heroines, who are held up to public imitation, he find one whom an impartial jury would even recommend to royal mercy'.[38] The Portia speech acquired significance for defenders of dramatic art against charges of irreligion or immorality. An address from the actor-manager Thomas Trotter at the new theatre in Worthing published in August 1807, for example, alluding to 'Mercy's voice with angel tone', asked: 'Can scenes like these which hallow'd minds may read | The cause of virtue and of truth impede'?[39] Should a Christian preacher ever adopt the tone and manner of an actor? According to one critic in the *Monthly Review* in 1792 this might be acceptable where 'serious paternal admonition or moral reflection without any other emotion than such as results from a sense of its importance and a desire of making a deep and lasting impression on the persons to whom it is addressed,' and instanced Portia's 'celebrated and beautiful pleading'.[40] Others pointed to Shakespeare's scriptural sources, for instance in 1795 one correspondent of the *Gentleman's Magazine*: 'Every one, surely, who has ever read or heard Portia's beautiful panegerick on Mercy, must have perceived that the turn, thought, and very language, were derived from the Scriptures.'[41] The New England *Church Monthly* treating Shakespeare as a Christian poet in 1864, referred to the two plays' argument for merciful goodness.[42] From which of your Christian teachers, asked an early-twentieth-century sermonist in the hallowed Stratford-upon-Avon's collegiate church, 'will you learn of that unstrained "quality of mercy" ... more unerringly than you will from Shakespeare?'[43]

Portia's speech exemplified the scruples of the religious anxiety about uttering God's name on stage, even in a reverential atmosphere. The *Literary Panorama* in 1808, noting God's name in 'pathetic speeches', commented that the 'mention of it in Portia's speech on mercy ... has been lately attended with great approbation: the Portia whom I recently saw ... merited it, and the whole speech is calculated to excite applause'. But, the critic added, 'who can afterwards hear the indelicacies uttered by the same mouth in the fifth act without a double disgust at the incongruity'.[44]

Intriguingly, the poet and playwright Samuel Pratt's *Essays on Select Passages of Sacred Composition* (1777) contrasted the speech with Matthew 23: 37 and the 'tenderness of our Saviour' and, while commenting that 'it were a kind of literary heresy' to omit the two, wondered whether to admire more the scriptural passage or Portia's argument.[45] The Scottish Methodist minister Valentine Ward's pamphlet against the stage included the speech, sent as proof of the utility of plays by the 'comedians of Peterhead' in 1818.⁴⁶ 'I not only assert that Shakespeare holds a high station as a moralist,' said a visiting Londoner, at Sheffield's Shakespeare Club in 1827, 'but that he may rank with our orthodox divines and could I do justice to his sublime apostrophe to mercy it would in a moment prove the truth of my assertion.'⁴⁷ The *Theatrical Times*'s response to criticism of the theatre in the London press in 1847 noted Portia's speech and Isabella's pleading for mercy.⁴⁸ That rare figure, a public female lecturer in the early-Victorian era, Clara Lucas Balfour, associated the speech with 'the sublime inspirations of holy writ' in 1847.⁴⁹

Because of the fame of Portia's speech and since the politics of mercy was central to early modern authority, other plays from the early seventeenth century onwards commented on mercy's princely exercise. Thomas May's comedy *The Heir* (1620) debated the demands of justice and mercy through Euphues and Polymetes.⁵⁰ Nicholas Rowe, editor and biographer of Shakespeare, featured discussion of royal mercy in *Lady Jane Grey* (1715) a work included under that head in *A Dictionary of Quotations from the British Poets* in 1824, alongside apposite quotation from Eudosia in John Mottley's tragedy of Carthage, *Imperial Captives* (published 1720).⁵¹ Aaron Hill's character Scroop, in his 1723 adaptation of Shakespeare's *Henry V*, declares, 'Mercy is a topic, copious and fair; but men, who counsel Monarchs, | must smile at naked Nature's moral Dreams, | and, skill'd in manly Rigour, cast off Pity.'⁵² John Banks's Queen Elizabeth in *The Albion Queens* (1684, but unperformed until the early 1700s) declares, 'My throne's an altar with soft mercy crown'd.'⁵³ John Gay's *The Captives* (completed in 1724 and dedicated to the princess of Wales, consort of the future George II) figures comments by various characters on mercy, thus Astarbe advises her husband, king of Media, 'Be firm in justice, nor give way to mercy, 'Tis the mind's frailty, and the nurse of crimes. | Punish: and root out treason from the land.'⁵⁴ William Thompson's verse tragedy *Gondibert and Birtha* included dialogue on the righteous king: 'Justice supports but mercy fills his Throne.'⁵⁵

Mercy appeared in Isaac Bickerstaff's burletta *Recruiting Serjeant* of 1770, in a loyal air set in a village ale-house, toasting the health of a king 'merciful, pious … prudent and just'.⁵⁶ The milk-woman, anti-slavery poet and novelist Ann Yearsley's *Earl Goodwin* in the same year, dramatized justice and mercy and discussed the problem of punishment in a note, referring to some twenty men hanged in a morning in London 'under the cognizance of our *Most Gracious Sovereign George III*'.⁵⁷ George Colman the younger's *Surrender of Calais* (1791) unsurprisingly featured intercession from Philippa of Hainault: 'mercy, valour, and compassion; do characterize the Englishman'. It finishes on the refrain, 'Yet on the victor's heart let truth engrave | That heav'n-born mercy best becomes the brave.'⁵⁸ The Anglo-French *The Deserter of Naples, or Royal Clemency*, performed in various versions, was advertised in 1801–2 as a 'grand, serious, pantomimical ballet'.⁵⁹ Other Napoleonic-era plays in exotic settings permitted mercy's association with Britain and her monarch, thus Richard Cumberland's comic opera *The Jew of Mogadore* (published 1808) features a British sea captain's intercession with the emperor and empress of Morocco (the latter representing mercy). The emperor Selim's homily on security in ruling in justice tempered by mercy follows the captain's assertion that he 'cannot execute my king's commands more to his royal pleasure and content, than when I am able to demonstrate, that mercy is a duty he expects from all his officers by land or sea'.[60]

Schiller's play about Mary Stuart, in a translation by the naval chaplain Hugh Salvin in 1824, bore the Shakespearian imprint, in 'Mercy, Not severity, | Should shine the brightest gem in the king's crown'.[61] Other nineteenth-century plays depicting monarchs enacted the granting or withholding of justice and mercy, not all on the high political plane. The Scottish professor of Moral Philosophy John Wilson's *The Convict* (1816) figured pleas for mercy. The wife of the innocent Francis Russel desperately awaits the verdict at his murder trial, imagining news of deliverance conveyed to her by an angel's hand, or flinging herself before the feet of the 'kind-hearted' monarch, for 'mercy dwells with the King – and he is merciful!' Though there is no such royal deliverance the murderer reveals himself by mistake just as Russel is to be executed.[62]

This is a brief overview rather than representing the full extent of direct and extended appeals to mercy in a variety of different forms (tragedy, comedy, burlettas) over our period – the works referred to here being cited in contemporary books of quotations and encyclopaedias, or uncovered through the digitization of justly obscure, and once-famous plays. Scholars have pointed out the theme of mercy and clemency in opera, which I have not discussed.[63] I revisit mercy's staging when a later chapter briefly studies gesture. The next section considers works of non-dramatic poetry.

Poetic mercy

Despite Samuel Johnson's suggestion in an essay on the seventeenth-century poet Edmund Waller in 1779, that man, 'admitted to implore the mercy of his Creator, and plead the merits of his Redeemer, is already in a higher state than poetry can confer', there was a sacred poetry of mercy.[64] Necrological and anniversary poems invoked royal mercy. Anti-slavery, anti-gallows and petitionary poetry were directed to the throne.[65] As one early-nineteenth-century writer observed, 'Mercy and benevolence may be treated poetically, because they are in unison with the mild spirit of poetry'.[66] Another, reviewing Wordsworth's *The Excursion* in 1815, complained inaccurately that too few contemporary poets seemed interested in philosophical reflections, such as the scale and sword of divine justice and mercy.[67] A defence of sacred poetry argued (against Johnson) the propriety of tackling the theme: 'And while science explores, may not poetry celebrate the glories and the mercies of our God!' asserted 'Christopher North' of *Blackwood's Edinburgh Magazine* in 1828 (probably the John Wilson whose play I cited above). Another essayist concerned with sacred poetry thought that while God's mercy was unmagnifiable, 'yet how necessary is it to dwell upon it constantly, in order to impress our hearts with a lively and permanent conviction of it!'[68] A mid-Victorian formalist defence asserted that metre and musicality combined to deeper effect in stirring emotions: comparing the 'quality of mercy is not strained' with the prose assertion 'mercy is spontaneous in its nature, and two-fold in its blessing – to the giver and receiver'.[69]

Victorian literary criticism explored mercy and justice in older poetry, exemplified by the treatment of Giles Fletcher's *Christ's Victorie and Triumph in Heaven and Earth*, *over and after Death* (dramatizing heavenly debate between justice and mercy, in 1610) by the clergyman-scholar, Alexander Grosart. The 'dispute between Justice and Mercy, such as is often represented by the Theologians' occasioned a debate about the theologic-poetic with the poet and novelist George Macdonald.[70] Verse on the same 'fair sacred sisters' by another seventeenth-century poet, Joshua Sylvester, was also reprinted and studied by Grosart.[71]

Perhaps the most famous poetic representation in the eighteenth century was William Collins's *Ode to Mercy*. This was linked to the Jacobite rising in 1745 and designed to 'excite sentiments of compassion in favour of those unhappy and deluded wretches who became a sacrifice to public justice'. In Collins's poem mercy was no mere abstraction, as it might be in later Georgian odes, but a well-understood word to plead clemency.[72] As I show later, the poem stimulated visual representation. The magistrate John Langhorne, who memorialized Collins, in *The County Justice* of 1777 appealed to the healing wings of Mercy, 'thron'd on his eternal breast'.[73] And poetry directed towards magistrates enjoined or extolled mercy: Isaac Watts's 'Psalm 101. The Magistrate's Psalm' (1719) began 'Mercy and Judgement are my song'.[74] Edward Ward's 'The Severe Magistrate: Or, The Proud Man in Authority' (1708) argued 'Mildness and mercy, ought to be | The gentle Gifts and Grace | Of Persons in Authority, | Who sit in lofty Places'.[75]

Many nineteenth-century versifiers and hymnologists reflected on mercy. Edward Trapp Pilgrim, sometime 'thread laceman' in London, described the angel of mercy as 'Ever near the throne on high', in hymning divine attributes in 1832. The working-class John Critchley Prince's 'Mercy' (published 1856) depicted the virtue with 'beauteous and beseeching face, | And wedded hands upraised with supplicating grace': 'Not Truth, nor Justice, must we put away, | But lean towards Mercy whensoe'er we may'.[76] A discussion of divine mercy figured in more ambitious poems in the surgeon George Eveleigh's *Science revealed* (1863).[77] The carter George Blyth in Fifeshire wrote about justice, mercy and humility in his collection in 1874. It inspired competitive poets in eisteddfods.[78] The essayist Pauline Roose collected extracts on mercy, from illustrious contemporaries, such as Tennyson, George Macdonald and Sidney Dobell.[79] The clergyman and friend of Gerard Manley Hopkins, Richard Watson Dixon's 'Mercy' imagines a 'sad earth' with clouds of 'hanging judgement'.[80] More compellingly Thomas Hardy's 'A Plaint to Man' (1909–10) imagines man-created God in dialogue with humanity, ventriloquizing the thought that man needed 'to conceive of a mercy-seat | Somewhere above the gloomy aisles | Of this wailful world'. Hardy's 'Immanent Will' has no mercy.[81]

The context of global warfare explained the frequent injunction to mercy-in-victory in late-eighteenth-century British poetry. A versifier claimed in 1782 that 'Valour and mercy have one throne, | And that Throne, a Britain's heart'.[82] Victorians continued the tendency to sing of British imperial mercy, Eliza Cook's 'The Flag of the Free', stating 'Tis the herald of mercy as well as of might', for instance.[83] The poetry of late Victorian and Edwardian imperialism, as if cued by Kipling's 'Recessional' (1897) deploys mercy stridently, in the Boer War era of international odium. Algernon Swinburne's ode 'Astraea Victrix' spoke of 'English men | Ashamed of shame and strong in mercy'[84] and in sustained patriotic fervour his 'England. An Ode' imagined the smiting activity of British justice and mercy, 'Justice bright as mercy, mercy girt by justice with her sword, | Smote and saved and raised and ruined.'[85] Contrastingly the Welsh Liberal Lewis Morris's 'Meliora' refers to 'knowing one limit alone to the Commonwealth's province of mercy | That no action of all shall mar the life-giving effort of each.'[86] 'The Fortunes of Britain', dated April 1898, asks that his dear Motherland be based not on military might but on 'Mercy and Right.'[87] Published in 1894, Frederick William Orde's patriotic 'Pax Britannica', asserted 'Your Mercy is a fortress free | For all who ill endure'.[88] His 'The Walls of England', spoke of the law 'which lights our progress and scatters plenty wide, | Co-partner with the mercy that sitteth at God's side, | The justice joined to pity | Above an action mean'.[89] The Tory Thomas Crosland's Anglo-Saxonist 'The Blood' asserted, 'For your law is a law for the makers of laws, | Builded of justice and mercy and right.'[90] William Watson, critic of the war, in 1909 maintained that the Empire 'despite her faults and sins, | Loves Justice, and loves mercy, and loves truth'.[91] He already asserted 'her all living lands above, | In Justice, and in Mercy, and in Love', in a poem of 1899, 'On being styled unpatriotic'.[92]

Particular episodes as here, called forth for mercy. The prolific George Barlow's 'Kritzinger Sonnet' of 1902, for example, concerning the fate of the Boer Commandant Pieter Kritzinger, asked, 'Let mercy, not crude "Justice," win the day! | Forgive; and be for many a sin forgiven.'[93] British justice in India and Ireland was excoriated by the English Tory Wilfrid Scawen Blunt in 'The Canon of Aughrim' (1888), whose scant references to modern mercy included 'death is done with a sigh, and mercy tightens the noose'.[94] Mercy crops up in verse of shocking realism in John Masefield's controversial narrative about a drunken poacher, *Everlasting Mercy* (first appearing in October 1911). The hero sees Christ ploughing to make the 'holy bread', the mercy of the title. One reader accused Masefield of selecting the title to attract the 'sentimentally religious public' and tricking out a vicious and sordid tale with 'Brummagem religious symbols'.[95]

Then there is the campaigning poet: examples of these feature in Chapter 6's exploration of anti-slavery agitation. Poetry about penal reforms tends to include mercy.[96] In 1842 the capital-punishment abolitionist *Morning Advertiser* responded to the poetic apology for the gallows by William Wordsworth ('Hence thoughtful mercy, mercy sage and pure, | Sanctions the forfeiture the law demands') by defending godlike mercy from 'impious sophistry'.[97] On other occasions, philanthropy called forth mercy: winter-time charity for instance.[98] Poetry about condemned and executed capital convicts queried human justice.[99] These include a poem calling for mercy purportedly from a man in possession of a printing plate for counterfeit bank notes, hanged at Ilchester in 1819.[100]

Essaying mercy: Mercy in periodical and newspaper

Poetry extolling mercy appeared in newspapers and was slipped into such leading Victorian periodicals as Dickens's *Households Words*.[101] There were also essays and essay-writing exercises on virtues like clemency in the eighteenth and nineteenth centuries. They include an essay on revenge and cruelty in the *Universal Magazine* in 1748, an essay on mercy in war in the *Public Ledger* in 1760, an essay on clemency in the *Oxford Magazine* in 1769 which argued for a monarch 'to acquire the reputation of a merciful prince … Histories are full of the happy reigns of such princes' and a prize essay in *St James's Magazine* in 1775. There was another in the *Town and Country Magazine* in May 1788. An essay on mercy was published in the *Ladies' Monthly Museum* in November and December 1821.[102]

Thoughts on mercy as asides or queries appear in other essays, thus in the 'Oracle or Quaerist' section of the almanac *Ladies' Diary* of 1751: 'We are taught to do *Justice* and to love *Mercy*: How is Mercy to be shewen where Justice ought to take Place? And, if Mercy takes Place, can *Justice* be distributed by either *Bishop* or *Judge*?'[103] An essay on 'Dress' in the *Ladies Library* of 1739 decried indiscriminate clemency and lenity.[104] The refusal by the captain of the royal yacht *Midina* to pillage fishermen was pressed into the argument that 'mercy and Justice always accompany true courage', in the *Kentish Register* for September 1795.[105] For this writer, 'X.Y.Z.' of York Coffee House, deeds of mercy provided a 'demarcation between the civilized and uncivilized parts of the Creation' and defined true valour or courage.

The *Blackburn Standard* in 1895 ran a competition for the 'best postcard essay on mercy' in which competitors discussed judgement versus mercy, just deserts, the relationship of humans to animals ('for "The merciful man is merciful to his beast"').[106] By the 1890s as shown by the *Standard*'s contributors it was common to discursively extend mercy: 'perhaps more than any other virtue far-reaching in its effects; it blesseth the receiver, whilst the giver is not impoverished'. Essay-writing for newspapers was one method to develop children's animal-welfare sentiments.[107] Newspapers were an important site for presenting or challenging platitudes; religious sections sermonizing on mercy especially during such occasions as Hospital Sunday.[108] Religious magazines for the laity presented discussion on errands of mercy, essays on theology and sermons on the Beatitudes.[109] Book reviewers might touch on mercy themes, such as Peter Bayne's critique of Thomas Carlyle's hero-worship involving a 'more and more express contradiction to every common idea of mercy, justice, and even truth.'[110]

Unsurprisingly, newspapers responded to contentious acts by local magistrates, courts of justice and home secretaries. Editorials debated justice and mercy in relation to penal reform or particular criminal cases.[111] Correspondents aired views on particular cases, general questions of mercy and the royal prerogative. Mercy was also raised in commentary on philanthropy, economics, foreign policy and conduct of war. How was this public discourse on mercy presented, analysed and problematized? Hackneyed use of Shakespeare's 'quality of mercy' is notable: in reported speech or headlines. Critics described mercy appeals as 'plausible clap trap' in the 1820s.[112] Public discourse on mercy half a century later was dismissible as sentimentality, 'sham humanity' and 'popular clamour'; the home secretary in the 1920s, William Joynson-Hicks, referred to a 'mob mercy' of public outcry and press agitation.[113]

Mercy in prose fictions

Debates on mercy figure in novels and short stories. There is the comment on 'mistaken' mercy from Allworthy to the eponymous hero in Henry Fielding's *History of Tom Jones*

(1749) after Bliflil's fraud is discovered.[114] More obscurely, there is brief discourse on mercy in the former Unitarian minister William Pitt Scargill's *Usurer's Daughter* of 1832 as 'a word of wide, weak and foolish meaning' in a novel set in the Gordon Riots era.[115] Purgatory, 'this consciousness that the mercy of God will take place of his justice,' is consolatory in Agnes Stewart's *Justice & mercy, or, A Tale of All Hallow's Eve* of 1858.[116] A trope of 'tempering' justice surfaced in treating relationships outside legal plots. A character like George Macdonald's Lady Clementina, in *The Marquis of Lossie* (1877) helped examine the nature of mercy.[117] Macdonald had been a Congregational minister: literary scholars have explored public and private ruminations on mercy by other Victorian novelists.[118]

The role that law and legal discourse played in novels brought in mercy as a theme. These might be a few lines, in the case of Phineas Finn, on trial for the murder of a fellow MP in Trollope's *Phineas Redux* (1874).[119] Some were explicitly campaigning: John Oxenham's *God's Prisoner* (1898) was a call for treating the murderer more mercifully. Religious bodies used fiction to depict divine mercy: the Society for Promoting Christian Knowledge's *Barzillai; or, The Triumph of Mercy* (1860) had a biblical setting; short stories presented the power of mercy over the delinquent.[120] The phrenologist Stackpool O'Dell's *Merciful or Merciless* of 1886 dealt with sacred matters differently. The *Pall Mall Gazette* called it 'moral philosophy decoratively treated', a vindication of God's justice and mercy which rejected eternal damnation. Through the character of a rector O'Dell offered reassurance about God's infinite wisdom, justice, love and mercy against doctrines of predestination, election and vicarious sacrifice.[121]

Imaginative literature is envisaged by some ethicists as having agency in relation to the virtues. Charles Barker's work on Christian ethics (1947) declared mercy dependent on imagination.[122] Martha Nussbaum, examining mercy's relationship with the literary imagination, argues 'attentiveness to particularity … capacity for sympathetic understanding' renders the form something 'prepared for equity and, in turn, for mercy'. For Nussbaum, the novel is an 'artificial construction of mercy'.[123] Thomas De Quincey claimed in an essay on Alexander Pope that the 'literature of power' (great works such as *Paradise Lost*) taught by moving, providing 'sufficient illustration': 'Tragedy, romance, fairy tale, or epopee, all alike restore to man's mind the ideals of justice, of hope, of truth, or mercy, of retribution.'[124]

Schramm's study of atonement in nineteenth-century narratives argues that the mid-Victorian novel 'battles to keep mercy located firmly in the public sphere'.[125] The 'theological' work of fiction, Schramm notes, included dramatizing mercy and embodying it in female form, and is exemplified by Charles Dickens's works such as *Bleak House* and *Great Expectations*, Elizabeth Gaskell's *Mary Barton* and George Eliot's *Mill on the Floss* and *Middlemarch*.[126] Indeed, 'Victorian literature tended to advocate mercy and forgiveness as the appropriate individual response to human error.'[127] The justice tempered with mercy acknowledged by Rochester, reunited with Jane Eyre, represents this shared culture.[128] Study of any Victorian novelist might reveal themes and characters embodying mercy, quite apart from those like Matilda Charlotte Houston's *Recommended to Mercy* (1862) with the title rendering the theme explicit, or like Wilkie Collins in the *New Magdalene* (1873), naming their heroine Mercy.[129]

Johann Bohnstedt's appraisal of Dickens (1854) exemplifies the nineteenth-century tendency to identify and praise novels' morality: 'All his writings abound with stern reflections on Mercy, Charity, Forbearance, Self-Examination and Self-Control, they make us recollect Universal Love as our principal Duty.'[130] Analysis of his theology in *The Homilist* in 1871 also stressed, in Dickens's appeal to God's mercy in his will and testament, evangelical credentials. The late Victorian novelist George Gissing praised him for giving 'form and substance' to mercy and other ideals, for the 'dim multitudes'.[131]

Was there any recognition of literature's role in extending mercy and kindness beyond humanity? The anti-vivisectionist Edward Berdoe (an expert on Robert Browning) argued animal welfare owed more to men of letters and poets in the era after the French Revolution, than to religion.[132] James Routledge's study of 'popular progress' asserted that 'no … priest preached with greater force of the quality and grace of mercy than Burns preached from the text of "The Wounded Hare," and "The Tim'rous Cow'rin' Mousie"'.[133]

Representing mercy in sculpture and painting[134]

This section of my examination of mercy's representation in British culture surveys sculpture and painting over the 'long nineteenth century', reserving modern representation in art and literature to the final chapter. Mercy's place was predictable in a culture prizing moral themes: art was defended on the basis of 'purpose' by pre-eminent writers like John Ruskin, who thought 'justice and Mercy … are fastened in the hearts of men'.[135] The artist's moral mission was exposition of the 'abstract qualities of virtue'.[136]

The context for this representation is a longer history of personification of mercy, depiction of scenes of mercy exercised or withheld in Western art.[137] Justice was recognizable in allegory throughout the period – equipped with scale, perhaps blindfolded, and wielding a sword.[138] Related to this was the depiction of judgement, including the final judgement.[139] Mercy seemed harder to depict for modern artists unless beside her sister virtue or as a supplicant for others,[140] although Kenelm Henry Digby argued, from the vantage point of lengthy study of medieval Catholicism:

> The symbol which has superseded it in the modern civilization, representing a woman blindfolded and holding a balance, is never found on any monument of the middle ages. No foolish Pagan allegory was then used, to instil proud thoughts into human breasts. The balance was for the hand of the archangel; – the justice of man was mercy.[141]

Yet the symbolism of pagan antiquity was reflected in commonplace talk of 'veiling' the statue of mercy during war.[142]

Mercy and justice took their predictable place in decorating judicial, penal and civic buildings in London and across the British isles. London's Old Bailey was a place of royal justice: the emblem of the sheathed sword surmounted by crown – visible in a variety of printed depictions by Thomas Rowlandson and others – affixed to a crimson cloth-covered panel, conveyed this eloquently.[143] The old Newgate incorporated statues of justice, mercy and truth in niches (these reappeared in the new gaol).[144] The Court of King's Bench depicted justice, mercy, fortitude and clemency. The north wall of Lincoln's Inn had a fresco inspired by Raphael's 'School of Athens' by the young George Frederic Watts, the apex of the design three massive statues of justice, mercy and religion.[145] 'Now', asked the *British Quarterly Review*, 'as it has been very truly remarked mercy can have nothing to do with law, for law presupposes retribution. Why was Truth ignored?'[146] The Edwardian Central Criminal Court, where Newgate had stood, included sculptural mercy with supporters, by Frederick Pomeroy, as interior decoration of the dome. From the same era, the Law Society's Chancery Lane extension had Charles Pibworth's representations of mercy in the exterior.

In 1844 *The Athenaeum*, condemning workmanlike representation of Justice 'poising a steel-yard; a Mercy sheathing her sword', commented that it was 'precisely such things as we see every day on prominent town halls and law courts – beneath all criticism'.[147] Justice was hackneyed by sword and scales – images 'for the adornment of a police court' as the *Morning Chronicle* commented in 1845.[148] Representations of mercy at these civic and judicial sites were sculptural or two-dimensional. The courthouse for Middlesex, Clerkenwell Sessions House, was adorned with a relief chiselled by Joseph Nollekens (with separate representations of justice, and the king, over other windows) in 1780. Mercy held 'the blunted sword and the sceptre surmounted with British crown on which as emblematic of the mildness of the British laws rests a dove with an olive branch in her mouth'.[149] The eighteenth-century decoration of the lord mayor's court at York figured emblems of justice and mercy in 'fine painted glass'.[150] Statues of justice and mercy were pedimented at Stafford Shire Hall (1794) by John Charles Felix Rossi. In 1815, the Earl of Lonsdale presented to the magistrates of Cumberland Rossi's marble bust of George III to be placed over the judge's seat in the new crown court in Carlisle, between figures of mercy and justice.[151] Dublin's law courts had pedimental justice, mercy, wisdom and Moses by Edward Smyth and incorporated mercy among colossal bas-relief stucco renditions of appropriate legal virtues in the interior.[152] In Cork the court in George Street had justice, law and mercy on the pediment constructed in 1828.[153] Similar adornment was provided in Victorian judicial edifices, Edward Godwin's Gothic Town Hall at Northampton having pillars and statues representing justice and mercy in the vestibule: mercy breaking the sword of justice, with other decoration including the prodigal son's return.[154] The iconography of mercy and justice appeared in civic and municipal ritual with the scales of justice and sword of mercy embellishing the Lord Mayor of London's state coach. Appropriately the London-made 'warming machine' for the House of Burgesses in Richmond in the state of Virginia, given by the governor in 1770, bore the figures of justice and mercy.

What did mercy's representation in the iconography of civic government and justice amount to? That these were public sites adhering to a Christian vision of authority with an accepted place for mercy? The audience for such artworks was intended to read them as messages of ideal rule. Yet a late Victorian satirical image (reproduced as a postcard) on mercy and other judicial virtues, as external adornment but denied to the poor inside Dublin's Four Courts, shows such representation might be read ironically.[155] As well as warnings for judges and the multitude (as the architect Alfred Waterhouse suggested, of Thomas Woolner's statue of mercy for the judges' lodgings, and justice for the people's entrance to the Manchester assize courts), iconography presented that pardoning power wielded by the monarch.[156] In *The Royal Throne of Mercy* I studied John Gibson's statue of Victoria between justice and clemency. For, apart from its understandable presence alongside associated virtues in civic, legal and judicial contexts, mercy – conceived as a royal attribute – appeared on structures and objects associated with monarchs. Representations included Antonio Verrio's painting of Anne (*c*. 1703) in the Queen's Drawing Room at Hampton Court, attended by mercy and justice. Mercy with other virtues and attributes feature in Sir James Thornhill's decoration of George I's royal state coach, *c*. 1718. Thornhill's scheme on the north side of the Great Hall of Greenwich Hospital were the 'social virtues' in *chiaroscuro*, mercy with humanity, benignity, goodness, generosity, liberality, magnanimity and hospitality.[157] Medallioned trophies with justice and religion adorn the temple in the queen's honour after George III's recovery, at Stowe in Buckingham in 1790.

Mercy appeared in allegory and historic garb in the rebuilt Palace of Westminster, beyond Gibson's monumental sculptural group. Marochetti's equestrian Richard the Lionheart bore a bas-relief which one writer saw as 'key-note by which our old institutions keep in touch with the unchanging instincts of the human race', Richard's mercy towards the archer who inflicted the fatal wound.[158] Twenty years before these reliefs had been affixed to that monument, *Punch* might have alluded to the proliferation of medievalizing virtues when talking about mercy and all the virtues leaving their skiey home for the peers' housewarming in 1847.[159] The convention of representing mercy and justice as female allowed artists to include women in the proposed decorations; the historian Henry Hallam raised the point that for any attractive historical pictures series it was 'essential to intermingle female beauty and this … a strict adherence to our authentic records will not adequately supply … the most beautiful and interesting women in English history must be painted if at all upon the scaffold'.[160]

Mercy offered eminently suitable decoration for church and chapel. Justice and mercy figured in Chatsworth House chapel, and, to designs by Joshua Reynolds, in Oxford's New College chapel. Mercy appeared in funerary art: 'acts of mercy' were sculpted by William Theed for the Duchess of Gloucester's monument in St George's Chapel, Windsor. Mercy was apposite in memorials to judges. Lord Chief Justice John Holt's tomb at Redgrave in Suffolk displayed mercy and justice as did John Flaxman's memorial to Lord Chief Justice Mansfield at Westminster Abbey. Flaxman also represented acts of mercy in drawings 'in the manner of Ancient Sculpture', reproduced as aquatints by Frederick Lewis.[161]

Perhaps surprisingly, mercy did not join the virtues arrayed on the Albert Memorial's Gothic canopy in Hyde Park (but a later chapter notes Scott's memorial to Governor Hotham in the Australian state of Victoria).[162] Yet Gothic Revival and Oxford Movement further encouraged mercy's ecclesiastical presence. The publisher of Augustus Pugin's *Present State of Ecclesiastical Architecture in England* (1843) advertised the Catholic convert Eleanor Agnew's *Illustrations of The Corporal and Spiritual Works of Mercy*.[163] Wakeling's recollections of the movement identify the construction of the Church of All Saints, Margaret Street, London (its foundation stone laid by Edward Pusey in 1850) with a growth of 'very spiritual and corporal work of mercy'.[164] The revival of stained glass stimulated frequent Anglican memorial acts of mercy like the window for Harpenden church in Hertfordshire exhibited at the international exhibition in London in 1862 (see Figure 2.1); Pusey's memorial window in 1884 presented the same subject. Little wonder a late-nineteenth-century lecturer spoke of the country overrun with acts of mercy, miracles and other medievalizing scenes: the series became a stock item.[165]

Since mercy featured in public sculpture it also figured in models for exhibitions such as Charles Summer's prize-winning 'Mercy interceding for the Vanquished,' a

Figure 2.1 'Act of Mercy Window': Designed by Heaton, Butler and Bayne for St Nicholas Church, Harpenden. Engraving. Author's collection.

woman restraining a man raising a dagger to a prostrate man, in 1851.[166] Summer was probably influenced by the painter William Etty's 'The Combat: Pleading for the Vanquished' (1825) reproduced as an engraving by George Doo as 'Mercy Interceding for the Vanquished' (Figure 2.2) leading to the comment that the 'impassioned abandonment of the beautiful creature, who is hanging, *body* and soul, on the infuriated victor, is not the conduct of divine and dignified MERCY. It is that of WOMAN – loving, natural, genuine woman, – not that of a spirit of virtue in woman's *form*'. For this critic, 'Mercy, in her female impersonation, would surely be represented as a calm and dignified female, simply arresting, with sedate and commanding power, the arm of the conqueror; and with a countenance, implying the retaliative vengeance of heaven, forbidding, rather than appealing against, the fulfilled vengeance of man.'[167]

The theme reappeared in plaster in Edward Stephens's 'Mercy on the Battlefield' at the International Exhibition in London in 1862. Bronze copies were made for the Art Union of a design which appeared to one critic to show the virtue encouraging a wounded man to run for his life (a provincial critic detected 'mercy … in every feature').[168] A military setting was evident in the Royal Academy schools in 1887, mercy 'glar[ing] at the spectator from every side'. In Henry Pegram's work shrouded Death extended mercy to a mortally wounded soldier. George Frampton showed a 'pathetic figure of a little child offering a cup of water to an old man, a prisoner.'[169] Frampton's

Figure 2.2 After William Etty, 'The Combat Woman Pleading for the Vanquished'. Wood engraving *c.* 1880. Author's collection.

'Acts' accompanied similar efforts in 1888, including Goscombe John's 'Greeks tending an Amazon'.[170] Hamo Thorneycroft exhibited allegorical reliefs of justice and mercy which became depictions of justice and charity for the national memorial of General Gordon in Trafalgar Square in 1888: in 1918 he projected a statue of mercy interceding for the vanquished.[171]

I turn now to painted treatment outside architectural decoration. Mercy was allegorized in the artistic mission to use depiction of the virtues for moral instruction. G.K. Chesterton satirized 'meek Victorian allegories which showed Mercy and Foresight urging men to found a Society for the Preservation of Young Game'.[172] Representations might, as in the proposals for Westminster, include historical acts by the good and great. Depictions of actual monarchical mercy – a European-wide genre which was a 'traditional subject-type of history painting', included the prize-winning design by John Cross of Richard I's clemency for his killer, Bertrand de Gordon, engraved by Henry Shenton (given to subscribers of the Art Union of London in 1857).[173] The scene need not relate to British monarchs: John Vinter's 'An Act of Mercy' depicted Blanche, regent of France, liberating prisoners in Paris in 1512, a prize-winning competition for students at the Royal Academy in 1849 (see Figure 2.3). Other historical depictions, without monarchs, included John Millais's 'Mercy during St Bartholomew's Day' of

Figure 2.3 'An Act of Mercy', after J.A. Vinter, *Illustrated London News*, 29 December 1849, p.441. Author's collection.

1886, and worthies such Thomas Guthrie of Glasgow on a 'Mission of Mercy' of 1862, and Elizabeth Fry likewise, 'to the Prisoners in Newgate in the Year 1816' of 1860.[174]

There were also renditions of the virtues and passions. 'Mercy: David Sparing Saul's Life' was in a series on the 'passions' by the parricide Richard Dadd at Bethlem hospital in 1854.[175] George Frederic Watts's mercy was in the traditional guise of a mother with children. Other paintings related to acts (or errands) of mercy may be mentioned. Thomas Gainsborough depicted a servant giving food to a poor woman and children within view of a cathedral.[176] Jessie Macgregor's painting, exhibited in 1872, was suggested by the sermon on the Mount and Edward Armitage exhibited a series of acts of mercy at the Royal Academy in 1881 (see Figure 2.4).[177]

Figure 2.4 'An Act of Mercy', engraving after Jessie Macgregor, *The Graphic*, 20 January 1872, p.45. Author's collection.

Unsurprisingly, there were biblical scenes such as John Martin's 'David Spareth Saul at Hachilah' of 1831. In the 1850s Holman Hunt's first version of 'The Scapegoat' figured God's rainbow of mercy: he accentuated the sense of desolation and despair in a second version.[178] The Pre-Raphaelite Arthur Hughes completed an ethereal and light-suffused scene of angels at the 'door of mercy' in 1905. The prodigal son's return also attracted artists, Edward Prentis setting the scene in a modern parlour with the song 'Home Sweet Home' on the piano and a parable picture on mercy and forgiveness hanging on a wall.[179] Frederick Goodall's 'Misery and Mercy', figuring Christ and the woman taken in adultery, was displayed at the same time as Millais's Huguenot-themed painting on mercy, at the Royal Academy in 1887. Bernard Shaw described it as potboiler and 'tea-board painting' in *Fun*.[180] The Pre-Raphaelite Evelyn de Morgan also presented the biblical 'Mercy and Truth met together' (1898).[181]

Secular literature provided further inspiration, such as Shakespeare's Portia in the trial scene, with an anonymous cartoon in Westminster Hall in 1843[182]; a version by Millais and a watercolour by the Pre-Raphaelite George Smetham-Jones. William Collins's memorialist in 1765 suggested 'the scene and figures described [in his ode to mercy of 1746] … are exquisitely striking, and would afford a painter one of the finest subjects in the world'.[183] William Artaud attempted this in 'The Triumph of Mercy' (sometimes styled, 'Mercy: Lady Hamilton as Thetis pleading with Achilles before Troy') displayed in Macklin's Gallery of Poets in London, engraved by Francesco Bartolozzi and published in 1794.[184] Authors of the Gothic Revival such as Kenelm Digby provided stimulus for images of merciful Christian knights, like Edward Burne-Jones's watercolour of 1863 or unmerciful ladies illustrating John Keats' 'La Belle Dame sans Merci'.[185]

In printed form, the circulation of images included engravings of graces and virtues. Laura Valentine's *The Nobility of Life* – a presentation volume for the Christmas market c. 1869 contained, alongside texts, engravings of mercy interceding in knightly combat by the engraver Dalziel, vignettes of merciful errands, and a splendid chromolithograph of Edward Poynter's painting of the prodigal son embraced by his aged father (see Figure 2.5). More ephemeral images included the transparency of 'justice, truth and mercy' and temple of concord in Dover's New Theatre in 1791.[186] A masonic ball in Ireland had 'admirably painted' transparencies of females representing justice and mercy; freemasonry claimed these were 'great masonic attributes'.[187] There were tableaux such as that showing the 'classical' theme of intercession for the vanquished praised in a review of the Canterbury Music Hall in 1873.[188] Mercy and justice were suggested in the United States as themes for children's tableaux, with the injunction, 'justice must be a larger lady than Mercy. Mercy kneels in attitude of prayer with clasped hands; Justice stands erect holding sword and scales'.[189] The harder-edged virtue of justice was probably a more prolific figure in trade-union imagery such as that selected by a Victorian tinplate workers' union.[190]

In the sculptural and painted rendition of mercy the virtue generally took female guise.[191] Artists depicted abstract personifications and angels of mercy.[192] Avoiding an excursus on the belief in heavenly spirits, a few words are appropriate about mercy as angelic and people as 'angels of mercy'.[193] The *Illustrated Police News* imagined an angel hovering over the Prince of Wales's sickbed in December 1871.[194] Carlo Marochetti's

Figure 2.5 E.J. Poynter, 'Mercy. The prodigal son', colour print from L. Valentine, *The Nobility of Life, its Graces and Virtues* (London: Warne, 1869), after p.60. Author's collection.

marble angel overlooked the memorial well at Cawnpore, a sacred place for Britons after the massacre of women and children during the Mutiny.[195] The angels in Victorian cemeteries might represent mercy weeping: the Gothic revivalist Augustus Pugin, criticizing a proliferation of non-Christian funeral art, wanted angels and 'emblems of mercy and redemption'.[196]

As a description, 'angel of mercy' was applied to Florence Nightingale: paintings and engravings of Nightingale in Scutari were entitled 'An Angel of Mercy' (Butterworth) and 'Works of Mercy' (Henry Barraud).[197] Representations of nuns appeared in British art as 'sisters of mercy', for example Henriette Browne's painting of 1859. *The Graphic* depicted French nuns as 'angels of mercy' during the Franco-Prussian War (see Figure 2.6). Sisters of mercy were controversial in Protestant Britain: anti-Catholics scorned the idea of mercy 'clad in garments nightlike and forbidding' or 'by stern rule' plying 'Mercy's execution'.[198] Less problematic was the association between nursing and mercy. Nurses and doctors were devoted to acts of mercy – one professor of medicine in an early number of *The Lancet* saw the profession 'approaching to the power and purity of mercy'.[199] The next chapter turns to the gendering and embodying of mercy.

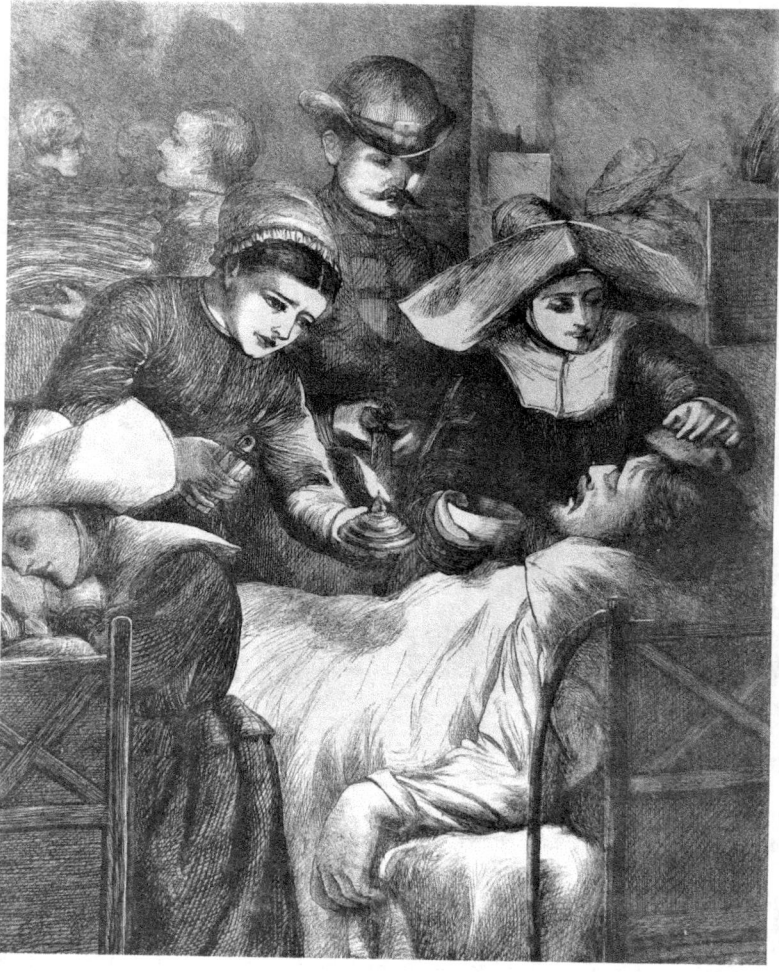

Figure 2.6 'Angels of Mercy', *The Graphic*, 3 September 1870, p.217. Author's collection.

3

Merciful agents and subjects

Having established mercy's cultural dimension through presence and representation in literature and art, this chapter looks at its embodiment, identifying important categories of agents and subjects. Ideas about the nature of human mercy are examined firstly by considering how Britons thought about it as subjects responding to royal or elite mercy; then its relationship to ethnicity, race and nationality are explored. I turn to mercy's gendering, its relationship to childhood and pedagogical link to kindness to animals. The broader field of philanthropy or active benevolence – a key arena for women – is considered from mercy's perspective.

British subjects of mercy

The powerful grant, bestow, show, extend, withhold or deny mercy to subjects. The language of mercy from petitioners' or supplicants' viewpoints is recoverable in legal cases through petitions and utterances, such as the Old Bailey reports. The proper response in criminal cases was of course gratitude and humility. I am interested here to give some recognition to the agency and voice of those seeking or receiving mercy. There are eighteenth-century examples of State mercy spurned (or its claims to be merciful denied). Sometimes newspapers reported refusal of the terms and a choice of ignominious death rather than transportation. The apprentice and forger Samuel Burt, whilst praising George III's humanity, 'only … equalled by his love of virtue', astonished a court in 1787 by initially refusing the mercy of transportation to New South Wales since 'life was no longer an object with him, as it was utterly impossible that he could be joined in union with the person that was dearer to him than life itself'.[1] The youthful Sarah Cowden refused exile, for robbery in a house of ill-fame in Petticoat Lane, despite the efforts of William Garrow and the Recorder's admonition in a 'very humane and sensible speech' in 1789. This was an 'affront to the humanity of her Sovereign'.[2] In this case the Ordinary (chaplain) persuaded her otherwise.[3] In 1792 a convict called Jones refused transportation to Botany Bay.[4]

We might think of mercy in terms of relations between social groups and classes. The American Ralph Waldo Emerson commented in 1856 that an Englishman 'shows no mercy to those below him in the social scale, as he looks for none from those above him: any forbearance from his superiors surprises him, and they suffer in his good opinion'.[5] Yet mercy was precisely what was shown between classes, through those interventions paternal, benevolent, or charitable, discerned as 'acts of mercy'. Recipients were supposed to be grateful: sometimes the historical record shows otherwise. The satirical *Punch*, in its radical phase, reproduced a letter from John Shelly and William Lewis, erroneously sentenced to fifteen years' transportation, being too poor to bring witnesses to prove their alibi, for an assault on a Devon yeoman, James Reddicliffe in 1848: 'It does somehow strike us, and we must be bold enough to ask it, – if you can only forgive folks for being innocent, what sort of mercy do you show them as is guilty?'[6] Other subjects of royal mercy in Britain's empire, in particular in Ireland and India, are studied in later chapters.

Racializing mercy

How was mercy imagined by Christian writers to exist in the racial and religious 'other'? This is a large topic, complicated by pre-modern understanding for when people extolled or urged national virtues they were not thinking in racial terms.[7] Nevertheless, it is clear that a supposed disposition to mercy marked difference or similarity between Britons and non-Britons.[8] Another perspective is British mercy as described by the non-British: an important subject treated here only cursorily.[9]

Others have explored British encounters with non-Christian 'natives' where notions of the merciful were expressed. Mercy might be embodied by individuals (a Pocahontas pleading for Captain Smith, see Figure 3.1) or providential acts rather than choices made by native peoples.[10] Unmerciful acts in these non-British cultures could be the consequence of heathenism – *sati* in India or widow-strangulation in Fiji – furnishing

Figure 3.1 'Rescue of Captain Smith by Pocahontas', wood engraving, *Pictorial Times*, 1846, p.340. Author's collection.

justification for missionaries and European influence.[11] Unmercy was identified with particular peoples or nations – the west-African kingdom of Dahomey for instance, the leading source of slaves bound for America and ruled by Gezo, from 1818 until his death in 1858, in whom 'the very ideas of mercy and clemency are unknown'.[12] Critics of British imperial cruelty might stress, as Robert Martin did during war against the Xhosa of 1851–2, capacity for clemency in *non*-white peoples.[13] Some races or nations were identified with cultures of magnanimity, like the Japanese in early-twentieth-century discourse.[14]

Mercy's use as a justification for empire is detailed in Chapter 6, but it is worthwhile noting the examination of mercy as a British characteristic made in the nineteenth century. Thomas Fowell Buxton identified a disjunction between harsh laws and a people 'so merciful and humane' in a Commons debate on removing the capital penalty for forgery in May 1821.[15] In 1854 the American Harriet Beecher Stowe, recounting the anti-slavery agitator Thomas Clarkson's life, wrote of Anglo-Saxons as 'justly called the Romans of the nineteenth century', conquering and breaking 'weaker races … with little regard either to justice or mercy'. Yet she identified a 'peculiar efficient' philanthropy created by individual compassion tempered by the 'vigorous sense of justice as appears in our habeas corpus, our jury trials, and other features of state organization'.[16]

Race mixed with gender in one account of the Celtic propensity to mercy contrasted with the English for justice and truth. In the *National Review*, in 1864, it was claimed that scholastic division of virtues into moral and theological reflected a truth shown in individuals, the sexes and nations: 'The Saxon is wanting in much of the tenderness and religious patience of the Celt and the Celt seems too rarely able to grasp the fundamental notion of the inherent sanctity of abstract truth and justice.'[17] Writing on Ireland in *Fraser's Magazine* in 1865, the Anglo-Irish Frances Power Cobbe treated mercy as a 'virtue much preferred to cold justice'.[18] The *Londonderry Sentinel*'s point in 1876 was that Irish mercy was unsullied by the sort of press commentary on the accused in England, 'silent on whatever might militate against him'.[19] In a similar Celtic vein, we might note the merciful disposition reputed to Fingal 'of the mildest look', king of Morven in ancient Caledonia, in Ossianic poetry and asserted to be remembered among modern Highlanders (or so it was claimed of this eighteenth-century forgery).[20]

Acts of mercy might be seen as foundational to British North America, in the story of Pocahontas – represented on the American and British stage in our period.[21] Yet the merciless savage was a trope as enduring as the noble savage. John Trenchard and Thomas Gordon's essays on bigotry in Anglicanism in the 1720s noted the cruelty of the Iroquois, but observed that they were 'merciful and good-natured to one another'.[22] Tales of 'Indian' cruelty were prominent during the Revolution. Later writers such as Richard Dodge in the 1880s presented the native American as a 'ferocious beast of prey, unsoftened by any touch of pity or mercy'.[23] Cruelty, pity and justice were central to nineteenth-century histories written of Native American experience at the hands of Europeans.[24] Absence of mercy and justice justified destruction, as Henry Rowe Schoolcraft recalled (1845), 'It was always represented as a meritorious act in old revolutionary reminiscences to have killed one of them in the border wars and thus aided in ridding the land of a cruel and unnatural race in whom all feelings of pity, justice and mercy were supposed to be obliterated.'[25]

Encountering the non-European, it was asserted that the concept was absent or that it and related qualities lacked expression in 'native' languages. Montaigne's 'Des cannibales' (published 1580) presented a Brazilian society without words for lying, treachery, envy but also none for pardon: the vanquished were eaten rather than shown mercy.[26] In the Tonga Islands, higher qualities such as mercy and justice (or their 'vicious' counterparts) were absent from native vocabulary according to a British account published in 1818, except through recourse to *ofa* meaning 'friendship'.[27] Even in 1918, it was deemed a remarkable fact 'that among most non-Christian peoples there is no word for mercy'.[28] The ethnologist William Baucke suggested European dissatisfaction with one Maori word, *aroha*, to cover love, pity, mercy, failed to understand the indigenous understandings conveyed through inflection, intonation and context.[29] Yet Baron Suyematsu's elegant work on Japan (1905) suggested complexity and sophisticated Confucian vocabularies of the virtues, including those related to magnanimity.[30] Perhaps none spent longer on the contradictory texts of missionaries, travellers and scientists than Herbert Spencer, in *Synthetic Philosophy*, seeking to understand the temperament and moral qualities of 'primitive man' as data for his sociology by accumulating references to philoprogenitiveness, cruelty and mildness.[31]

The non-Western response to discourses of mercy was encountered in the preceding chapter's brief study of response to missionary and proselytic discourse. Nitobe's late-nineteenth-century *The Bushido: The Soul of Japan* is an interesting presentation of Japanese values with 'sympathy and pity' and allied virtues treated as 'the highest of all the attributes of the human soul'. Nitobe wrote, 'We needed no Shakespeare to feel – although, perhaps, like the rest of the world, we needed him to express it – that mercy became a monarch better than his crown'. Justice and mercy are gendered in his account as masculine and feminine.[32] I turn now to the gendering of mercy in British culture.

Gendering mercy

The last chapter ended with preliminary observations on mercy tending to be represented in feminine form. This was no mere artistic convention but a feature of the language and as Alexander Bain, professor of logic at Aberdeen, noted in 1863, the 'English practice of confining distinction of gender to difference of sex, renders those occasional deviations very impressive, by actually suggesting to the mind the idea of personal existence and attributes'. Bain explained that things 'remarkable for strength, superiority, majesty, sublimity' such as death or time were looked upon as masculine, while 'gentleness, beauty, and grace, fertility or productiveness, belonging, or imagined to belong to things, suggest a feminine personification, as the Earth, Spring, Hope, Virtue, Truth, Justice, Mercy, Peace'.[33]

As a disposition or emotion, mercy was associated with women as in this assertion by James Hodges (in a work dedicated to Queen Anne) in 1710, 'this stronger

Disposition to Mercy in the Nature of Woman cannot but make her Nature more Glorious, than that of Man less disposing to Mercy, seeing it is a certain Effect and Evidence of a stronger Love'.[34] The Talmud asserted women are merciful (Meghilah 14). Catholicism – to its nineteenth-century British apologists – seemed to equate female nature with mercifulness. Kenelm Henry Digby spoke of the angel-like perfection of the woman's heart contributing to the 'reign of mercy upon earth' in envisioning the Middle Ages in 1846.[35] The Anglo-Catholic Edward Pusey discussed the 'Romanist' notion of the Virgin as queen of mercy during Tractarian controversy and others at the time commented on the 'Romish' tendency to present Christ or Mary as more merciful than God or leave Jesus 'only in the stern unapproachable character of a Judge'.[36] Later in the century the clergyman George Cobbold noted a similar shift from masculine to feminine personification in the Buddhist goddess of mercy, Kwannon, and commented that the 'Blessed Mother has ... been made to encroach upon the prerogatives of her Divine Son'.[37]

British women spoke and wrote about mercy.[38] Private correspondence referred to their lives' small or great mercies as seen in the letters and diaries of the Quakers Mary Waring and Eliza Southall ('mercy is a broader thing than our most earnest prayers suppose').[39] As Chapter 5 shows, during heightened debate about mercy in the French Revolution, they had opinions to share. Some mercy was mere figure of speech: Jane Carlyle's letters habitually exclaimed 'mercy'. Frances Power Cobbe argued in 1869 that the tenderness and mercy of woman's nature was a defect of their 'quality', leading them to honour less 'stern justice and veracity' whereas men were prone to 'exact justice and vengeance, and to forget mercy and charity'. This was amendable through education.[40] The early-twentieth-century *American Women and Social Progress*'s discussed the idea that 'the concept of sympathy was first developed by women' and asserted they 'feel pity more keenly than men'.[41] But the popular novelist and animal-lover Ouida's essay 'The Quality of Mercy', in 1896 argued that with their power to shape infants and lovers in the ways of mercy women did not 'use this unlimited power ... to breathe the quality of mercy into the souls of those who for the time are as wax in their hands ... Mercy is not in them, nor humility, nor sympathy'.[42]

Texts as varied as play, poetry, novel, collective biography (see Figure 3.2) and sermon, connected gender and mercy. Male poets including Walter Scott, George Crabbe, Charles Kingsley, and John Critchley Prince, expressed belief that women were naturally ministering angels.[43] George Crabbe's 'Woman!' (a poem of 1807 asserting women's compassion regardless of race) stated: 'Man may the sterner virtues know, | Determined Justice, truth severe; | But female hearts with pity glow.'[44] Thomas Norton and Thomas Sackville's sixteenth-century *Gorbudoc* asks, 'O where is ruthe? Or where is pittie now?' and ends, 'If not, in women, mercie may be found.'[45] The previous chapter noted other British plays presenting mercy. Often, a female character implored mercy. Friedrich Schiller's *Mary Stuart* of 1800 has Lord Burleigh comment, in one translation, 'The sword of justice that so graces man | Is odious in a woman's hand.'[46] Harrison Ainsworth's bestselling *The Tower of London* (1840) depicted a character imploring Mary Tudor for mercy, 'A woman's heart can never be closed to the pleadings of the unfortunate of her own sex.'

Figure 3.2 Frank Mundell, *Heroines of Mercy* (London: Sunday School Union, 1896). Author's collection.

Statements about women's exercise of mercy concerned the distribution of power. Man was a being of justice but woman was one of mercy, went a transatlantic aphorism entitled 'parallel of the sexes' in the early nineteenth century.[47] A correspondent in the *Gentleman's Magazine* in 1788 in calling for women to be admitted to Parliament argued this would temper 'the stern mind of man with feminine delicacy and by that means [season] justice with mercy'.[48] The Reverend Watts Lethbridge's *Woman the Glory of the Man* (1856) argued woman was better out of the law: 'She and justice never agree. Mercy is her strength. Portia as judge is most eloquent on mercy. Nature has made woman merciful ... The guilty would take advantage of her merciful disposition.'[49] The juxtaposition continued through the century, finding utterance in William Lecky's *History of European Morals* in 1869, 'men lean most to justice and women to mercy' and Herbert Spencer's thoughts on abstract justice in *The Study of Sociology* in 1873.[50]

Anthropologists sought to explain feminine propensity to pity and mercy to animals and humans.[51] Modern research on 'value orientation' claims to uncover gendered differences in caring values.[52] The nineteenth-century habit of describing the virtue as 'sweet' from Shakespeare's famous lines from *Titus Andronicus* might even, though linked to 'nobility's true badge', have feminized it.[53] Infrequent references to manly mercy, clemency and pity could be framed as fatherly, following the pattern of God as the 'father of mercy'.[54] It could be linked to Christian tenderness and recognition that the Son of Man combined 'all that was most tender and merciful in woman, and all that was most strong and courageous in man'.⁵⁵ It was an attribute associated with chivalry or identified in recent military leaders (as explored in Chapter 7).⁵⁶ It can be seen in discourse on boxing as manly and generous. 'An Englishman learns from His youth,' John Farington the artist reported a dinner conversation in 1815, 'to depend upon his unarmed personal valour, and to spare His antagonist when conquered and at His mercy.'⁵⁷ In the Commons in 1834 the MP for Birmingham Thomas Attwood defended pugilism for 'qualities of the highest order – forbearance, mercy, a manly control over the bad passions, exhibited in the prize-fighter'.⁵⁸ The popular Anglican preacher Frederick Robertson of Brighton referred to 'manly mercy' in a sermon in 1849.⁵⁹ Discourse on prayer emphasized how intercession (for divine mercy) was manly.

Female emancipation might be thought to alter mercy discourse: the *Law Journal* in 1912 felt moves to drop the marriage vow of obedience took away 'much of the idea of special mercy to offenders of the weaker sex which is inherent in British justice'.⁶⁰ There was discussion about propensities to mercy in debates about women jurors (and barristers) – women jurors were permitted in 1919 but not empanelled until 1920.⁶¹ The journalist Florence Fenwick Miller argued for a female presence in court to make men involved (as jurors, judges and so on) 'talk, and even think more decently'.⁶²

Mercy was also discussed in relation to fallen women: the historian John Seeley explaining, in his widely read life of Christ (1866) why mercy failed 'even in the tender hearts of women', why it tended not to be shown by virtuous women to fallen sisters: 'Why is it that in this one case the female sex is more hard-hearted than the male?'⁶³ 'A Song of the Perplexed', dissecting inconsistent conventional ideas on female abilities and qualities in *Women's Franchise* in 1909, observed, 'she's prone to mercy – so unjust', as a consequence.⁶⁴

The creation of Sisters of Mercy in Protestant England (Catherine McAuley founded the Catholic Sisters of Mercy in Ireland in 1831⁶⁵) stimulated discussion of female propensities and anti-Catholic reflections on abusing women's merciful nature, the 'marvellous skill with which [Popery] seizes on every true principle of grace or of nature, and so perverts and misapplies them', while a 'true' mercy was not based on self-righteousness, as the Reverend Hetherington argued.⁶⁶ Works of mercy could not be works of merit in this interpretation. In the next section, however, those works are explored from philanthropy's perspective. To recognize philanthropic mercy is to recognize a collective act or emotion – not just the fate of individuals before God or the magistrate.⁶⁷

Acts of mercy: Framing philanthropy as merciful

Oh Charity! Thou fairest birth
Of heavenly mercy! Sent on earth⁶⁸

… it was with genuine relief that men and women betook themselves to the helpful works of charity and mercy as a way of escape from the battle of the chasubles, and from the arithmetic of Bishop Colenso.⁶⁹

Acts of mercy extend beyond the clemency bestowed or withheld in law courts though the corporal act might involve quasi-judicial judgements in philanthropic institutions. When unmarried women applied for relief at the Foundling Hospital in London, the evidence of the petitions and statements, the moral crimes of the woman and 'seducer', might call for a response of mercy from the governors (one of these, the painter Joseph Highmore, depicted c. 1746 an angel of mercy stopping a mother's attempts to strangle her baby with a ribbon).[70]

Denominational congregations, philanthropic movements and reform agitations appealed to notions of Christian mercy and justice: going beyond concern with individual souls to wider social justice. But critics stressed the need for individual responsibility that nurtured independence rather than the 'fidgety kindness of modern mercy' in the *Morning Chronicle*'s phrase in 1815.[71] And as indicated by the second quotation heading this section, works of mercy might be attractive alternatives to theological controversy, religious doubts and personal unhappiness.[72]

There are appeals to 'shewing mercy to the poor' in New Poor Law polemics in the mid to late 1830s. Working-class radicals were scornful of the 'mercy' of magistrate, commissioners and guardians.[73] Pamphleteers stressed Christian duty: debating mercy's role in implementing social policy. The former MP for Derby, Sir George Crewe, discussed the implication of Portia's speech in a pamphlet against the Poor Law's principle and practice in 1843.[74] 'If the New Poor-Law be true, mercy is a crime,' commented the Welshman George Baxter.[75] Kay of Abingdon contrasted the blazing abroad of a religion of mercy with the grinding of poor Britons and suggested 'new charity-bastiles' be emblazoned, from Prov. xii.10. 'THE TENDER MERCIES OF THE WICKED ARE CRUEL.'[76] The interpretation of a heartless system ensured the resonance of appeals to mercy decades later: Charles Keene's *Punch* cartoon in 1866 depicted an unfeeling beadle confronting a Sister of Mercy, 'You're the sister of mercy is you? Well, we ain't got that name in the house, so toddle!'[77]

Factory reformers of the 1830s mobilized mercy against mammon.[78] Two decades later a laissez faire attitude to protection from machinery seemed more concerned with mercy to owners than to workers endangered by accidents, according to Henry Morley's controversial essay in Dickens's *Household Words*, in the year *Hard Times* was serialized. Morley quoted Dryden's lines from *Absalom and Achitophel* (1681) on mercy 'become our crime'.[79] The Free Trade agitation used the figure of mercy alongside truth, and justice. A sonnet to Richard Cobden at the great free-trade banquet in Glasgow in January 1844, described a 'high Apostle in the holiest cause | That Truth and Mercy ever smiled upon'.[80] Mercy was unsurprisingly mobilized in prison reform. The novelist Matthew Lewis's poem on 'The Felon' memorably ends, 'There's Mercy for each creeping thing; – | But MAN HAS NONE FOR MAN!'[81] Mercy framed the discussion in Dickens's *All the Year Round* of local responses to the Lancashire cotton famine in 1862; articles entitled 'An Act of Mercy' detailed 'the actual working of the machinery of mercy which has been set in motion by means of public benevolence only.'[82]

'A child's life,' a clergyman wrote in a study of Dr Barnardo, 'is the mercy-seat of Christian ministry.' In child-welfare mercy was naturally invoked by the evangelical Barnardo and his biographers: although an essay about the National Society for the Prevention of Cruelty to Children by the Reverend Benjamin Waugh stated that the

'Angel of Mercy herself must wield the sword of justice' against cruelty.[83] Barnardo's movement encompassed a branch of the Humane Society entitled 'Merciful Brigade', promoted through the periodical *Our Darlings* (see Figure 3.3).[84]

Royal involvement in philanthropy, studied by Prochaska, ensured mercy's association with royalty in eulogy. Royalty patronized a League of Mercy fundraising for hospitals, George V being Sovereign of the Order of Mercy which his father helped found in 1899. The order's cross depicted children clambering over a maternal figure. Its leading supporters included members of the aristocracy. Given the mixed motives in philanthropy, mercy could be seen here as endangered by a glittering show, 'Ostentation, Display, Forgetfulness, and False-kindness' in the words of a Quaker

Figure 3.3 First page of *Our Merciful Brigade* no.2, June 1883. Author's collection.

journal.[85] Yet achievements in mercy fed national pride: *Britain's Record, What She Has Done for The World* was the title of one work detailing the various 'waves' of mercy.[86] The imperative to perform acts of mercy legitimized women's public involvement. The Conservative politician Lord Sandon spoke of Crimean War nurses and others in medical tasks being protected by their moral sense and higher feelings in performing these works of mercy.[87] But late-nineteenth-century mercy was identified as amateurish: 'The complaint of the Charity Organisation Society, slightly varied from Shakespeare, is that The quality of Mercy is not trained.'[88]

Mercy towards the brute creation

'I think I mentioned mercy to animals as rather a *new* feature of our national character, brought out by laws and education,' Lucy Aikin commented in 1838, a suggestion of an important recent development in the operation of merciful sentiments in Britain.[89] Women were accorded a central part in this more merciful sensibility. The vegetarian Alice Marie Lewis, arguing for the 'Rights of the Non-Human Races,' claimed in 1889 that female emancipation should be accompanied by 'hostility towards deeds of violence, and by the spread of the instinct of pity and mercy'.[90] *Woman's Signal*, organ of the British Women's Temperance Association, created a 'mercy department' for animal welfare in 1895.[91] I noted above the link between child welfare and kindness to animals by Barnardo. His merciful brigades followed Bands of Mercy (1875) created to protect animals from human cruelty.[92]

This association between human mercy and non-human animals developed from the call for compassion for the 'brute creation'. Sermons, tracts, hymns and newspaper articles linked kindness to animals with mercy. There were texts like the anonymous *Clemency to brutes; the substance of two sermons* (1761), Humphry Primatt's *Dissertation on the Duty of Mercy and Sin of Cruelty to Brute Animals* (1776), the evangelical Sarah Trimmer's *Fabulous Histories* for children (1786); the 'tender-hearted [English] member of the *Club des Jacobines*', John Oswald's *The Cry of Nature* (1791); and John Lawrence's treatise on horses 'and on the moral duties of man towards the brute creation' (1802).[93] This movement attracted royal patronage. Abraham Smith's scriptural and moral catechism, 'designed chiefly to lead the minds of the rising generation to the love and practice of mercy, and to expose the horrid nature of cruelty to the dumb creation', was dedicated to Princess Alexandrina Victoria, the future Queen Victoria, in 1833.[94]

'Mercy Recommended' was often the title to an anthologized passage in Laurence Sterne's *Tristram Shandy* (1759) where uncle Toby frees a fly.[95] Among early-nineteenth-century hymns intended to promote the cause was the evangelical Rowland Hill's 'Cruelty to Brutes': 'Sweet it is to see a child | Tender, merciful, and mild – | Every ready to perform | Acts of mercy to a worm.'[96] The popular poet Martin Tupper's 'Mercy to Animals. A Ballad of Humanity', appeared in newspapers in the 1840s.[97]

Considerate treatment of animals was certainly seen as a matter involving the Christian virtue.[98] Those writing against cruelty to the brute creation sought to render the characterization of a 'merciful man' problematic, by showing that to limit this mercy was unscriptural. Trimmer enjoined mercy as scripture stated that 'merciful man is merciful to his beast'.[99] In fact this claim, often made, was based on a misquotation from Proverbs xii.10 or a distortion of the beatitudes (Matthew v.7, 'Blessed are the merciful: for they shall obtain mercy').[100] Sermons on animals presented scriptural texts in arguing for God remembering 'even mercy to animals'.[101] In commenting about the relative mercy towards animals in other religions it was sometimes noted that Turks were remarkably merciful to brute creation, following the Quran, if not so merciful to humans.[102] In other instances of advocacy of animal kindness, Shakespeare's 'quality of mercy' speech was employed.[103]

The Quaker social reformer Thomas Clarkson's *The Diversions of the Field* (1806) spoke of men who performed 'numerous acts of mercy' yet did not 'deserve the character of the thoroughly merciful man'.[104] The Irish Unitarian minister William Drummond's *The Rights of Animals* (1838), on the basis that Christianity was 'throughout a religion of mercy', asserted mercy could not be limited by tribe, nation 'or rationality'.[105] Other essays on animal rights used this argument.[106] A review of a tract by James Macaulay, editor of the Christian periodical *The Leisure Hour*, stated of cruelty to animals:

> In its grosser forms, it may be prevented or punished by law; but for the most part the happiness of animals will always depend upon the mercy of man, and hence it is a duty springing directly from the Christian religion to assist by all means in one's power in raising the tone of public opinion upon the subject, and particularly in educating the conscience and affections of the young.[107]

Sometimes a lexical distinction was attempted: the American *Advocate of Peace* spoke of 'kindness towards Animals, Mercy Towards Human beings'.[108] If man was lord of all, 'mercy is the charter of his sovereignty'.[109] Here, in relation to brute creation, mercy was the opposite of cruelty. Others argued justice was necessary 'because mercy implies somewhat of indulgence', rather than right.[110]

Experimentation on animals foregrounded questions of mercy and justice. Anna Barbauld explained her poem 'The Mouse's Petition' (published 1772) was about these.[111] Fanny Kemble mused in her diary in 1831 that 'perhaps some of our more immediate mercy is to be sacrificed to our humanity in the lump', apropos of Jean-Baptiste Bouillaud's vivisection (in the Faculty of Medicine in Paris). Britons condemned his contemporary François Magendie's physiological experiments in the first half of the century using the scriptural language of mercy.[112]

In anti-vivisection debates from the 1870s mercy still figured, with the sort of scientific education proposed by Thomas Huxley seen as contending with the sentiment inculcated in religious education; the physiologist disregarding 'looks for mercy' from the animal victim.[113] Women might be especially equipped to lead, 'as the chief possessor of the prerogative of mercy' they should give this 'new education … in relation to Mercy'.[114] The vegetarian mystic Dr Anna Kingsford presented her anti-vivisection campaign as an education in 'justice and mercy' for medical men.[115] The transatlantic activist Thomas Timmins was described as the 'Apostle of Mercy'. Tracts such as *Plea for Mercy to Animals* by the Reverend George Weldon (1876) invoked mercy.[116] Visual propaganda referenced mercy though it was the 'Genius of Pity staying the Vivisector's hand' after a painting by the German Gabriel Max that was sold by the anti-vivisectionist Victoria Street Society.[117]

Kindness and mercy to animals figured in the early Sunday School movement; children's essay competitions similarly framed the matter as one of mercy to animals.[118] The monthly *Band of Mercy Advocate*, with engravings, anecdotes, music and poetry, appeared four years after the first children's Band of Mercy formed by the Wesleyan Catherine Smithies. The periodical's estimated readership was 100,000 by 1888 in a Universal Mercy Band of the British Empire (see Figure 3.4).[119] 'Be kind to animals' was the movement's motto. Smithies was active in anti-slavery, temperance and other causes; her son, the publisher Thomas Smithies, learned 'mercy took all living creatures

Figure 3.4 Front cover illustration, *Band of Mercy*, December 1891. Author's collection.

into its sympathy'. Like other movements geared to children and adults, the message was promoted through hymns.[120] Women played a central part.[121]

The language of mercy featured in animal-welfare discourse well into the twentieth century.[122] This is unsurprising given the role of clergymen such as Hardwicke Rawnsley. In *Nature Notes*, the Selborne Society's magazine, his appeal, 'Ad Misericordiam', linked God's mercy to humanity with man's mercy towards birds, against 'murderous millinery' and the sacrifice of horses in the Boer war.[123] In Rawnsley's discourse animals appealed for mercy – his verse 'My Feathered Lady', has thousands of birds 'in silence to entreat | For mercy, round the murderers' feet'.[124] Appeals to clergy and ministers referenced not only 'enlightened' and 'humane' principles but 'the best interests of a religion of mercy'.[125] This particular campaign frequently contrasted mercy with human activity – as in the Cockney refrain to 'Murder Hats', 'They loves mercy, yes, they do, | They loves pity, it is true, | But they mostly and especially loves their hats' and James Buckland's attack on 'befeathered Herodias'.[126]

Justice and mercy could be seen as central not simply to religion but to the practice of science.[127] Were Christian ideas about justice and mercy inimical to emerging 'scientific' ideas of nature? Sympathy and pity were presented as *underlying* natural selection, by one anti-vivisectionist, the Reverend Arthur Ingleby.[128] It was a question of the 'triumph of Mercy over false science'.[129] The *Zoophilist* argued, a 'doctrine that mercy is to be measured, not by the sensitiveness of the sufferer, or the extent of his sufferings – but solely by his likeness to our own dear selves, is a beautiful example of neo-scientific morality'.[130] Anti-vivisectors saw their role as imparting mercy (and justice) to the struggle for existence.[131]

The ultimate act of human mercy might be to avoid killing for food and other needs, becoming 'more merciful' than the lions, tigers and vultures, according to a vegetarian ballad. Organized vegetarianism beyond narrow religious sects in Britain was a product of the 1840s. The *Vegetarian Advocate* of 1848 and early volumes of the *Vegetarian Messenger* in setting out the movement's claims asserted merciful principles and identified the trinity of justice, truth and mercy, optimistically seeing in disquiet with capital punishment growth of merciful sentiment: 'Is mercy to extend itself to the murderer, and not to the innocent and unoffending victim of the slaughter-house system?'[132] A shield emblazoned 'mercy and truth' figured in decorations at soirées and annual Vegetarian Society banquet and the message of mercy was contained in tracts.[133] One in 1898 about a vegetarian hospital was entitled *Mercy, not curiosity, the mother of medicine*. The *Herald of the Golden Age* argued in 1900 that only by basing the diet 'upon an eternal principle, that of mercy' rather than selfish motives would it last.[134] Improvements in abattoirs were framed by non-vegetarians as an advance in mercy.[135] On the other hand, reported scenes of animal-slaughter cruelty were used to advance the campaign: Thomas Hardy's *Jude the Obscure*, for instance.[136]

The idea that animals themselves felt or showed mercy was entertained. Pliny the Elder claimed lions showed mercy to suppliants.[137] The moral nature of animals is something present-day philosophers and others debate.[138] A contributor to *Our Animal Friends* (motto: 'Blessed are the merciful' Matt.v.7), organ of the American Society for the Prevention of Cruelty to Animals, in 1895, was sure a higher morality allowed them to feel sympathy and benevolence, and cited John Lubbock's admission that feelings of humanity – the quality of mercy – were displayed by the ants he studied.¹³⁹ Anecdotes about the ourang-outang claimed it sometimes showed mercy to humans.¹⁴⁰ The naturalist Jonathan Couch found birds who showed 'deliberate affectionate disposition', rather than mere 'involuntary compassion', for neglected fledglings.¹⁴¹ St Bernards were trained for missions of mercy and presented to juveniles and others in texts and images from the early nineteenth century onwards – and anecdotes suggested canine mercy beyond the Alps.¹⁴² There were also the appeals to mercy discerned in the animal gaze confronting the vivisecting scientist.¹⁴³

Lessons in mercy

The propriety of representing MERCY as a Youth, the season of life when our affections are most compassionate and tender, need not be insisted on.¹⁴⁴

Mercy is as much a lesson to be learned as any other maxim in moral philosophy. Savages and children are cruel, simply because they don't know cruelty when they see it.¹⁴⁵

> 'Tis to Thy sovereign grace I owe
> That I was born on British ground;
> Where streams of heavenly mercy flow,
> And words of sweet salvation sound.¹⁴⁶

The quotations heading this section express several distinct nineteenth-century views on mercy related to childhood and youth: that there was a developmental stage when a human was particularly merciful and that mercy needed training. The third quotation might suggest British compassionate exceptionalism: in fact Isaac Watt's 'divine song for children' (published in 1715) stresses the boon of being raised in a Christian country. Mercy, even if accepted as an innate human feeling or emotion, required instruction, whether weekly schooling, Sunday School lessons in divine mercy (*Teacher*: 'What does mercy mean, Nathaniel?' *Nathaniel*: 'I suppose it's when a boy deserved a whipping and don't get it'¹⁴⁷) or moral culture within the home.¹⁴⁸ Women as mothers played a key role in this sentimental or moral instruction.

Religious education concerned itself with mercy as part of the divine perfection which man ought to imitate.¹⁴⁹ Scripture classes might be supplemented with 'general history and biography', in instructing about this cardinal virtue; or the teacher's notebook could be a treasury of the social virtues 'to make a favourable impression on the minds of the children'.¹⁵⁰ Composition classes set essays on mercy.¹⁵¹ A practice developed in early-modern grammar schools of culling aphorisms from learned texts for notebooks and commonplace books, was part of the process by which ideas on mercy figured in education.¹⁵²

For Christian writers, keen to avoid 'mere natural compassion, in which there is no exercise of judgement, and no moral control' (in the words of one minister of religion from New South Wales) education was necessary to instruct in acts of mercy and so practice mercy-as-virtue. Sentimentalism, mere feeling or 'natural sensibility' were distinguished from the consequence-regarding Christian principle of mercy.[153] The lesson of mercy is seen in Thomas Arnold's project of reform where the older Rugbeians experienced a 'New Testament' approach to misdemeanour.[154] Freethinkers might have different views: one Edwardian seeking a *non*-religious basis for ethical education, argued against basing lessons on scripture which portrayed a god of both mercy and revenge.[155]

The second of the quotations heading this section, from an Anglican clergyman, Joseph Owen, was uttered during a high-Victorian lecture on cruelty to man and brutes. The Band of Mercy should be seen in this context: raising children in habits of mercy through its branches and illustrated hap'penny monthly *Advocate* (1879), its medal (the reverse bearing the legend around a royal coat of arms, 'BE MERCIFUL AFTER THY POWER. JUSTICE – KINDNESS'), hymn book and school activities. A branch of the Children's Humane Society was called the 'Merciful Brigade'.[156] Cruelty or kindness to animals were presented as one of the 'surest tests of true worth of character'.[157] Through their progeny parents could be educated in 'deeds of kindness, mercy and protection'.[158] As Monica Flegel argues, this was about the right exercise of power by infants whose power was otherwise limited.[159]

How mercy should be taught was discussed before Smithies formed her association in 1875. *Advice to Parents* by John Mortimer commanded in 1704, 'inure them to a merciful Charitable Temper; remember them often that *the merciful shall receive mercy*, and do what you can to beget a compassionate Temper in them', and advised against spectacles of cruelty and cruel sports, 'use them to Pity and Tenderness'.[160] The Reverend Edward Whitaker in 1788 saw the propensity to cruelty first exercised by children against brute creation as something to work with, through emphasizing the agonies caused, and then exercising their developing powers of reasoning.[161]

Nineteenth-century educationalists such as Louisa Hoare touched upon the pedagogy of mercy, recommending learning at home the poem 'On Cruelty to Animals' which circulated in evangelical journals.[162] In class, precepts of mercy ought to be 'inscribed in large characters on the walls' to impress youthful minds, and as writing exercises.[163] The Reverend Thomas Spencer's extensively circulated tract suggested weekly orations by schoolboys on mercy and other important themes.[164] The advocate James Simpson reflected on the lesson of 'practical mercy' in class, when juvenile moralists resisted killing a caterpillar, in *Necessity of Popular Education*.[165] In the 1850s the educator Thomas Turner Tate imagined a 'happy' schoolroom diffusing mercy and other virtues through the school and quoted Shakespeare's 'quality of mercy' lines for good measure.[166]

An article in the *Educational Reporter* in 1869 on the humane treatment of animals emphasized that boys lacked the sympathy to feel the pain of helpless others (man and beast). To reform 'uneducated nature' and create a public in favour of mercy and kindness involved attention to minds 'susceptible of impressions'. Teachers should (even with concerns about fitting this into a system governed by the Revised Code of Minutes on Education) teach by precept and themselves show no cruelty to vermin, stray dogs or cats. Mercy might be a habit established by the teacher's example; better still to teach 'the beauty, the nobility, the Godlikeness of mercy and pity', by precept and the idea that they emulate God's mercy. Since animals only communicated through the 'meek pleading of the eye', one should teach children to be their friends.[167] The American reformer George Angell observed that in England (and France) the message of animal kindness 'during many years has shown that children taught kindness to animals only, became not only more kind to animals, but also more kind to one another'.[168] For Angell and others, teaching kindness to animals created traits that could help reduce criminality in the future.

As several British writers quoted, the fabulist Jean de La Fontaine observed of infancy, 'Cet âge est sans pitié.'[169] The idea of mercy in relation to pedagogy and child-rearing is connected to that transformation from one view of the child's nature, to, in the late-Victorian Sidney Colvin's view, 'what it really is'.[170] Early in the next century the American academic Granville Hall characterized puberty as the age when children started to judge motives and concluded there was 'with increased years a great development of the quality of mercy'.[171]

Literature for infant and juvenile presented a message through tales involving animals or errands of mercy for people.[172] The prolific writer Dorothy Kilner's *First Going to School*, one of the earliest school stories, argued for mercy to animals and conveyed the knowledge that animals lack the rationality or understanding to know vice and virtue, cruelty and mercy.[173] The utilitarian John Bowring's unappetizingly entitled *Minor Morals for Young People* in 1834 (illustrated by George Cruikshank) exemplified mercy among other virtues for the 'coming generation' as part of a utilitarian-based morality.[174] Instruction encompassed hymns and poetry such as Laura Watts's 'The Happy Condition of the Merciful' in 1850, the second stanza concerning the hungry ragged boy who might steal and swear, 'The child that's merciful will feel | He must his pity share.'[175] Children's tales such as *Susy's Flowers* (1862) preached the text.[176] Publishers provided collections of precepts including passages on mercy.[177] Illustrated children's periodicals and postcards depicted children out in the snow or other hazards on 'errands of mercy'.[178]

Education concerned with feeling – lessons in benevolence – naturally considered mercy.[179] The manner of teaching was also relevant as educationalists reflected on the roles of strict justice or mercy in dealing with wrongdoers: the eighteenth-century headmaster Vicesimus Knox asking adults to 'learn mercy' and avoid outdoing Nero as pedagogues. Samuel Johnson eloquently asked, 'Shall I, whom thousand free-will acts disgrace | Petition mercy at the throne of grace; | Yet dare with heavy punishment assault | A wretch, when nature is alone in fault?'[180] The Society for the Diffusion of Useful Knowledge enjoined infant-school instructors to be 'slow to anger, and of great mercy'.[181]

Education was crucial to the imperial project, for by raising God-fearing men and women, there would develop that manliness, fairness and unselfishness, which, so one late-nineteenth-century newspaper commentator claimed, 'make the name of Englishman and the rule of England in the furthest corners of the earth, a synonym for that Justice, Mercy and Truth, which are alone the justifications of our Empire's greatness and the final sanction of our imperial away'.[182]

The somatic location for sensations of mercy might be the heart – the key site for kindly emotions in Western culture after talk of 'bowels' of mercy ceased amid embarrassment about intimate bodily functions. The merciful were mild hearted, the merciless were heartless.[183] Mercy is 'a lively emotion of the heart which is excited by the discovery of any creature's misery'[184]; that 'sympathetic sense of the suffering of another by which the heart is affected', in one early-nineteenth-century religious encyclopaedia; a 'feeling in the heart, or a desire of the mind to relieve another in suffering ... a sensation as well as a virtue' in Reverend William Hutchings's sermon of 1871; one of the 'intensities of divine feeling', alongside pity, clemency and long-suffering according to the American Methodist John Miley.[185] Because feelings of mercy could be blunted by acts of violence butchers were supposedly barred from juries.[186]

Mercy came with its gestural practices – of supplication (spreading abroad the hands to Jehovah[187]) and imploring: 'The bended knee is the attitude of imploring mercy or forgiveness.'[188] John Bunyan wrote of the posture signifying 'a heart in good earnest for mercy' in prayer.[189] In visual art this is recognizable: in Millais's depiction of a nun begging a man not to participate in the St Bartholomew's Day Massacre of 1572 (1886), and in the woman keeling and clasping hands, as Christ walks with his disciples in a wood engraving accompanying Alan Brodrick's verse 'Have Mercy on Me' in the late-Victorian periodical *Quiver*, for example.[190] There is also the 'powerful arm' of Christ's mercy.[191] In Augustus Egg's meticulous 'Past and Present No.1', of 1858, the gesture has failed and the adulterer lies prostrate with hands still clasped, the husband sits crushed by the terrible knowledge. A set of evocative gestures included clasping the knees and 'eyes wide staring'.[192] There was the glance of mercy too.[193]

The theatre's repertoire of counterfeit or simulated emotions included 'attitudes of supplication', with hands clasped outstretched (Henry Siddons said 'this gesture may be often observed in children, when entreating forgiveness').[194] Sometimes, the pose of mercy-seeking was detected in circumstances lacking urgency: William Tooke's account of the characteristics observed, as chaplain to the English resident in Catherine the Great's Russia, noted of the people, 'When they have any thing to request, they assume a tone and gesture, as if they were imploring mercy.' Perhaps, as modern anthropology suggests, a cross-cultural awareness of mercy exists in gestural terms.[195]

We are told that merciful or clement nature was visible in the countenance. Sir Thomas Browne in 1643 commented that 'master mendicants' looked out for a physiognomy bearing a 'merciful aspect, and will single out a face wherein they spy the signatures and marks of mercy'.[196] The physiognomy of mercy might be subsumed within ideas about amiability and benevolence.[197]

This chapter studied those key objects of mercy: children and the brute creation, and considered the discourse generated by ideas of the racial other, in terms of merciful propensities. Education and religious instruction brought an understanding of justice and mercy to the child, whether Christian or (through missionary and other European agencies), heathen.[198] How mercy was embodied, as emotion and gesture, concluded the chapter. Woman's agency as the merciful gender has also been studied: in *The Royal Throne of Mercy* I show a woman's merciful nature was a key aspect of appeals made to Victoria throughout her reign.

Part Two

Mercy challenged

4

Mercy for Ireland

Ireland – that 'cardinal point of our domestic politics' in the phrase of the *Annual Register* in 1837 – was a significant theatre for British mercy, the royal prerogative of mercy's exercise being 'a key point of negotiation and communication between the state and local communities on questions of law, crime and justice in the pre-Famine and Famine period'.[1] Confessional divisions led to partisan assertions for or against Ireland's merciful culture using the evidence of history. Catholic Ireland, with its Sisters and Houses of Mercy, was a society where mercy ('trocaire') was a prominent concept.[2] Historical research justified the idea that while early English laws were savage the Irish 'erred on the side of mercy'.[3] Catholics proudly expressed the view that the papacy was a source of mercy and exercise of mercy towards errant priests triggered a defence of Catholic mercy.[4] Reference was made to the mercy shown to English refugees from Mary Tudor's persecutions, to 'stamp the Irish character with mercy, benignity, and forbearance'.[5] The Protestant Irish took a different view of Catholicism 'teach[ing] the gospel of mercy in the agonies of the scaffold'.[6]

As part of the Anglophone world Ireland shared in the mercy discourse associated with Shakespeare, the 'quality of mercy' speech used in agitation and print commentary, and by defendants in criminal cases, as in England.[7] As subjects in rebellion, recourse to royal mercy was common: but sectarian politics ensured it was especially politicized – it is unsurprising to read of the 'pale of mercy' in an Irish context. The British, or English, reputation for perfidy – making a ruse of mercy – also relates to the bloody interpretation of mercy in the early-modern subjugation of Ireland.[8] The plight of the peasant in terms of rights and access to the land was treated as a question of justice and mercy – ironically did the Catholic priest of Ballibay in County Monaghan describe in 1850 the office of the landlord's agent as 'spotless shrine of justice and mercy'.[9] A 'virtuous and suffering nation' was presented by Irish Catholic 'patriots' for independence as meriting God's mercy.[10]

This chapter explores mercy's operation in Ireland in the modern age and the claims made for and against it in British, Irish and American-Irish press newspapers, memoirs and histories, focusing on the rebellion of 1798–1803, Viscount Mulgrave's rule, the aftermath of the 'Young Ireland' rising of 1848 and Fenian outrages of the 1860s, and the Easter Rising in 1916. In opening Part II of the book, the chapter shows the long history of a discourse of unmercy in 'English' domination in the British archipelago. By highlighting unmercy, critics underscored a state of injustice and dramatized this unchristian exercise in power to obtain concessions or undermine moral authority.

The plausibility of the charge of unmerciful rule from afar (through lord lieutenant), as well as through the agency of sectarian Protestant Ascendancy on the ground, gained force in the eighteenth century through earlier rebellion in another part of the empire, the American colonies, where, as a later chapter in Part II shows, unmercy was also a frequent charge levelled against the British and loyalist forces. Yet, opposing this charge of unmerciful British power in an Irish context was the loyalist Briton's presentation of the French revolutionary allies of rebellious Irish, as exemplars of unmercy at large. This chapter ends with the British state's response to the events of 1916, when the propagandist opposition of British mercy and unmercy was similarly played out in a context of global war.

Rebellion and mercy in eighteenth-century Ireland

The quelling of rebellion provided a common environment for royal mercy's exercise. Religious and political commentary discussed the challenges. William Sheridan, non-juring Bishop of Kilmore and Ardagh (in the Church of Ireland) reflected on Christian duty to forgive enemies in *Several Discourses c.* 1705.[11] In 1725 the collected works of another non-juror, Thomas Ken, Bishop of Bath and Wells, were published, including an essay of 1699 in which a king's throne being established by mercy, was linked to the rebellion in the early reign of Solomon. The divine argued that in dealing with rebellion, the king's ministers should use as much mercy as justice.[12]

The rebellion of 1641, as presented by the Irish lawyer and politician Sir John Temple in 1646, helped establish a representation of the Irish as cruel in pro-English writing, apparent in texts on the rebellion of 1798.[13] Daniel O'Connell noted in 1843 after describing Cromwell's words on the massacre at Drogheda in 1649 as 'truly an *English* mercy' that English writers 'should have preserved so many traits of humanity and mercy on the part of the Irish; while at the same time they have not attempted to state a single act of kindness, charity, humanity, or mercy amongst the leaders of the English Protestant party'.[14] The use of the word 'mercy' was misapplied by Cromwell to brutality in Drogheda and Wexford according to the miscellaneous English writer John Tillotson's history in 1865.[15]

In 'all Ages they have mock't and abus'd the Clemency and Mercy of the English Government', the Irish Protestant Michael Jephson sermonized in Dublin following the 1688 rebellion.[16] In the Irish rebellion in 1798 the king's 'parental desire of extending mercy' and the clemency of the lord lieutenant similarly faced counter interpretations.[17] This section studies the treatment of mercy, merciful acts and mercilessness in writing produced during the rebellion, such as the United Irishman *Northern Star* and *The Press*, treatment in other Irish and British newspapers, and texts produced after the rebellion was routed. The discourse includes revealing allusion and more extended reflections on mercy.[18] Michael de Nie suggests 'arguments for mercy or for the victimhood of the Irish peasantry were widespread in the British press'.[19] The sources are deeply biased: as the Irish lawyer and politician Jonah Barrington noted in 1835, no history of the rebellion 'contains any thing like an impartial or adequate delineation of that dreadful conflict'.[20]

The events preceding rebellion brought claims and counter-claims for mercy. Discussion about civil inequality, one of the injustices animating the United Irishmen, was framed partly in the language of mercy (referring to the 'ancient Romans' and the 'attribute of their greatest deity, Jupiter Capitolinus') by 'Philadelphus' in *Freeman's Journal* in 1788.[21] The privately circulated prospectus of the Society of United Irishmen (penned by Wolfe Tone in June 1791), hailing an independent Ireland's rights and prerogatives, ended with the 'cry of Mercy, – of Justice – and of Victory'.[22] The lord lieutenant's exercise of the prerogative of mercy was watched.[23] In *A Letter to His Excellency Earl FitzWilliam* in 1795, the new lord lieutenant was urged by the Ulster Presbyterian and United Irishman William Drennan to be prominent in benevolence, and 'by thus anticipating your parliament, let it appear the work of private mercy, rather than of public justice; and thus gratitude will be secured to your person'.[24] The statue of mercy was placed on the pediment of the new Courts of Justice in Dublin by 1796, a year of abortive French invasion, counter-revolutionary violence from torture to murder and the imposition of martial law. How was mercy exploited by government, loyalists and United Irishmen?[25]

'Mercy had no seat' in government councils in suppressing the United Irish societies towards the end of 1797, according to the United Irishman Charles Teeling.[26] Generous forbearance and a 'magnanimous oblivion of the past', Teeling claimed, was the demeanour Lord Edward Fitzgerald (speaking in the spring of 1797 in Kilmainham gaol) hoped to inculcate in the United Irishmen, 'confident am I that they will exercise a clemency and forbearance, which no people, under heaven, similarly circumstanced, was ever known to practice!'[27] Meeting in Kilmainham, Teeling and Fitzgerald expressed concern that retributive justice for torture and oppression would overtake 'the milder feelings of mercy'.

The United Irishmen's Belfast paper foregrounded the cause of justice as a supporter on the masthead. Mercy was referenced in the *Northern Star* in verse, news reports and commentary. The Dublin United Irishmen's *The Press* also featured mercy in dealing with the trial of Presbyterian farmer William Orr of Farranshane in County Antrim.[28] When he was executed for administering an oath for an association for seditious purposes, *The Press* on 17 October 1797 spoke of the 'sword of justice' and asked what had happened to 'that most sacred principle of coronary discretion, that brightest gem in the Royal diadem – the sacred and awful duty of executing justice with mercy'.[29] A subsequent number, 26 October, printed a letter by Deane Swift under the signature of 'Marcus', addressed to Lord Camden, the Lord Lieutenant, about the failure to exercise the prerogative of mercy – for which the publisher Peter Finnerty was indicted for libel. Further evidence (28 October) was given of the attempt to 'intercept the stream of mercy' in Orr's case. Clemency to loyalists was contrasted with Orr's treatment, 'let a representation be made for *mercy – Royal mercy !!!* Ever beaming, ever open, ever tender, bright attribute, Godlike prerogative'.[30] A nationalist press remembered Orr's martyrdom.[31]

Finnerty's trial in December 1797 heard that it was (in the judge, William Downes's words) impossible for the lord lieutenant to ignore any evidence of Orr's innocence, 'for there is no man whose heart is so steeled against mercy and humanity, as to have refused it'.[32] 'It is a wicked doctrine,' the attorney-general told the jury, 'endeavoured to be read abroad, that the Lord Lieutenant will not extend mercy where it ought to be extended.'[33] John Philpot Curran, pleading for the publisher, commented on the viceroy's mercy in a speech cherished as an instance of Irish eloquence: it was not a 'gaudy feather stuck into the diadem to shake in the wind, and by the wearing of the gaudy plumage, to amuse the vanity of the wearer'.[34]

The Press sought to run down in the popular mind the Irish system of justice, critics said.[35] Yet *The Press* hoped in mid-January 1798 that the United Irishmen, despite persecution, 'would be merciful, temperate and just ... by acts of mercy and forgiveness, more sublime than fortune has yet put in their power to exercise, that virtue, which it shall be our province to cultivate and foster'.[36] Foreign invasion necessarily complicated mercy's exercise. 'Mercy and faith to every Irish man who would show mercy and faith, was his motto; but to invaders, no mercy', says the Elizabethan marshal of Munster in the Englishman Charles Kingsley's Victorian novel *Westward Ho!*[37] The French troops under General Humbert in August 1798 'cried for mercy', so an officer in the British forces claimed.[38] At the battle of Ballinamuck at Longford they pretended to offer up arms but were 'received to composition'.[39] No mercy 'of course' was shown to Irish rebels, who expected no quarter and were 'cut down without mercy'. The French are credited with acting as a force of restraint for their Irish allies.[40]

Teeling's brother Bartholomew who landed at Killala with Humbert's troops was executed despite the 'humanity which he so effectually exerted in restraining the excesses of vindictive warfare', and the 'usual ceremony of reliance on the justice and mercy of the court, and some personal compliments to the Lord Lieutenant' at his trial.[41] Denying he pursued humanity 'under the influence of any selfish impression allianced with future consequences', he claimed to be 'merciful for mercy's sake, and from the conviction that it should ever influence the conduct and the decisions of power. As a Roman Catholic too, I had learned that it was my duty, as it was surely my inclination, to love and to protect my fellow-creatures.'[42]

The oaths of privates in the rebel army were meant to avoid the 'spilling of innocent blood' and 'have mercy where it can be given'.[43] The trial of the Sheares brothers (barristers from Dublin – eventually executed for high treason) witnessed the assertion from John Sheares, after sentence of death, that there was no sentiment more foreign to him then the charge 'that he should have felt reluctance to extend mercy to the submission of any class, or a supplicant foe'.[44] But the loyalist Reverend James Gordon's history (published in 1801, and more temperate on the rising than Sir Richard Musgrave's treatment), pausing on the sanguinary tone of a manifesto found with the United Irishmen, anticipating control of Dublin, wondered if shutting the 'gates of mercy on mankind' was not a 'maxim with revolutionists'.[45]

For the pseudonymous historian 'Brian Borohme the Younger' in 1843, rebellion made the 'angry passions ... excited': 'the exercise of mercy was called weakness, and cruelty firmness'.[46] Some of the atrocities of 1798 involved 'infuriated mobs' including women.[47] The supplicatory role expected of women included written or physical acts. Orr's wife, for example, begged Countess Camden's intercession with her husband in an eloquent letter full of the 'phrenzy of a distracted woman': 'Despair has almost made me mad! I call on you – in the name of the gentle mercy that warms thy bosom – in the name of that pity which should ever find a refuge in the female heart.'[48]

The rebellion was remembered for the atrocities experienced by Protestant loyalists – slaughtered at Wexford bridge on 20 June 1798 ('97 human victims sacrificed to the God of Mercy'[49]) with priests withholding 'Roman Catholic mercy'.[50] They were luridly depicted in the nineteenth century in Lyttelton's history (see Figure 4.1), and by George Cruikshank and *The Terrific Register: Or, Record of Crimes, Judgments, Providences, and Calamities* in 1825. George Taylor wrote of the 'merciless pike-men … no mercy for any man who bore the name of *Protestant*' and gave harrowing details of what took place in a barn at Scollabogue in June: 'Humanity had fled the place, and mercy was not known.'[51]

Sir Richard Musgrave's partisan account (1801) emphasized priestly complicity with Father Roche's ambiguous sermon about mercy to a congregation of Catholic pikemen and fearful Protestants at Wexford (10 June 1798) dramatizing this.[52] An anonymous collection of 1798 published in Dublin extracted the lesson that 'the merciful Creator of all things did not favour their [Catholic] horrid acts of massacre and devastation'.[53] Quaker writings exemplified the moral power of their passive resistance and appeals to rebels grounded in Christian mercy and forbearance.[54]

Other histories emphasized merciful efforts to stop the murder of Protestants at the 'fatal bridge' by the Catholic Reverend John Corrin.[55] Notoriously, loyalists used tortures such as the pitch cap and 'walking gallows' in 1795–6.[56] The Orange yeomanry were condemned for retaliatory mercilessness in accounts by United Irishmen such

Figure 4.1 'The Massacre of the Irish Loyalists on Wexford Bridge', engraving by Ambrose William Warren after Woodruffe, from G.C. Lyttlelton, *The History of England, from the Earliest Dawn of Authentic Record, to the Commencement of Hostilities in the Year 1803* (1804). Author's collection.

as Teeling, in *The Press* and in the rebel leader Thomas Cloney's recollections.[57] The justification for retaliation and an 'inhuman system of warfare' where the defenceless and weak had no mercy, was reflected upon by Teeling in referring to the massacre of yeomanry in Wexford town.[58] Animosity was stirred by enormities on both sides; the 'humane and merciful' were powerless to repress it.[59]

After the rebellion, mercy was shown to all but the leaders according to the English *Monthly Magazine* in October 1798.[60] But for *The Oeconomist, or Englishmen's Magazine* published in Newcastle, the Dublin citizens and freeholders were merciless: 'The pages of history scarcely present a fact, which more strongly marks that implacable fury which intestine discord is so apt to generate,' as the petitioning *against* any pardons.[61] Charles Cornwallis, the Lord Lieutenant appointed in June 1798, may have been more merciful in India than in America (his role in this context is examined in Chapter 7), wrote William Bailey, but in Ireland he oversaw merciless repression with gallows so frequently employed that it became a sight of 'comparative indifference'.[62] 'Rob not Justice of her Triumph; but, seated in all the majesty of order, and in all the loveliness of mercy, let her punish where she must,' said Arthur O' Connor in 1798, addressing the electors of Antrim and fellow Irish citizens against British tyranny, 'let her save where she can!'[63] But the martial courts were designed in Teeling's view to free Cornwallis 'from importunate appeals to mercy' and speed up retribution.[64]

Accounts of the rebellion, such as 'General' Joseph Holt's (1838) or Edward Hay's (1842) history of events in Wexford, were bleak records of rebel cruelty and military vengeance with 'in several instances no mercy from the indiscriminate fury' of the troops – against not only countrymen but women and infants; sectarian violence where individuals who had shown 'benevolence and humanity' were treated as criminals; but also where instances of humanity by aristocrats, such as the family of the earl of Donoughmore, ensured the 'gates of mercy' were open.[65]

In Croker's edition of Holt's memoirs, we are told that there were 'brilliant examples of mercy and humanity, but they were not so many or of such frequency as the "milk of human kindness" would have hoped for.'[66] Holt (who died in 1826 after returning from transportation in New South Wales) included passages on the conduct of the yeomanry and rebels, the 'demon of revenge', and the sense that 'cruelty was ... a part of their duty', on the part of 'tigerlike monsters'. 'To meet with any one who was merciful in those days, was an uncommon occurrence, so much had men been corrupted and depraved by circumstances.' He extended mercy to his enemies once he had sufficient power over forces in Wicklow, 'feeling satisfied that humanity is never allowed to go without its reward, even in this world'. A Protestant, his memoirs recalled the Sermon on the Mount's words on mercy and his hopes that the 'acts of mercy I had done to the unfortunate who had fallen into the hands of my people', would be pleasing to the Almighty and 'vouchsafed to myself in my misery and distress'.[67]

Rebel humanity did not mean merciful suppression. The Protestant clergyman James Gordon's history refers to John Kelly of Killan who fought at the battle of Ross as an example: 'A display of humanity by a rebel, was in general, in the trials of court-martial, by no means regarded as a circumstance in favour of the accused.'[68] Teeling, discussing the bill of amnesty and oblivion of past offences, issued in July 1798, also argued that it did not deliver mercy to the Union's leaders, those who had shown public integrity and moral worth: a 'too confiding people anticipated the merciful dispensation of the measure'.[69] Weighing up the Irish executive's response, the Scots-Irish military novelist William Hamilton Maxwell – in an anti-rebel account of 1845 – accepted that 'in some cases, mercy might have been judiciously extended', nevertheless severity was a 'stern necessity' in other cases. Where there was mercy, it might be down, as in the case of Arthur Wolfe, Chief Justice of the Court of King's Bench in Ireland (ennobled as Lord Kilwarden), to his own character, 'an extreme respect for human life. He delighted in mercy … he was … inflexibly merciful'.[70] A distinction was made between the humanity of judges presiding at the criminal court in Wexford ('actuated by the godlike virtues of justice and mercy') and the vengeful treatment of prisoners before court martials.[71]

Edward Wakefield's early-nineteenth-century study praised the policy of conciliation by Cornwallis (sworn in as lord lieutenant on 20 June 1798) as re-erecting the 'altar of mercy'. The Reverend Gordon called it the 'necessary system of mercy'.[72] Sympathetic Irish papers, critical of any attempt to 'poison the stream of mercy', hailed the 'sun of clemency' and praised the king's 'mild and paternal' disposition.[73] The Irish Parliament's act for the king's most gracious, general and free pardon preambled his continuous desire to 'show his royal inclination to mercy' and pointing out that the only way to evade the highest penalties for this 'unnatural' rebellion was through his 'great goodness and clemency'. Mercy after rebellion, as ever, was presented as an act of grace.[74] It was necessary to use the language of contrition in bestowing royal clemency to emphasize the rebellion was crushed, hence the formula of 'humbly imploring mercy', which Arthur O'Connor took exception to, as admitting guilt and expressing remorse.

The liberal Protestant lawyer John Philpot Curran organized an address to Cornwallis, circulating in Dublin for signatures on 30 June 1798, praising him for sparing those he had subdued and for conciliation rather than destruction, 'such a system of mildness and mercy hath had so rapid an operation in giving new energy to the loyalty of Ireland'.[75] Examples of Cornwallis's mercy publicized in the Irish and English press included pardoning the wool merchant Oliver Bond of Dublin in 1798. *Freeman's Journal* which eulogized the 'peculiar privilege' of royal mercy and mentioned the coronation oath, praised the 'benevolence of his Excellency the Marquis of Cornwallis, for the most *wise and salutary* purposes', and asserted it was not for critics to question this prerogative or expect a 'digressive account' of government motives. Bond and William Michael Byrne of Wicklow were the focus of bargaining by the state prisoners as a whole: they offered to acknowledge their guilt if the two men were reprieved but Byrne was executed and Bond died of apoplexy.[76]

The *Anti-Jacobin Review*, attacking Cornwallis's 'falsely lenient system' in October 1798, identified an attempt to 'persuade the noble Viceroy that justice was a crime, and that virtue and magnanimity consisted only in mercy and lenity' by the supporters of O'Connor and Lord Edward Fitzgerald.[77] The Protestant ascendancy opinion, unsurprisingly, thought him too lenient, as Bishop Thomas Percy of Dromore told his wife.[78] They complained of a *cruel mercy* leading to a political Union with Britain: 'Peace, justice and mercy were among the means employed.'[79] William Plunket protested in the Irish House of Commons in May 1799 that 'all the rays of mercy and forbearance are reserved to gild the brow of the Viceroy, and that all the odium of harshness and severity are flung upon the Parliament'.[80] The MP for Armagh in the Union Parliament, the Anglican Patrick Duigenan ironized on the clemency of the marquis, 'his liberality, his mercy, his clemency, his wisdom, &c' praised in the Catholic press of Dublin, and the London Whig press of *Courier* and *Morning Chronicle*.[81] By contrast Lord Donoughmore, in the Irish Parliament's debates on union, defended the principle of forbearance, the 'salutary mercy', of the lord lieutenant.[82] An artefact of Cornwallis's viceroyalty commenting on his mercifulness is a creamware jug in which the figures of justice and mercy surround him (Nelson appears on the other side of the jug), with an inscription 'to whose Clemency & Bravery | Ireland owes her Preservation'.[83]

The British press at the time praised 'mercy and Cornwallis' and histories took a similar line.[84] 'He united conciliation with firmness,' a continuator of Goldsmith's *History of England* judged in 1805, 'whilst displaying a system of moderation and mercy to the infatuated rabble.'[85] Richard Madden's history of the United Irishmen (1842) includes an incident, in the trial of the Sheares brothers in July 1798, where Cornwallis's scruples to start his reign withholding clemency are claimed, and his young nephew Horace is recalled imploring him on his knees for mercy.[86] Madden reprinted an essay on forgiveness by the father of John and Henry Sheares: 'pity, patience and benignity' were God's favourite offerings.[87] Cloney's memoirs recalled the efforts of his sister after his sentence of death at Wexford: supplicating on her knees in Dublin in the presence of Lord Castlereagh, the secretary.[88]

In the 1830s the English writer Thomas De Quincey judged of the rebellion, 'the worst results of vengeance the fiercest, and clemency the most undistinguishing, without any one advantage of either'.[89] But the *Dublin University Magazine* described the response, from the distance of 1844, as a 'magnanimity of mercy which has no parallel in history', when eighty 'chiefs of the conspiracy' were pardoned.[90] Differing assessments appeared through the Victorian era: Henry Milman's *Annals of St Paul's* (1868), apropos of the memorial there to Cornwallis, asserted 'when mercy was on all sides an exploded virtue, he dared to be merciful'.[91] The historian James Froude excoriated as naïve Cornwallis's clemency: Ireland needed, as in Cromwell's time, the 'gentleness of inflexible authority and the kindness of even-handed justice'.[92] William Lecky more judiciously accepted the repression of a peasantry 'much more deserving of pity than of blame' was merciless and acknowledged the dilemma of rebel leaders acting in a way that made strong claims on government clemency.[93]

With the repeal movement's emergence under Daniel O'Connell, the justice of the cause also raised the figure of mercy in rhetoric and iconography. The Vicomte de Cormenin's study of orators presented the transition in O'Connell's speech from supplication to invective, from rage to 'mercy and pity'.[94] The Scottish artist David Wilkie supposedly painted the Liberator attitudinizing 'demanding from Justice, what he could not hope from Mercy, for Ireland' in 1838.[95] Tory papers associated O'Connell with the Whig Lord Lieutenant in Victoria's first years as queen: controlling a puppet in a 'mock-regal court'.[96] Mulgrave was ironically called 'Viceregal Liberator' for spectacular acts of mercy (see Figure 4.2).[97]

Figure 4.2 The Earl of Mulgrave. Portrait by H.P. Briggs, engraved by H. Robinson (London: Fisher, Son, 1838). Author's collection.

The viceroyalty of Constantine Henry Phipps, Lord Mulgrave

In the summer of 1836, according to Mulgrave's own account, he attempted to combine 'attachment with obedience' by releasing well-behaved minor offenders. One eyewitness to his visit to Sligo in August 1836, through triumphal arches followed by thousands, spoke of the 'prison gate thrown open … I beheld the poor captive on his emancipation from the gloomy dungeon look with rapture and delight upon the splendid prospect before him'.[98] In the ensuing controversy Mulgrave presented remission as involving painstaking consultation with judges and blamed the outcry on sustained press misrepresentation.[99] Mulgrave was appointed in April 1835; his mercy was defended from Conservative critics in William IV's final months through the royal prerogative of pardoning.[100]

In 1838, shortly after Victoria's coronation, the Liberal London *Morning Chronicle* published a response to his actions, which picked up on the symbolism of the sword of mercy: 'By that sword, pointless but trenchant, has been gained that splendid victory which all the mortal engines in the armoury of this martial kingdom never achieved ... The natural instinct of a female dynasty will revolt from the rough instruments of power that generate hatred without establishing authority. The Queen of England will reign with the sword of mercy.'[101] It was asserted, 'we have happily, at present [1838], both a Sovereign and a viceroy to whom the imploring cry of the injured does not rise in vain.'[102] Pro-ministerial papers delighted in the continued confidence shown in Mulgrave as the crown's representative.[103]

Contemporary apologists saw Mulgrave's predicament as the result of Ascendancy reaction; Orangeism thwarting 'all his benevolent designs'.[104] For supporters of Whig policy in Ireland like the *British and Foreign Review*, mercy 'had a most useful effect' for a people previously prejudiced against a constitution seen in Coercion Acts and a legal system equated with tyranny: 'It was reserved for Lord Normanby [his title on elevation to marquessate] to show to them the mercy as well as the majesty of justice and they now begin to respect what they had formerly detested and opposed.'[105] Public justice hitherto wore 'Orange robes, and the question of guilty or not guilty is the question of Catholic or Protestant'.[106] A justice-loving people were conciliated by laws 'administered with equity indeed and mercy'.[107] The prisoners released had been remorseful, were punished enough and now restored to their families.[108]

Opposition in the Irish and British press, and in British party politics, ignored the usual courtesies. Mulgrave was described as a foppish aristocrat and 'tinsel hero of the Minerva press' (he had published several novels) and his previous gubernatorial role in Jamaica was mocked.[109] The *Church of England Quarterly* (formed in 1837 against liberalism and popery) characterized his viceroyalty as a profanation of the queen's name 'on every trivial occasion, scattering on all sides the royal patronage, till men "surfeited with honey"'. The abuse of the prerogative was part of the charge: quoting Shakespeare's Henry IV, the *Quarterly* said he rendered this mysterious power 'common, hackneyed ... stale and cheap' and, it was alleged, violence and crime increased.[110] The interpretation was current outside Parliament: for the Peel Club of Glasgow, among a multiplicity of shabby acts was this degradation of mercy as the 'means of acquiring mob-popularity'.[111]

The hyperbole of the Ascendancy may be seen in equating Mulgrave's acts with the 'evil practices' of the Stuarts. While Irish pro-Liberal papers and *Morning Chronicle* and other ministerial papers in London defended him, Mulgrave's use of the prerogative was criticized in the Ascendancy press and *The Times*.[112] It was discussed in Parliament: Conservatives disputing the claims of the 'Mulgrave tranquillizers'.[113] A petition to the Lords followed a mass meeting of Protestants at Dublin Mansion-house in January 1837 (just before the parliamentary session). This described the prerogative as 'so injuriously exercised as to bring if that were possible our incorruptible judges into disrespect and to deprive the laws of their salutary sanctions'. The petitioners alleged that as a result trial by jury was by accomplices rather than one's peers.[114] Representation of Mulgrave's governing style by opponents in the Lords likened his acts to the amnesties of medieval monarchs, a 'full display of royal state' as the Earl of Powerscourt described it. Mercy by 'wholesale' was an abuse of the prerogative: 'That was not the idea that was entertained of the quality of mercy by the greatest moralist and truest observer of a by gone age.'[115]

'Fortunate island, that an O'Connell supplies with justice, and a Mulgrave with mercy; the severer quality typified by a murdered Protestant, the gentler attribute only by the release of a Papist convict,' wrote Benjamin Disraeli in *The Times* in February 1837.[116] 'Had there not been some seeking of popularity,' Wellington asked fellow peers in November 1837, 'in the undue exercise of the prerogative of mercy.'[117] Sir Robert Peel gave a notable speech on 15 April 1839 after Lord John Russell's motion of confidence in the government of Ireland in which he affirmed the need to exercise mercy with 'caution and judgment' as a 'strictly judicial proceeding,' rather than 'a matter of public display for public applause'.[118] Mulgrave's return of the number of memorials presented to the lord lieutenant, the Protestant Ultra Lord Winchelsea's requests for a return of coroners' inquests in cases of murder and homicide from 1 January 1827 to 31 December 1837, a return of trials of persons charged with murder and homicide 'and for similar returns for England during the same period', showed the politics of Irish justice and mercy played out in statistics and pamphlet.[119]

The government hit back, with Russell defending Mulgrave in the Commons.[120] Lord Morpeth, secretary for Ireland, explained how mercy was triggered by inquiries before any prisoner was released (on their health, conduct in prison, previous character). The attorney-general informed constituents at Cashel to cheers, that they were 'libellers' who spoke of the 'too merciful and beneficent' Mulgrave – yet contrasted him with the charge against former governments of too much shedding of blood. *Ireland Under Lord Mulgrave*, published in 1837, asserted the government used the prerogative with the 'soundest discretion and the strictest impartiality ... Tommy Downshire in the North has been treated with as kind consideration as Captain Starlight in the South.'[121]

Defenders of Mulgrave turned to county addresses, local meetings and press reports to criticize a factional assault and assert the value for ensuring the Catholic peasantry's loyalty, of the 'principle of mercy' in law.[122] The episode of Mulgrave's lord lieutenancy shows how significant the politics of mercy was in the 1830s and early 1840s. According to Tories, his viceregal use of the prerogative risked damaging the brightest jewel in the crown, 'and the condition of the wearer rendered such as to be envied only by the slave'.[123] A Tory pamphlet imagined a pro-Orange Victoria critical of her viceroy.[124] Practically, the Tory opposition wanted to constrain Mulgrave, as one journal expressed it, 'fettering the prerogative of the Crown by laying down certain abstract rules for its guidance in the exercise of mercy wisely placed at its discretion by the constitution'. Yet regardless of the party in government, mercy and justice constantly surfaced in commentary on British rule in nineteenth-century Ireland. The poetic effusions about viceregal rule which appeared during the eighteenth century and Mulgrave's era continued. At his departure his Irish Catholic supporters eulogized his legacy (the more to hold his successor to the same policy) but with every new lord lieutenant a poet hailed the arrival of justice and mercy.[125]

A fine medal of 1837, designed by Bernard Mulrenin, bore the olive-wreathed legend, 'The Tribute of a grateful people to Constantine Henry Earl of Mulgrave'. The cartoonist John Doyle satirized his clemency as farce, a late-Victorian representation by Henry Paget shows stunned and delighted 'Irish prisoners liberated during Lord Mulgrave's Progress'.[126] Mulgrave – created marquess of Normanby in 1838, was briefly Home Secretary from 1839 to 1841: his detractors treated this as fitting for one who had shown 'generous sympathy with crime' and who now demonstrated 'sympathising clemency' with English criminals – though gaol-deliveries 'will not, my lord, do, I think in England'.[127]

'Mighty Monarch! Pardon Smith O'Brien': Mercy in a time of famine and rebellion

For contemporary critics, the Irish famine was a failure of British social justice and mercy. John MacHale, Catholic Archbishop of Tuam, in a letter to *The Freeman* in April 1849, scrupulously avoided criticizing the queen, blaming 'those ministers who exercise of the duties and prerogatives of royalty everything but its benevolence and its merciful justice'.[128] Naturally sermons to raise funds for Irish victims appealed to Christian ideas of charitable acts. Although MacHale's pastoral in 1848 told his flock that chief reliance 'in this awful crisis must be in the mercy of the Almighty', who should be besought to 'soften the hearts of our rulers and legislators',[129] others commented on how long failure in government produced 'an outrage on God's merciful providence, and a defiance of his merciful laws'.[130] The Irish poet Aubrey de Vere spoke of Providence's 'merciful severity' and the Irish Dean of Ripon published *The Famine a Rod of God: Its Provoking Cause, its Merciful Design* in 1847.[131]

The pious appealed to divine mercy, including through national fast and humiliation in March 1847; a more sinister variant in the discourse was uttered by the nationalist Thomas Meagher at a public meeting of the Irish Confederation in 1847, quoting *The Times*, 'great organ' of English opinion, 'Ireland is now at the mercy of England. For the first time in the course of centuries, England may rule Ireland, and treat her as a thoroughly conquered country.'[132]

Justice and mercy figured in nationalist discourse against British rule: in general when in Meagher's terms the situation was Ireland at England's mercy; in critiquing the landlord and tenant relationship; and lambasting the criminal justice system. The nationalist journalist James Fintan Lalor, in a letter to the new *Irish Felon* in 1848, arguing against qualms about taking back property and land, declared that mercy was for the merciful, and 'you may think it pity to oust and abolish the present noble race of landowners, who have ever been so pitiful and compassionate themselves'.[133]

When it came to mercy's operation in criminal cases, it was recognized that Ireland was different from other parts of Britain. The *Leinster Independent* had claimed in 1838, 'In Ireland the term "conviction" is not always associated with deep guilt. When the rage of faction demands a sacrifice, many men are convicted of crimes they never committed, and sentenced to punishment they never deserved.'[134] In 1848 *The Irish*

Felon pointed to the hostility expressed in the legal system, with articles like 'Trial by Jury in Ireland,' on the sectarian nature of John Mitchel's treason trial.[135]

The 'Young Ireland' rebellion in July 1848, and its suppression, inevitably led to new appeals for mercy. One of the rebellion's supporters, the journalist Charles Gavan Duffy, editor of *The Nation*, sought to distinguish in his journal (as leaders of the United Irishmen had tried to) between rebels' response to the system and their intended merciful behaviour to individuals merely the 'instruments of that system' … 'teach them to be majestic in their force, generous in their clemency, noble in their triumph'.[136] John Martin's last article for *The Tribune* associated rebellion with the 'God of Justice and mercy'.[137] James Whiteside QC, in October 1849, appealing to jurors at the trial for sedition of William Smith O'Brien (Protestant landowner and MP for Limerick), one of the rising's prominent participants, linked their judicial role with the queen's coronation oath, that 'great compact between the people and the crown', to execute justice in mercy, reminding them 'you administer – no rigorous, remorseless, sanguinary code – but justice in mercy'.[138]

Appeals to the queen for mercy to rebel leaders appeared in the Irish press, thus a 'Stanch Tory' in the nationalist *Freeman's Journal* in October 1848 asked, 'Are the lives of Irish subjects to be in the hands of a Viceroy, while subjects may appeal to their young and merciful Queen for the clemency which heaven itself has placed in her hands.'[139] The rhetoric of appeals played on the queen's gender through references to her conquest of loyal subjects' hearts.[140] The *Cork Examiner* in the same month, anticipating O'Brien's sentence, reflected:

The great prerogative of the crown is mercy. In this, the monarchical principle approaches nearest to divine. In woman it is part of her being. The Queen is merged in the wife and mother; and this gentlest but most magnanimous of human virtues, 'dove-eyed and robed in white', is prominent in the character of the woman-sovereign of Great Britain and Ireland.[141]

The *Cork Examiner* noted later, the allusion to convictions for atrocious murder after the Act for the Prevention of Crime and Outrage in Ireland, in the queen's speech in proroguing Parliament in early September: 'The announcement is made graciously to proceed from a monarch, merciful – and a woman.'[142] For *Tait's Edinburgh Magazine*, reflecting on O'Brien, the 'sceptre is grasped by hands too weak for brave men to dash it rudely … The Crown sits on a brow too fair and free of crime against the people'.[143] A year later, in August 1849 Victoria visited Ireland (the hostile *Galway Vindicator* clear 'no act of mercy piloted the royal yacht to our shores'[144]). *Freeman's Journal* advised a postponement unless she was transported by 'favouring gales', 'With mercy in her train, | Aye, mercy telegraphed before, | She anchors off the Emerald shore.'[145] In Dublin efforts were made to raise the question of the state prisoners' fate: one of the North Dublin Union guardians, James Nugent, addressed her, 'Mighty monarch, pardon Smith O'Brien' and the single word 'MERCY' appeared on a banner as she proceeded through a triumphal arch.[146]

Petitioners in Ireland reminded the queen of the 'divine right to forgive', the 'most precious portion of the royal prerogative'.[147] The effort was extensive, to suggest a 'universal national voice'.¹⁴⁸ Petitions for vice-regal and royal mercy were printed in the Irish press: 'Let tyrants guard themselves by terror, they dare not be merciful,' argued the inhabitants of West Carbery in Cork, 'your illustrious reign shall not be clouded by so dark a spot – history shall shew your Majesty's power, for it shall tell that you feared not to be clement'.¹⁴⁹ The *Cork Examiner* felt, in its editorial, that as it was a work 'purely of mercy and love, so should the female population bear a part in expressing the public voice'.¹⁵⁰ The *Examiner* explained the response to O'Brien's fate as 'woman is compassionated for the weaknesses'.¹⁵¹

Legislation was passed to allow the sovereign to substitute life imprisonment for the capital sentence for treason, following the rebellion, on the home secretary or lord lieutenant's advice. After the trial the earl of Clarendon, the Whig Lord Lieutenant, appealed to by Irishmen – Orangemen and Catholics, to exercise mercy – was reported as commenting in the press that 'humanity was a cheap virtue'.¹⁵² The sentence on O'Brien was commuted to transportation to Tasmania. The earl's role unsurprisingly divided opinion.¹⁵³ When he appeared haughty in receiving a deputation of Irish MPs on Gavan Duffy's behalf, the *Galway Mercury* declared, 'heaven-borne attribute, mercy finds no niche in the Temple of Whiggery'.¹⁵⁴ In March *The Economist*, briefly assessing Clarendon's rule, suggested that among other things in governance, the 'utmost forbearance, and the kindest indulgence', would not have prevented insurrection, given the nature of Ireland.¹⁵⁵ A few years after the rising, a bill to abolish the role was debated: Disraeli expressed opposition based partly on the prerogative of mercy.¹⁵⁶

The politics of mercy were understood: the *United Irishman* scorned a 'boasted act of amnesty [by which] his gracious Majesty excludes from his royal mercy all who were in custody at any time since the year 1794'. Those involved in the rising of 1848 were critical of official mercy during their trials: John Martin declaring 'I cannot condescend to accept mercy where I believe I have been morally right. I want justice, not mercy'.¹⁵⁷ When O'Brien and others rejected transportation as no mercy, discussion in parliament and press brought out the sense that it was indeed the reverse of clemency.¹⁵⁸ Irish papers scorned the 'merciful Whigs' for O'Brien's antipodean imprisonment.¹⁵⁹

The ensuing campaign to liberate the exiles through petitions naturally pointed towards the prerogative.¹⁶⁰ The queen's Irish popularity was at stake. There was protracted cheering at a meeting at the Dublin mechanics' institute in 1850 when Gavan Duffy contrasted O'Brien imprisoned in Maria Island off Tasmania, with the queen, 'they shall not dare to bring the Queen of England into this island'.¹⁶¹ Yet hopes of queenly mercy were uttered in the campaign to release O'Brien from prison: 'I believe in my soul that the heart of the monarch of this mighty empire is full of tenderness and compassion,' said Maguire at a meeting of the Town Council of Cork in early March 1852, 'she would be glad to obey the dictates of her woman's nature' but was worried about the role of government.¹⁶² Of course the position of queen regnant in relation to British rule (or misrule) in Ireland was fraught with tension, between appeals to 'Irish' chivalry and Irish nationalists' awareness of the strategic value of feminine rule for the British state.¹⁶³ As Charles Gavan Duffy wrote in response to outraged Cork politicians in July 1850, there was 'dextrous casuistry, that personal devoirs to the woman of the queen compromised no man's opinions or principles'.¹⁶⁴

The *Irish Examiner* contrasted the call for capital punishment in *The Times*, with the position of the *Liverpool Albion*, 18 September 1848, which advised 'let mercy step in and let its mild and gentle voice be heard, and see what effect that will have upon the people'.[165] Interest in justice and mercy was international, given the Irish diaspora. Exercised about the possibility of a hideous traitor's execution for O'Brien, the American reformer Charles Spear's *Prisoner's Friend* contrasted the reputation Britain had for emancipation in the West Indies, missionaries and bibles, with the prospect of a grisly traitor's death: 'England! On whose throne is a woman – God's best gift to a man … why this gathering up of names to petition the Queen to save life … Will they send a quarter to the Queen to be hung in her palace!' Let there be, he determined, a stench in her nostrils if he was executed.[166] Émigré commentators discussed the royal mercy for the rebels: the New York *Nation*, created by one of the *Dublin Nation*'s editors, Thomas Darcy M'Ghee, discussed 'the Queen's mercy' in its second number in 1849: 'Our souls sicken at this base prostitution of God's two primal attributes, Justice and Mercy.'[167] A similar internationalism developed in the next significant episode where mercy prominently figured in Anglo-Irish politics. But unlike the 1848 rising, mercy was not extended in the 1860s to Fenians, with lengthy sentences after treason trials for Flood, Duffy and Cody; and execution following their trial and conviction, for Michael Larkin, William Allen and other Fenians, for killing a policeman whilst attempting to rescue the Irish-American Fenian leaders Deasy and Kelly from a police van in Manchester.

Unsurprisingly, the Irish press and diaspora concerned itself with debating the British State's mercy and justice in the aftermath of these trials, executions and imprisonments. History showed the enduring severity of British rule. *The Shamrock* of Dublin published a tale of the 1798 rebellion beginning, 'The snowy ermine of Justice, covered with blood, trailed its loathsome length through the mourning towns and villages of Ireland.'[168] Irish commentators knew the limits of royal power – the *Cork Examiner* in 27 August 1868 admitted that the queen was 'unoffending and irresponsible' and that it was her government which 'sought to employ the influence of her assumed opinions against a great measure of justice'.[169] The *Nation*'s comment on the 'clemency movement' was cynical in mid-May 1869: the government had European and American public opinion to consider and would get up an 'edifying appeal for the Queen's benign clemency and gracious mercy' itself.[170] In Toronto in 1873, the Irish-Canadian James J. Gahan publicly asserted that if the lady 'whose virtues have been proclaimed in every tone from the bass to the treble takes an active part in the government, then I blush for female clemency, I blush for womanly mercy, I blush for womanly tenderness'.[171]

The memory of British injustice and merciless was cultivated by nationalists in the late nineteenth and early twentieth centuries. Appeals to British mercy weakened the cause, it was said.[172] A biography of the republican politician Michael Davitt, published in 1881, referred to 'mock pardon' with 'British mercy' firmly in ironic quotation marks.[173] The tenth volume of *Irish Penny Readings*, by *The Nation*'s editors, included 'British mercy to Ireland' in 1885: a paragraph reprinting Smith O'Brien's sentence in 9 October 1848, without indicating how the sentence was commuted.[174] The *United Irishman*'s first editorial, in March 1899, stated that it would not 'at any time support an appeal to any such myths as English Justice or English Mercy'.[175] The *Irish News*'s article on the 'noble martyrdom' of Allen, Larkin and O'Brien stressed the unmercifulness of government, in 1902.[176] Cartoons depicted Erin 'at the mercy' of England: on the block of English prejudice, eyes blindfolded by 'cloture' and about to be executed by the axe of coercion wielded by Gladstone while John Bright looked on approvingly, in the *Weekly Freeman*, 8 April 1882. British fear could explain prominent acts of clemency: the socialist and republican James Larkin's release from prison as an act of the prerogative was dismissed by its recipient thus, 'Mercy be damned', in 1913.[177]

Mercy during the Easter Rising

The picture of British clemency promoted during the Great War (studied in the penultimate chapter) looks different viewed across the Irish Sea following revolt in 1916. The Irish were told that the war was concerned, like British rule 'on the whole', with justice and mercy.[178] The prime minister, Asquith, emphasized to the Commons the desire to show clemency to the rank and file and inflict the death penalty 'as sparingly as possible'.[179] Naturally in the British press, Britain was presented as merciful: with images of injured rebels being nursed alongside, as well as guarded by, soldiers, for instance (see Figure 4.3).[180] From America, William Dean Howells (author of the novel *The Quality of Mercy*) implored a 'golden hour for the sort of justice which we misname mercy', rather than overmatching the rising's madness 'with the madness of English resentment'.[181] His essay was quoted in the British press.[182]

The sectarian Irish press debated the wisdom of mercy and the necessity of justice. Notoriously the *Irish Independent* led a 'howl' against clemency whilst the 'quality of

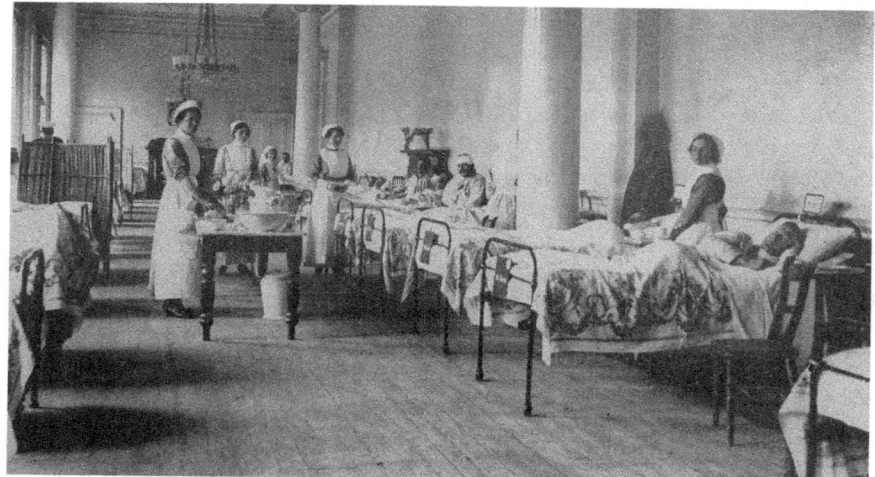

Figure 4.3 'Dublin Castle as Hospital for Casualties in the Rebellion', *Illustrated War News*, 10 May 1916, p.41. Author's collection.

mercy' was extolled in a paper such as the *Skibbereen Eagle*.[183] The Irish press reprinted the essayist 'Judex' in the English *Fortnightly Review*, 'Vengeance has heretofore followed every revolt in Ireland; it is about time that mercy should at last be given a trial'.[184] John Dillon complained of press censorship in the Commons in August: '*Freeman's Journal* had been warned against publishing articles urging clemency to rebels, and the warning was conveyed to the editor by a soldier carrying a fixed bayonet.'[185] Irish appeals for funds for a National Aid Association for relatives of the imprisoned or executed men mentioned the virtue of mercy.[186]

John Mahaffy, the classicist and Provost of Trinity College argued, in *The Times*, for stern justice for the leaders, 'much pity … large mercy' for the followers.[187] 'You took care that no plea for mercy should interpose on behalf of the poor young fellows who surrendered to you in Dublin,' Sir John Maxwell (overseeing the military response) was told by the bishop of Limerick when Sinn Fein leaders who surrendered – Joseph Plunkett, Edmund Daly, Michael Hanrahan, William Pearse and John McBride – were shot on 4 and 5 May. Clemency was appealed to for the rank-and-file: 'pity for its dupes and victims'.[188] Catholic priests were 'ardent and unanimous in favour of a policy of mercy', Judex argued in the *Fortnightly Review* in June 1916: their views should carry weight given their role in brokering a surrender.[189] The Presbytery of Dublin did not forget 'the claims of mercy … in so far as they are pleaded on behalf of the misguided among the rebels'.[190] Telegrams to Asquith pleaded for executions to stop.[191] In the Commons, calls for clemency were led by John Redmond, the nationalist leader. In October the nationalist MP and T.P. O'Connor identified an 'instinctive cry for humanity and mercy', in denying it was an Irish 'waywardness and unreasonableness' that resented the executions. Joseph Devlin told the Commons the British 'should have treated these men more mercifully, and, as you were powerful, you should have been generous and magnanimous'.[192]

Petitioners for clemency towards the Irish rebels and others, alluded to Botha's merciful handling of Boer revolt in South Africa (in 1915 his clemency was praised as evidence he 'grasped British methods of government'[193]). A West Australian 'monster meeting' which sent its resolutions to John Redmond, for example, alluded to this in August.[194] In Chicago a mass protest against the executions had James Larkin on the platform. The Senate passed a resolution calling for clemency.[195] The *North American Review*, accepting the justice of executing the ringleaders, argued for 'magnanimous clemency'.[196]

In England the response included the headlines of *The People* (London) on 7 May: 'IRISH REBELS' FATE. U.S.A. AND THE GERMAN NOTE. EIGHT REBEL LEADERS SHOT BUT MERCY EXTENDED TO MANY', and comment that Maxwell tempered 'stern military justice' with mercy.[197] The *Leeds Mercury* thought 'severity at the right time is in reality the truest form of mercy for the leaders'.[198] The *Pall Mall Gazette* feared mercy brought 'recrudescence', asserted English justice was unvindictive and argued for 'no further mercy' for treason against the 'usual appeals from the besotted sentimentalist'.[199] Another newspaper decried 'sentimentality' in the Commons by English radicals.[200] *The Spectator* weighed up the claims of 'strict justice' or 'inglorious leniency' for the leaders.[201] The socialist Harold Laski mourned the loss of a Labour figure in James Connolly and called for mercy since Sir Edward Carson and Asquith bore some blame.²⁰² The Liverpool Railwaymen's Vigilance Committee, 'whilst dissociating ourselves entirely from the Sinn Fein revolt, strongly protest[ed] against the merciless treatment that is being meted out to the Irish rebels', it informed Asquith.²⁰³ Scottish newspapers reported the meetings of Irish Scots, such as the Croy Ancient Hibernians who hoped the government 'would forgive and forget and show to these men now a hand as merciful as in the days gone bye they showed a merciless hand'.²⁰⁴

Protestant critics in Ulster feared nationalists saw 'every act of clemency as a sign of weakness' and recalled the 'extreme clemency of a pliable and sympathetic Lord Lieutenant', misusing the prerogative. They blamed the chief secretary for Ireland, Augustine Birrell.²⁰⁵ In the colourful words of *Ballymena Weekly Telegraph* in May 1916, 'Jail became a vestibule of the Viceregal Lodge.' The prerogative had been abused to release nationalists in the viceroyalty of the Liberal earl of Aberdeen: the rebels were not fit subjects for mercy. 'Mercy to traitors is rank injustice to the loyal,' it starkly concluded.²⁰⁶ For such critics the Irish insurrection attempted the following year emphasized the danger of 'magnanimity and clemency carried to the point of criminal weakness; they do not admit that the quality of mercy has been strained in their interests'.²⁰⁷ In fact, Lord Wimborne, who succeeded Aberdeen, revealed to the Royal Commission on the rebellion his largely nominal or ceremonial role as power was concentrated in the hands of the chief secretary for Ireland in the Cabinet, even if the royal prerogative of mercy remained.²⁰⁸

The press reported public resentment at the executions.²⁰⁹ Government mishandling of repression and mercy led, according to F.S.L. Lyons, to 'deep and permanent alienation of Irish opinion'; a contemporary privately wrote of the need to 'pour' out love and mercy on Ireland to prevent the executed leaders becoming national saints.²¹⁰ The long history of British violence in Ireland meant that historic instances of mercilessness were rehearsed in nationalist propaganda. The Irish-American Patrick Lally's *Facts of Irish history and English propaganda* of 1916, for example, referred to Oliver Cromwell.²¹¹ The politics of mercy was contentious in the ensuing Anglo-Irish war. Mercy in the case of one eighteen-year-old Sinn Feiner involved in the death of four soldiers in 1920 was discussed by Britons as an appeal to an 'emotional people'.²¹² The message of mercy and forgiveness in post-partition, sectarian Ireland, remained compelling.²¹³

'In this plea for clemency, the Government should avoid history repeating itself in the too extensive making of martyrs now by excessive punishments,' the *Leitrim Advertiser* of 11 May 1916 argued, referring to the nationalist Constance Markievic brooding over the rebellion of 1798 as a child.²¹⁴ Writing shortly after the Rising, the Irish-American John Regan looked to the Society of United Irishman's prospectus written by Wolfe Tone and circulated in Ireland in June 1791, which based the struggle for freedom in the rights of man for Ireland, and ended with the cry of 'mercy, of justice and of victory'.²¹⁵ The French revolutionary context which stimulated these men, provided another arena in which to rehearse claims of mercy and denounce unmercy. Mercy in the context of this global struggle, is now turned to.

5

British mercy and the French Revolution

Its discursive use during the French Revolution is of fundamental importance to mercy's modern history. The focus of this chapter is how Britons interpreted the era as an absence: exposing the mercilessness of revolutionary and imperial regimes in propaganda and presented a contrasting British clemency. It contributes to the scholarship on the revolution's emotional aspects that include work on pity.[1] Its sources are the newspapers, contemporary histories and pamphlets, pouring out translations of French discourse and offering British reflections on events in continental Europe, and images.[2] The revolution stimulated a graphic discourse of unmercy, replacing the figurative gates of mercy shut on mankind with images such as 'the reeking heart of Mercy' hurled to murderous *sans culottes*, as one American wrote.[3]

Those contemporaries witnessing the revolution, or looking back at it as recent history, lamented mercy's absence. Edmund Burke's *Reflections on the Revolution in France* in 1790 argued that the 'reforming doctors in Paris' attacking the Catholic Church, unlike their English counterparts, forgot that 'justice and mercy are substantial parts of religion'. Burke held that order would be restored with a 'discriminating, manly, and provident mercy'.[4] Thomas Paine advocated mercy for the French king on 19 January 1793 after the Convention voted for death, 'If on my return to America, I should employ myself on a history of the French Revolution, I had rather record a thousand errors on the side of mercy, than be obliged to tell one act of severe justice.'[5] The Oxford don Henry Kett's tract of prophecy in 1799 commented that Jacobin power 'absolute in all things else, disdained to preserve the prerogative of mercy' … 'There was no forgiving power in any part of the executive government … application for mercy was rejected with the declaration that, they had no power to pardon or to save'.[6] It was a 'fearful period, when justice and mercy seemed banished from the world', a sermonist recollected in 1814.[7] Thomas Carlyle described (in 1837) the transition from Terror to Thermidor as the triumph of public opinion, Desmoulins's failure to secure a committee followed on after 9th Thermidor by the 'whole Nation' resolving into a Committee of Mercy.[8] Louis Blanc cast the Revolution in terms of mercy's impotence, taxonomizing the factions as Terror (Hébert), Justice (Robespierre) and Mercy (Danton) in 1858.[9]

Mercy and the Terror

Mercy was a treasured aspect of sacred monarchy and a subject for Enlightenment thought in France.[10] By contrast, revolutions were understood to tend to mercilessness.

British thought on the phenomenon of revolution before 1789, assumed violence: David Hume identifying only two instances from antiquity where revolution was not associated with 'great effusion of blood in massacres ... Caesar's clemency ... would not gain great applause in the present age'.[11] Some explained the revolution in Louis XVI's too tender mercy – James M'Queen of Glasgow arguing 'he hesitated – he leaned to mercy when he should have wielded the sword of justice; and he was therefore undone'.[12]

Mercy's role became problematic for the new republican state, even as the radical Helen Maria Williams (living in France) hoped, with the Bastille's demise, for justice to 'erect, on eternal foundations, her protecting sanctuary for the oppressed! and may humanity and mercy be the graceful decorations of her temple!'[13] The Terror – during which Williams was imprisoned – starkly demonstrated to the world that mercy was not to interfere with the justice of revolutionary tribunals. Mercy was no *vertu républicaine*: in fact an English poet imagined mercy and other virtues fleeing for Britain.[14] Pity became suspect, 'all tears, all commiseration, were rigorously forbidden'.[15] Ironically in the guillotine revolutionaries had a symbol of justice devised for merciful execution: 'It is curious, and ought to be to theorists an instructive lesson, that this bloody implement was at first proposed on a combined principle of justice and mercy'.[16]

In the anonymous *First Fruits of the French Revolution* (after November 1793), 'Humanity and Mercy' is the title to a summary of 'butcheries, and wanton cruelties, the assassinations, massacres, and bloody executions' and detailing the counter-revolution in La Vendée and 'reduction' of Lyons with Collot d'Herbois and Fouché's joint statement '*we distrust the tears of repentance – Nothing can disarm our severity*' italicized.[17] From Philadelphia Cobbett's *The bloody buoy* (1797) documented the atrocities to show what humanity or mercy to expect from French republicans.[18] Other British works provided anecdotes of women pleading for lives: the heroic Mademoiselle Elizabeth Cazotte begging mercy for her father after saving him from summary execution at the Prison de l'Abbaye in September 1792, vainly expecting mercy to be one of the attributes of magistrates, and appealing through the 'voice of nature'.[19]

The most extended discussion of the French removal of the right of pardon, in the English language, seems to be Jacques Necker's. The Swiss-born former French finance minister (see Figure 5.1) devoted a chapter to the prerogative of mercy, in *Du pouvoir exécutif dans les grands états*, translated as *An Essay on the True Principles of Executive Power in Great States* and published in London in 1792.[20] He claimed 'the word clemency has been blotted from our language', and that no other people on earth had removed the right of pardon. At the same time the establishment of juries, which might have mitigated sentences (Necker disputed this), had not taken place:

> The spirit of philosophy, that spirit, which by asserting the rights of humanity has attracted so great attention, is so disfigured by its usurpers, that they have proposed the abolition of the right of pardoning as a reasonable and becoming measure ... Meanwhile from the reign of the national assembly the monarch has found himself divested of the most august of his prerogatives.[21]

For Necker, a republic where there was 'a sort of kindred spirit and moral feeling, circumstances which throw a shade of mildness and forbearance over all acts of authority' *might* not regret removing this prerogative.²² This was not the case in France, where the people were now aware of strength, spoke a language of menace, were agitated, and sanguinary in their passions. The revolutionaries 'dared to confide in a justice so sure, impartial and intrepid, as to authorise the abolition of the prerogative of mercy'.²³

In Necker's account, demand for irrevocable judgement appealed to vanity. Contrasted with this new 'cold and logical system' was the English king's signature necessary (Necker believed) to execute criminal sentences, the judges returned from circuit to 'instruct the monarch as to the circumstances of each particular offence'.²⁴ The 'empire of sentiment, and of all those grand and simple ideas which follow in its train', were banished.²⁵ Not only that, a chain of virtue linking man to God that

Figure 5.1 Jacques Necker (1732–1804), stipple engraving *c.* 1800. Author's collection.

'most precious resemblance to his divine perfections' was removed.[26] Necker's chapter rehearsed the oaths sworn during the English coronation ('Words like these give us as it were at one stroke the character of a nation') and, flattering his English readers, in that 'wise and virtuous nation', it was contrived that 'the first intimations addressed to the king of England upon his accession to the throne, and the first engagements into which he enters, are calculated to impress his duties and his rights of clemency and mercy'.[27] It was a matter of national honour, France's reputation for 'manners', 'justice is not more a debt that we owe to the political institution of society, than mercy is a debt we owe to our common nature'.[28]

'Legislators, away with pity, away with mercy, let us put between them and us, a barrier of eternity,' Jean-Nicholas Pache, Mayor of Paris, declared in the National Convention in September 1793.[29] Camille Desmoulins's argument in *Le Vieux Cordelier* in 20 December 1793, for the 'revolutionary' status of clemency organized through a *comité de clémence* to strengthen liberty was ignored.[30] The imprisonment of the royal family led to British calls for mercy, thus in the work of one Irish and Foxite member of the British Parliament dedicated to Burke in 1793 appeared the lines, 'In noble minds the love of mercy reigns, | But dire revenge a Nation's glory stains'.[31] The republic showed the king no mercy; after regicide, hopes that the festival of the Supreme Being signalled mercy's return, as Helen Maria Williams reported in her published account of 1795 was the hope of prisoners, went unrealized ('while Robespierre behind the scenes was issuing daily mandates for murder, we see him on the stage the herald of mercy and of peace').[32]

The Terror's end – with the death of Robespierre whom the young poet Robert Southey extolled from Somerset as a 'ministering angel of mercy' – was not perceived by Britons as ushering in mercy's sway.[33] Pierre Claude François Daunou might speak, in a widely reported speech, of the laying of the altar of Clemency during the festival of 10 Thermidor 1795.[34] But a writer in the *British Critic* spoke of 'the dissembled clemency which the successors of Robespierre have assumed'.[35] The interpretation of the post-Thermidor regime in nineteenth-century British discourse was one where mercy was the 'fashion', used pragmatically for self-advancement as in the case of Jean-Lambert Tallien whose advocacy of justice and mercy in the Convention, on 21 January 1795, was seen as merely 'puling'.[36] Pardon and mercy remained absent from the French law code of 1798; as a writer commented, a democratic republic lacked the blessings of a monarchy where mercy arose 'from a discrimination of the nature of crimes, which laws cannot always notice … revision of judgments passed under the influence of popular delusion or popular prejudice'.[37]

Britons understood their intervention in the revolutionary crisis as an act of mercy or justice, as one poet stated in 1793: 'Britannia's Genius, to whose hand is given | The first and noblest attributes of heav'n; | Justice and Mercy, all her sons to arms, | To arbitrate, and rectify those harms'.[38] 'Give them, o'er MERCY'S FOES triumphant pow'r,' implored another at the time of threatened invasion in 1803, of the Almighty.[39] The poetic response also involved extolling the opposite of mercy: 'If the foe, misjudging, read | Dismay in Pity's gentlest deed, | And construing mercy into fear,' the poet laureate Henry Pye said in 1796.[40]

The withholding of mercy by an anxious British State during this existential conflict is understandable: Ruti Teitel notes 'though clemency appears to be built into ordinary notions of the rule of law, there are also significant differences in its exercise in periods of heightened political change'.[41] A declared war of extermination on the French side led some Britons to eschew talk of 'moderation, mercy, and tenderness'.[42] The centrality of justice and mercy to British discourse on the meaning of the revolution is unsurprising. As Douglas Hay argues, defence of the 'majesty of law' was renewed at various crises points such as the food riots of 1766 and Gordon riots of 1780: 'The justice of the English law was ... a powerful ideological weapon in the arsenal of conservatives during the French Revolution.' The ideological aspect to the law meant instances of judicial fairness such as the execution of malefactory aristocrats, and the palladium of freedom which was the jury (or habeas corpus), featured in counter-revolutionary discourse.[43]

Examination of the revolution's meaning in the newspaper press included reports of the parliamentary debates on revolutionaries' acts of injustice and unmercy.[44] Parliamentarians discussed the claims made for the new state in terms of justice and mercy. Burke argued against Sheridan on this subject; his letters on 'regicide peace' presented peace overtures as a humiliating supplication for mercy from the 'People-King'.[45] When planning counter-revolutionary measures in Britain, parliamentarians referred to mercy and justice.[46] Trials of radicals invoked mercy and justice – seemingly by contrast with the French example, although radicals also used the coronation oath to administer justice with mercy, to indict the monarch. One example is the trial of Thomas Hardy of the London Corresponding Society in 1794.[47] *The Times* reported that transported Scottish seditionists were reprimanded for relying on opposition politicians rather than appealing to the throne's mercy.[48] In the same year, a report of John Thelwall's trial for high treason included assurance that 'the Jury were to administer justice in mercy, as was always the case in this country'. A similar claim figured in the case of William Stone in 1796.[49] The action of United Irishmen was contrasted with the blessings under a merciful king at the head of a free constitution.[50] Unsurprisingly the judge in the case of the loyalist John Reeves, charged with libel for *Thoughts on the English Constitution*, asserted the requirement to administer the law 'with every fair leaning to mercy'.[51]

Optimistic initial commentary, it is true, beheld or foretold revolutionary mercy. One Norfolk farmer, a Whig and Baptist, Mark Wilks, argued in a sermon in July 1791, against Edmund Burke's critical view, that the National Assembly was one, 'where mercy and truth meet together ... that wisdom, mercy, fidelity, and disinterested virtue, which have appeared on the very face of all the actions of the National Assembly'.[52] At the outset of the French crisis, the British press reported the hopes of orators in the National Convention, that 'plunder and Tyranny are ready to yield room for Mercy and Justice'.[53] Alexander Pirie, a minister in the independent church in Scotland, wrote of this hopeful era, promising the 'return of the golden age, in which mercy and truth, righteousness and peace should embrace each other'.[54] In the Tory John Gifford's four-volume history of France (translated from the work of French historians and appearing from 1793), the frontispiece by Henry Singleton included 'time breaking the Clouds which had obscured the Genius of France, who is sitting between Justice and Mercy'.[55]

But female personification of mercy or clemency was absent from revolutionary iconography; the feminine aspect to violence exemplified in the furies of the guillotine featuring in post-Revolutionary literature.[56]

Douglas Hay notes the role that ideas about French legal tyranny played. The English system compared favourably with the *ancien régime* of *lettres de cachet*, aristocratic tyranny, and inquisitorial processes.[57] The poet laureate Pye, in 'Naucratia, or Naval Dominion; a Poem', described the 'semblance of mercy' of the *ancien régime* as a sign of its sickness. On the other hand, the Marquis de Rivarol's lines, 'Maria Antoinette's Lamentation at the Conciergerie', translated in the British press, claimed that the French nation had ever been a refuge for mercy.[58] The king, just before his execution, British reports stated, on the basis of the official account from general Santerre, wished to reflect publicly on mercy: 'Louis Capet wanted to speak of mercy to the people, but I would not let him.'[59] His brother, the self-proclaimed Louis XVIII, sought to present himself as ruling (in exile) in mercy and justice.[60] At the Bourbon monarchy's first restoration in 1814, Sir Richard Bedingfield at Bath presented a transparency of olive branch and Dove with the French Crown, with the motto adapted from Shakespeare, 'Sweet Mercy now, is Royalty's True badge.'[61]

The propaganda war involved counter claims of British mercy. For the *British Critic*, finding ammunition in William Cobbett's popular *Democratic Principles Illustrated by Examples* (1798), atrocities and perversion of justice demonstrated the 'pretended philanthropy of Republicans'. Necker had referred to the coronation oath's requirement to exercise justice in mercy and the *British Critic* commented in September 1798 that it was a noted void in the republican code that there was nothing on pardon or mercy.[62] In 1798, responding to the French legal system imposed on Algeria an amateur poet in the *Derby Mercury* contrasted bloody 'tyrannic democrats' with the heirs to Alfred's laws: 'If death their fiat, streams of mercy flow from George's throne to check desponding woe, | Ye ancient Numas of this envied realm! Let Mercy, Truth, and Justice guide the helm!'[63]

British royal mercy and Blackstone's comments on the royal prerogative were invoked during the trials for sedition of the political reformers Thomas Muir and Thomas Palmer in 1794.[64] It was even claimed in the press, that as the king signed their warrant of transportation he read 'with peculiar emphasis, and from the known humanity of his heart, we doubt not with all appropriate feeling, the lines from the *Merchant of Venice*.'[65] In July 1797 there were appeals to mercy after the naval mutinies, the *Hampshire Chronicle*, for example, quoting the 'beautiful lines of Shakespeare' about mercy when imagining the generous-hearted seamen in the 'lowly posture of contrition': 'They appeal to the charities of his heart, they conjure the amiable prerogative of his crown.'[66] The previous chapter studied the response of the British to rebellion in Ireland during this era. In *The Monstrous Republic: or, French Atrocities Pourtrayed* (1799), the Irish scholar and clergyman William Hales linked 'softening rigour of justice' with effeminacy and lassitude, and pointed out the danger of mercy towards Irish rebels (he played an active role in responding to the French invasion of Killala).[67]

A later chapter studies the mercy claims made in the conduct of late-eighteenth-century warfare. The revolutionary regime was anathematized for its uncivilized mode of war by Edmund Burke who scorned the defence of assassinations as merciful because they might prevent battles.[68] The duke of York's response to the proclamation that all

Figure 5.2 Lithograph, *c.* 1840s. *L'enfant de Giberne. Clémence de Napoléon no.4* (Paris: A. Bes and Dubreuil). Author's collection.

English and Hanoverian soldiers would be killed (discussed by Robespierre in the Jacobin Club on 21 June 1794) – that clemency was the brightest gem in the character of soldier – was ridiculed by the French revolutionary leader as an impossibility between a free people and satellites of despots.[69]

Public and private commentary on the absence of mercy during the revolution included the responses of women such as the poet Anna Seward, sharing with her fellow writer Helen Maria Williams, then in Paris (and later in that year, to be imprisoned) her views on the Convention, 'the few, few pleaders for mercy, who, conscious that their lives must probably expiate the generous attempt, deserve statues to their memories'.[70] The novelist Laetitia Hawkins's *Letters on the Female Mind* (1793) took comfort from a superintending providence whose mercy, balancing justice, reconciled her 'to the stupendous scenes of violence and anarchy, which great parts of Europe now presents', yet saw the only power to stop France's slide into famine was 'Heaven in mercy' checking republican delusion.[71]

Napoleonic mercy

As the Triumvirate was established and Napoleon rose to supreme power, the British papers reported and commented on Bonapartean clemency. On the credit side was clemency in Cairo in 1798 and 'transcendent sentiments of mercy' in response to the conspirators of the Council of Five Hundred and others in 1797.[72] In exile his own utterance was recorded by de Las Cases: 'A sovereign should be regarded only as a blessing to his people; his acts of severity must be overlooked in consideration of his acts of clemency; mercy must still be held to be his chief attribute.'[73] Historians have shown some interest in what was an important element of contemporary assessments of Napoleon. His acts are studied in relation to Machiavelli's *The Prince* (where the Italian argued for the political use of cruelty and clemency) by Peter Hicks.[74]

The artistic representation of Napoleonic mercy (see Figure 5.2) has stimulated several exhibitions.[75] For official art extolled Napoleon's mercy as part of a long tradition in French art of the *exemplum virtutis* proliferating from the 1760s and using classical subjects.[76] Artists depicted the emperor's pardoning of rebels and granting mercy to figures such as the Duc de Saint-Simon through his daughter's agency, for instance Charles Lafont's *Clémence de Napoléon envers Mademoiselle de Saint-Simon* (1808); or the mercy given to the traitorous Prince de Hatzfeld (painted on several occasions and reproduced in several early-nineteenth-century engravings); and battlefield mercy. Marguerite Gérard's *Clémence de Napoléon* was bought by Napoleon for Josephine after exhibition in 1808. Napoleon's status as a man of mercy was also asserted by later British apologists, for instance William Ireland in his *Life of Napoleon Bonaparte* published in 1828.[77]

Contemporary English literary representation stressed his unmercy, for instance the scene between Madame Moreau and the emperor in the play *The Caitiff of Corsica* in 1808. Treatment of General Jean-Victor Moreau was further evidence of his cruelty in William Burdon's character assassination of 1804.[78] British propagandists made visual representation of Napoleonic unmercy. From Sir Robert Wilson's account appeared depiction of the poisoning of sick French soldiers at Jaffa, in broadsides and sheets on the *Tender Mercies of Bonaparte in Egypt! Britons, Beware* as part of a series by the London publisher, Asperne. The prints by George Cruikshank c. 1814 depicted Napoleon's unmerciful acts from the massacre at Toulon, blowing up comrades, burning mosques, shooting prisoners in Egypt and poisoning at Jaffa.[79]

As Napoleon's attempt to regain power failed in 1815 what to do with 'the Monster' became a 'problematic of mercy' for Britons.[80] Capel Lofft's call for clemency stimulated Bulmer and others to debate Napoleon's lack of mercy in prose and verse.[81] Would not humanity in the circumstances be the extreme of madness, asked a newspaper correspondent calling himself 'Alfred'?[82] Others described such mercy as immoderate, spurious humanity, unprincipled clemency and fantasized in poetry that with mercy's sweet voice unheeded, Napoleon would be killed.[83] In the words of the patriotic William Fitzgerald, in May 1815: 'MERCY, too long abroad, will cease to plead, | When the WORLD dooms the MAN OF BLOOD TO BLEED.'[84]

For some, the ex-emperor's journey via Plymouth to St Helena, instantiated British mercy and generosity, 'By GEORGE, blest Prince, was life of peace insur'd, | From Europe's vengeance free,' in the words of one 'old naval officer'.[85] Indeed, readers of a published letter purporting to be from an officer on the *Northumberland* learned that Napoleon decided to sue for mercy from Britain because of the generosity of the national character. Elsewhere it was reported of the conversation that he had with

Admiral Hotham on the *Superb*, he placed hope in the mercy of this nation whereas with any other member of the Holy Alliance it would have been the 'caprice and will of an individual'.[86]

A creamware Staffordshire mug of about 1803 has a transfer print of Napoleon crying 'mercy, mercy, mercy' to a British soldier who is punching him, a gibbet and hanged man conveying the message of justice.[87] Justice figured prominently in anti-Napoleon imagery: Edward Baldwyn's etching of justice punishing Napoleon after his flight from Elba has the figure of mercy grasping his decapitated head (the *Bellerophon* in the background indicating the British have him at their mercy), the 'ballace [sic] of power' weighed justice with piety exemplified by Louis XVIII, and truth, as heavier in the scales against the emperor, for the abolition of the French slave trade was evidently a false mercy, joined as she was by sin, death and the devil, in Humphrey's splendid satire of 1815.

Mercy appeared in public celebration in Britain in 1814.[88] A transparency by the blind-maker Murray of George Court showed 'Britannia supported by Mercy and Justice with Plenty and Commerce' and elsewhere peace and mercy were tastefully depicted.[89] 'Fair mercy pleads to smooth the warrior's frown,' commented one poet, apropos of the Congress of Vienna. Yet mercy's role in contributing to the resurgence of Napoleon was also bewailed, in the initial treaty with France: 'Mercy, here much worse, than vain | Lighted war's fell torch again' – France could not expect such mercy again.[90] With European peace, mercy figured alongside sister virtues, in celebration of Napoleon's defeat (after being momentarily imperilled again, by the Hundred Days[91]). 'A View of the Grand Triumphal Pillar', an etching, after George Humphrey, of 12 May 1815, has Napoleon flogging mercy with the words, 'There you good for nothing jade, take that for persuading the Allied Sovereigns to send me to Elba.'

Mercy's restoration and the memory of revolution

The Charter of the Bourbon restoration restored monarchical clemency and it was the occasion for French commentary, such as Charles Vernay's *De la restauration de la Monarchie, ou la clémence de Louis XVIII* in 1814 and *Un Mot sur la clémence du roi* in 1815.[92] The politics of mercy in the restoration was picked up in Britain, in William Ireland's *The Napoleon Anecdotes* (1822), which referred to a French caricature ironically contrasting Louis XVIII's clemency with the tyranny of Napoleon.[93] Mercy's place in nineteenth-century French law was dissected by British commentators, referring to Louis's *ordonnance* of 1818, and the conditions for mercy and pardon it entailed.[94]

Enduring fascination with the first French Revolution meant that the debates about mercy in the Terror were presented in British works of history. These include the radical James Bronterre O'Brien's eulogy to Robespierre as the projector of France's regeneration, 'based on justice and mercy to all that would be just and merciful', and George Lewes's biography in which Robespierre's response to the call for Marie Antoinette's execution became 'ideas are pitiless, but the people ought to have mercy'.[95] Mercy's absence in the revolution figured in British art, prose and drama through the

Figure 5.3 *An Appeal for Mercy, 1798*. Engraving of the picture by Marcus Stone painted in 1876. Author's collection.

course of the century.⁹⁶ At the Royal Academy in 1875, for example, Marcus Stone (who developed a penchant for eighteenth-century scenes) presented *An Appeal for Mercy, 1793* in which a prostrate woman appeals to a hard-hearted member of the Convention (see Figure 5.3). By contrast to this enduring sense of French unmercy, mercy's presence in the British imperium was often asserted. I quoted Necker's eloquent phrase concerning the empire of sentiment early in this chapter: the next chapter studies the discourse of merciful imperial sentiment and action.

6

Empire of mercy

'Spread it then, | And let it circulate through every vein | Of all your empire; that where Britain's power | Is felt, mankind may feel her mercy too,' William Cowper's lines, from his anti-slavery *The Task* (1785) were cited through the nineteenth century by Christian missionaries and promoters of the high-minded empire.[1] 'British power is mercy: whom it controls it saves,' asserted the Reverend William Shrewsbury, Methodist missionary in the Caribbean and South Africa.[2] 'Might with mercy constant blended', sang the chorus of *India*, an imperial show by Imre Kiralfy performed in London in 1895–6.[3] Discourses of the empire present (to quote Richard Frohock) 'crass acts of appropriation as acts of mercy, justice, lenity, or charity'.[4] The association of power with mercy was discernible to contemporaries studying the empire. Robert Martin's *History of the British Possessions in the East Indies* of 1837, glossed British control over the territory of 'stipendiary princes' as a response to their tyranny 'which in mercy to the unhappy sufferers we could no longer permit to exist'.[5] In New Zealand the Maori awoke, Godfrey Lagden's imperial study of 1924 complacently said, 'to the inevitable and recognise[d] the power of the British, who had shown on many occasions how to temper justice with mercy and displayed the desire both to forgive and to govern the natives fairly with every intention to enlighten and uplift them'.[6]

This chapter looks at the empire from mercy's perspective *not* to argue for a more merciful nature to the imperial project. The empire was a criminal history for the American editor of *The Irish World* in 1881: a pamphlet reprinting his verdict in 1915 displays as frontispiece a venomous serpent circling the globe, a trope of wickedness and malevolence echoed in other anti-British iconography.[7] Scholarly work on the empire's demise emphasizes the brutality with which it sought to sustain itself.[8] Robinson and Gallagher comment that the imperial historian was 'very much at the mercy of his own particular concept of empire': this chapter places mercy among imperialism's 'idioms and imaginaries'.[9] Nor was it simply about 'making selfishness seem noble'.[10] Scholarship has studied the role of sympathy in British imperialism.[11] Supporters of the *imperium Britannicum* recognized power required tempering by mercy to last.[12]

For children given the coronation volume *King Edward's Realm*, the empire was presented as simply expressing love of 'justice and fair-play'.[13] But in a longer catalogue of supposed imperial virtues mercy was present. For the imperial races 'took it for granted', a Canadian, Arthur Lower, recalled of his late-Victorian childhood, 'that honesty, decency, mercy, justice, the love of freedom, were the peculiar prerogatives of the British world'.[14] Non-British observers – such as American visitors to the Raj, weighed up force and mercy's roles in imperial rule.¹⁵ The colonized paid homage to it: a claimant to the Awadh (Oude) throne, Nawwab 'Iqbal-al-daula Bahadur in 1834 asserted '*clemency* to captives, and *mercy*, is perfected in them! *These* alone are the principles which are the causes of their supremacy and dominion'.¹⁶ The sultan of Perak in Malaya claimed that what struck him after months in Britain in 1902 was the 'three qualities in British rule without which, he believed, no rule could be successful— they were strength, justice, and mercy'.¹⁷ Recognition of, or appeals to, British mercy were not limited to ruling elites: social reformers and writers alluded to it.¹⁸ Though Rabindranath Tagore decided of the British in India, 'they do not show mercy but do good; do not love but protect'.¹⁹

Yet when British imperialism is studied by historians, historic claims of 'mercy' are often forgotten outside specialist literature on missionaries. Jack Greene's work on the empire in eighteenth-century culture considers the languages of humanity and justice with almost nothing to say about mercy or being merciful.²⁰ Studies of British imperialism and the military find no call to invoke mercy.²¹ This is odd because apart from the habit of describing their rule as justice-with-mercy (following the scriptural command to act justly and love mercy), moments calling for mercy are obvious in the empire's history.²² Acts such as slave-trade abolition, now seen through the lens of humanitarianism, were presented as acts of mercy and not simply of justice.²³ There were also episodes when mercy and forbearance were prominent by absence: as in the war 'without pity' after Indian rebellion in 1857–8.²⁴ The judicial processes and discourse which attract attention from legal and imperial historians cannot be separated from that of mercy, though mercy might seem to be inferior to, as following on from, justice.²⁵

Attending to mercy leads us to texts about imperialism's ethical dimension – the claim that the empire was or should be a moral endeavour.²⁶ Not infrequently the empire was defended as a Christian enterprise and agent of God's will.²⁷ For George Troup's *The British Empire and the Christian Faith* (1852), the task above all was the 'justice of conveying to [fellow-men, still debased in idolatry] the message of mercy which you have received'.²⁸ This was famously represented in Thomas Barker's *The Secret of England's Greatness* of c. 1863.²⁹ Measured by Christianity's yardstick the empire might be found wanting: Gladstone publicly asked in 1857 whether Britons had given the 'full benefit of Christian example ... set before them the pattern of moderation and truth and justice and mercy', in India.³⁰ Yet the ideal endured: in 1890 the Catholic bishop of Salford, when imperial federation was promoted, admitted seeing the empire as instrument of mercy and salvation.³¹

William Cowper's poem can be viewed alongside other poems of slavery abolition as, in the words of Pramod Nayar, offering 'moral imperialism ... that brings the distant parts of the world into Britain's civilizational domain'. Moral improvement was a 'mode of global conquest'.³² Cowper's poem was employed, beyond the ambit of anti-slavery, to justify the higher purpose of British [evangelical Protestant] Christianity.³³ Mercy also figures in the work of Victorian poets, such as Martin Tupper ('May British mercy more than British valour, | Gain from the world its laurel and its olive,' the pious hope of the moralizing poet in 1832).³⁴

The survey that follows in the first section of this chapter, draws on texts from nineteenth-century historiographers, newspapers, colonial magazines and royal eulogists.[35] I earlier detailed mercy's artistic representation in judicial contexts, history paintings and religious iconography in Britain. Across the British world, the figure of mercy is found in similar locations: Christian sites of worship, colonial administrative centres, law courts and funerary monuments. Some prominent sculptural or painted images of the empire incorporated mercy, like Marochetti's angel of Cawnpore, sometimes called an angel of mercy. Gilbert Scott's gothic memorial to Hotham of Victoria, designed in 1857, and erected in Melbourne cemetery, had mercy among the virtues 'which ought to characterise a governor'.[36] There was the classical angel embodying one of three imperial virtues carved by Simonetti, for the colonial secretary's building in Sydney, New South Wales, in the late 1870s: imploring mercy through a scroll in one hand and her other on her heart.[37] In Bombay in the 1870s, the gothic High Courts were topped by colossal statues of mercy and justice in Christian garb.[38]

Discussing mercy in the British Empire

Surveying the discursive associations made between the empire and mercy over the British long nineteenth century, various manifestations are apparent. There is mercy's natural (scriptural and long-standing cultural) association with justice. In criminal law this covered clemency to capital criminals and a politics of mercy (as discerned in parts of Australia) towards 'aborigines'.[39] On the other hand, justice was appealed to without invoking mercy: as in a pamphlet on taxation in British India in 1839.[40]

There are plenty of references to mercy in the sense of subordination to Britons, as at Oude in 1800.[41] Appeals to 'mercy's sake' included requests to be placed under British rule.[42] As 'agents of emancipation' Derek Peterson notes, nineteenth-century British rulers in Africa faced appeals from minorities 'position[ing] themselves as objects of mercy'.[43] Sometimes mercy was urged in battle, 'be still the British nation prompt to save' as one eulogist of Nelson hoped in 1806.[44] The *Calcutta Review* cast the second Sikh war (1848–9) as warriors guided by 'rays of Christian mercy' though merciful disposition was also discerned among the Sikhs.[45] In New Zealand in the 1840s the British way of mercy was presented to the chieftain Tamati Waaka Nene in conversation, 'it was not the custom of the English to injure any defenceless people, though they might be enemies,' and the reply, 'You are more merciful than we are, and what you say is good and right.'[46] Peace treaties, traditionally, invoked mercy – supplication and its bestowal.[47]

In the next chapter the ways in which mercy was summoned from the eighteenth to early twentieth century in warfare are studied: the discourse represented Britain standing for mercy (and justice).[48] War stimulated much bad poetry including the poet laureate Alfred Austin's 'Mercy of the Mightiful' in 1900 piously hoping of an empire 'least avenging when victorious most', that 'Might's twin Mercy heal the wounds of war, | Solace the heart and cicatrice the scar'. Quelling rebellion brought out the discourse of justice and mercy; mercy claims were most prominently ignored in the Indian rebellion.[49] On these, and other occasions, we hear of God's mercy to the British. British rule was presented providentially as 'a wise and merciful arrangement' between a superior race and subject races.[50] The journalist and reformer Ganapati Subramanya Iyer even claimed during the Indian National Congress in 1885 that British rule was a merciful dispensation of Providence.[51] The counter to that is the idea of Britain's undeserved mercy, as Mrs E. Burrows has a character utter in *Our Eastern Empire* (1857), 'We are so apt to pride ourselves upon our own superiority, and to forget that we do not owe our greatness to any inherent merit of our own, but to God's free mercy and protection.'[52]

Unsurprisingly a future colonial bishop, Daniel Wilson of Calcutta, looked to imperial 'works of mercy ... as the proofs of faith and love'.[53] The missionary discourse of the long nineteenth century was concerned with mercy.[54] For clergymen, exertions were necessary (to quote Samuel Cox in 1833) 'in the cause of God, lest judgments might take the place of mercies'.[55] Catastrophe such as the Indian mutiny required 'solemn fast and humiliation ... a whole people prostrate before God, to beseech Him for pardon and mercy'.[56] Mercy was part of the discourse of imperial philanthropy. The language of mercy with its Christian associations is not our modern secular language of human rights.[57] To be an 'island of benevolence' Britain must be seen as a place where people act justly, love mercy and work humbly with God.[58] Acts of mercy writ large through imperial benevolence proved Britons' 'merciful and loving side'.[59] The Christian theology of mercy also relates to power, as a theologian pointed out, 'to punish and to destroy; for mercy to some implies danger to all. There are not vessels of mercy, unless there are also vessels of wrath.'[60]

Sometimes it is clear how suspect British mercy was: in 1849 in British India, Lionel Trotter's *History* tell us, 'exceeding mistrust in British mercy' was felt by the 'arch-rebel' Moolraj, vassal ruler of Multan.[61] When Britain was condemned for brutality or oppression, as in the slave trade, appeal to mercy is frequent.[62] Mercy is also mentioned in reference to racial prejudice, in the 1830s, Thomas Pringle's South African ballad of 'The Forester of the Neutral Ground', who marries 'Brown Dinah', ends thus (invoking Boer prejudices): 'Shall the Edict of Mercy be sent forth at last, | To break the harsh fetters of Colour and Caste?'[63]

On other occasions mercy was located with royalty. As Mithi Mukerjee notes in *India in the Shadows of Empire*, justice and mercy flowed from Victoria, with the demise of the East India Company, after 1857.[64] Allusions to her status as 'merciful Empress' appear in verse.[65] We are told 'they picture to themselves the Queen-Empress seated on the throne of justice under the canopy of mercy'.[66] Flora Annie Steel stressed the greater power of the 'woman's hand', as Kaiser-i-Hind, the power of the Queen's sympathy.[67] Eulogies to Victoria in 1901 in the *Indian Review* (Madras) claimed she filled the new constitution 'with the shining spirit of her love. We know that the justice, sympathy, toleration, and mercy which so nobly characterise the Proclamation of 1858 really sprang out of the womanly kindliness of Her Majesty's loving heart.'[68] At Edward VII's accession, readers of the *Indian Review* had details of the coronation oath's reference to justice and mercy: Lord Curzon's Durbar Speech asserted, 'to the masses it [the King's Government] dispenses mercy in the hour of suffering' (alongside justice, protection, etc.).[69]

Mercy was part of official rhetoric, as satirized in one Anglo-Indian novel in 1875 where the official gazette reports the annexation of a province, the British government 'in tones of splendid generosity ... would temper justice with mercy so far as to respect existing rights of property'.[70] Here mercy's association with imperial extension is apparent. Just as with acts of justice, mobilizing these sentiments served British power, sometimes in conflict with other imperial powers. One early-nineteenth-century poem about Canada – in the context of French revolution – claimed that British control brought justice and mercy.[71]

The use of mercy in justification is undeniable – expansion on the basis of wars for a just cause being 'tempered with mercy', for example.[72] Having been victorious the *Evangelical Magazine and Missionary Chronicle* (1853) hoped the Cape Colony government would 'be so just and merciful that numbers of the Kaffir nation may seek its protection; and thus be brought again within the civilizing and sacred influence of Christian missions'.[73] 'Mercy to the Zulu people asks that they should be taken under our administration,' it was asserted in 1880.[74]

Peter the Pearker's tract *Caste in India* appealed to readers for patience to hear the 'arguments for mercy' in 1858. I am not asking the reader to accept a claim that the British Empire *was* based on mercy, benevolence or disinterestedness: there were contemporaries who condemned imperial violence, admitted guilt, injustice and the need for atonement.[75] 'We have yet to learn,' the *Indian News* commented in 1851, of the deposition of the Ameers of Sindh, 'to temper mercy with our cravings after universality of dominion.'[76] Yet recognition of a mercy discourse is needed, whether it be anti-slavery advocates asking Britain to exercise her power 'in mercy to mankind', by enforcing treaties[77]; or the *Fortnightly Review* hoping that it be 'known through the length and breadth of Africa', that 'where Englishmen go there justice and mercy follow', or Golden Jubilee pieties about a 'constantly increasing' assault on oppression and a desire to do justly and show mercy.[78]

Much of this is chauvinism, the unjustified assertion, for instance, that 'poor old England [was] so brimful of mercy' and an assumption that 'the strength and mercy of civilisation' came with British rule.[79] Thomas Babington Macaulay is an illustrious example, identifying the 'mightiest empire' with the 'strong moral feeling of the English people', his utterance was strategic in an anti-slavery context in 1824.[80] Rudyard Kipling's *Recessional* invoked mercy, his verse 'adopted by the clergy as the Imperial Anthem, because its appeal for mercy upon contrition has a soothing effect on the conscience', in *The Nation*'s words (1909).[81] The American William Parker described *Recessional*'s impact as resounding 'through England like a great organ note'.[82] But Kipling could be ironic since he referred to the Father of Mercy in the scathing 'Supplication of Kerr Cross, Missionary': implored by a missionary for arms and ammunition, and safe passage of smuggled guns, to teach 'goodwill to men and peace on earth'.[83]

Complaints of unmercy circulated in English-language texts. These include commentary from transported Canadian rebels, references to the killing and mutilation of the Kaffir chief Hintza (an atrocity alleged against the officer George Southey in 1835), criticism of Governor Torrington's martial law in Ceylon after mid-century rebellion, the shooting down of natives in Bambireh by Henry Morton Stanley in 1876 and failure to honour the flag of surrender in the Bambaata campaign, when killing the chief Mudhlogozulu and followers in Natal in 1906.[84] They include Walter Walsh's *The Moral Damage of War* (1906) in the aftermath of war with the Boers, restyling the beatitudes for 'imperialistic heathenism', along lines such as 'blessed are the merciless: for they shall not need mercy'.[85] Critics close at hand, the Irish nationalist press highlighted atrocities, the *Irish News* referring in 1899 to the crushing of rebellion in Bechuanaland as an act of the 'mild and merciful British regime'.[86]

Some *advocated* an imperial policy of unmercy, reacting in the late nineteenth century against humane sentiment in British middle-class culture. The journalist George Steevens offered 'bracing tonic to our later morality' in an essay on the new humanitarianism in 1898: 'We ought not to forget to temper mercy with justice – even that rude and brutal exercise of superiority which may be called natural justice'.[87] There should be no mercy to the weak. Others deplored a future guided by Charles Darwin and 'it seems by no means improbable that the twentieth century will be brought up in its earlier years on Nietzsche and water', the *Indian Review* prophesied in 1901.[88] The concentration camps of South Africa were known unironically as 'Camps of Mercy' in the British press, defended from Emily Hobhouse's criticisms, as havens of mercy in 1901.[89] That year, Algernon Swinburne's 'On the Death of Colonel Benson' asserted: 'Nor heed we more than he what liars dare say | Of mercy's holiest duties left undone | Toward whelps and dams of murderous foes, whom none | Save we had spared or feared to starve and slay'.

The exercise of mercy reflects security of power. So Meer Ali Moorad of Upper Scind's fate after forging a claim to additional territory after the treaty of Nounahar was to be stripped of these lands and not hanged, 'It is lucky for him ... that he lives in 1852, when our power is irresistible, and we can afford to be merciful.'[90] The *North British Review*'s comment in 1853, 'In our relations with savage tribes, we are strong, and can therefore afford to be merciful and forbearing,' is telling.[91] Mercy, as Žižek points out, is linked to sovereign power.[92] To invoke mercy is to justify power: so discourses of mercy offered one of the 'protective colours' selfish imperialism employs, in J.A. Hobson's classic critique (1902).[93] Mercy and justice would eventually be understood as ruling ideas, by 'capable races' such as the Fulani of Northern Nigeria under British tutelage, Frederick Lugard reported in the 1900s.[94] Even at the end of the empire, it was explicitly asserted that young imperial officers enjoyed the power to act as 'the arm of justice and the hand of mercy to millions'.[95] Mercy and justice were part of discursive justifications for autocratic and imperial rule, against democratic and indigenous self-rule.[96]

The tarnished crown of slaves

The second section of this chapter studies mercy's place in a key imperial episode: efforts to link slave-trade abolition with the monarchy in the reigns of George III and his sons. Nineteenth-century Britons were proud of their role in anti-slavery efforts, supposing that abolition in the British Isles and emancipation in the empire in August 1838 expressed a national disposition. The oft-quoted lines from Cowper about Britain's power and mercy concerned slavery.[97] Its abolition in the empire was frequently seen, as for the *Christian Observer* in 1834, as a 'great measure of national justice and mercy'.[98] Abolition was presented as adding lustre to monarchy but it was an untruth to describe it as bringing immortality to the king's memory in John Rippon's funeral sermon for George III, as the king had been unsympathetic.[99]

British abolitionist efforts were described in various terms: as Christian benevolence, the recognition of common humanity or the demands of justice (a fresco design on justice for the new palace of Westminster in 1845 by William Salter includes West Indian emancipation – one art critic thought the depiction of so many 'negroes' was in bad taste[100]). These springs of action or motivation are complicated and problematic. Because mercy is associated with inequality rather than rights, as something unmerited or undeserved, the idea of abolitionism as an act of mercy may be alien to us – redolent of the clemency to the conquered. Slaves do not get to display mercy.[101]

John Wesley characterized slavery 'as irreconcilable to justice as to mercy'.[102] 'I could venture to the foot of the throne,' wrote George Whitfield, Wesley's travelling companion, in his letters on slavery republished in 1827, 'to supplicate, not so much for mercy as justice, in advocacy of this most injured and most insulted part of the human family'. The crown was most 'fearfully tarnished, whose sovereign lends not his aid to effect the emancipation of the imprisoned African!'[103] Others linked abolition to Micah's injunction to do justice, love mercy and walk humbly with God. A study of British culture in this period must acknowledge the centrality of the slave trade and the institution of slavery, its abolition the performance of a national act related by its advocates to divine mercy for a guilty nation. The desire to act mercifully may have been genuine but mercy was also part of abolitionism's discursive arsenal. Was there mercy in any part of the slave system, the Reverend Benjamin Godwin of Bradford asked? [Apologists made mercy claims: for Enoch Lewis, the institution *encouraged* acts of mercy by masters – a point obviously disputed strongly.][104]

In the formal discourse of parliamentary petitions, abolitionists spoke of an act of equity, benevolence, mercy and justice. Specific tactics such as boycotting slave-produced sugar were linked to mercy's agency: 'Blest be that holy tear in Mercy's eye,' versified *Gentleman's Magazine* in December 1791, 'That bids from taste the *sweet indulgence* fly, | The price of Justice, and a brother's weal, | Which all confess, and all but INTEREST feel!'[105]

Verse in praise of abolitionists associated them with mercy and imagined, in James Montgomery's lines, the slave pleading 'mercy, mercy' (Montgomery's poems appeared in *Poems on the Abolition of Slavery* in 1809 with Smirke's engraving of Justice hovering above Britannia, implored by slaves).[106] When abolition of slavery was achieved in the empire in 1835, one commemorative poetry collection invoked divine mercy, represented mercy pleading, presiding over the law, her long-restrained voice bidding 'Afric's sable sons rejoice'.[107] Mercy was imagined as a heavenly power with agency to abolish the trade, in the evangelical Hannah More's 'The Slave Trade' of 1788 where, having begun with the sober goddess Liberty she concludes by calling on the 'cherub Mercy' who softly descends from the sphere of love to spread 'soft contagion' of heavenly peace, end oppression, captivity and war, her 'healing smiles' restoring natural joy in the tropics and establishing liberty's banner. The 'dusky myriads crowd the sultry plain, | And hail that Mercy long invok'd in vain.'[108] Helen Maria William's *Poem on the Bill Lately Passed for Regulating the Slave Trade* (1788) had similar reference following a title page with Shakespeare's 'quality of mercy' lines: 'To Mercy consecrate the hour! | Risque something in her cause at last, | And thus atone for all the past.'[109] This exemplary act was linked to imperial power: 'O, spread thy blessings; be the glory thine, | The first in mercy, as in pow'r, to shine.'[110]

At the pinnacle of the empire, one might suppose that the monarch had an important role in abolitionist strategy and imagination.[111] Consider James Grainger's *The Sugar Cane*, published in 1764, on the tender muse who might 'knock off the chains | Of heart-debasing slavery' if possessing the power that 'monarchs have, and monarchs oft abuse'.[112] The duty and role of kings in relation to abolition was emphasized by Ottobah Cugoano in 1787.[113] The Commons' address to the prince regent in 1814, on the African slave trade, hoped 'nations may be taught a higher respect for justice and humanity by the example of their Sovereigns'. There is evidence that African rulers believed in the monarch's agency.[114]

In the era before organized abolitionist efforts the Crown was a key supporter of the slave trade. King George III commanded Virginians to pass no law to prohibit or obstruct imports of slaves in 1770; American opponents like Thomas Jefferson blamed him for the trade.[115] The Crown was linked through legal process: through the use of the royal prerogative of mercy by slaves before the courts of the British Caribbean.[116] The monarch had troubling associations with slavery after king and Court opposition were defeated in 1807. The *Anti-Slavery Reporter* was horrified by the Crown's direct ownership of slaves in March 1830. Forfeited to the king at Grenada and working under the whip 'for his benefit' on a sugar plantation, it was disgraceful.[117] The trade was still seen as falling under the protection of king and council.[118]

Metaphorically, liberation was presented as the 'brightest gem in the British diadem', an event to be emblazoned with a crown of glory according to Reverend Hugh Stowell at the anniversary of the British and Foreign Bible Society in Exeter Hall in 1835. Such figures of speech reflected the force of the image of the royal crown of mercy. Beyond metaphor was the appreciation of the monarch's political and cultural power to enhance or impede the cause.

Petitioning the Crown and appealing in propaganda to patriotic and loyalist notions of what a monarch should be were important strategies. In 1793 the American abolitionist Anthony Benezet sent a letter to queen Charlotte (with tracts) 'which was graciously received' that referred to Britain's 'national authority … exerted in support of the African slave trade'.[119] The Society of Friends sent tracts to the king, queen and prince of Wales. In 1788, when the newspapers discussed abolition, a letter in the *Public Advertiser* replying to a supporter of slavery, hoped that 'the mildness of heart which actuates our present Sovereign may be led to add his weight in favour of his country's honour, and the future peace of Africa!'[120] The king received private letters advocating abolition in 1798.[121] In 1803, with disgust at the hunting of Maroons (escaped Caribbean slaves) by dogs, reported in the *Gentleman's Magazine*, another effort was made to associate the cause with the 'amiable character of its Sovereign, who has constantly tempered justice with mercy'.[122] Attempts to persuade the king to aid the campaign failed.

Appeals for support on the basis of the damage to the royal prerogative were made by early abolitionists such as Granville Sharp in 1769.[123] William Pitt the younger's failure, for one reviewer of Thomas Clarkson's history of the movement in 1808, was linked to royal power: 'Had its tendency been not to redress the wrongs of Africa but to increase the prerogatives of the crown he would instantly have forced it through both houses even though it had been opposite to the wishes of nine tenths of the kingdom.'[124] A later pamphlet, by James Stephen in 1826, ingeniously appealed to Tory loyalty to throne and church by noting that colonial tyranny established 'intermediate' kings between subject and throne. The monarch was rendered an 'empty name' and rule was by sword and not 'sceptre'. Thus 'the authority of the Sovereign is so degraded as to be actually made subordinate and ministerial to that of the master'. Private slavery subverted the British monarchy, since the slave could be no object of mercy, its 'most glorious and darling prerogative ... No royal grace can absolve him from those harsh penalties which the master thinks fit to adjudge'.[125]

Abolitionists addressed the wider royal family. The abolitionist and Whig MP for Tewkesbury, James Martin, in a Commons' debate on the motion for the abolition of the slave trade, argued in 1792 that the 'first persons of Royal dignity in this country' had 'merciful and benevolent dispositions' and that their offspring were inspired 'with the same sentiments'. This being so, 'We might justly entertain the warmest hopes of the countenance and support of every part of the Royal Family.'[126] But association between these efforts and the royal family was weak. The Anti-Slavery Society's patronage by William Frederick, Duke of Gloucester, was exceptional (see Figure 6.1). Oldfield notes that 'abolition was not publicly commemorated in Britain'.[127] When the celebratory abolitionist image by Henry Moses was published showing Britannia with justice and

Figure 6.1 White metal medal of William Frederick, Duke of Gloucester as Chancellor of Cambridge University, 1811. Author's collection.

religion, reference to royal patronage in its iconography comprised a flag bearing a crown – surmounted by a cap of liberty – and Gloucester's coat of arms, to whom it was dedicated on 4 June 1808 by Joseph Collyer, engraver to queen Charlotte.[128] Oulton's life of the queen claimed she and the princesses expressed 'great satisfaction' at abolition.[129] Yet 'Anti-Saccharite' satires on Charlotte linked the campaign against slave-produced sugar with royal miserliness in the 1790s (in cartoons by Gillray and Cruikshank).

It was odd to congratulate Gloucester's uncle for abolition, as the General Assembly of the Church of Scotland did in 1807, as in line with the king's uniform zeal for religion, justice and humanity. But having developed an iconography of merciful Georgian monarchy in the face of rebellion abroad and at home, and in victorious combat with atheistic French republicanism, it was to be expected that a link was asserted between a national act of virtue and a virtuous monarch, 'render[ing] the circle of glory playing around the head of our beloved monarch complete ... he touched the fetters of Africa with the golden sceptre of mercy, and they fell to the ground.' So eulogized William Benzo Collyer, Congregationalist minister of Peckham, in a royal jubilee sermon. The reviewer in Flower's *Political Review* in 1810 was scornful as 'all Europe' knew only Gloucester supported abolition.[130] Robert Southey thought Clarkson's *Abolition of the Slave Trade* forbore to notice the 'notorious predilection of the royal family for the African slave trade'. Clarkson had expected the royal family from 'their known benevolence' to support abolition.[131]

Privately, William Wilberforce's diary for 1807 noted 'the Princes canvassing against us alas', with 'Clarence worse in point of execution than usual'.[132] In public, the press made the contrast with Gloucester.[133] The *Edinburgh Review* in 1812 noted the 'melancholy but unquestionable fact' that the king, his heir and the whole of the royal family 'with the honourable exception' of Gloucester, 'uniformly and zealously opposed the abolition of the Slave-Trade'.[134] For the *Review* (actually the words were Henry Brougham's), this represented courtiers' harmful influence. The *Colonial Review* thought such comments on the royal family 'treacherous' in 1818, acting as 'powerful instruments, to render unpopular the prince, the royal family, the ministers, and to lessen public respect for our courts of justice'.[135] The contrast was repeated in publications like the *Monthly Repository* in 1813, *Encyclopaedia Americana* in 1835 and *Popular Encyclopedia* of 1841.

It is difficult to present George IV as having any interest in the question. His humanity and mercy tend to be stressed in relation to qualms about capital punishment in Britain. But as prince regent he was pressurized about the abolition of the trade undertaken by foreign powers and publicly committed in an answer to a parliamentary address to 'use his best endeavours to accomplish that object'.[136] He was praised for exertions 'in obtaining the consent of the Government of Sweden and still more that of Holland to an immediate and unqualified Abolition of the Slave Trade', but disappointed in the effort to 'obtain a Convention of the Powers of Europe for the immediate and universal Abolition of the African Slave Trade' in 1814.[137] He seemed unmoved by parliamentary addresses as prince regent in 1819, on the 'more effectual' abolition of slavery.

The failure to send the royal mercy in time for the missionary John Smith – sentenced to execution in Demerera for contributing to a revolt, but dying in prison of illness in

February 1824 – was reported but not apparently used against the king personally.[138] At the time of George IV's demise, his successor was addressed on anti-slavery by citizens of Leeds, it being regretted 'that the efforts of his late most Gracious Majesty ... and of Parliament, have been productive of so little benefit to that unfortunate class of your majesty's subjects, the negro Slave'.[139] The situation now appeared altered. A review of Benjamin Godwin of Bradford's anti-slavery lectures in the *Imperial Magazine* thought the time ripe in November 1830, partly due to the accession: an 'energetic, and merciful prince is placed at the head of the British Empire [the agitation] will offer ample scope for the exercise of mercy and justice, those heaven-born attributes, whose living temple should ever be the monarch's breast'.[140]

Perhaps the king's popular association with parliamentary reform played a part in perceptions of willingness to continue reform in relation to slavery. Anti-slavery support for parliamentary candidates in the Reform era associated the question of slavery with the Crown – thus support for Henry Brougham's candidature in the general election of 1833, in the representation of Yorkshire, spoke of the king's sceptre and the 'brightest glory' of reigning over freemen.[141]

George Wright's posthumous biography of William IV linked the measure with his character as 'peculiarly suitable to the reign of a monarch distinguished in early life for an overflow of kindly and affectionate feeling to his companions, fellow-sailors, and fellow-creatures, and whose advanced years were graced by innumerable acts of the most unostentatious benevolence'.[142] This passed over the fact that as duke of Clarence in 11 April 1793 the future king had – 'warmed by the subject', as the *Parliamentary Register* phrased it – described abolitionists as 'fanatics and hypocrites, among whom he included Mr Wilberforce by name'.[143] In Huish's royal biography, William IV's opposition to abolition was said to have 'alienated from him many individuals of high character and distinction, and with whom he had hitherto lived on terms of the greatest intimacy'.[144] His maiden speech on 3 May 1792 defended the trade (and, ominously for the future Reform crisis) the natural and constituent balance of a powerful House of Lords against the Commons' dictates.[145] His speech of 5 July 1799 was published at the request of the West India Merchants and Planters and the 'mercantile interest of Liverpool'. For the *Monthly Review*, disputing the prince's arguments on the basis of humanity, it did 'considerable credit to the industry and research of the royal orator'.[146] Robert Bisset, apologist for slavery, in a history of George III's reign published in 1811, described the prince's 'masterly view' as 'clear and manly' and 'the most satisfactory and complete treatise which has hitherto appeared on that side of the question'.[147] The duke's presentation of petitions from the merchants and mortgagees of Liverpool *against* abolition, was reported in 1804. In the parliamentary debate on 30 May 1804 he spoke of experience of life in the West Indies (he was rumoured, and satirized by Gillray, as having a black mistress, 1787–8[148]) 'that the treatment of the slaves did not deserve the imputations which were cast upon it'.[149] He defended the trade in 1807: report of an often-inaudible debate described Gloucester's speech as one 'worthy of a descendant of the House of Brunswick' when he 'combated the arguments of his Royal relation'.[150] An anonymous pamphlet in 1808 observed that while the 'West-India Planters and Liverpool Merchants praised his oratory, hallowed love of liberty, and steady patriotism. – The Blacks were not deficient in sagacity; they declared that such an advocate against their cause was an auspicious omen, and promised an happy success'.[151]

The king was appealed to in petitions for emancipation, the Sheffield Auxiliary Anti-Slavery Society condemning any denial of the 'clemency and mercy of your majesty's crown' in 1833.[152] When emancipation was partially effected the king was associated through image and texts.[153] The *Christian Penny Magazine* noted '1 August 1834' was doubly auspicious as the day set for 'what has transpired under the British crown of so godlike a character as that which is celebrated on this day' and the anniversary of Hanoverian accession. Esther Copley's *History of Slavery*, in 1836, noted he left 'to his successor the monarchy of a free people; for among all the millions of his subjects there shall not be found a slave'.[154] A further stage in emancipation (of 'apprentices') came with Victoria's accession in 1837: her predicament as a queen of slaves is explored in *The Royal Throne of Mercy*.

We might take the discussion elsewhere: to representing the unmerciful imperial 'other' in British political commentary, like that relating to Russians and Ottomans in the long nineteenth century. The trope of the 'merciless Turk' (qualified by a counter-discourse of kindness to animals, noted earlier) was current in English discourse for centuries.[155] It was expressed in a variety of sources, from plays to passing allusion.[156] James Cobb's comic opera *The Siege of Belgrade*, in 1828, ended with (according to one critic) a 'puff direct on Christian mercy and forbearance and all that sort of thing; as if the banner of the cross were not a whit less blood-stained than that of the

Figure 6.2 Benjamin Constant, *'Mercy!'* 'A Bulgarian village retaken – the Inhabitants brought before the Turkish commander', *The Graphic*, war number, 29 September 1877, 10–11. Author's collection.

crescent'.[157] Lord John Russell's *The Establishment of the Turks in Europe* of the same year, expounded on a government by terror, using capital punishment 'without delay, without mercy, without limit'.[158] Comparison between merciful Christianity and cruel Islam was long-standing – with such contrasts made between Richard Coeur de Lion and Saladin.[159] Poetry and play compared the violence of the Muslim warrior with the Quranic message of pity and mercy; contrasted the Western idea of the cruel Muslim ruler with Western hypocrisy.[160] The trope gained force with the Bulgarian atrocities, response to Armenian genocide and was rehearsed in the early-twentieth-century chaos of Ottoman collapse and Turkish nationalism (see Figure 6.2).[161]

The next chapter studies another location for mercy discourse as a way of 'othering' an external threat. In war, against rebellious eighteenth-century colonials in America or early-twentieth-century Germans, mercy was a casualty of conflict and the means of conducting that struggle through propaganda. The performance of mercy, leniency and clemency was a necessary counterpart of the force and violence inherent in imperialism and warfare.

7

The mercy of war

This chapter explores mercy's relationship to Britain's military activities from the mid-eighteenth century to the Great War's end. Here it was most starkly wielded in a relationship of power by the state's forces on the battlefield (and at sea). Mercy in war was the avoidance of unnecessary killing but severity (as in the crushing of rebellions) was defended as the avoidance, in the long term, of further bloodshed.[1] Considering an environment where men were at the mercy of others, also raises the idea of release from misery for the grievously injured. The subject of mercy killings on the battlefield has been studied before from ethical and legal perspectives.[2] Eighteenth-century regulations for conduct in war did not require mercy to an enemy but proportionality became an ideal: the Continental Army boasted merciful treatment of enemy combatants where Britons seemed to deny mercy to Patriot soldiers giving quarter.[3] The renewed influence of chivalric ideals, blending martial and Christian values, secured mercy a place in the age of Walter Scott. The Victorian Catholic apologist Kenelm Digby claimed for the Middle Ages the exercise of mercy in battle.[4] Out of such individual acts evolved conventions of justice and humane behaviour, *jus in bello*, and ultimately international conventions culminating in the convention of 1949.[5]

The sources for this chapter are varied, including newspapers, martial biography, military dictionaries, contemporary histories of conflict and poetry. The section on the Great War draws on visual sources and Allied pamphlets. Efforts to inculcate habits of mercy were important in the peace movement, and so the literature of peace activists provides another angle on mercy in warfare.[6]

Military mercy in the eighteenth and early nineteenth centuries[7]

Cultural scholars and art historians have shown how the figures of soldiers and sailors emblematized national humanity in the course of the eighteenth century: balancing manliness with compassion, magnanimity and sensibility.[8] 'Heroes became merciful men,' an essayist wrote in 1795.[9] The reality was different especially in colonial wars and sometimes against rebellious subjects at home but the public reputation was one of the merciful Briton at arms.[10]

The exercise of mercy and clemency might be linked to the Crown in military matters. 'For in imitation of their magnanimous King,' one sermonist after George II's death in 1760 said of the nation in arms, 'their Clemency to the Vanquished has been no less remarkable than their Bravery and Intrepidity in the Field'.[11] Representation of martial clemency included Francis Hayman's *The Humanity of General Amherst*, at Montreal's surrender in 1760 (the inscription: 'Power exerted, Conquest obtained, Mercy shewn') and Lord Clive shown *Receiving the Homage of the Nabob* after the battle of Plassey in 1757, both images in the great hall of Vauxhall Pleasure Gardens in 1760 and reproduced as engravings.[12]

George III's reign was characterized by global warfare, with rebellion in North America, revolution in Europe and threats of revolution in Britain: mercy might be a dangerous virtue in statecraft.[13] With rebellion's outbreak, separate discourses of British and American behaviour developed: a rhetoric of British cruelty unsurprisingly promoted by rebels.[14] Nicole Eustace has shown how tensions in late 1760s saw American 'spirit' contrasted with British assumption of colonial submission to mercy.[15] The revolutionary war became a conflict over merciful 'character' in warfare.[16] From the outset mercy was much invoked. British artists and poets offered the king as a figure of mercy, with the laurel or olive branch and 'merciful forbearance' of loyal addresses. From the Kentish Weald, one loyalist wrote in 1771, 'you are happily situated under the best established government in the world, with a King, who is a friend to mankind, whose heart is disposed to every virtue, and the diadem of his Crown is MERCY and HUMANITY'.[17]

Open rebellion initially stimulated conventional words about penitent subjects. In the Commons on 30 March 1775, the Whig MP Temple Luttrell hoped the colonies would not be treated as rebels but 'whatever may be the hazard of battle, will be entitled to the same military honours, to the same acts of clemency and of grace that are usually practised, according to the system of war, by every civilized nation in the world'.[18] The British press accessed colonial claims of patriot mercy early on in the conflict, reprinting the boast of *Essex Gazette* (Salem) of 25 April 1775, after Lieutenant-General Thomas Gage's confrontation with the American militia, that 'not one instance of cruelty … was committed by our victorious militia; but, listening to the merciful dictates of the Christian religion, they "breathed higher sentiments of humanity"'.[19]

There were hopes that, as the poet Whitehead phrased it 'mercy [might] gild the ray … still avert impending Fate', in a royal birthday ode in 1775, the 'assurance of the royal mercy was given, as soon as the deluded multitude should become sensible of their error'.[20] Gage issued his proclamation of harangue and mercy in June 1775 – and by opponents of the war in the British press.[21] Gage claimed in a letter to the new commander in chief of the Continental Army, George Washington, on 13 August, reprinted in Britain, to 'the glory of civilized nations, humanity and war have been compatible; and compassion to the subdued is become almost a general system. Britons, ever preëminent in mercy, have outgone common examples, and overlooked the criminal in the captive'.[22] Calculated displays of British mercy – combated in American counter-propaganda – included General Guy Carleton's release of prisoners in August 1776.[23]

The king stated in a reply to a petition from the Corporation of London on 23 March 1776, against the miseries brought upon by his American subjects, he was 'ready and happy to alleviate those miseries by acts of mercy and clemency, whenever that authority should be established, and the now existing rebellion at an end'.[24] An 'old officer', detecting absolutist pretensions in calls for complete submission before clemency, wrote to the *Public Advertiser* in 1776 to criticize an 'Asiatic' language of clemency and mercy towards the Americans.[25] William Gordon's history of the rebellion (1788) suggested it was as much clemency 'as could be expected, considering what coercion was going forward'.[26]

The muse of poetry was harnessed to implore mercy. In 1776 the poet Thomas Penrose (soldier turned curate), deploring the government's attitude, called on mercy to intervene by whispering forgiveness in the royal ear, 'nor thou, great | George | Disdain the muse's prayer; most loyal she ... Urg'd by the plaintive call | Of meek humanity, O! pardon, now'.[27] Verse at a 'Caractacan Meeting' at Longnor in Shropshire in the month Congress declared independence, declaimed 'Victory O yet may Britons, in whose gen'rous breasts | Firm Valour is with gentlest Mercy join'd, | (Noblest distinction of the brave and good!) | Learn to forgive e'en blind deluded zeal'.[28] John Fletcher, vicar of Madeley in Shropshire, imagined the king's parental mercy to contrite rebels, in a pamphlet. George III was implored to exercise regal mercy, 'O let that jewel shine in this cloudy day and it will reflect the light of the Sun of righteousness across the Atlantic and cheer the western world.' Royal mercy would melt into tears, rash patriots and fiery heroes.[29]

The generosity of royal mercy as hailed by these voices was starkly different to the official discourse. Benjamin Franklin, representing the Second Constitutional Congress in Paris, in January 1777 learned that 'the King's ambassador receives no application from rebels unless they come to implore his Majesty's mercy'. 'Thus wantonly and wickedly', observed the historian William Belsham, 'were the horrors of war deepened and thus the eternal principles of justice and mercy sacrificed to the barbarous and wretched etiquette of a court.'[30] *Freeman's Journal* on 28 January referred to Britons' vain boast to 'being ever preeminent in mercy'.[31] Lord Chatham, opposing the hostilities, in the Lords on 13 May regretted the door of mercy being shut: 'Mercy cannot do harm; it will seat the King where he ought to be, throned on the hearts of his people; and Millions at Home and abroad, now employed in Obloquy or Revolt, would pray for him.'[32] General John Burgoyne's proclamations presented the king as a source of mercy when properly sought, in June 1777, but the grandiloquent language of magnanimity was satirized: 'A.B.C.D.' in the *New York Journal* on 8 September, referring to the 'sublime, and irresistible proclamation' opening the 'doors of mercy'.[33] In the Commons, on 4 December 1778, Coke deplored the commissioners' proclamation issued in New York by the earl of Carlisle, Sir Henry Clinton and William Eden: Englishmen were 'so far degenerated as to forfeit the noble pre-eminences they maintained over every nation on the face of the globe, those of justice, lenity, clemency, and mercy'.[34]

Washington denied the attributes of justice and mercy to Britons and their German allies in 1777, 'their mercy ... conspicuous only in their inhuman treatment of their prisoners ... inhuman treatment of their prisoners ... cold-blood slaughter, consummated by the tender mercies of the Indian tomahawk'.[35] Yet the troops of Hesse-cassel were described as enjoying 'the plenitude of American pity, tenderness, and mercy' as prisoners that year.[36] The Congress told Americans that British victories had been 'followed by the cool murder of men no longer able to resist', the *Scots Magazine* reported in 1778.[37] This included 'savage barbarity' towards civilians and massacres such as that of Colonel George Baylor's regiment in September 1778. The

British enemy 'most infamously outraged all the laws of humanity ... destroying the character of their nation', to quote James Thacher, surgeon in the revolutionary army.[38] The British soldier-turned-American patriot John Robert Shaw offered grisly insight (in 1807) on 'cruel carnage' by General Grey's troops in Tappan near New Jersey – butchery that 'melted into compassion the heart of a Turk or a Tartar'.[39]

Despite these British atrocities, clemency from the rebels at Stoney-Point in 1779 heeded the British garrison's cry for 'Mercy! Mercy! Dear Americans! Mercy! Quarter! Brave Americans!'[40] Royalist and patriot press reported mercy and humanity's triumph there.[41] An icon of British military cruelty, Colonel Banastre Tarleton's public humiliation by exclusion from the banquet hosted by Washington after Cornwallis's surrender at Yorktown in October 1781 also exemplifies mercy's public significance, Colonel Laurens telling the Englishman (in one nineteenth-century account), 'there are modes, sir, of discharging a soldier's duty, and where mercy has a share in the mode, it renders the duty the more acceptable to both friends and foes.'[42]

Press report, parody, anecdote, song and painting offered American patriot commentary on British mercilessness or battlefield clemency. One privately circulated patriot newspaper, the *Pasquin or Minute Intelligencer* (near Egg Harbor, New Jersey) in 1778, had a mock advertisement for the British commander-in-chief General Howe's miscellaneous works' in which one of the articles was 'A dissertation on the cardinal virtues, in which it is proved that justice and mercy ought to be excluded from holding any rank amongst them'.[43] The *Pennsylvania Packet* claimed an anecdote in 1780 that at the coronation the symbolic sword of justice was brought but the sword of mercy left in the Tower, and rather than delay the ceremony the lord mayor's sword was substituted.[44] Cornwallis was a cruel general ordering no prisoners at Camden in August 1780, 'however supplicating for mercy they may be found!!' according to an account 'from England' reprinted in New Jersey in 1781.[45] American patriot song referred to a struggle against 'merciless tyrants'.[46] The visual arts' response includes John Trumbull's famous *Death of General Warren at the Battle of Bunker's Hill, June 17, 1775* (1786) showing John Small staying a fellow Briton's bayonet (see Figure 7.1). Trumbull also depicted Washington's treatment of the wounded officer Johann Rahl, in *Capture of the Hessians at Trenton* (begun 1787) expressly to give a lesson 'to show mercy and kindness to a fallen enemy'.[47]

Thomas Paine recoiled from the prospect of receiving mercy from such a figure as George III – characterizing Howe's offer as 'a trick of war'.[48] Intervening for Charles Asgill (a British captain handed over to the mercy of revolutionaries in reprisal for the execution of Joshua Huddy by loyalists in April 1782, and whose life was successfully pleaded for by his mother, appealing to Louis XVI and Marie Antoinette), Paine critiqued the British discourse of mercy. In a public letter to Sir Guy Carleton, he disputed talk by British generals from Gage onwards, in proclamation and communications with Washington and Congress, of British honour, generosity and clemency. They spoke 'in language they have no right to ... as if those things were matters of facts'.[49]

British mercy claims were disputed by civilians such as Eliza Wilkinson, responding to treatment in Charleston after surrender in May 1780. She claimed initial disbelief in the tales of British misbehaviour coming from the north, which went against 'humanity and every manly sentiment' which she had believed inherent in Englishmen. Then she

Figure 7.1 Detail from steel engraving by J.C. Armytage after John Trumbull, *Death of General Warren at the Battle of Bunker's Hill, June 17, 1775* (1786), from *The History of England. With a Continuation to the Year 1859 (Present Time). From the Invasion of Julius Caesar to the End of the Reign of James II*, by David Hume; Continued from the Reign of William and Mary to the Death of George II by Tobias Smollett; and from the Accession of George III to the Twenty-third Year of the Reign of Queen Victoria by E. Farr and E.H. Nolan (3 vols; London: Virtue, 1859), vol.3, p.79. Author's collection.

experienced 'the loving-kindness and tender mercies', she wrote ironically in 1782.[50] Wilkinson contrasted American patriot behaviour, echoing the 'attributes of heaven', against the enemy 'deaf to all the cries of mercy' on the battlefield.[51]

News of British massacres stimulated critics to write and publish in the British press: the *Public Ledger* printed one lengthy anti-ministerial letter from 'J.S.' in September 1777 contrasting the 'immaculate Being' sworn to uphold mercy and righteousness, with the countenancing of the 'horrid act of employing the TOMAHAWK and SCALPING KNIFE against innocent women and children.'[52] In the *Dublin Evening Post*, in September 1778, a critical poet offered the euphemism for scalping, of 'Scots mercy'.[53] John Wilkes spoke against Burgoyne's proclamation announcing this use of Native American forces.[54] Burgoyne later claimed in the Commons he intended the threat to 'speak daggers but to use none'.[55] The policy of using native forces was controversial because of their alleged cruelty, David Ramsay's history of the wars recording concern in Britain about the strategy and explaining it thus, 'every appearance of lenity, by inciting to disobedience, and thereby increasing the objects of punishment, was eventual cruelty', whilst noting the 'extremity of military vengeance' meted out to American royalists.⁵⁶ (The legacy of British use of native troops was the excuse it offered for severity by white Americans against nations symbolized by tomahawk and scalping-knife.⁵⁷) Mercy and clemency, on the other hand, signified timidity by the British according to the proclamation of pardon by the revolutionary governor and commander-in-chief of South Carolina, John Rutledge.⁵⁸ The problematic of pardon and forgiveness was confronted by Americans too: Governor William Livingston querying 'lenity' before New Jersey's general assembly, 29 May 1778.⁵⁹

Mercy figured in memorials, including the monument erected in 1821 in Westminster Abbey to the British officer and spy, Major John André, executed in 1780.⁶⁰ His fate was a theme for painters, historians, memoirists and playwrights (see Figure 7.2). The Anglo-American William Dunlap's *André* of 1798 favoured clemency: 'By such an act | The stern and blood-stain'd brow of War | Would be disarm'd of half its gorgon horrors; | More humanized customs be induced; | And all the race of civilized man | Be blest in the example.'⁶¹

The Irish republican and American John Burk's *Bunker-Hill; or the Death of General Warren* had Warren scorning Gage's offer of pardon, despising the Briton's pity and suggesting mercy be shown to Boston.⁶² For the appropriately named Mercy Otis Warren, also a revolutionary dramatist, whose history of the conflict appeared in 1805, the tendency to 'trumpet forth the godlike attributes of justice, equity, mercy

Figure 7.2 *The Death Warrant of Major John Andre.* Steel engraving by G.R. Hall after the painting by Alonzo Chappel *c.* 1855 (New York: Martin & Johnson). Author's collection.

and above all, that universal benevolence and tenderness to mankind', was too familiar in the etiquette of modern courts waging undemocratic warfare.[63] For the American patriot, William Bailey, in 1822: the monarchical governments of Europe knew 'nothing of forgiveness ... Mercy is continually in the mouths of all of them, as are justice, magnanimity, and many other of the amiabilities; but they are only there, and woe betide the man that puts an iota of confidence in them'.[64]

Memories of unmercy endured. The war of 1812 sustained the discourse: with references to 'suppliants and victims to the altar of British mercy'.[65] Gilbert Hunt's *The Late War* has a line about the 'insignia of British mercy! – a human scalp!'[66] After this conflict one survivor of British 'cold, calculating cruelty' judged Americans to possess 'as much generosity towards an enemy they have vanquished, and who is at their mercy, as any people to be found in the records of the human kind'.[67] The Founding Fathers' writings show their preoccupation with British unmercy.[68] But the 'British have too many documents to prove that American mercy was as far from universal as British mercy was', Rupert Hughes's pioneering demythologizing biography of Washington suggested.[69]

Mercy and the Victorian military

Early Victorians were able to imagine a warfare progressively more merciful: *Chambers's Information for the People* complacently concluded 'the object is less to kill than to disperse and terrify into subjection; and therefore, among civilised nations, mercy is always shown when asked'.[70] True, there was concern about whether one could be a 'man butcher' and Christian yet this was the era in which the hymn 'Onward Christian Soldiers' was penned by Sabine Baring-Gould (1865).[71] From sermon to fundraising poetry the message of force tempered by mercy endured.[72] Mid-nineteenth-century evangelicals emphasized God's mercy through *The British Flag and Christian Sentinel*, organ of the United British Army Scripture Readers' and Soldiers' Friend Society. For the art-viewer, as the discussion of representations in Part I suggested, there were various depictions of battlefield mercy. To this might be added the illustrated press's visions: 'On the Battlefield of the Alma: The Mission of Mercy' showing emergency medical aid in the Crimea in 1854 and scantily clad native women giving water to thirsty English soldiers in 'The Afghan War – A sister of mercy' (1879). Charles Hunt's children playing the roles of officers and soldiers, presents the *Plea for Mercy* (1872) with traditional roles of supplicant, for the girl, kneeling before the officer with letter of petition, the executioner ominously ready.[73]

British brutality in punitive campaigns could be condemned: a provincial paper was shocked in 1843 at the statement that in one Afghan city, 'Not a man was spared, whether with or without arms; not a prisoner taken; hunted down like vermin mercy never dreamt of. Verily, we have been avenged.'[74] Against this slander there was poetry based on General Nott's account concerning the forbearance of soldiers at the town or village of Rosa near Ghazni: 'Yet discipline and mercy joined | To keep the Christians back; | ... They bade fierce fiery passion yield | To mercy's gentle rein, | And so our British soldiers raised | Their glory above gain!'[75]

The figurative crown of mercy was employed in praising the 'extreme moderation of Lord Hardinge in victory' by a speaker at East India House in 1846 and extolling troops in supposedly treasure-laden Govinghur and Umritsur, 'all at their mercy, but all untouched … through the noble conduct of the Governor-General and the army, that diadem now sparkles with gems far brighter, and more valuable – justice, clemency, and generosity to the vanquished'.[76] A decade later mercy was a much-debated response to Indian mutiny but one cyclopaedia of battles claimed of Delhi, 'the British soldier is merciful in victory, as he is irresistible in battle. To armed rebels, no mercy was shown; but women and children, and the defenceless citizens, were spared and protected'.[77] Sir Norton Knatchbull's defence of the British soldier was recorded in 1858, 'not unmindful' of the precepts of the Bible, 'he would carry out that merciful justice which was due to the outraged honour of an insulted country'.[78] In another theatre of war in the same decade, the 'kind-heartedness of the English soldier', was claimed to be acknowledged by all, 'even Russians', and acts of mercy were the subject of soldierly discourse.[79]

A key mid-Victorian development was the Geneva convention, bringing neutrality for sick or wounded in war and field or military hospitals. European rulers signed it in 1865, and the red cross became a familiar symbol in war. The 'self set task of mercy' and the 'appeal of the moved heart' during the Franco-Prussian War needed to be balanced in one commentator's view, against Britain's position of neutrality in this and future conflicts. Some discussion of this development such as reference to 'elementary principles of humanity' might not employ the word mercy but 'humanitarian' had still to divest itself of pejorative connotations.[80]

The establishment of concentration camps in South Africa during a war in which the British flag was the herald of mercy as well as might (the *Newcastle Chronicle* maintained) damaged British reputation at the end of Victoria's reign.[81] Defenders of the policy cast the camps as 'a stupendous work of mercy which is being carried out with all possible humanity'.[82] An English newspaper defended 'CAMPS OF MERCY … the Imperial Government, with a chivalrous generosity which no conquering Power has ever displayed towards its foe, has sheltered, fed, doctored, and nursed over a hundred thousand of the enemy'.[83] For the *Belfast News-letter*, criticizing Campbell-Bannerman's attack on the policy, it was 'act of mercy without parallel in the history of warfare, either Christian or barbarian'.[84] For another prominent critic of the war, W.T. Stead, the British people ignored the 'instinct of chivalry'.[85] 'As a matter of fact', an essay he published on the end of the war asserted, 'it has been waged with a merciless barbarity that has only been tempered by the good-heartedness of individual soldiers', rather than, as the English pretended, 'unexampled humanity'.[86] Another critic, the MP Thomas Shaw, argued, 'our prestige as a military and merciful nation was in peril in the face of the civilised world'.[87]

Then there was the punishment of defeated rebels. The relish with which *Black and White Budget* reported Kitchener's public hangings in that 'nest of treason', Graaf Reinet, and the unavailing cries for mercy is disturbing: it was asserted that the Cape rebels deserved not the least mercy.[88] (Kitchener was described by one lady-in-waiting to the queen in 1896 as not of the type to temper justice with mercy.)[89] Opponents of pro-Boer sympathies feared a sapping of the nation's morale: clemency a 'vice' in this context indulged by 'social philanthropists and weak and sentimental men and women'.[90] It represented 'pseudo-clemency' towards traitors.[91] The Royal Commission studying martial-law sentences in South Africa was condemned on those grounds, or praised as an example of Britain's exceptional mercy towards rebels.[92] The fate of one prominent Boer, Commandant Kritzinger, focused discussion about national acts of mercy.[93]

The reporting of this conflict showed awareness of changing attitudes to soldiers' conduct. The right of quarter was 'now recognised as one of peculiar sanctity'.[94] Episodes of British mercy to Boer were reported but also instances of mercilessness.[95] Thus *Melbourne Argus*'s correspondent described Tommy Atkins as a 'very demon of death' with bayonet at night in the siege of Ladysmith, as 'there is necessarily great uncertainty as to what may follow, so there is no time for making prisoners' – the few appeals for mercy were ignored.[96] Macdonald blithely reported the 'quality of mercy is not being strained by the Gordons', and was graphic about a lust for vengeance, sloughing off centuries of civilization in delirium during the hour of victory: 'Kill, Kill, Kill … For them is no salvation, save from the conqueror who is all mercy.'[97] The enemy might be acknowledged as merciful – as Kruger was in William Regan's *Boer and Uitlander* in 1896, or presented as merciless towards British 'Kaffirs' and Britons who surrendered.[98]

In the aftermath of the South African war: in a culture where militarism and invasion fear were significant features, how did military mercy fare? In 1909 one military man told civilians gathered to hear about the new Territorial force that 'the merciful soldier was not a good type', echoing an old adage about clemency during active warfare.[99] On the other hand, mercy figured in war memorials.[100] With efforts to enshrine international arbitration through new conventions and structures, the British decorative contribution to the Hague Palace of Peace was reported in 1911 to include mercy meeting with truth (or righteousness and peace kissing) in stained-glass form.[101] There was an appreciation of the adoption of the codes of civilized warfare by non-Westerners. The Japanese, signatories to the Geneva convention, reportedly fought 'upon purely civilised lines', treating with the 'utmost kindness and care … all the wounded'. The Japanese state promoted this message in their English-language press during war with China, framing it as a conflict against barbarous forces.[102]

At the end of the new century's first decade despite contrary evidence a chauvinist press believed the British soldier alone had 'ingrained the sense of mercy. Though Tommy Atkins fights like a lion, and throws away his life a hundred times, yet in action he is the most merciful soldier in the whole world.'[103] Such platitudes were elaborated within a few years when the exceptional cruelty of the enemy was the necessary contrast.

Mercy and justice during the Great War

Mercy was invoked in newspaper editorial and paragraphs, in sermons, poetry and plays during the Great War.[104] Postcards provided a new medium for expressing anxieties about safety in conflict in the traditional language of intercession for mercy

Figure 7.3 'Holy Father in Thy Mercy', postcards in a wartime series by Bamforth and Co. of Holmfirth. Author's collection. Reproduced with permission of Bamforth & Company.

(see Figure 7.3). A counter-discourse of stern justice, unsurprising when Britons were anxious about possible defeat and victory was hard-fought, also prevailed. In 1917, understandably, 'The Reign of Justice' figured among lithographs illustrating *Britain's Efforts and Ideals* by Edmund J. Sullivan.[105]

Study of the chivalric discourse of the war reveals some of the representations of mercy; Frantzen relates this period to medieval culture with its cycles of revenge and mercy.[106] Not that Allied propagandists acknowledged German chivalry: the American William Roscoe Thayer stated bluntly Germany repudiated 'the claims of chivalry and of mercy' while Anglo-Saxons embraced 'Justice, Mercy, Veracity, Honour and Reverence for one's plighted word'.[107] Elsewhere Germans were described as 'brutal transgressors of the laws of mercy and chivalry'.[108] On the side of civilization was a 'keener sensitiveness to Mercy' in Thayer's words; on the German was Nietzsche and the negation of 'the emotions of mercy, self-sacrifice and pity', a religion of valour in which mercy and pity were absent.[109] (The Vorticists commented that Nietzsche enjoyed an English sale 'such as he could hardly have anticipated in his most ecstatic and morose moments'.[110])

German battlefield cries ('Kamerad! Kamerad! Mercy!') figure in contemporary and subsequent accounts, often associated with the white flag of surrender.[111] Several paintings depicted this, including one by Fortunino Matania in 1915 derived from the testimony of Sergeant Megarry of 'A' Company, the Northamptonshire Regiment, reproduced in newspapers and postcard.[112] In this way German lack of fighting spirit or duplicity (with tales of abuses of the flag common from August 1914) was conveyed, whilst Britons were told, 'There is no English equivalent on the French front for "Mercy, mercy, kamerad!"'[113] British forbearance was the subject of visual comment.[114] Cinematic newsreels and stereoscopic photography animated and re-presented the trope (see Figure 7.4).[115]

The propagandist use of mercy and revenge was frequent. These included ironic reference to German mercy in a 'Hymn of Disgust' replying to Ernst Lissauer's notorious 'hymn of hate'.[116] British writers maintained their enemy lacked scruples, 'pity, mercy, humanity, and meaningless terms'.[117] Evidence presented to the British (and American) public stressed the unmerciful German conduct of war with those who 'betrayed symptoms of mercy' being punished.[118] *Shrecklichkeit* was contrasted with 'fair play' or humanity. Atrocities were linked to this mercilessness; talk of pity

Figure 7.4 '"Kamerad!" Bewildered Huns come out of their dugouts at Thjepval in answer to our bombs'. Realistic Travels Publishers. Author's collection.

for Germans was condemned.[119] 'Great Britain trusts in this war', said one reviewer of Cloudesley Brereton's *Who is Responsible?* 'to show that the virtues of freedom, honour and mercy have a real value in the struggle of nations'.[120] Whereas the Germans were taught from childhood to 'shoot down everything that cries for mercy'.[121]

Mercy metaphorically provided 'ammunition for civilians' with the Kaiser's words to German troops bound for China in June 1900, 'Let all who fall into your hands be at your mercy' being cited (this supplied the quotation for the Dutch Louis Raemaker's cartoon, 'Kultur has passed here').[122] The *Daily News*'s editor characterized the German state as without the bowels of compassion, divorced from 'mercy ... justice ... pity'.[123] 'Pity! The Hun knows not the word! In Kultur's dictionary it has no place,' said the *Sunday Mirror*.[124] The campaign to disseminate tales of atrocity relied on an understanding of the rules of war and civilization as guided by a spirit of mercy: hence publicizing outrages to women and children, the sinking of neutral vessels and attacks on hospital ships and sisters of mercy.[125]

Portia's words retained force. Keble Howard's *'The Quality of Mercy': How British Prisoners of War Were Taken to Germany in 1914* exemplifies this.[126] The novelist Marie Corelli's 'The Quality of Mercy', high-flown banality in response to a request from the American Committee of Mercy, presented the work of mercy as a means to display 'the spirit of the young New World'.[127] The scholar Walter Raleigh contrasted Shakespeare's speech with a doctrine of unmercy and declared mercy the 'creed of the Navy'.[128] In one compilation of Allied deeds, Edith Cavell's biography ends by quoting on mercy seasoning justice.[129] Shakespeare was mobilized through the fund-raising associated with the tercentenary of his death in 1917, for the British Red Cross, National Committee for Relief in Belgium, and the League of Mercy.[130] The *New Crusader* (a 'journal of enquiry for all seekers after a new way of life') on 18 October 1918 published the verse in full on the front page with the headline, 'Shakespeare's Peace Terms'.[131]

Cavell became an icon, symbolizing as the journalist James Douglas wrote, 'the spirit of pity, mercy and compassion'.[132] Mercy was one of the gendered attributes restored in this conflict, according to the novelist and soldier Coningsby Dawson, detecting a medievalism in which women were no longer treated like men as pre-war suffragettes had demanded, but made their contribution in 'mercy and motherhood'.[133] The National Union of Women's Suffrage Societies, wrote *The Scotsman*, 'sunk its own particular aspirations and devoted its energies to works of mercy in the nation's hour of need'.[134] Mercy work was the obvious lens by which to view women's expanded activities.[135] In Catholic Ireland one fund-raising priest acclaimed this 'one of the bright and illuminating features of the terrible time, for they had indeed proved themselves to be in truth and in fact ministering angels'.[136] German women, like their menfolk, were condemned for cruelty as 'jeering, spitting, vindictive "angels of mercy"'.[137] The propaganda of German Red Cross nurses pouring water away rather than give it to the British POWs is well known.[138]

Soldiers wrote of their recovery under 'angels of mercy'.[139] The international Red Cross was described as 'mercy-workers of the war' in a work of 1916 which, admitting 'no one race in this war belongs exclusively the work of mercy', noted the Ottoman Red Crescent's 'corps of mercy-workers'. 'Mercy', this syndicated interview with the chairman of the British Red Cross Society commented, 'so often beaten under in the actual conflicts of the belligerents, has survived gloriously among those whose function has been to relieve, where possible, the victims of shot and shell'.[140] The Red Cross was discursively militarized as 'soldiers of mercy' (alongside army chaplains and doctors).[141] Suffragettes reproduced this language of an 'army of mercy'.[142] The field of mercy was reported in the American Frances Huard's account of nursing in France in 1917 and a post-war *Pictorial Library of the World War* devoted a volume to 'The Armies of Mercy. The Vast Relief Work in All the Nations'.[143] A 'militia of mercy' was invoked in *Defenders of Democracy* of 1918.[144] Fund-raising for Belgian children in Christmas 1916 had 'envelopes of mercy' but no British posters directly appealed for mercy like Albert Herter's splendid American appeal for the Red Cross.[145] Red Cross activity appeared in photography (see Figure 7.5) and newsreels under the familiar label of mercy.[146]

Figure 7.5 'The Angel of Mercy'. One side of a stereoscopic card image. Author's collection.

Perhaps at no time before was there such a volume of musings on mercy withheld or performed in war, towards fellow humanity and animals.[147] Street placards bore the legend 'Peace with no Mercy'.[148] Illustrated lectures presented 'deeds of bravery and mercy in the great war'.[149] As a non-combatant, the philosopher Bertrand Russell would tell a pacifist gathering in 1915 of encountering a seemingly innocuous Scotsman, who boasted of bayoneting a disarmed German weeping for mercy.[150] Much appeared in the British press about such craven German soldiers under headlines like 'Cried for Mercy'.[151]

Testimony from the Western Front in newsprint and in books shows the struggle between humanity and revenge for combatants. 'Sometimes', Corporal Treadway of the 1st Middlesex Regiment wrote in a letter printed in the newspapers, 'I feel I could shoot them all, and at other times I pity them'.[152] A rifleman, from Birmingham, his letter reprinted with the usual emphasis of panic-stricken Germans crying for mercy, admitted, 'I am afraid some of them received no mercy'.[153] A private in the Royal Scots Fusiliers contrasted the pity he could not help feeling for wounded Germans with the assertion that the enemy 'don't think twice of putting another bullet' in British soldiers.[154] A private, a Highlander, in the early compilation *In the Firing Line*, reflected on the vengeance meted out to German cavalrymen for slaughtering Irish soldiers, they 'howled for mercy, but I don't think they got it. In war mercy is only for the merciful', a sentiment uttered in other reflections on battle experience.[155]

A more critical post-war account, Stephen Graham's *A Private in The Guards* (1919), tells of a sergeant who 'had once been a religious man but the war had caused him to swear and to kill without an idea of mercy'; Graham was blunt about the brutalities from the British side.[156] The American Benjamin Muse's later memoir reflected that men had not been told not to harm enemy combatants who 'threw themselves on our mercy', the assumption being 'instinctive English decency' dealt with it.[157] Women involved in nursing also considered the toll on sympathy and sensibility: one example is Florence Flamborough's exchange with a fellow nurse in 1915, where her comment that the numbing of feeling was perhaps *merciful* provoked the response, 'Merciful ... to be hardened, petrified, against all feeling!'[158]

Beyond the musings over mercy and reprisal in policy and propaganda was the moral problem.[159] Soldiers' diaries might reflect on the quandary of reconciling divine mercy with the conflict's horrors.[160] The morality of the war occasioned comments from ministers of religion on the legitimacy of indignation and the roles of pity and mercy.[161] The British press reproduced the Lutheran pastor Fritz Philippi's sermon on a 'Divine mission of Germany' in cleansing humanity, requiring the soldiers to 'strike without mercy ... Let it then be a war without pity'.[162] Newspaper correspondence reflected on the fearsome and unpitying Jesus of the Book of Revelations meting out retribution for wrong-doing.[163] In 1918, the archbishop of Canterbury's response to the imploring of mercifulness at the peace conference was insistence on stern but righteous vindication.[164] Three years earlier an essayist in the philosophical and theological *Hibbert Journal* detected something revelatory in the 'spirit of sympathy and brotherhood' – that Divine attributes of justice, mercy, liberty, sympathy were 'in the world'.[165] James Drummond's 'God's requirements', in Joseph Estlin Carpenter's *Ethical and Religious Problems of the War* discussed the duty of mercy.[166] The ex-Royal

Marine and Congregational minister Alexander Irvine's *God and Tommy Atkins* (1918) studied the demands of mercy and compassion.[167]

The victors presented themselves as 'merciful conquerors' and memorials asserted that the war was fought for mercy, freedom and justice.[168] For an acerbic view of such wartime rhetoric one turns to Edward Garnett's extraordinary 'Truth's Welcome Home', of June 1918, a satire of an Assembly of the Virtues 'arrayed in khaki', from which all the chief virtues went to the front, and only truth and justice appeared apart. Powerless mercy pled with death to visit the tormented dying in shell-holes.[169] Four years before, Arthur Clutton-Brock's humane *Thoughts on the War* imagined a god without pity, amused at the separate prayers for victory of combatant nations, before hoping that 'we could pray to God that He would have mercy upon our foolish little planet, there would be some chance of an answer to the prayer, and that we should have mercy upon each other'.[170]

As after the global conflict of a century before, the public reflected on the balance between mercy and 'stern' justice for the vanquished.[171] Did Germany and her allies deserve 'merciful justice' as there were no extenuating circumstances, asked Lord Chief Justice Reading, in October 1918? Mercy could be false or in error.[172] A peace treaty where mercy destroyed justice was unchristian, declared American Secretary of State Robert Lansing.[173] Sermons, electoral addresses and editorials commenting on the conferences, debated the enemy's fate in terms of the demands of justice or the force of 'New Testament Ideals'.[174] 'Anti-patriots' were deplored by the weekly *Bystander*, 'with their poisonous prattle about pitying the "poor, Hungry Hun" and handing out, not justice but mercy'. Sourness about the civilian population crept in to reporting the army of occupation's experience. In 'Smuggler Huns', the writer concluded that mercy for smuggling goods beyond the Rhineland was viewed by most Germans only as an invitation to redouble efforts.[175]

General Botha's widely reported words in July 1919 before returning to South Africa, were that 'it should be the privilege of Britain, just as she has led the war, also to lead in the mercy of peace'.[176] Idealists hoped for a 'new spirit and a regeneration' where mercy and truth met.[177] The League of Nations would enshrine 'international virtues': Christian internationalism, Lord Robert Cecil hoped, would be guided by 'broad principles of mercy and pity, of truth and justice'.[178] *The Scotsman*, reporting on Jan Smuts's plea after signing the treaty of Versailles, for 'all-embracing pity', argued qualities of 'mercy, pity, and forgiveness ... constitute the very essence and differentia of our religion', and saw their practical application to international affairs as obvious.[179] While a study of English-language publications by the League or about the new organization suggests mercy was invoked less than justice and humanitarianism, my final chapter reveals a continuing discourse of mercy.[180]

Conclusion: Modern mercy

The preceding chapters studied mercy as a disposition, act or mission carried out by Britons. I studied mercy enjoined towards vanquished foe, slave and 'brute creation'. The mercy discourse on government or misgovernment in Ireland was surveyed. Mercy (alongside justice, and other virtues) offered justification or condemnation of the imperial enterprise in Christian missionary enterprise and acquisition of territory. Mercy's roles in the propaganda and memory of the American and French revolutionary era were detailed. In a separate study I argue for mercy's significant role in presenting the relationship between a monarch and subjects into the Victorian era. This concluding chapter examines key elements of twentieth-century discussion of mercy in British culture.

Prospects for mercy in the new century

As something so centrally involved with Christian discourse, mercy was unsurprisingly part of post-Great War culture. Linking the concepts of mercy, justice and truth was one way in which Christianity remained a framework for national identity and response to national or international problems. Science might have led to a certain disenchantment: 'to talk', the *Saturday Review* said in 1896, 'about any majesty or mercy greater than that of the mayor and the stipendiary magistrate is to dub oneself a fossil or a buffer of the most musty type'.[1] Yet for worshippers mercy *was* familiar: one anti-vivisectionist informed his audience in 1899 of the word's use on thirty occasions during a Sunday service.[2] Humanitarianism was not a term enjoying unqualified approval in the nineteenth century since it was linked to enthusiasts for the rights of humanity who permitted the French Revolutionary Terror, and described as 'sentimentalism' when directed towards capital punishment, penology in general, or vivisection.[3] C.S. Lewis, during the Second World War, decried 'covert propaganda for cruelty which tries to drive mercy out of the world by calling it names such as "Humanitarianism" and "Sentimentality"'.[4]

It seemed obvious in the new century that society was more merciful: a sermonist pointing out, one Edwardian Hospital Sunday, abundant charities, animal and child welfare societies, the conduct of war and 'daily business ... private lives'.[5] The campaign against atrocities in the Belgian Congo brought calls in 1907 for the 'race of Clarkson and of Wilberforce' to head the 'cry of Justice and Mercy'.[6] When disaster struck Britons and others, such as the sinking of RMS *Titanic* in 1912, God's mercy was the topic of sermons.[7] Civil disorder through suffragette destructiveness could be framed in newspaper discourse, propagandist speeches and theatre, as the pursuit of justice, mercy and truth.[8] As a cause, it involved the gender forwards in 'works of mercy' and standing 'with unpolluted hands at the altar of mercy', saving mankind from barbarity.[9] The poet John Masefield, in 1910, ironically talked of Parliament free of 'puling womanly sentiment' about 'mercy and justice and commonsense'.[10] Suffragettes, in confronting male and State power, politicized unmercy in prisons and Home Office, arguing against the government's treatment of 'political reformers' as mere criminals rather than first-class misdemeanants.[11] *The Vote* pointedly imagined the minister faced by William Dyce's fresco of mercy in the Sovereign's Robing Room in Westminster.[12] Liberalism's claims to mercy were disputed by suffragettes.[13]

Liberalism fostered mercy in executive administration and other fields, the Liberal grandee John Morley argued, in a memoir published in the midst of the Great War he opposed.[14] Unfortunately, it became a century of hatred and cruelty on a global scale. The previous chapter demonstrated how mercy was challenged, mobilized and politicized in the First World War. Massive-scale mercy assisted the claim to greatness among her allies on the part of the new superpower: writers asserted America's 'more humanitarian' nature.[15]

The reverse of mercy might be extolled or normalized. *The War of the Worlds* (1898) asked readers whether Europeans were such 'apostles of mercy'. The hero of Wells's *Mr Britling Sees It Through* (1916) admires the 'creative energy' of hate and sees anger in its ultimate quality as greater than mercy.[16] In *The Shape of Things to Come* (1933) Wells argued cruelty and gentleness were simply responses to circumstances: cruelty originating in the attempt to subdue. The kindly and merciful man of 1900 encountered by a 'visitor from another sphere' would appear, 'under different conditions of stress' in 1940, as diabolic. Mercy and generosity were merely 'change of phase'.[17] Surveying the situation in 1937, Ivor Brown's essay on 'The Quantity of Mercy' clung to the belief that among 'our people' there was 'increasing virtue' and 'surely more gentleness year by year'. To avoid pessimism about human nature was 'less difficult, I think, for the British citizen who keeps his eyes narrowly fixed upon the domestic scene'.[18]

Imagining and presenting mercy in interwar British culture

Novels and plays are fruitful places to start an examination of mercy's interwar representation. This was a heyday of the detective and thriller genres where mercy might be expected to be discussed. Some novels were explicitly anti-capital punishment.[19] The melodramatic flavour of the phrase 'without mercy' lent itself to titles like John Goodwin's, subtitled, *The Story of a Mother's Vengeance* (1920), serialized in the popular weekly, *Answers* and a Hollywood film in 1925.[20] The essay 'Christian Moral in the Detective Story' published in America in 1943, referring to the popular doctor-detective created by Englishman Henry Bailey, observed 'Reggie Fortune has taken over the whole doctrine of justice and mercy straight from the New

Testament'.²¹ Contrasting with such middlebrow works, no significant fiction appeared with the word 'mercy' in the title after the Great War until Belloc's satirical *Mercy of Allah* in 1922 and in translation Alfred Döblin's *Men without Mercy* (*Pardon wird nicht gegeben*).²² One critic discerned too much exposure of unpleasant truths in art: to be 'merciless' was a 'compliment eagerly accepted by playwrights, storytellers, historians, and even house decorators'. Heartiness and cheerfulness were unremunerative.²³

Joseph Conrad referred to life's 'merciless logic for a futile purpose' in *Heart of Darkness*.²⁴ By contrast George Bernard Shaw sought in his anti-Darwinian way, we are told, to bring back justice and mercy to the universe, while identifying through Undershaft in *Major Barbara* (1905), mercy and other graces as luxuries of 'a rich, strong safe life'.²⁵ For later Modernists, mercy had a 'Victorian' odour: satirizable as an evangelical troupe of angel-winged singers under a mercenary American in Evelyn Waugh's *Vile Bodies*.²⁶ Lytton Strachey's famous dissection of Victorian character began with Henry Manning's moral accountancy of God's special mercies towards him, 'list upon list', including being saved six times in his life during such perils as 'falling nearly through the ceiling of a church'. Evangelical alertness to divine mercy was, by implication, part of the absurdity.²⁷ For Aldous Huxley in *Jesting Pilate*, in 1925, inherited 'cracker mottoes' included talk of the quality of mercy, about which in 1925 contemporary ideas depended 'on whether we are followers of Gandhi on the one hand, or of Sorel, Lenin and Mussolini on the other'.²⁸ How did mercy relate to such anti-Modernist interwar figures as the Inklings – to Charles Williams for instance, whose gravestone presented the enigmatic phrase, under the word 'poet', of 'under the mercy'?²⁹ Or to Catholic converts such as G.K. Chesterton, whose essay 'On the Mercy of Mr Arnold Bennett' criticized the popular novelist's call to judge less, as the opposite of mercy, and who associated the 'representative' modern, Bernard Shaw, with 'morbid mercy'?³⁰

How did the interests in 'human mercy and justice' which Vera Brittain in a eulogy of Winifred Holtby referred to, appear in her friend's works of fiction? In *Mandoa, Mandoa!* (1933), Jean Stanbury's ideals are equality and 'reform illumined by mercy' and the socialist Bill Durrant, with the gifts of civilization, 'Profit, Power and Pity', shows mercy to the natives.³¹ In another novel of empire, *A Passage to India* (1924), Forster's Hindus and missionaries debate God's infinite mercy, discomforting the Christians by questioning what was included, from monkeys to bacteria.³² Other postwar novels such as Francis Brett Young's *Portrait of Clare* (1927) expressed patriotic identification: the novel's paean to Englishness includes the 'cult of liberty, mercy, justice, gentleness'.³³

There was dramatic interpretation: a reviewer of the Jewish-Russian actor Maurice Moscovitch as Shylock at the Whitechapel Pavilion in 1919, for the left-wing *Daily Herald*, thought 'Portia's declamation of mercy becomes two-edged. Could the Christians' mercy not rise above the old racial and religious antagonisms?'³⁴ Two decades later the Jewishness of Shylock and the play's association with the quality of mercy were used by British anti-Semites in response to calls for assistance to European Jewry.³⁵ One staging – using modern dress and dance tunes – even dropped Portia's speech.³⁶

Memoirs of the Great War, as indicated in the previous chapter, made reference to mercy. If we turn to contemporary histories, the conservative Arthur Bryant's *Unfinished Victory* (1940) claimed the 'natural disposition of Englishmen' against a vindictive peace and explained British response to Jewish refugees as a hatred of cruelty.[37] He contrasted individual tolerance, forbearance and good sense, with a harshness in democracy at large. Human nature was 'temporarily soured' so that forgiveness and forbearance were in short supply and Britons had forgotten their fighting code and chivalry in dealing with Germans.[38] The pacifist Caroline Playne's study of the psychology of war fever viewed mercy and judgement as warped by propaganda.[39] Playne recalled of the impact on civilians who were 'whole-hearted followers of mercy and truth', that they 'broke down under the prolonged moral shock'.[40]

In art work the chief expression of a tradition might be the English symbolist Frederick Cayley Robinson's *Acts of Mercy*, for Middlesex Hospital, 1915–20, representing mercy for the wounded, orphans and others.[41] How frequently did war memorials incorporate the iconography of mercy, beyond textual traces such as prayers to 'Jesu Mercy,' imploring mercy for the departed or in thanksgiving for combatants' safe return, inscribed and carved into the countless individual and group memorials in church and chapel?[42]

Theologies and philosophies of mercy in the interwar era

Despite the horrors of the interwar period, no profound philosophical or theological discussions of mercy and justice were apparently generated in Britain. Spiritualism – stimulated by mass slaughter – assured that the future state was merciful. Arthur Conan Doyle told his audience messages about hell 'were couched in the terms of mercy and kindness which went with the higher religious thought'.[43] Awareness of non-Christian religious concepts such as *karma* brought new points of discussion regarding mercy for those interested in theosophy and mysticism.[44] That temple of freethought, the Ethical Church in Bayswater planned to display an antique statue of the Chinese goddess of mercy Kwan-yin, who refused to leave the world until everyone was in heaven: Stanton Coit stating the sentiment harmonized with freethought.[45] Kenelm Foss's poem on the goddess, her mercy seemingly 'inscrutable', appeared in the *English Review* in 1935.[46]

More traditional religious themes of mercy and justice featured in essays from correspondents in *The Times* and occasionally other national newspapers.[47] Some provincial newspapers, publishing sermons from local ministers, presented the Christian theology of mercy.[48] Others discussed it more secular terms, for example as the fitness of humanity and as a condition of 'joy'.[49] George V was eulogized for his mercy in obituaries in 1936.[50] The coronation in 1937 permitted an emphasis on the difference between usurpers and those anointed and given the kingly gifts of 'peace, justice, mercy'.[51] The *Church Times* then, and later, described charitable acts and philanthropy in terms of Christian mercy.[52] Yet, as the Reverend Cyril Tompkinson contended, this was a generation 'far more interested in humanitarianism than in God's mercy'.[53] William Wallace's *Scientific World View* (1931) dismissed the notion of a divine mercy operating in the universe. Seeking definitions of such things as goodness or mercy as 'abstract moral qualities that have a real existence of their own, according to divine pattern or model' was idle.[54]

The mercy of the magistrate and the law

The judicial sphere remained a key site for mercy. Newspapers reported appeals to the royal prerogative in the reigns of Edward VII and George V.[55] A flurry happened during the mayor of Cork's hunger strike in 1920, with Arthur Balfour publicly explaining the prerogative.[56] There was a last whimper of the tradition of verse on acts of reprieve.[57] Arthur Keith included the prerogative of mercy and justice in *The King and the Imperial Crown* in 1936, and commented that had the monarch been a woman the decision to execute a mother, Dorothea Waddingham, in April 1936, 'clearly' could not have been taken.[58]

The frequency with which newspaper items on local justice by judges, jury and magistrates – and in obituaries of Justices of the Peace – mentioned mercy in headlines is striking.[59] This reinforced the idea of a British legal system where mercy played a significant role. John Cairns, a well-known London magistrate, offered thoughts in the weekly *Answers* in 1932: the law could only be 'just and merciful' while the public should show magnanimity and sentiment to those who served their sentences. He had earlier reflected on the 'generosity and understanding' of the modern legal system.[60]

The significant change of women as jurors, barristers and judges led to debates about their qualities: whether they were more broadminded than male jurors, for instance. One writer described women dressing in unwonted robes of justice, so that 'natural soft-heartedness is momentarily lost in its folds' … We prefer to think … that Portia's sense of justice tempered by mercy is natural to the sex'.[61] Death-penalty abolitionists of the interwar period (and post-1945 campaigners) continued to present the case in terms of mercy.[62] The colourful campaigner Violet van der Elst's propagandism included a placard asserting 'mercy is not weakness'.[63] Critics of the treatment of women convicted of infanticide with jury recommendations to clemency, also identified this with mercy.[64]

Mercy in domestic politics and philanthropy

Historians of interwar philanthropy seem inattentive to mercy discourse yet domestic news coupled voluntary support for hospitals with mercy.[65] Appeals for the League of Mercy were heard through the medium of radio in the 1920s.[66] As the situation worsened in Europe appeal to mercy and pity in charitable donations was joined by the awareness, according to a bishop in 1938, that 'those glorious qualities … [were] in danger from disappearing from the earth'.[67] In that year, framed in the context of 'the great defence and armament programme', *The Sphere* advertised 'Munitions of Mercy Needed!' for charities.[68] Mercy figured in public talk about euthanasia: a news item on sterilizing the mentally defective in 1935 subtitled, 'Death would be merciful'.[69] A series of criminal cases publicized the idea of 'mercy murders'.[70] Instances of animal cruelty led to reflections on the depth of merciful sentiment too.[71]

The eugenics movement related mercy to voluntary – or forcible – sterilization. The sterilization of the feeble minded, for the avowedly Christian Dr Herbert Gray in 1933, was 'in the name of mercy'.[72] 'A biologically inferior class', the Bishop of Southwark told readers of *The Spectator* as he explained 'Christian Eugenics', 'owing to its having been treated with special care according to Christian standards of mercy, pity and love, has tended to increase to such an extent that it is already becoming a difficult task for the rest of the population to support it'.[73]

Given the condition of international affairs newspapers reported non-British individuals and groups 'at the mercy' of others; while asserting that the Royal Navy was *not* at the mercy of air attack, or with the refinement of poison gases that civilian populations *were* at the mercy of chemists.[74] The readers and writers of Lady Houston's right-wing *Saturday Review* in the 1930s saw the empire and British isles at the 'tender mercies' of MacDonald, Baldwin, British Bolsheviks, Indian Congress and Germany. The magazine appealed to the archbishop of Canterbury to show mercy, quoting Portia, to the ex-king Edward VIII.[75] The press detailed British Red Cross and Red Crescent 'missions of mercy' to victims of imperialist and fascist terrorism in the Riff in 1924 and Abyssinia in 1935.[76]

British perspectives on the unmercy of interwar totalitarianism

Correspondents in the Conservative *Daily Telegraph* asserted the state's moral nature – the 'non-moral State is a Prussian idea' – in 1920, including its role in justice and mercy.[77] Liberal British interwar political commentary could hardly ignore the 'philosophy of force, on which modern dictatorships, whatever their complexion, are based' and praised democracy and fellowship 'in which merciful dealings were cultivated between man and man', seeing commitment to mercy and other high ideals as the reason why Britain 'remained the sole repository and guardian of democratic principles'.[78] The anti-fascist novelist Rex Warner argued in 1941 that the only response to exultation of individual or racial power and violence was 'the actual practice of general justice, mercy, brotherhood and understanding'.[79]

Langdon Everard's verse 'Heil, mercy!' on the Spanish civil war in the socialist *Tribune* in April 1938 ironically commented on Francoist radio appeals to red militia men to trust in Franco's mercy.[80] Winston Churchill – his son interviewed Franco for the *Daily Mail* – also stressed mercy's importance for British public opinion.[81] The Anglo-Irish Arland Ussher's reflection (1959) on the conflict was *Spanish Mercy*: for contemporaries evidence of the conflict's unmercy came through newspapers and books.[82] British organizations collected funds under the appeal of mercy and relief.[83] Lord Halifax asked Franco to 'show mercy' when attacking Madrid in February 1939: *Punch* that month represented mercy accosting Franco with the words, 'Whoever recognises *you*, I hope you will recognise *me*' (see Figure C1 below).[84] Yet British fascists used the idea of mercy *against* communists in their paper *Action*, presenting atrocities committed against Catholic priests.[85]

The communists – through the Third International – were described by Fritz Voigt of the *Manchester Guardian* as spreading 'disregard' for mercy and truth.[86] From the 1920s the Soviets banned the Russian word usually equated with mercy (*miloserdie*) in the context of institutional charities such as 'sisters of mercy' alongside the word

Figure C1 E.H. Shepard, 'The Highest Cause', *Punch*, 22 February 1939, p.211. Reproduced under licence from Punch Cartoon Library / Topfoto.

for charity.[87] 'We will make our hearts cruel, hard and unmovable, so that no mercy will enter them,' British readers were told the Red Army declared in 1919. The regime's mercilessness was publicized through a White Paper (the *Daily Telegraph*'s editorialized this as 'Bolshevism without Mercy') and reinforced through reports of execution of agitators and 'counter-revolutionaries', repression of Christianity and de-kulakization.[88] The press covered appeals for clemency when notable victims of the anti-religious campaign such as Archbishop Ciepliak and Father Budkevich in 1923 faced execution; and reported how these efforts were countered by reference to British unmercy in Ireland, India and Egypt. *The Times* headlined 'Soviet "Justice." Clemency for Murderers' in October 1927 while the *Daily Telegraph* highlighted 'Soviet Terror and Mercy'.[89] English-language Soviet propaganda proudly proclaimed ruthlessness towards enemies, such as 'Trotskyite-Bukharinite spies, wreckers and diversionists'. The socialist *Daily Herald* entitled its report of the Soviet response to Labour requests for an independent trial of Zinoviev and others in 1936 ('in accordance with the ordinary canons of justice and humanity', in Sir Walter Citrine's words), 'Attack on Labour's Plea For Mercy'.[90] The *Daily Express* headlined this 'Red Chiefs Beg Stalin for Mercy'.[91] The prominent Anglo-American politician Lady Astor, who had spoken of women's incursion into national politics as bringing in mercy to complement male justice[92] asked in 1937 after visiting Stalin and hearing his admission that there was no justice in Russia: 'How can you have civilization without first justice and mercy? They are the foundations of the English way of thinking.'[93] Gollancz published *Soviet Justice* in that year: Dudley Collard's work found scant need to refer to mercy.[94]

No great perspicacity was needed to appreciate the Nazi attitude to mercy. Lord Lothian commented on Nazism in 1935 as having 'none of the Christian quality of mercy which power should show to opponents when they are defenceless and weak'.[95] Voigt, as the *Manchester Guardian*'s diplomatic correspondent, noted the hatred of mercy present in the Nazi 'Brown Terror' and corruption of the young. Teutonic paganism (Wickham Steed's phrase) inculcated mercilessness in children. 'An unscrupulous man', the Dean of Bristol said, on a day of national prayer in March 1941, 'had so trained the youth of a great nation to denial of all religion that justice and mercy no longer found their place in the Germans' vocabulary.'[96] Nor was it seen as just a Christian inheritance that was rejected: Jewish writers asserted the origin of justice and mercy in their faith.[97] The Nazi rejection of Christian ethics that included mercy and pity was presented in Elizabeth Burdekin's feminist dystopian *Swastika Night* (1937); a year later in a book also published by Victor Gollancz, the Hungarian Aurel Kolnai commented on an assault on the 'ethic of mercy'.[98]

Mercy and interwar imperialism

The Whig politician and historian Thomas Babington Macaulay described the imperialism of the early nineteenth century as 'the strength of civilization without its mercy'.[99] *Recessional*, Rudyard Kipling's verse of the Jubilee year of 1897 anxiously pled, 'For frantic boast and foolish word, | Thy mercy on Thy people, Lord!'[100] Mercy was implored against punishment for hubris rather than for the victims of British violence. An obvious area where mercy was discussed in the interwar period was an empire experiencing the Irish civil war and violence in India. The Amritsar massacre of 1919 caused by General Dyer was characterized by Churchill (quoting Macaulay's words in the House of Commons against Dyer) as an exception to an inclination to kindness and mercy.[101] Dyer told the Committee of Investigation it was 'a merciful thing. I thought I should shoot well and strong, so that I should not have to shoot again.'[102]

The *Daily Herald* under the heading 'Imperial Atrocities' suggested Dyer's failure to offer medical assistance to the wounded 'was done in order to teach men and women of a different civilization and a different religion what a beautiful and merciful thing Christianity is'.[103] A few years later in a public talk in Oxford Churchill emphasized the combination of power and mercy as a key to imperial rule.[104] Royal mercy was still bestowed in India; when a political amnesty was declared 'the effect of mercy always is good', the *Herald* commented.[105] The *Daily Worker* ironized that 'blessed be the merciful, for they shall obtain mercy' was chanted by the Royal Air Force before bombing on the North-West Frontier.[106] Austen Chamberlain's description of the use of such bombardment in 'police expeditions' as 'merciful' was returned to by the *Daily Herald*.[107]

Indian nationalists made capital from British unmercy. The *Indian Sociologist* – banned in India – ironically referred to 'howls of delighted English mercy and loving kindness', when thousands died through plague in 1907.[108] John Gwynn, formerly of the Indian Civil Service, reported a comment to readers of the *Manchester Guardian* that the new generation of Indians lost 'the old faith in English justice and English mercy' in 1924; the polemical *Sister India* referred in 1945 to the British habit of emphasizing India dependence 'solely and wholly on British mercy'.[109] Elsewhere, capital punishment meant colonial mercy remained an element of British rule.[110]

Mercy appears in discussion of 'Bloody Sunday' – the targeting of British officers and the wounding and killing of civilians at Croke Park football grounds, Dublin, on 21 November 1920. The Auxiliaries of the Royal Irish Constabulary gained the reputation in West Cork as killers 'without mercy'.[111] As Ireland descended into violence in the next few years, the Catholic archbishop of Tuam and others preached mercy. *Dublin Weekly Freeman's Journal* reported on the unmercy of the anti-Treaty IRA, the Irregulars and *their* appeals to mercy.[112] In the Dáil, the war of the Irregulars was called a 'peculiarly cowardly form' and they were 'asked to show mercy'.[113] Mercy was identified as a defining element of the Irish Free State's national army faced by 'mutiny' in 1922, and figured in English press reporting.[114] The witness statements given afterwards are sprinkled with allusions to republican mercy, British soldiers' pleas for mercy and mercy withheld by the British state to figures like Casement.[115]

G.K. Chesterton, writing in 1920, identified pride and provincialism in 'suggestions that the English alone can establish anywhere a reign of law, justice, mercy, purity and all the rest of it'.[116] Yet mercy was represented in imperial iconography: in a memorial to David Livingstone at his birthplace, for example, alongside faith and courage.[117] As might be expected of the Religious Tract Society, the lesson of the school book *How the Empire Grew* of 1920 was that empires were secure only if power was exercised with mercy, justice and humility.[118] Plenty of imperialists complacently argued for British rule's Christian basis in 'liberty, justice, mercy and truth' by contrast with Soviets and Nazis.[119] Their appeals to resist the Axis threat asserted the principles of justice and mercy. For example, Lady Reid, the governor of Assam's wife, we are told, held 'aloft the lamp of mercy, of compassion and of kindness'.[120]

British mercy and the Second World War

Winston Churchill's response to Hitler's attack on him, Anthony Eden, Duff Cooper and others as warmongers in November 1938 was to imagine the world's joy and Hitler's enhanced historical reputation if he showed toleration, magnanimity, pity and mercy.[121] A year later Lord Halifax said in a broadcast that the fight was to 'maintain the rule of law and the quality of mercy in dealings between man and man in the great society of civilised States'.[122] Readers of Hitler's response to Britain's war aims in 1940 had his riposte: Britain, 'wallowing in the Bible', always claimed to be fighting for God and religion, 'for truth and justice and the protagonist of all virtues'.[123] It was a claim shared with other Allies. Roosevelt's characterization of the American Red Cross undertaking 'the greatest single crusade of mercy in all history' stated it was a war 'to decide whether all our concepts of mercy and human decency are strong enough to survive. In the Axis nations mercy and decency are regarded as synonyms for weakness and decadence. In our land it is from our great tradition of mercy that we take part of our strength.'[124]

Churchill's broadcast as First Sea Lord on 1 October 1939, well received by Mass Observation diarists, registered an intention that was linked to religious sentiment, to preserve the navy's mercifulness while rigorously pursuing U-boats.[125] Mercy remained a keyword in a war which might, as one theologian argued in 1941 be seen not as conflict of capitalism or imperialism but 'of religion'.[126] How was one to reconcile faith in 'God's love and mercy' with Nazism's apparent success?[127] This is not the place to uncover in detail the discourse of mercy and equivalent non-Christian concepts in the war which would requires study of Axis propaganda like *Contemporary Japan* (published in Tokyo) emphasizing *bushido* in treatment of enemies.[128]

Few works published during the war referenced mercy in titles: a hymn by Noel Bonavia-Hunt entitled *Father, in Thy Mercy Hear Us* (1940); the American classicist Macurdy's study of mercy in Greek literature (1940); reprints of the nineteenth-century Dutchman Jan de Liefde's *Errands of Mercy*; a work on the First World War entitled *War without Mercy* by a pro-German Swiss.[129] British works published at the time reflect on mercy and cruelty. Arthur Bryant's history of the last century asserted that without 'moral justice, honesty, truth, mercy, charity and a humble belief in a divine purpose', England was a 'barbarous Teuton island' (1941).[130] The pacifist Vera Brittain in *England's Hour* (1941) presented the reader with a bomb-damaged church crucifix looking down in 'sorrowful pity for the sins of the world'. This vignette of the 'merciful Son of Man' was followed by a quotation from the Prayer for Protection against Air Raids, imploring the 'most merciful God' to protect church and home.[131] *Testament of Experience* (1957) recounted response in the British and American press to the concluding chapter 'Forever London' which took to task vengeful journalism such as 'Can we Forgive?' Brittain's regular *Letter* sustained a message of mercy.[132] She was instrumental with her husband, Victor Gollancz and Sheila Hodges, in a short anthology on kindness between enemies, *Above all Nations* (1945), demonstrating 'that even amidst the illimitable degradation of modern warfare men of all nations can be decent and merciful to those who at the very moment are their mortal enemies', and which one reviewer thought would 'delight a few and infuriate many'.[133] Brittain's commitment to mercy, pity and love was also expressed in public speaking and poetry.[134]

The Congregational minister R.M. Goodfield in the *London Quarterly*, discussing the cardinal virtues in 1943, included mercy though preferring to call it 'compassion'. Works of theology like John Cowper Powys's essay on St Paul in 1938 ('something coming from behind the whole System of Things, that finds in forgiveness and mercy and pity and magnanimity exultation larger than space, older than time, and able to melt the very bones within us in a feeling for which there is no name'[135]) or C.S. Lewis's *The Problem of Pain* (1940) discussed divine mercy.[136] The professor of theology Herbert Wood's *Christianity and Civilisation* (1942) observed the 'constant downward pressure leading us to ignore our professed ideals in practice', too much wartime talk about justice, mercy and truth led to hypocrisy. These virtues, seemingly part of the 'permanent vocabulary of mankind', were imperilled by Axis and Marxist ideology.[137]

From the late 1920s, T.S. Eliot's religious poems, *Ash-Wednesday* included mercy but it was not a prominent interwar poetic theme; one commentator on the abstractions of justice, mercy and peace, described the 'chill of a convention in which nobody to-day, not even the poet himself, really believes'.[138] Some poets held on to moral values in a darkening world: Laurence Binyon's 'The Winds of all the World' of 1943 for instance, where amidst the torments and agonies, 'I thought of beauty, justice, mercy, peace.'[139] George Fraser dealt with mercy, justice and the death of the innocent, in a memorial to the refugee children of SS *City of Benares* in 1941.[140] Yet poetry by young men and women of the armed forces seemingly had little time for thoughts of mercy, if one can judge from the infrequency of 'mercy' and 'merciful' in the collection *More Poems from the Forces*.[141]

The war began with a stark demonstration reported in the British press: '"No Mercy!" Says Hitler! Seething with baffled rage at the heroic resistance of Poland's gallant troops, Hitler gives vent to unbridled and maniacal ferocity. "Destroy them all without mercy," he screams', went the *Sunday Pictorial* headline and opening paragraph in September 1939.[142] Like the Great War there was the sense that Britons fought for 'right, justice, and mercy', that the enemy thought these 'sentimental nonsense' and 'knew no mercy'. The Nazis, commented Neville Chamberlain in April 1940 after Norway's fall, shut the 'gates of mercy' upon mankind, the religious turn of phrase perhaps explained by his National Free Church Council audience (though the radio broadcaster Hans Fritzsche had been reported as declaring this).[143] On the other hand, it was suggested a more merciful treaty than Versailles might not have led to the rise of Hitler.[144]

The sense of a Nazi war against God and Christianity, in which the ethics of mercy, love and humility were rejected as 'slave morality' was expressed in sermons, in the press and by-election literature.[145] Consider *The Scotsman*'s headline in September 1939: 'A merciless regime. Christian Culture repudiated'.[146] Or this comment at a Salvation Army Hall in Lanarkshire in October 1939: that the gospel was the only hope as it embodied 'a system of mercy which all the present day "isms," Communism, Nazism and Fascism, lack'.[147] Pity was 'one of our national virtues', characterizing British Legion veterans and the 'very solvent of ruthlessness and the best antidote to the horrors of War'.[148] Attacks on wounded soldiers in Dunkirk in May – June 1940 were used to contrast Red Cross with German pitilessness.[149] (In Bernard Partridge's appeal in *Punch*, 5 June 1940, 'The Banner of Mercy', the symbol was 'honoured by every nation in the world except Germany'.) British newsreel presented wartime Europe in terms of the discourse of mercy. Pathé News showed civil war Athens under the title 'The Quality of Mercy' in January 1945 as crying out to the grace of mercy and answered by the International Red Cross.[150] Churchill's Christmas broadcast to his transatlantic audience in 1941 invoked God's mercy at its end.[151] In Bradford in 1942 he contrasted an Allied cause of law, mercy and tolerance with Nazi tyranny.[152]

The *Sunday Express*'s John Gordon called for raids on Germany whether reprisals or 'plain ruddy murder': 'No feeling of mercy, no feeling of pity should hold us back', another of his articles was entitled, 'No Mercy for the Germans Now'.[153] The churches might attempt to preserve a more merciful outlook. Privately the poet (and wartime fireman) Stephen Spender tackled the bishop of Southwark about this in a letter in 1944 critical of the Anglican church's support of the war 'almost without reserve'.[154] Concern was publicly uttered by some churchmen, such as Herbert Hensley Henson, about the impact on British mercy claims from 'reprisals' for German total war (using the homely image of putting justice and mercy on and off 'like winter pants').[155] Vera Brittain quoted the *Sunday Express*, 6 June 1943, in the context of massive bombing raids:

NO PITY! NO MERCY!

If we are to succeed we must not harbour cant and humbug. Voices are already heard, crying that mercy must temper justice, that vengeance belongs alone to God ... All these sentimental appeals are bunkum and hypocrisy ... whether they come from a familiar prelate or some unsuspected quisling.[156]

Air Marshal Arthur Harris's statement that the Germans would cry for mercy as a result of saturation bombing was widely reported.[157]

Some Britons hoped during the conflict for a 'real new order' expressed through the Atlantic Charter and recognition that justice with vengeance must be replaced by justice with mercy; 'but not too much mercy' in Labour peer Lord Nathan's words in May 1942.[158] The power of 'fellow-feeling' and compassion was 'drawing together not only individuals but nations, as never before', a *Times* correspondent hoped in 1941, writing on 'Compassion'.[159] Organization of relief and reconstruction through the UN, announced in 1943, was framed in terms of work of mercy.[160] The home front had 'mercy squads' of firefighters and others during the blitz.[161] Meanwhile the press complained of bureaucracy tying mercy in red tape in dealing with the bomb damage.[162]

Printed comment gave the public evidence of a deliberate mercilessness in Poland and other occupied states: readers were told that propaganda urged Germans to 'show no pity, to have no mercy', towards Poles.[163] Evidence of the attitude to 'unnecessary humanitarianism' in the Eastern Front, via *Pravda* and *Soviet Documents of Nazi Atrocities* published by the Soviet embassy ('Exterminate mercy and compassion within you'[164]) was presented through newspapers. The Reich's policy of euthanasia was 'Nazi Mercy': 'upholding death as their outstanding act of kindness to the German people' and warping the 'humanitarian side of the theory'.[165]

What happened to mercy discourse with growing awareness of systematic and mass extermination of European Jewry? Well might the Chief Rabbi Joseph Hertz point out in 1941 that in 'our day of diminishing mercy the larger world hardly took any note of the hideous mass execution of Jews'.[166] Details of unparalleled violence towards Jews in Germany and Europe, the deliberate rejection of mercy by Goebbels in *Das Reich* in early 1942, appeared in the British press.[167] Evidence of the plan to exterminate European Jewry was published, with information on Treblinka in 1943.[168] The fate of Jews was linked to mercy in reported speeches: the Jewish Labour politician Harold Laski (contrasting 'appeasement' for fear of British anti-Semitism being stimulated by

Jewish refugees, with acts of mercy), or General Smuts in Pretoria in December 1942 (pleading for a policy of mercy but fearing the consequence for Germans in terms of retribution for atrocities), the archbishop of York concluding fear was sometimes 'effective when mercy makes no appeal' in warning of impending Allied punishment of Nazi criminals in 1943, or Anthony Eden advising the 'merciful' within the Balkan satellites of the Reich to 'multiply their acts of humanity' in 1944.[169]

The liberation of the concentration camps was framed in terms of Allied works of mercy (the 'brighter side', as one Methodist chaplain to the armed forces described it), but also in the realization that there had only been the mercy of death.[170] Language's inadequacy in articulating a response shows in the letter of one British soldier on the horrors of Belsen contrasting the generous qualities of the 'sportsman' in victory with Nazi actions, ending with the prayer that no divine mercy be shown to the guilty.[171]

Charles Morgan, in the *Spectator* in 1940, described Germans as unappeasable 'by what we call justice or mercy, for these they despise, giving or receiving', nevertheless 'we must still exercise mercy and justice as parts of our own integrity'.[172] There was pessimism about how vanquished Germans could be dealt with: 'proposals for the forcible re-education … in the virtues of humility, and pity and mercy are futile'.[173] Mass Observation research in 1942 on attitudes about after the war found one participant wishing that continental Europeans and Russians would be left to deal with Germany, for 'they have suffered, and will give no mercy', rather than the 'sloppy and sporting' British.[174] The *Daily Mirror*'s question about what to do with German boys who fired on American soldiers in 1944 suggested that of the thousands replying, half suggested extermination.[175] Fear of inadequate severity was expressed by women liberated across the Channel in the autumn of 1944: the *Daily Mirror* reported bitter hate for Germans in France and Belgium, and outrage when its chief correspondent said 'it was very difficult for the people of England to be merciless', and that 'in Britain there was always pity'.[176]

Mercy in victory and peace

Churchill said the Axis powers had to yield absolutely to the Allied forces' justice and mercy and in the Commons discussed the need for mercy in handling Germans, as victory looked possible in early 1945.[177] Mercy was also invoked by him after atomic bombs were used in August 1945, identifying God's mercy behind mankind's delayed understanding of these destructive forces and Allied outpacing of Nazi scientists.[178] God's providence for the crowning mercy of Japanese surrender figured in George VI's reply to a parliamentary address on 21 August 1945. Newspaper correspondents and columnists – without the horrific details conveyed in John Hersey's *New Yorker* essay in August 1946 – sought to justify the bombs' use by Axis unmercy, the 'merciful' results of saving thousands of Allied solders' lives, or coupled Hiroshima and Nagasaki's fate with the mercy of providence, if this war or all war was over. Mass Observation's interviews indicate the language of mercy was absent from people's thoughts about the atomic bomb, or post-war peace.[179]

With victory there followed 'days of retribution'.[180] Mercy was involved in press reporting of the fate of British traitors,[181] the Vichy leaders,[182] and trials for war crimes; and was appealed to at the gallows in Nuremberg. The British press reported the prayers for mercy left for the condemned by the Protectant pastor at Nuremberg, and the final words of the executed Nazis Ribbentrop, Keitel and Frank, for divine mercy for themselves or Germany. The *Daily Mirror*'s columnist William Connor referred to 'merciful violence' when Japanese were executed by British military police in 1947.[183] At least one editorial reflected on mercy as a 'spiritual force for good' in opposing death sentences.[184] Portia's speech appeared in an editorial on the judicial spirit of the non-Soviet members of the tribunal.[185] Harold Nicholson wrote of decency and mercy when deploring photographs of the corpses of Mussolini and other enemies.[186] In the war crimes trials in the Far East, the need to temper victors' justice with mercy was also raised.[187]

Mercy, alongside sister virtues of justice and truth, was a commonplace of wartime discourse: the scriptural trinity resonant as shorthand for what the Allied cause meant and what 'Germanism' with its monstrous efficiencies lacked.[188] W.H. Auden's *For the Time Being. A Christmas Oratorio* (1944) imagined secularized Britons wanting a God on a more mundane plane of domestic needs than in relation to eternal or ideal values.[189] For what ordinary Britons thought about justice and the virtues of truth and mercy in such pressing times, one turns to newspaper correspondence, Mass Observation and diaries.[190] A 'false satisfaction with small mercies' blunted people to the real issues, a newspaper article asserted in 1941.[191] The words of one speaker at a women's guild meeting were headlined 'Remember Nazi Crimes': after the war they would 'face the danger of allowing pity and mercy to overcome justice. The Germans have neither pity nor mercy.'[192] Correspondents naturally fell on both sides in answering the *Daily Herald*'s 'should we pity the Germans?' in February 1945.[193] Study of the national and provincial press uncovers debates about dealing with Germans in terms of ideals or self-described 'realism'.[194]

The *Daily Record*, publishing letters in response to extended rationing, included one extolling British self-denial as 'merciful and gracious gestures' under the headline, 'Our Mercy is our Glory'.[195] The 'Save Europe' campaign used the trope of British pity and mercy in late 1945. 'Mercy needed in Europe', was Father Gilbert Shaw's plea – calling for aid to Central Europe, it was 'a great moral problem crying out for a Christian solution'.[196] Mercy ships, mercy trains and justice-and-mercy appeals were practical responses to liberated Europe and occupied Germany.[197] Lectures promoted the United Nations Relief and Rehabilitation Administration's activities, 'the greatest work of mercy the world had ever known'.[198] As an American wrote, 'Reconstruction automatically includes the extension of mercy even to the undeserving.'[199] The contrite German response to Allied aid might accept that this *was* mercy rather than a human right.[200]

Memorialization of the war does not appear to have invoked mercy: though civilian 'acts of mercy' by first-aider, firemen and air-sea rescuers were commemorated in stained glass by Nora Yoxall at Muswell Hill Methodist Church in 1949. The inscription 'Father Forgive' in the bombed Coventry cathedral chancel was one response for divine mercy during the war.[201] Concern with Christian forgiveness and reconciliation with Germans caused the cathedral's provost to condemn display of Holocaust-related photography in June 1961.[202]

Mercy in post-war Britain, Europe and the empire

Planning for the peace stimulated talk of ensuring a future of justice and mercy. An educationist and secretary of the League of Nations Union, James Clerk Maxwell Garnett, suggested 'psychological' planning: an 'education must add a mutual friendliness that makes for justice and mercy and a common supreme purpose'.[203] Churchill's speech promoting a 'United Europe' led by France and Germany, delivered at Zurich University in 1946, was framed as a call for mercy (alongside justice and freedom) in the press.[204] Robert Boothby, Conservative delegate to the consultative assembly of the Council of Europe, identified mercy as one of three essential qualities sustaining a new united Europe, in 1949.[205]

The World Council of Churches at Geneva in 1948 appealed for 'mercy not vengeance'.[206] At a humbler level, ministers of religion commented on the mercy and justice demands of European states: a series of Sunday evening talks by a Methodist minister in Rochdale argued these were 'not alternatives … in the post-war world'.[207] Their apologetics might also, as the 1949 edition of the Congregationalist-turned-Anglican David Davies's *On to Orthodoxy* did, consider mercy's place.[208] Clergymen enjoined mercy's influence, alongside justice, in pre-election religious services. A defender of the established church, the historian and journalist Arthur Bryant, presented this relationship as a safeguard of the 'eternal laws that ultimately govern the world – of justice, love, mercy, truth and respect for the individual'.[209]

Labour's 'New Jerusalem' did not emphasize mercy: before 1945 the labour movement sought a national health service, not the 'mercy of charity'.[210] Rejection of voluntaristic and charitable solutions explains why one clergyman's public concern about the state taking over 'humanitarian service', made a link with mercy in 1952, 'the appalling dangers which confront us in the matter of mercy – one of the most vitally important elements in human intercourse. Wherever there is a move towards totalitarianism in a state mercy flies out of the door.'[211] The League of Mercy was dissolved in February 1948: its records passing to the Ministry of Health.[212] Elsewhere in the popular press concerns were raised about the 'growth of State welfare services', curbing initiatives for voluntary work.[213] This was not new: in the interwar period Christian virtues such as mercy, 'thought to be personal affairs', were contrasted with the 'Social Conscience' of the democratic mind.[214]

In post-war discourse, mercy's absence from politicians' speeches continued the pre-war situation though my study has not extensively examined their writings. Beaverbrook's reflections on mercy appear in *Success* (1921) as self-interest ('Those who exercise mercy lay up a store of it for themselves') and 'tenderness springing out of harsh experience'.[215] Attlee asserted the moral basis and values underpinning the state, including 'truth and justice, mercy and liberty', to an audience of children organized by the World Forum of Youth and Council for Education in World Citizenship in 1949.[216] Parliamentary debate rarely referenced mercy unless discussing capital punishment.[217] The Cold War sustained discourse on communist unmercy in Europe and in European colonies: Koestler's conception of Satan's chilly arithmetic of mercy in *Darkness at Noon* (1941) being applied to communism, for instance.[218]

Decolonization and struggles for independence generated references to justice and mercy from the colonized, the late-imperial state and imperialists. Bishop Woods of Lichfield, in a new year's address in 1949 asserted 'the British Commonwealth, have a mission in the world to show that it is possible to achieve a new and better social order without the loss of justice and mercy'.[219] In 1960 another clergyman, in Commonwealth Week, acknowledged the need for greater social justice, yet mercy was also referenced.[220] Sir Arthur Bryant in *Illustrated London News* in 1968 defended the empire in terms of justice and 'a certain kindliness and mercifulness of dealing'.[221] At this late stage in the empire mercy still provided justification.

Examples on the opposite side are no doubt countless: continuing the anti-imperialist critique of British rule as merciless. They include a text from 1946, Rāmeśvara Vidyārthī's *British Savagery in India*, 'Feelings of tenderness, and mercy are said to be inherent in man ... But alas! there is no "point" at which any sense of mercy or feeling could arise in the steel-framed British administration in India or its officers'.[222] Given the appalling cruelty of partition it is surprising to see mercy in British texts in the aftermath: *Mission with Mountbatten* presents the former vicereine's 'errands of mercy' as she helped coordinate a United Council for Relief and Welfare in September 1947.[223] Late-imperial violence also stimulated calls for intervention, as an 'act of mercy' in relation to the high death-penalty rate for minor offences in Kenya.[224] The exercise of the royal prerogative of mercy would be one of the controversies in the Rhodesian crisis when the illegal Salisbury regime refused to accept a recommendation to mercy for three Africans condemned to death in 1968.[225]

A declining discourse of mercy?

In the *Commonwealth and Empire Review* in 1945, it was noted, quoting the Chinese novelist Lin Yutang (writing for a wartime Western audience), that 'we are to-day scared of the old simple words like "goodness" "justice" "mercy". This age shuns moral platitudes and goodness, justice and mercy seem like overused coins.' Yutang was concerned with modern English's 'mechanisation': 'We create euphemisms for these words and would rather speak of them as anything but goodness, justice and mercy'.[226]

Yet mercy was still extolled: George VI's death stimulated those eulogies to royal mercy that I explore elsewhere.[227] Mercy retained allegorical force: Ernest Shepard used her figure to protect a child from the ghost of a Dickensian beadle in dramatizing child neglect for *Punch* in 1945 (see Figure C2).[228] In the 1950s and 1960s, the press and the increasingly pervasive medium of television debated mercy in the form of euthanasia.[229] The prerogative of mercy kept hanging going, *The Spectator* argued, at the time of Ruth Ellis's execution in 1955.[230] Adolf Eichmann's trial in Israel was followed in Britain; a report of British Jews urging clemency appeared in *The Economist* in 1962.[231] Proposals to reform the laws against homosexuality alluded to mercy.[232] Critics of permissiveness and leniency towards offenders characterized 'social mercy' without punishment for social justice, as a 'public breach of law ... licence and moral indifference'.[233] Mercy was used to characterize the humanizing of industrial or managerial relations.[234] More existentially, Churchill suggested America's monopoly in atomic weaponry could bring peace by stimulating mercy and a return to sanity in

Figure C2 E.H. Shepard, 'The Neglected Child', *Punch*, 21 February 1945, p.153. Reproduced under licence from Punch Cartoon Library / Topfoto.

the brief respite it afforded.²³⁵ Where Churchill acknowledged the strangeness whilst emphasizing the mercy, of American nuclear defence in 1950, others stressed the 'large mercy' of escaping nuclear annihilation.²³⁶

For an Anglican readership, appeals for victims of Cold War and postcolonial conflict still presented claims for charitable contributions as works of Christian mercy.²³⁷ The tragedy of the Rosenbergs in 1953 brought an international campaign for mercy in which Catholic assertion of a principle 'superior to other human values' was broadcast.²³⁸ Newspapers reported St John's Ambulance Brigade's work as merciful – but also made the term 'mercy squad' familiar in the context of dealing with myxomatosis.²³⁹

How far did the discourse of mercy survive in the second half of the century as others emerged into prominence, such as that around humanitarianism? There are hints: a public and shared language of mercy, with familiar touchstones of scripture and Shakespeare, was deemed old fashioned. C.S. Lewis asserted in 1949 that the trend for a 'curative' and humanitarian theory of punishment was a mere 'semblance of mercy': no longer was there a belief in sin and thus the need to acknowledge guilt and seek pardon. He offered the paradox of mercy, detached from justice, becoming unmerciful.[240] The philosopher Harry Roberts, in the 1960s, responding to Alwynne Smart's philosophical thoughts on mercy in the law, commented: 'It must be some time since a judge has been importuned by an advocate to temper his justice with mercy!'[241] The Anglican commentator Rosamund Essex in 1977, taking her cue from a complaint about the lack of mercy from striking firemen or power-station workers, and towards Vietnamese 'boat people', commented, 'apparently Christian mercy has gone out of fashion'. Justice had replaced it as a cry; mercy 'deteriorated in value because people say that those who show mercy are putting themselves on a higher plain [sic] than others, exalting themselves, being paternalistic and condescending'.[242] From a legal studies perspective Carolyn Strange notes the 'old-fashioned ring' which mercy has 'increasingly', and theologians have identified it too as an antiquated term.[243]

Like those anxious about the threat to acts of mercy from the welfare state in the 1940s, Margaret Thatcher stressed the 'many deeds of mercy, the myriad acts of human kindness' of individuals as opposed to state social services and insisted that 'exercise of mercy and generosity' could not be delegated.[244] Thatcher's presentation of her spiritual values before the General Assembly of the Church of Scotland in 1988 stimulated discussion of social justice's role compared with individual compassion, pity and mercy.[245] (Thatcher's journalism and speeches tended to refer to people and businesses being *at* the mercy of strikers and closed shops).[246]

The discourse of mercy was not seen as antiquated in the first quarter of the twentieth century, given its rhetorical and practical mobilization in the 'thirty years' war'. This chapter studied its appearance in interwar discussion of domestic social problems, law and crime reporting. Some of this was at the level of cliché and stock phrasing but reflected an enduring Christian culture. Its decline – but not complete disappearance – in British discourse, took place after the Second World War, with secularization and talk of a 'post-Christian' society whose extent has been challenged by recent scholars.[247] Late-twentieth-century British journalism would still employ the shorthand of 'mercy planes / ships' and the tabloid press might splutter at judicial miscarriages of mercy.[248] But 'humanitarianism', universal in scope, provided the Cold War era with a different and 'modern' vocabulary.

It may be that humanitarianism is part descendant of mercy – though the United Nations Declaration of Human Rights in December 1948 made universal claims about these rights without invoking it (justice *was* mentioned). A point made throughout this study is that mercy is a central idea in Christian theology, and recent events provided a context for its discussion by post-war Christian theologians.[249] Part I touched upon missionary discourse in which it prominently featured in the nineteenth century. Mercy was still a keyword in this activity in the mid-twentieth century. The Church Missionary Society's *Dynamics of Mercy* concerned medical work, in 1949. Swallow's history of the humane movement in the United States (1963) was entitled *Quality of Mercy*.[250] Works of the interwar period and commentary in the 1950s described philanthropy and social work in terms of mercy. The American Alice Menken's study of problems in 'social readjustment' was *On the Side of Mercy* (1933) whilst the American Episcopalian church's magazine *The Living Church* (1951) equated social work with the works of mercy of a century before. Later commentary described Christian social action as ministries of mercy.[251]

It is not time to speak of mercy as a lost emotion or 'disposition whose emotional power has more or less vanished'.[252] For the orthodox Christian, mercy remains an important virtue and divine attribute, as the Roman Catholic jubilee year of mercy announced by the papal bull *Misericordiae Vultus* and Pope Francis's *The Name of God Is Mercy*, and Protestant theological conferences, testify.[253] There has even been an attempt to argue for the everyday mercies.[254]

This historical study is driven by a belief in the importance of understanding mercy as a virtue and disposition. Anglo-American scholarship in modern times is motivated by a desire to 'rescue' mercy as a virtue in jurisprudence, or – in the context of penal or immigration policies, to halt the fall in its status in the face of retributionism, victims' rights claims, or a more general decline in the virtue in 'public life'.[255] It is studied in relationship to charity and social justice, with critical perspectives on recent or ongoing humanitarian disasters examining the limits of 'organised mercy / compassion'.[256]

Mercy may be degenerate: mere reflex of 'lax indulgence'.[257] One particularly tart discussion in the 1820s in a legal context characterized the virtue as 'treason to society, the worst injury to the common safety' and commonplace talk of tempering justice with it as 'plausible clap trap'.[258] If some of the many voices heard in this study thought there could be too much or the wrong sort of mercy, whether in peace or in the exigencies of war and rebellion – producing unjust, sentimental or cruel mercy (*crudelis misericordia*) – our world seems to have the right sort in short supply.

At the same time, the chapters studying discourses concerning Irish, French or American revolutionaries, demonstrated mercy's enduring rhetorical force. The word could be uttered in ironic or derisory fashion by those who craved its exercise or belittled its value. I am wary of establishing a transition towards a more ironic discursive use of mercy in the twentieth century since this mode can be found in the criticism in previous centuries of English rule, for example in relation to Ireland. There the trope was mercy with a vengeance, thus the *North American Review* responding to Dr Johnson's claim that 'English mercy wars not with the dead,' asked the question, 'when has English mercy spared the living?'[259] Frank Hugh O'Donnell, a Home Ruler, referred to the chain gang and ordure bucket of English mercy.[260] Earlier, the verse of the Glaswegian James Grahame (advocate-turned-Anglican curate) on the slave trade, addressed to England 'whose mercy is but love of gain?' ended with the words 'English mercy said, let millions bleed!'[261]

Mercy is a vastly complicated subject. On the one hand it has been presented – both non-ironically and ironically – as among 'eminently British qualities'.[262] On the other hand, some Britons also reflected on mercy's existence in other cultures. Yet mercy discourse has continued to be used, in the era of the New World Order and the 'war on terror', against the non-Western 'other'.[263] We often esteem it, and yet mercy is mobilized against authority as the cry of the impotent, and has never been a stirring catchword of modern revolutionaries.[264] Mercy, it seems, is a virtue in a fallen world – 'mercy no more could be | If all were as happy as we,' in William Blake's words.[265] Throughout this book and in the previous study where I focused on mercy in relation to the British monarchy, I have been acutely aware of the risks of single-mindedly pursuing mercy's trail, and reminded myself that it is comprehended in the context of other virtues (and vices) and, especially, often applied to people in particular states of helplessness. The Victorian Anglican clergyman Robert Whytehead noted the word 'involves the idea of misery, guilt, and unworthiness, as belonging to those who are the objects of its unfavourable regard'.[266] In the period under study there were some British people who were aware of the fact, and willing to acknowledge in their commentary, that there were other religions and cultures where the attribute or concept of mercy was valued, despite the conventionality of claims made for Christianity being *the* paramount religion of mercy outlined in the first section of the book.[267] More needs to be done to understand how other people have thought about mercy beyond the British world. A transcultural study of mercy is required.

Notes

Introduction

1. There are studies of mercy and closely associated concepts taking historical perspectives, and this introduction surveys the existing historiography, e.g. in relation to histories of monarchy, and law and society. M.B. Dowling, *Clemency and Cruelty in the Roman World* (Ann Arbor: Michigan University Press, 2005), refers to mercy/pity; and G. Sanchez, *Pity in Fin-de-Siècle French Culture: 'Liberté, Égalité, Pitié'* (Westport, CT: Praeger, 2004). For other contributions to histories of mercy in literature, see, for example, D. Quint, *Montaigne and the Quality of Mercy: Ethical and Political Themes in the 'Essais'* (Princeton, NJ: Princeton University Press, 1998). On mercy as a virtue, see D. Konstan, 'Clemency as a Virtue', *Classical Philology* 100:4 (October 2005), pp.337–46; B. Harding, *Augustine and Roman Virtue* (New York: Continuum, 2008); essays on 'Anger' and 'Clemency' translated and published in R.A. Kaster and M.C. Nussbaum, *Anger, Mercy, Revenge* (Chicago, IL: University of Chicago Press, 2012). For Christian reflections on the virtues without considering mercy in detail, D. DeMarco, *The Many Faces of Virtue* (Steubenville, OH: Emmaus Road Publishing, 2000).

2. G.H. Macurdy, *The Quality of Mercy: The Gentler Virtues in Greek Literature* (New Haven, CT: Yale University Press, 1940). That famous line is applied to other non-Western topics, e.g. B.E. McKnight, *The Quality of Mercy: Amnesties and Traditional Chinese Justice* (Honolulu: University of Hawaii Press, 1981).

3. Translations were available, *Seneca's Morals: By Way of Abstract. To Which Is Prefixed the Life of the Author* (Bristol: Lansdown, 1807); *Moral Maxims* (London: Millar, 1749), p.22, 'The Clemency of Princes is often but a Piece of Policy to gain the Affections of their Subjects.'

4. M. Stokes, *Justice and Mercy in Piers the Plowman* (London: Croom Helm, 1983); F. Botana, *The Works of Mercy in Italian Medieval Art; Working for the after Life (c.1050–c.1400)* (Turnhout: Brepols, 2011).

5. E. Tonge, *Popish Mercy and Justice, Being an Account of Some Later Persecutions of the French Protestants Set Forth [by L. de l'Isle and others] in Their Petition to the French King* (London: Dawks, 1679); T. Puller, *The Moderation of the Church of England* (London: Chiswell, 1679); E. Lane, *Mercy Triumphant. The Kingdom of Christ Enlarged* (London: Crooke, 1680), on prodigies, see ch.1 below.

6. See Francis Bacon's advice to Sir George Villiers, in *Cabala, Sive Scrinia Sacra: Mysteries of State and Government, in Letters of Illustrious Persons, and Great Ministers of State* (London: Sawbridge, 1691), p.41, 'The execution of justice is committed to his judges which seemeth to be the severer part but the milder part which is mercy is wholly left in the king's immediate hand and justice and mercy are the true supporters of his royal throne.' Texts to study for eighteenth-century discourses of the virtues might include P. Warwick, *A Discourse of Government* (London: Wotton, 1701), where clemency appears, pp.69–70; J. Hartcliffe,

A Compleat Treatise of Moral and Intellectual Virtues (2nd edn; London: Hooke, 1722), pp.114, 185, 195.

7   E. Coke, *Third Part of the Institutes of the Laws of England: Concerning High Treason, and Other Pleas of the Crown, and Criminal Causes* (London: Flesher, 1644), ch.105, 'Of Pardons'. This and the next chapter, 'Restitutions' are classed in the table of contents as 'Works of mercy'.

8   *The Lady's Companion; or, an Infallible Guide to the Fair Sex* (4th edn; London: T. Read, 1743) ch.4, 'Of Compassion'.

9   For reflections on mercy from legal perspective, L.R. Meyer, *The Justice of Mercy* (Ann Arbor: University of Michigan Press, 2010); D. Cornwell, 'Justice and Punishment: Myths, Mercy and Anglo-Saxon Attitudes', in J. Blad, D.J. Cornwell and M. Wright, eds, *Civilising Criminal Justice: An International Restorative Agenda for Penal Reform* (Winchester: Waterside Press, 2013), pp.49–79.

10 J. Stefancic and R. Delgado, *No Mercy: How Conservative Thinktanks and Foundations Changed America's Social Agenda* (Philadelphia, PA: Temple University Press, 1996); A. Donini, *The Policies of Mercy: UN Coordination in Afghanistan, Mozambique, and Rwanda* (Providence, RI: Watson J. Watson Jr. Institute for International Studies, 1996); D. Dijkzeul, *Between Force and Mercy: Military Acts and Humanitarian Aid* (Berlin: Berliner Wissenschafts-Verlag, 2004).

11 J.J. Rousseau, *Emile* (1762), for comments (in translation) on sensibility, justice and mercy; Sarah Scott, for Ellison being chided, and defending his forgiveness, in *The Man of Real Sensibility: Or, The History of Sir George Ellison* (Edinburgh: Shireffs, 1797), p.15; John Thelwall's 'A Midnight Ramble', in J. Thelwall, ed., *The Peripatetic; or, Sketches of the Heart, of Nature and Society* (Southwark: the author, 1793), p.77, 'the pure and simple form of a milder persuasion, whose universal benevolence smiles endearment to the heart of Sensibility, whose cheerful precepts are founded on the convictions of reason; and which promises the perfection of Justice without the immolation of Mercy'.

12 On their definitions of emotions, see U. Frevert et al., *Emotional Lexicons: Continuity and Change in the Vocabulary of Feeling 1700–2000* (Oxford: Oxford University Press, 2014), this does not mention mercy or deal, p.4, with individual specific emotions. F. Nietzsche *Zur Genealogie der Moral* (1887), transl. H.B. Samuel, *On the Genealogy of Morals: A Polemic* (Edinburgh: Foulis, 1910), Essay II, '"Guilt" "Bad Conscience," and the Like', p.94.

13 J. Hanway, *An Earnest Appeal for Mercy to the Children of the Poor* (London: Dodsley, 1766).

14 For scripture marshalled by Protestants against salvation by good works, *The Protestant Magazine*, 1 December 1860, pp.101–2. The London publisher Joseph Masters included a reward book, *The Seven Corporal Works of Mercy – In Seven Tales. In a Packet*, see catalogue, July 1850, p.40.

15 *Encyclopaedia Metropolitana, or, Universal Dictionary of Knowledge* (London: Fellowes etc., 1845), vol.22, p.104; E.N. Hoare, *Exotics: Or, English Words Derived from Latin Roots: Ten Lectures* (Dublin: Hodges, Smith, 1863), p.299.

16 J. Derrida, *The Death Penalty* (2 vols; Chicago: University of Chicago Press, 2017), vol.2, eds. G. Bennington and M. Crépon, transl. E. Rottenberg, p.165. As this form of forbearance 'was attributed to courtesy and not to covetousness, the word "mercy" took the general sense of kindness', according to R.C. Brown, ed., *English Poems by John Milton* (2 vols, 2nd edn; Oxford: Clarendon Press, 1872), vol.2, p.323.

17 The original, 'novum imperium inchoantibus utilis clementiae fama', in Rochefoucauld, *Moral Maxims by the Duke de la Roche Foucault. Translated from the French with Notes* (London: Millar, 1749), p.22, from book 4 of Tacitus's *History*.
18 E.g. *The Popular Lecturer* vol.1, n.s. (Manchester: Heywood, 1856), p.141.
19 'Of Ethics, or Moral Virtues', in *Bibliotheca Technologica: Or, a Philological Library of Literary Arts and Sciences* (London: Noon, 1737), p.26.
20 J. Claude, *An Essay on the Composition of a Sermon*, tr. by R. Robinson (2 vols; Cambridge: Hodson, 1779), vol.2, p.150.
21 *Encyclopaedia Britannica* (18 vols; Edinburgh: Bell and Macfarquhar, 1797), vol.11, p.403.
22 G. Crabb, *English Synonymes Explained with Illustrations and Examples from the Best Writers* (London: Baldwin, 1824), p.222.
23 G. Crabb, *English Synonymes*, p.428, 'gracious, merciful, kind': 'Gracious, when compared to merciful, is used only in the spiritual sense, the latter is applicable to the conduct of man as well as of the Deity.'
24 W. Parks, *Notes on Sermons Hitherto Unpublished* (London: Collingridge, 1868), sermon XXV, 'Who Are the Blessed?' p.123.
25 *The Art of Knowing Mankind* (London: Wilkie, 1766), pp.208–9.
26 It is described as common-place, and by-word, criticized in G.S. Weaver, *Hopes and Helps for the Young of Both Sexes* (New York: Fowlers and Wells, 1854), p.156.
27 On the reasoning behind the phrase 'bowels of mercy', *The Works of Thomas Goodwin* (Edinburgh: Nichol, 1861), vol.2, p.179: 'Now there is no thing so intimate or so natural to man as his bowels are.' See J. Staines, 'Compassion in the Public Sphere of Milton and King Charles', in G.K. Paster, K. Rowe and M. Floyd-Wilson, eds, *Reading the Early Modern Passions: Essays in the Cultural History of Emotion* (Philadelphia: University of Pennsylvania Press, 2004), pp.89–110 [pp.100–1]. The Victorian Swedenborgian J.J.G. Wilkinson, in a work that refers to the breath of mercy, refers to the bowels as the site of sensibility 'or by a privileged name, the sense of mercy', *The Human Body and Its Connection with Man: Illustrated by the Principal Organs* (Philadelphia, PA: Lippincott, Grambo, 1851), p.241 (see also pp.226–8). See also J.D. Peters, 'Bowels of Mercy', *BYU Studies Quarterly* 38:4 (1999), pp.27–41.
28 See, as part of the mercy/justice trope in illness, 'On recovering from a Fever', *British Magazine*, February 1762, pp.103–4; *Gentleman's Magazine* 76:1 (1806), p.455, anniversary festival of the Royal Jennerian Society: 'O, shield us, shield us, MERCY, or we die | O shield us, MERCY: is a nation's cry.'
29 See 'fair' by Philip Durkin at http://keywords.pitt.edu/keywords_defined/fair.html. For a useful discussion of Williams's keywords as concept (and words and concepts), see R. Kalas, *Frame, Glass, Verse: The Technology of Poetic Invention in the English Renaissance* (Ithaca, NY: Cornell University Press, 2007), pp.80–1.
30 M. Fortier, *The Culture of Equity in Restoration and Eighteenth-Century Britain and America* (London: Routledge, 2015). On altruism, see T. Dixon, *The Invention of Altruism: Making Moral Meanings in Victorian Britain* (Oxford: Oxford University Press for the British Academy, 2008). Further references to works on pity and forgiveness appear below.
31 On bringing amnesties – previously an unfettered exercise in 'mercy' by a sovereign power – under international law, K. McEvoy and L. Mallinder, 'Amnesties in Transition: Punishment, Restoration, and the Governance of Mercy', *Journal of Law and Society* 39:3 (September 2012), pp.410–40.

32 Monographic treatment of mercy in relation to religion, legal and political perspectives includes J. Murphy and J. Hampton, *Forgiveness and Mercy* (Cambridge: Cambridge University Press, 1988); K.D. Moore, *Pardons: Justice, Mercy and the Public Interest* (New York: Oxford University Press, 1997); C. Strange ed., *Qualities of Mercy: Justice, Punishment and Discretion* (Vancouver: UBC Press, 2001); J. Rothchild et al., eds, *Doing Justice to Mercy: Religion, Law, and Criminal Justice* (Charlottesville: University of Virginia Press, 2007); A. Sarat and N. Hussain, eds, *Forgiveness, Mercy and Clemency* (Stanford, CA: Stanford University Press, 2006); J.E. Gilman, *Christian Faith, Justice, and a Politics of Mercy: The Benevolent Community* (Lanham, MD: Lexington Books, 2014).
33 See M. Welker, 'The Power of Mercy in Biblical Law', *Journal of Law and Religion* 29:2 (June 2014), pp.225–35; L.E. Newman, 'Balancing Justice and Mercy. Reflections on Forgiveness in Judaism', *Journal of Religious Ethics* 41:3 (2013), pp.435–56.
34 See W. Zyzak, 'Mercy as a Theological Term', *The Person and the Challenges* 5:1 (2015), pp.137–53; A. Keaty, 'The Christian Virtue of Mercy: Aquinas' Transformation of Aristotelian Pity', *Heythrop Journal* 46:2 (2005), pp.181–95.
35 On Aristotle and Plato on pity, Keaty, 'The Christian Virtue of Mercy', pp.181–5.
36 Zyzak, 'Mercy as a Theological Term', pp.138–9.
37 A. Smart, 'Mercy', *Philosophy* 43 (October 1968), pp.345–59; C. Card, 'On Mercy', *Philosophical Review* 81 (April 1972), pp.182–207. Card contributed 'Mercy' in L.C. Becker and C.B. Becker, eds, *Encyclopedia of Ethics* (New York: Routledge, 2001). John Kleinig's response, 'Mercy and Justice', *Philosophy* 44:170 (October 1969), pp.341–2, identified mercy in benevolence to those with no entitlement or claim and suggested this 'broader conception' is the 'ordinary' view. H.S. Hestevold, 'Justice to Mercy', *Philosophy and Phenomenological Research* 46:2 (December 1985), pp.282–91 acknowledges (p.288) 'acts of mercy' are left out of philosophical debate but merely suggests they are appropriately described as 'charity'. Perhaps, but this ignores historic usage.
38 H.R.T. Roberts, 'Mercy', *Philosophy* 46:178 (1971), pp.352–3.
39 J.G. Murphy and J. Hampton, *Forgiveness and Mercy* (Cambridge: Cambridge University Press, 1988); see also; J.G. Murphy, 'Mercy and Legal Justice', *Social Philosophy and Policy* 4:1 (1986), pp.1–14; J.G. Murphy, 'Repentance, Punishment, and Mercy', in A. Etzioni and D.E. Carney, eds, *Repentance: A Comparative Perspective* (Lanham, MD: Rowman and Littlefield, 1997), pp.143–70; J.G. Murphy, 'Remorse, Apology, and Mercy', *Ohio State Journal of Criminal Law* 4 (2007), pp.423–53. A good response is C.S. Steiker, 'Murphy on Mercy: A Prudential Reconsideration', *Criminal Justice Ethics* 27:2 (2008), pp.45–54; see also N.E. Simmonds, 'Judgement and Mercy', *Oxford Journal of Legal Studies* 13:1 (March 1993), pp.52–68.
40 M.C. Nussbaum, 'Equity and Mercy', *Philosophy and Public Affairs* 22 (1993), pp.83–125; P. Gallagher, 'The Grounding of Forgiveness: Martha Nussbaum on Compassion and Mercy', *The American Journal of Economics and Sociology* 68:1 (2009), pp. 231–52. See also C.A.H. Johnson, 'Entitled to Clemency: Mercy in the Criminal Law', *Law and Philosophy* 10 (1991), pp.109–18. On mercy's relationship to equity, A. Brien, 'Mercy within the Legal System', *Social Theory and Practice* 24 (1998), pp.83–106 [pp.90–5].
41 N. Walker, 'The Quiddity of Mercy', *Philosophy* 70 (1995), pp.27–37; J. Tasioulas, 'Mercy', *Proceedings of the Aristotelian Society* 103: 2 (2003), pp.101–32; N. Markosian, 'Two Puzzles about Mercy', *Philosophical Quarterly* 63:251 (April 2013),

pp.169–292; B.D. Marshall, '"Tolle me et redime te": Anselm on the Justice and Mercy of God', *The Thomist* 81:2 (April 2017), pp.161–81. See also A. Brien, 'Mercy and Desert', *Philosophical Papers* 20 (1991), pp.193–201 and G.B. Sadler, 'Mercy and Justice in St Anselm's *Proslogion*', *American Catholic Philosophical Quarterly* 80:1 (2006), pp.41–61.

42 Tasioulas, 'Mercy', pp.101–2, p.104.
43 H.S. Hestevold, 'Disjunctive Desert', *American Philosophical Quarterly* 20:4 (October 1983), pp.357–63. For a critique of Hestevold's position, W.F. Ransome, '"Above the Sceptered Sway": Retrieving the Quality of Mercy', *Critica, Revista Hispanoamericana de Filosofia* 40:119 (August 2008), pp.3–27 [p.7].
44 For further essays from this perspective, Brien, 'Mercy within the Legal System'; S.P. Garvey, '"As the Gentle Rain from Heaven": Mercy in Capital Sentencing', *Cornell Law Review* 81 (1996), pp.989–1048.
45 W.F. Ransome, '"Above the Sceptered Sway" …', p.5.
46 T. Tallbott, 'Punishment, Forgiveness, and Divine Justice', *Religious Studies* 29:2 (June 1993), pp.151–68; R. Hollyer, 'Justice and Mercy: A Reply to Thomas Talbott', *Religious Studies* 30 (1994), pp.287–94.
47 Hollyer, 'Justice and Mercy', p.290. Justifying hell in terms of God's mercy, see B. Brown, 'Raymund Schwager on the Dramatic Justice and Mercy of God', *International Journal of Systematic Theology* 17:2 (April 2015), pp.212–28.
48 J. Rothchild, 'Dispenser of the Mercy of Government: Pardons, Justice, and Felony Disenfranchisement', *Journal of Religious Ethics* 39:1 (March 2011), pp.48–70.
49 M. Whitebrook, 'Compassion as a Political Virtue', *Political Studies* 50 (2002), pp.529–44 [p.530] distinguishes between mercy, which involves the 'objective' situation of a perpetrator in a social or political context, and pity/compassion, expressing 'direct feelings towards the particular other'. But historic usage subverts neat distinction. N. Eustace, *Passion Is the Gale: Emotion, Power, and the Coming of the American Revolution* (Chapel Hill: University of North Carolina Press, 2008), defines pity as censorious emotion, combining sentiment and blame (p.270).
50 A. Osanloo, 'The Measure of Mercy: Islamic Justice, Sovereign Power, and Human Rights in Iran', *Cultural Anthropology* 21:4 (November 2006), pp.570–602; A.S. Mohamed and R. Ofteringer, '"Rahmatan lil-'alamin" (A mercy to all creation): Islamic Voices in the Debate on Humanitarian Principles', *International Review of the Red Cross* 97 (2015), pp.371–94.
51 Welker, 'The Power of Mercy in Biblical Law', p.231. Also note 'mercy' as a seemingly 'outdated' term in T.P. Daaleman, 'The Quality of Mercy. Will You Be My Doctor?' *Journal of the American Medical Association* 312:18 (12 November 2014), pp.1863–4.
52 Zyzak, 'Mercy as a Theological Term', quoting Terry A. Veling, 'In the Name of Mercy: A Meditative Exploration', *Pacifica-Australasian Theological Studies* 22 (June 2009).
53 Gilman, *Christian Faith, Justice, and a Politics of Mercy*.
54 *An Essay on Crimes and Punishments. By the Marquis Beccaria of Milan. With a Commentary by M. De Voltaire* (Edinburgh: Donaldson, 1788), pp.167–8.
55 Welker, 'The Power of Mercy in Biblical Law', p.231. Critics of mercy include A.T. Nuyen, 'Straining the Quality of Mercy', *Philosophical Papers* 23 (1994), pp.61–74.
56 W.F. Ransome, '"Above the Sceptered Sway …', pp.3–27, for a recent effort to restore the praiseworthy quality of mercy outside the law.
57 Walker, 'The Quiddity of Mercy', p.35.
58 J. Pearn, 'The Quiddity of Mercy – A Response', *Philosophy* 71 (1996), pp.603–4.

59 Zyzak, 'Mercy as a Theological Term', pp.145–6.
60 Tasioulas, 'Mercy', p.104.
61 C. Deane-Drummond, 'Empathy and the Evolution of Compassion: From Deep History to Infused Virtue', *Zygon* 52:1 (March 2017), pp.258–78.
62 B. Straight, 'Uniquely Human: Cultural Norms and Private Acts of Mercy in the War Zone', *American Anthropologist* 119:3 (September 2017), pp.491–505.
63 J.J. Exline, E.L. Worthington, P. Hill and M.E. McCullough, 'Forgiveness and Justice: A Research Agenda for Social and Personality Psychology', *Personality and Social Psychology Review* 7:4 (2003), pp.337–48, focused on forgiveness, identifies mercy as a 'related construct'. C. Van Oyen Witvliet, T.E. Ludwig, and D.J. Bauer, 'Please Forgive Me: Transgressors' Emotions and Physiology during Imagery of Seeking Forgiveness and Victim Responses', *Journal of Psychology & Christianity* 21:3 (Fall 2002), pp.219–33, examines the physical impact of 'imagery of forgiveness seeking and merciful responses from victims', studying emotional engagement and negative or positive emotions. On the philosophical dimensions to forgiveness, part from works cited already dealing with it alongside mercy, see L. Allais, 'Wiping the Slate Clean: The Heart of Forgiveness', *Philosophy & Public Affairs* 36:1 (Winter 2008), pp.33–68.
64 H. Lacey, *The Royal Pardon: Access to Mercy in Fourteenth-Century England* (York: York Medieval Press, 2009); For earlier kingly mercy, 'Christianisation of the Royal Duty' in W.A. Chaney, *The Cult of Kingship in Anglo-Saxon England: The Transition from Paganism to Christianity* (Berkeley: University of California Press, 1970), p.256. K.J. Kesselring, *Mercy and Authority in the Tudor State* (Cambridge: Cambridge University Press, 2003). K. Sharpe, *Rebranding Rule: The Restoration and Revolution Monarchy, 1660–1714* (New Haven, CT: Yale University Press, 2013), p.30, p.473. An overview of the wider history of the pardoning power is L. Sebba, 'Clemency in Perspective', in S.F. Landau and L. Sebba, eds, *Criminology in Perspective: Essays in Honor of Israel Drapkin* (Lexington, MA: Lexington, 1977), pp.221–40.
65 D. Hay, 'Property, Authority and the Criminal Law', in D. Hay, P. Linebaugh, J.G. Rule, E.P. Thompson and C. Winslow, *Albion's Fatal Tree: Crime and Society in Eighteenth-Century England* (London: Allen Lane, 1975), pp.17–63.
66 Hay, 'Property, Authority and the Criminal Law', p.54.
67 Hay, 'Property, Authority and the Criminal Law', p.39, p.49.
68 C. Strange, *Qualities of Mercy: Justice, Punishment, and Discretion* (Vancouver: University of British Columbia Press, 1996), p.3.
69 T. McGeary, *The Politics of Opera in Handel's Britain* (Cambridge: Cambridge University Press, 2013), p.244.
70 The literature is vast, but see J. Plamper, *The History of Emotions. An Introduction*, transl. K. Tribe (2012; New York: Oxford University Press, 2015); U. Frevert, *Emotions in History – Lost and Found* (New York: Central European University Press, 2011), ch.3 discusses compassion, and inter alia mercy and pity; S. Broomhall, ed., *Early Modern Emotions: An Introduction* (Abingdon: Routledge, 2017) includes K. Ibbett, 'Fellow-feeling' in II.10, pp.61–4 which notes the impact for the eighteenth century of mistranslating Aristotelian 'pity' as sympathy (p.63); see also J. McEwan's discussion of mercy under 'III.8 Judicial Sources', e.g. p.113.
71 On compassion, F. Mirguet, *An Early History of Compassion: Emotion and Imagination in Hellenistic Judaism* (Cambridge: Cambridge University Press, 2017); N.S. Fiering, 'Irresistible Compassion: An Aspect of Eighteenth-Century Sympathy and Humanitarianism', *Journal of the History of Ideas* 37 (1976),

pp.195–218; K. Ibbett, 'Fellow-feeling', in Broomhall, ed., *Early Modern Emotions* and her *Compassion's Edge: Fellow Feeling and Its Limits in Early Modern France* (Philadelphia: University of Pennsylvania Press, 2017); A. Cullhed, 'A World of Fiction: Bengt Lidner and Global Compassion in Eighteenth-Century Sweden', in G. Rydén, ed., *Sweden in the Eighteenth-Century World: Provincial Cosmopolitans* (Farnham: Ashgate, 2013), pp.301–24; L. Berland, ed., *Compassion: The Culture and Politics of an Emotion* (New York: Routledge, 2004). On mercy's relationship with compassion, see C.G. Finney, *Lectures on Systematic Theology, Embracing Moral Government, The Atonement, Etc. Revised, Enlarged, and Partly Re-Written by the Author* (London: Tegg, 1851), p.204. On pity, see D. Punter, *The Literature of Pity* (Edinburgh: Edinburgh University Press, 2014), and contrasting classical and modern pity, D. Konstan, *Pity Transformed* (London: Duckworth, 2001).

72 A. Garrett, 'Human Nature' in K. Haakonssen, ed., *The Cambridge History of Eighteenth-Century Philosophy* (2 vols; Cambridge: Cambridge University Press, 2006), vol.1, pp.173–7, citing Bernard Mandeville's *Fable of the Bees* (1714) and John Oswald's *Cry of Nature* (1791).

73 M.L. Frazer, *The Enlightenment of Sympathy: Justice and the Moral Sentiments in the Eighteenth Century and Today* (New York: Oxford University Press, 2010).

74 *Über den Prozeß der Zivilisation* (1939), translated in two volumes as *The Civilizing Process* in 1978.

75 Eustace, *Passion Is the Gale*, p.5 ('tempest'), p.13 (distinguishing pity and mercy). Eustace explores the vocabulary of this shared feeling in ch.6, '"The Turnings of the Human Heart": Sympathy, Social Signals, and the Self'.

76 Eustace, *Passion Is the Gale*, p.240.

77 Eustace, *Passion Is the Gale*, pp.267–8, p.274.

78 Eustace, *Passion Is the Gale*, p.275.

79 M.C. Oziewiz, *Justice in Young Adult Speculative Fiction: A Cognitive Reading* (New York: Routledge, 2015).

80 See, for discussion of mercy as part of self, R. Chambers, 'The Aliases of Self', in R. Chambers, ed., *Select Writings of Robert Chambers. Volume III. Essays, Moral and Economic* (Edinburgh: Chambers, 1847), p.59.

81 Napoleon's reputation concerning mercy is discussed in a later chapter, for Cromwell, O. Cromwell, *Memoirs of the Protector, Oliver Cromwell: And of His Sons, Richard and Henry* (London: Longman, Hurst, Rees, Orme, and Brown, 1820). For compassionate characteristics in earlier biography, I. Sulimani, *Diodorus' Mythistory and the Pagan Mission: Historiography and Culture-Heroes in the First Pentad of the Bibliotheke* (Leiden: Brill, 2011), pp.106–8.

82 E.B. Ramsay, *Diversities of Christian Character Illustrated in the Lives of the Four Great Apostles* (London: Blackwood, 1858), p.132.

83 Unsurprisingly, in Quaker biography, e.g. *Journal of the Gospel Labours of George Richardson: A Minister in the Society of Friends, with a Biographical Sketch of His Life and Character* (London: Bennett, 1864); reference to recording mercy appears in the obituary of Barbara Burn (1734–1810) of Hull, *Evangelical Magazine* 20 (January 1812), p.12.

84 On 'small mercies', W. Garden Blaikie, 'Are The Conditions of Life Improving?' *Quiver* 27:241 (January 1892), pp.758–60.

85 And accessed through digitized collections such as *British and Irish Women's Letters and Diaries* (Alexander Street).

86 Eustace, *Passion Is the Gale*, pp.271–5.

87 E. Cleall, 'From Divine Judgement to Colonial Courts: Missionary "Justice" in British India, c.1840–1914', *Cultural and Social History* 14:4 (2017), pp.447–61.
88 *Nineteenth Century Collections Online* (Gale) provides a useful means to access British (and American) religious newspapers, such as *The Friend* and *Expository Times*. The *Literature Online* database (ProQuest) was used to identify more obscure nineteenth-century poetry on mercy.
89 J. Hambleton, *Sermons on the Fifty-Third Chapter of Isaiah, The Beatitudes, and Other Subjects* (2nd edn; London: Hatchard, 1832), p.186.

Chapter 1

1 A. Alison, *The Philosophy and History of Civilisation* (London: Chapman and Hall, 1860), p.423.
2 For reviews, *The Athenaeum*, 22 December 1860, p.868; *Saturday Review*, 22 December 1860, p.802; *The Spectator*, 24 November 1860, p.1124; *London Review*, 8 December 1860, p.549.
3 As the Scottish surgeon James Meikle reflected in 1758, *The Traveller: Or, Meditations on Various Subjects, Written on Board a Man of War* (Pittsburgh: Patterson, 1815), p.149.
4 'Eumenes', 'The Triumph of Mercy', *Evangelical Magazine and Missionary Chronicle* 7 (1799), pp.61–4; 'Adolescens', 'Mercy and Judgment', *Evangelical Magazine* 20 (August 1812), pp.301–3.
5 J. Leifchild, *The Christian Temper, or Lectures on the Beatitudes* (2nd edn; London: Holdsworth, 1822), pp.180–216 [p.181, p.189].
6 W.J. Irons, *Analysis of Human Responsibility. Being Three Papers Read before the Victoria Institute, or Philosophical Society of Great Britain, on February 1st, March 1st, and June 7th, 1869* (London: Hardwicke, 1869), p.70.
7 *London Magazine*, July 1768, p.366.
8 See M.W. Chapman, ed., *Harriet Martineau's Autobiography* (3rd edn; 3 vols; London: Smith, Elder, 1877), vol.2, p.185, 'I had long seen that the orthodox fruitlessly attempt to get rid of the difficulty by presenting the two-fold aspect of God, – the Father being the model of justice, and the Son of love and mercy.'
9 J. Fleetwood, *Christian Dictionary* (London: Cooke, 1775).
10 J. Brown, *A Dictionary of the Holy Bible* (London: Tegg, 1824), p.455. See entries on 'mercy' and 'mercy of God' in C. Buck, *A Theological Dictionary* (2 vols; Whitehall, PA: Woodward, 1807), vol.2, pp.99–102.
11 *Passion Is the Gale*, p.268.
12 See L.M. Stretch, *Beauties of History; or, Pictures of Virtue and Vice* (1770; London: Brambles, 1808); [J.S. Robertson and T. Byerley], *Humanity – Beneficence* (London: T. Boys, 1820), vol.1 in the twenty-volume *Percy Anecdotes* series.
13 Thus, *The Earthen Vessel: And Christian Record & Review for 1850*, serializing Ralph Erskine's 'Prayer for Mercy, a Seasonable Duty in Times of Sin and Wrath', pp.72–4.
14 See *The Pulpit Cyclopædia, and Christian Minister's Companion* (London: Houlston and Stoneman, 1844), p.86, p.110, p.278. See, from Congregationalism, *Descending on Humanity and Intervening in History: Notes from the Pulpit Ministry of P. T. Forsyth* (Eugene, OR: Pickwick, 2013). For notes on mercy as a sermon subject from Reverend John Angell James in Birmingham, M. Broyles, ed., *A Yankee Musician in*

Europe: The 1837 Journals of Lowell Mason (Rochester, NY: University of Rochester Press, 1990), p.128; on James's 'Christian mercy explained and enforced', T.S. James, ed., *The Works of John Angell James* (London: Hamilton: 1860), vol.1, *Sermons*, pp.209–42.

15 H. Begbie, *The Latest Thing* (London: Hutchinson, 1920), p.115.
16 See 'Dr Southey's Sir Thomas More', an anonymous review in the utilitarian *Westminster Review* 11:21 (July 1829), pp.193–211 [p.199]: 'People thus assailed, are to be saved "by the mercy of God – only by the mercy of God!" as if that mercy was not as signally displayed through the instrumentality of man.'
17 *Letters of Anna Seward: Written between the Years 1784 and 1806* (Edinburgh: Constable, 1811), vol.6, p.240.
18 J.S. *Divine Judgment and Mercy Exemplified, in a Variety of Surprizing Instances* (London: 1746), p.2. The letters within, are dated 1692. 'Robert Burton' i.e. Nathaniel Crouch, *Wonderful Prodigies of Judgment and Mercy, Discovered in near Three Hundred Memorable Histories* (1682; 8th edn; London: Bettesworth, 1729), p.4. For earlier clerical authors, Thomas Beard, Samuel Clarke and William Turner, see D.D. Hall, 'A World of Wonders: The Mentality of the Supernatural in Seventeenth-Century New England', in D.D. Hall and D.G. Allen, eds, *Seventeenth-Century New England* (Boston, MA: The Colonial Society of Massachusetts, 1984), pp.239–74 [p.245] and ch.2 in Hall's *Worlds of Wonder, Days of Judgment: Popular Religious Belief in Early New England* (Cambridge, MA: Harvard University Press, 1989).
19 'Mercy', *Lady's Magazine*, May 1778, p.271, concerned with Christ's atonement and the mercy of God.
20 'On Mercy', in J. Grose, *Ethics, Rational and Theological: With Cursory Reflections on the General Principles of Deism* (London: for the author, 1782), p.180.
21 *Dublin Review*, July–October 1876, p.259.
22 See the review of a later edition of Cox, *Gentleman's Magazine*, April 1849, p.396; J. Culross, *Divine Compassion; or, Jesus Shewing Mercy* (London: James Nisbet, 1864).
23 R. Boswell, *Lines Sacred & Lyric* (Printed for private circulation, 1820), p.21.
24 'The Mercy of God' in T. Watson, *A Body of Practical Divinity, Consisting Of Above One Hundred Seventy Six Sermons on the Lesser Catechism, Composed by the Reverend Assembly of Divines* (3rd edn; Glasgow: Tweedie, 1759), p.56.
25 H.J. Berman, *Law and Revolution. II. The Impact of the Protestant Reformation on the Western Legal Tradition* (Cambridge, MA: Harvard University Press, 2003), p.329, for theological tension between justice and mercy in assize sermons, citing Zachariah Mudge's before the assizes at Exeter in 1732. See also T. Herring, *A Sermon Preached before the Right Honourable the Lord-Mayor, the Court of Aldermen, the Sheriffs, and the Governors of the Several Hospitals of the City of London: At the Parish Church of St. Bridget, on Monday in Easter-week* (London: Pemberton, 1739). See also J. Conybeare, *The Virtue of Being Merciful Stated And Enforc'd* (London: Birt, John and Rivington, 1751). For Victorian clergymen debating divine mercy and justice, e.g. F.W. Robertson, 'Lecture XLV' [12 December 1852], in *Sermons Preached at Trinity Chapel, Brighton* (2 vols; Boston, MA: Fields, Osgood, 1869), vol.2, p.342. For conventional reflections in context of a national day of humiliation, F.D. Gilby, '*Mercy Rejoiceth against Judgment*'. *A Sermon Preached in St James's Church, Cheltenham, on Tuesday, Sept, 25, 1849, In Aid of the Cheltenham Orphan Asylum* (Cheltenham: Davies, 1849); for another sermon on mercy, J. Gregg, 'Misery and Mercy', *Church of England Magazine* 29:840 (24 August 1850), p.135.

26 'Letter III. Propositions implied in the doctrine of satisfaction' in *Letters to the Revd. John Pye Smith, D.D., on the Sacrifice of Christ: Occasioned by His Sermon Preached March 11, 1813, before the Patrons and Students of the Protestant Dissenting Academy at Homerton* (London: R. Taylor, 1813), p.20.

27 *Christian Telescope* (Providence) 2:9, 1 October 1825, p.36.

28 'On Capital Punishment', *Baptist Magazine*, July 1839, pp.301–6 [p.301].

29 *Leeds Times*, 13 July 1839, p.5; *The Examiner*, 14 July 1839, p.2.

30 R. M'Gregor, *Truth Vindicated in a Letter to a Friend. By R. M'Gregor. Recommended by George Townsend* (Ramsgate: Townsend, c.1775?), p.5.

31 *The Grand Assizes; or General Gaol Delivery* (Dublin: Watson, c.1796); H. More, *The Works of Hannah More* (11 vols; London: Cadell, 1830), vol.4, pp.74–84 [p.74].

32 R. Phillip, *The God of Glory, or a Guide to the Doubting* (4th edn; London: Ward, 1836), p.88.

33 E.g. Methodist theologian Adam Clark, *Discourses on Various Subjects Relative to the Being and Attributes of God, and His Works in Creation, Providence, and Grace* (3rd edn; vol.1; New York: M'Elrath and Bangs, 1830), p.129; T. Cotterill, *An Assize Sermon, Intended to Illustrate the Nature and Necessity of Laws* (London: Cadell and Davies, 1816), p.30. See also, *The Whole Works of the Right Reverend Edward Reynolds* (6 vols; London: Holdsworth, 1826), vol.1, p.119.

34 W.M. Punshon, *The New Handbook of Illustration; or, Treasury of Themes, Meditations* (London: Eliot Stock, 1874), pp.272–6.

35 M. Cornwallis, *Observations, Critical, Explanatory, and Practical, on the Canonical Scriptures* (4 vols; London: Baldwin, Cradock and Joy, 1817), vol.1, p.34. Revelations, verse 3, 'And He that sat was to look upon like a jasper and a sardine stone', glossed in W. Ramsay, *Lectures on the Revelation* (Edinburgh: Grant and Taylor, 1850), p.96. See G.P. Landow, *Images of Crisis: Literary Iconology, 1750 to the Present* (London: Routledge & Kegan Paul, 1982). For the rainbow in arguments about mercy, H. Primatt, *The Duty of Mercy and the Sin of Cruelty to Brute Animals* (1776; Edinburgh, 1834), p.282, 'the Token'; for sermons on the rainbow, G.P. Hough, *Sermons Preached at St Andrew's church, Ham Common, Surrey* (London: Hatchards, 1849), pp.1–20.

36 Milton writes about divine mercy in Book III of *Paradise Lost*, 'but that which first and last shall shine the brightest, shall be Mercy'. See A.D. Weiner, '"Die he or Justice must": Justice, Law, and Mercy in Book V of *The Faerie Queene*, *Measure for Measure*, and *Paradise Lost*', in A.D. Weiner and L.V. Kaplan, eds, *On Interpretation: Studies in Culture, Law, and the Sacred* (Madison: University of Wisconsin Press, 2002), pp.102–26.

37 See *Methodist Review* (New York: Soule and Mason, 1819), March 1819, pp.110–13; *The Jewish Expositor, and Friend of Israel*, September 1818, p.344; *The Christian's Penny Magazine* 1 (1832), p.237.

38 G. Carlyle, ed., *The Collected Writings of Edward Irving* (5 vols; London: Strahan, 1864), vol. 2, p.163.

39 For defence, at mid-century, Burney Prize essayist, G.M. Gorham, *The Eternal Duration of Future Punishments Is Not Inconsistent with the Divine Attributes of Justice and Mercy* (Cambridge: Deighton, 1852).

40 B. Jowett, 'On the Interpretation of Scripture', ch.7 in *Essays and Reviews* (London: Parker, 1860), p.385.

41 On this point, in relation to the parable, 'The Prodigal Son. VII. The Way Home', *The Sunday at Home* 77 (18 October 1855), pp.657–62 [p.657].

42 J. Seeley, *Ecce Homo: A Survey of the Life and Work of Jesus Christ* (London: Macmillan, 1866), chapters 19–20, 'The Law of Mercy'.
43 F.W. Farrar, *Mercy and Judgement: A Few Last Words on Christian Eschatology* (London: Macmillan, 1881), p.448. See M. Wheeler, *Heaven, Hell and the Victorians* (Cambridge: Cambridge University Press, 1994) on divine mercy. See B. Hilton, *The Age of Atonement: The Influence of Evangelicalism on Social and Economic Thought, 1785–1865* (Oxford: Clarendon Press, 1988).
44 J.C. Morison, *The Service of Man: An Essay towards the Religion of The Future* (London: Kegan Paul, 1887), p.57.
45 A sermon at St Saviour's Church, Oxford Street, July 1876, widely reported in the press, e.g. *Manchester Evening News*, 17 July 1876, p.4.
46 *The Inquisition in Spain, and Other Countries* (London: Religious Tract Society, 1853), p.6.
47 J.M. De Maistre, *Letters on the Spanish Inquisition* (London: Keating, 1838), p.32. For Catholic critique of unmercy by Protestants, P. Maclachlan, *The True Religion, What It Is: Or, a Protestant's Objections to Catholicity Fully and Fairly Answered. In a Series of Letters to R. W. Kennard* (Edinburgh: Marsh and Beattie, 1855), e.g. pp.86–7 demand for the Catholic Earl of Huntly's death, even though suing for pardon.
48 K.H. Digby, *Mores Catholici: Or Ages of Faith* (London: Dolman, 1846), vol.2, p.286.
49 Ibid., p.306.
50 Ibid., p.511.
51 E.g. Church of Ireland dean, R. Graves, *Calvinistic Predestination Repugnant to the General Tenour of Scripture* (Dublin: Hodges, Smith, 1859), p.34.
52 J. Simpson, 'Phrenological Analysis of Eloquence', *Edinburgh Phrenological Journal*, reprinted in *American Phrenological Journal* 30: 6 (December 1859), pp.85–6. Actually Chalmers, 'The Effect of Man's Wrath in the Agitation of Religious Controversies', *Sermons and Discourses* (2 vols; New York, Carter, 1844), vol.1, p.256, speaks of justification by the righteousness of Christ. Chalmers refers much to the mercy of God in his writings.
53 J. Sturrock, *'Heaven and Home': Charlotte M. Yonge's Domestic Fiction and the Victorian Debate over Women* (Victoria, BC: University of Victoria, 1995), p.53; C.M. Yonge, *The Three Brides* (2 vols; Leipzig: Tauchnitz, 1876), vol.1, p.260.
54 *What One Work of Mercy Can I Do This Lent? A Letter to a Friend* (London: Burns, 1847), p.16, and pp.3–4, where mercy acts in Lent are listed as education, admonition of sinners, almsgiving and reconciliation of enemies.
55 C.I Foster's transatlantic study of evangelicalism is *An Errand of Mercy: The Evangelical United Front, 1790–1837* (Chapel Hill: University of North Carolina Press, 1960).
56 H. Budd, *Infant Baptism, the Means of National Reformation, According to the Doctrine and Discipline of the Established Church; in Nine Letters to a Friend* (London: Seeley, 1826), p.vi; on this latter point, see Reverend Hugh M'Neile, 'A Sermon, Preached at St Bride's Church, Fleet Street, on Monday Evening, 5 May 1845, before the Church Missionary Society', in *Proceedings of the Church Missionary Society for Africa and the East. Forty-Fifth Year. 1844–1845* (London: Hatchard, 1845), p.11.
57 R.J. Cruikshank, *Charles Dickens and Early Victorian England* (London: Pitman, 1949), p.182.
58 For divine mercy in wills, M.J. Trevelyan, *The Life and Letters of Zachary Macaulay* (London: Arnold, 1900), p.484. For mercy in hymns by evangelicals, e.g. Rowland Hill's 'Pastoral Hymn', and 'A Song in Adversity', reprinted in W. Jones, *Memoir of*

the Rev. Rowland Hill, M.A. (London: H.G. Bohn, 1845), pp.573–5. Mercy figures in hymnals of the Church of England, see sixteenth-century 'Lamentation of a Sinner' published in English in 1561 with words by John Marckant and reprinted, e.g. *The Book of Common Prayer, and Administration of the Sacraments and Other Rites and Ceremonies of the Church, According to the Use of the United Church of England and Ireland, Together with the Psalter or Psalms of David* (Cambridge: Smith, 1816), p.84.

59 *Some Account of the Life and Writings of Mrs Trimmer, with Original Letters, and Meditations and Prayers, Selected from Her Journals* (London: Rivington and Johnson, 1814), vol. 2, p.326; W. Roberts, *Memoirs of the Life of Mrs Hannah More* (2 vols; London: Seeley and Burnside, 1836), vol.2, pp.16–17; C. Buxton, *Memoirs of Sir Thomas Fowell Buxton, Bart* (5th edn; London: Murray, 1866), p.44.

60 W. Carus, *Memoir of the Rev. Charles Simeon. Late Senior Fellow of King's College and Minister of Trinity Church, Cambridge, with a Selection from His Writings and Correspondence* (London: Hatchard, 1856): refers to pardoning, free, unspeakable, rich, tender, peculiar, great, infinite, unbounded mercy; a similar frequency of mercy references is in *Memoir of the Rev. Edward Bickersteth: Late Rector of Watton, Herts* (2 vols; New York: Harper, 1851), from which the quote derives, vol.1, p.193. The heroine of the famous tract by the Reverend Leigh Richmond, *The Dairyman's Daughter; an Authentic Narrative* (Chelsea: Religious Tract Society, 1812), dies a 'vessel' and 'monument of the Redeemer's mercy', pp.46–8.

61 W. Wilberforce, *Practical View of the Prevailing Religious System of Professed Christians* (2nd edn; London: Cadell and Davies, 1797), p.124.

62 See J. Macpherson, *Life and Labors of Duncan Matheson, the Scottish Evangelist* (New York: Carter, 1876), p.176. The journal aimed to awaken and convert sinners.

63 J. Manners, *England's Trust and Other Poems* (London: Rivington, 1841), p.34. On controversy in British Protestantism see S. Mumm, *Stolen Daughters, Virgin Mothers: Anglican Sisterhoods in Victorian Britain* (London: Leicester University Press, 1999).

64 E. Cleall, 'From Divine Judgement to Colonial Courts'. Cleall considers compassion and mercy as 'specific aspects of justice', p.448 in her argument about gendering of justice but while justice is polyvalent, we should be attentive to separate but allied concepts (such as mercy, truth, humanity).

65 Report of the formation of the Cambridge Auxiliary Bible Society, p.47, quoted in *Reports of the British and Foreign Bible Society 3. For the Year 1814 and 1815* (London: for the Society, 1815), p.75, balances 'thunder of her power' with 'blessings of her beneficence', see E. Elbourne, 'The Foundation of the Church Missionary Society: the Anglican missionary impulse', in J. Walsh, C. Haydon and S. Taylor, eds, *The Church of England c.1689–c.1833: from Toleration to Tractarianism* (Cambridge: Cambridge University Press, 1993), pp.247–64 [p.263].

66 'Persecutions in Tinnevelly', *Church Missionary Gleaner*, November 1842, p.132.

67 E.P. Miller, 'Secluded Lives in Hausaland', *Church Missionary Gleaner*, 2 August 1815, p.118.

68 'Emulating Christianity', *Church Missionary Gleaner*, 1 December 1915, p.181.

69 See *Proceedings of the Church Missionary Society for Africa and the East. Eighteenth Year: 1817–1818* (London: Bensley, 1818), p.14; and, in the same, *Report of the Committee Delivered to the Annual Meeting Held May 5, 1818*, p.51; 'Compassion, a motive to missionary exertion', *Church Missionary Gleaner*, February 1842, pp.13–15.

70 H.C. Mullens, *Prsanna and Kamini. The History of a Young Hindu* (London: Religious Tract Society, 1885), p.115. This, by Hannah Mullens of Calcutta, was translated into Hindi and serialized in an Anglo-Hindi monthly.

71 For argument that all healing was an 'expression of the will of Christ', and a 'work of Christian mercy', see review of R.L. Langford-James, *The Church and Bodily Healing* in *Church Times*, 12 April 1929, p.444.

72 The introductory discussion by W.E. Burroughs, 'Our Title', *Mercy and Truth* in 1897, established the scriptural framework for this 'blessed and beneficent work', see p.2. It was renamed *The Mission Hospital* in the 1920s, supposedly to convey better the medical work it did, W. McAdam Eccles, *The Mission Hospital*, January 1922, p.9.

73 T. Paine, *The Age of Reason: Being an Investigation of True and Fabulous Theology* (Paris: Barrois, 1794), p.32.

74 W.H.R. Wood, *Infidelity Reclaimed; or Paine's Age of Reason Reviewed; Being a Defence of Christianity against the Attacks of Infidelity* (San Francisco, CA: Valentine, 1862), p.19.

75 *The Republican*, 11:14 (8 April 1825), p.446.

76 J. Walker, *An Expostulatory Address to the Members of the Methodist Society in Ireland: Together with a Series of Letters to Alexander Knox, Esq. M.R.I.A.* (Edinburgh: Ritchie, 1806), p.273.

77 For eighteenth-century discussions of divine mercy in anti-infidelity context, J.C. Ryland, *The Scheme of Infidelity Ruined for Ever: Or the Deistical and Socinian Schemes Demonstrated to Be Insufficient for the Happiness of Mankind* (London: Pasham, 1770), pp.71–2.

78 *The Republican* 11:24 (17 June 1825), p.762. On Perry, see 'Utilitarian Record', *The Reasoner*, 13 January 1847, p.13.

79 R. Carlile, *Every Man's Book: Or What Is God?* (London: Carlile, 1826), p.35, responding to an address by the Quaker William Allen.

80 *The Republican* 11:24, 17 June 1825, p.740.

81 Essay dated 19 December 1828, *The Lion* 3:1 (2 January 1829), the poem from *Poems and Translations with the Sophy Written by the Honourable Sir John Denham, Knight of the Bath* (1688).

82 *The Republican* 10:20, 19 November 1824, p.612.

83 *Manual of Freemasonry: In Three Parts, with an Explanatory Introduction to the Science and a Free Translation of Some of the Sacred Scripture Names* (London: Vickers, 1855), p.40.

84 A. Carson, *The Truth of the Gospel Demonstrated from the Character of God, Manifested in the Atonement. In a Letter to Mr Richard Carlile* (New York: Fletcher, 1851), p.241, p.245.

85 *The Influence of Christianity. Report of a Public Discussion Which Took Place at Oldham February 19th and 20th, 1839* (Manchester: Cave and Sever, 1839), p.38.

86 J.A. James, *Christian Mercy Stated and Enforced* (London: Westley, 1820), p.14.

87 C. Leslie, *A Short and Easie Method with the Deists* (7th edn; London: Strahan, 1745), p.68. See W. Stevenson, 'The Deist on a Deathbed' in *Original Poems on Several Subjects* (2 vols; Edinburgh: Donaldson and Reid, 1765), vol.2, p.220 for mercy withheld.

88 G.S. Faber, *The Difficulties of Infidelity* (London: Rivington, 1824), pp.30–5.

89 'Morley's Voltaire', *The Christian Observer* (March 1872), p.199.

90 Though he also argued that God would not shrink from justice, in 'Prevenient Grace', F.W. Newman, *Theism, Doctrinal and Practical: Or Didactic Religious Utterances* (London: Chapman, 1858), p.97.

91 H.G. Wells, *First and Last Things. A Confession of Faith and Rule of Life* (London: Constable, 1908), pp.196–8. In *The Undying Fire* (London: Cassell, 1919), ch.5, one character, Dr Barrack, argues that justice and mercy have no enduring criteria.

92 S. Gilfillan, 'On Forgiveness with God', *Discourses on Various Important Subjects, for the Use of Families* (Edinburgh: for the author, 1822), pp.1–9 [p.5].

93 Reverend Hugh M'Neile, 'A Sermon, Preached at St Bride's Church, Fleet Street, on Monday Evening, 5 May 1845, before the Church Missionary Society', in *Proceedings of the Church Missionary Society for Africa and the East. Forty-Fifth Year. 1844–1845* (London: Hatchard, 1845), p.7.

94 *Western Morning News*, 9 December 1882 [p.2]. This responded to the resignation of Riaz Pasha.

95 The Collects for Good Friday, *The Book of Common Prayer* (Cambridge: Smith, 1816), p.169.

96 See the Christian convert Abdool Messee's discourse on Christianity, combining justice and mercy, to Muslims in Lucknow, 30 July 1814, *Missionary Register* 3:8 (August 1815), p.408.

97 S. Gilfillan, *Practical Views of the Dignity, Grace, and Operations of the Holy Spirit* (Edinburgh: Oliphant, 1826), p.388.

98 R. Caldwell, *The Three Way-Marks* (Madras: Christian Vernacular Education Society, 1860), reviewed in *The Colonial Church Chronicle and Missionary Journal* 15 (1861) p.273.

99 This contrast of merciful Christian and cruel Muslim appears in theology and common journalism, see B. Porteus, *Summary of the Principal Evidences for the Truth and Divine Origin of the Christian Revelation* (1800; 19th edn; London: Cadell, 1840), pp.59, 65–6; 'The Question of the Near East', *Boston Guardian*, 10 January 1903, p.4. For recognition of the structuring role of contrast with the self-image of Christian mercifulness, see C. Forster, *Mahometanism Unveiled: An Inquiry, in Which That Arch-Heresy, Its Diffusion and Continuance, Are Examined on a New Principle, Tending to Confirm the Evidences, and Aid the Propagation, of the Christian Faith* (2 vols; London: 1829), vol.2, p.469, taking to task White's Bampton lectures. On divine mercy in Islam, J.M. Arnold, *Ishmael: Or, a Natural History of Islamism, and Its Relation to Christianity* (London: Rivingtons, 1859), pp.119–20; reprinted as *Islam: Its History, Character, and Relation to Christianity* (3rd edn; London: Longman, Green, 1874), pp.96–7. For a corrective to nineteenth-century prejudices, 'The benevolence of Muhammadanism', in 'Afrikander', 'The Reformation of Christianity and Islamism', *The African Times and Orient Review*, November–December 1913, p.209; and mercy and forgiveness realized in Muhammad rather than Christianity, 'Jesus, an Ideal of Godhead and Humanity', *African Times and Orient Review*, December–January 1913, p.218.

100 See T. Watson, *Popular Evidences of Natural Religion and Christianity* (London: Longman, Hurst, Rees, and Orme, 1805), p.351; and J. Fleming, *A Testimony for an Universal Church* (Edinburgh: for the author, 1826), p.595 on Muhammad as the reverse of Christianity (pure, peaceful, merciful); J. Alley, *Vindiciae Christianae: A Comparative Estimate of the Genius and Temper of The Greek, The Roman, The Hindu, The Mahometan, and the Christian Religions* (London: Cadell, 1826), p.574. For notes to missionaries on God's mercy, A. Brinckman, 'Short Argument to Prove the Truth of Christianity', in *Notes on Islam* (London: Church Press, 1868), pp.314–15. On discussion of the implications of justice and mercy for the divine attributes with a Muslim scholar, J. Selkirk, *Recollections of Ceylon after a Residence of Nearly Thirteen Years; with an Account of the Church Missionary Society's Operations in the Island* (London: Hatchard, 1844), p.541.

101 Thus in the Society [South Sea] islands, king Pomare of Tahiti's clemency to enemies after an attack on the Sabbath (12 November 1815) convinced many of the 'merciful religion', *Hampshire Chronicle*, 20 January 1817 [p.2]; see also W. Ellis, *Polynesian Researches, during a Residence of Nearly Six Years, in the South Sea Islands* (2 vols; London: Fisher, Son and Jackson, 1829), vol.2, e.g. pp.282–283.

102 Reverend John Nelson, 'Indian Relief Fund', *Greenock Telegraph*, 14 October 1857 [p.2]; lecture by Reverend N. Haycroft, Bristol Athenaeum, *Western Daily Press*, 9 March 1860, p.2.

103 'On the Necessity of imparting the knowledge of Christianity to the Hindoos', *Friend of India*, December 1818, p.296.

104 *The Bombay Quarterly Review*, vol.2 (July and October 1855), pp.341–71 [p.359, p.366], reviewing John Wilson's *History of the Suppression of Infanticide in Western India* (London: Smith, Elder, 1855).

105 See P. Anagol, 'Indian Christian Women and Indigenous Feminism, c.1850–c.1920', in C. Midgley, ed., *Gender and Imperialism* (Manchester: Manchester University Press, 1998), pp.79–103 [p.86].

106 E.J. Eitel, *Three Lectures on Buddhism* (London: Trübner, 1871).

107 Caswell, 'The Character and Influence of Buddhism', in 'Siam. Annual Report of the Mission', *Missionary Herald* (January 1848), p.16.

108 M. Symes, *An Account of an Embassy to the Kingdom of Ava Sent by the Governor-General of India, in the Year 1795* (London: Bulmer, 1800), p.303. The passage was repeated in reviews and informed encyclopaedia entries. See 'Clemency of the King of Burma', *Mission Field: A Monthly Record of the Proceedings of the Society for the Propagation of the Gospel at Home and Abroad*, 1 September 1870, p.276, on later royal mercy presented as the result of Western intercession by Reverend J.E. Marks.

109 R. Cust, *Clouds on the Horizon. An Essay on the Various Forms of Error, which Stand in the Way of the Acceptance of Real Christian Faith by the Educated Natives of Asia, Africa, America, and Oceanica* (2nd edn; London: Stock, 1891), p.22.

110 K. Suyematsu, *A Fantasy of Far Japan* (London: Constable, 1905); *Pall Mall Gazette*, 27 December 1905.

111 E.J. Eitel, *Buddhism: Its Historical, Theoretical and Popular Aspects. In Three Lectures* (2nd edn; London: Trübner, 1873), pp.102–9; *The Far East* 1:2, 20 March 1896, p.28, and frontispiece, 'Kwan-on, a Goddess of Mercy'. See T. Richard, *The New Testament of Higher Buddhism* (Edinburgh: T&T Clark, 1910), on common ground between Buddhism and Christianity, equating Kwanyin and Holy Spirit, p.16. B.H. Chamberlain, *The Handbook for Travellers in Japan* (London: Murray, 1901) detailed deities including Kwannon, see p.52. G.A. Cobbold, *Religion in Japan; Shintoism, Buddhism, Christianity* (London: S.P.C.K., 1894), p.65 indicates the Chinese making this translation when referring to the deity, with Europeans. See also R. Timothy, 'The Life of the "Goddess of Mercy,"' *The Sunday at Home*, 1 January 1896), pp.20–5. An exhibition in aid of China presented representations of the Chinese goddess of mercy, 'Art Exhibitions', *The Times*, 27 November 1943, p.8. On the goddess of mercy in Meiji-era Japanese art and its relationship to Western, Christian art, see C. Foxwell, '"Merciful Mother Kannon" and Its Audiences', *Art Bulletin* 92:4 (December 2010), pp. 326–47.

112 W. Clarkson, *India and the Gospel, or, an Empire for the Messiah* (London: Snow, 1850), pp.79–80.

113 S. Johnson, *Oriental Religions and Their Relation to Universal Religion by Samuel Johnson: India* (London: Trübner, 1873), p.535.

114 This is manifested in debates about policy towards China, see House of Lords debate on the Chinese War, *London Evening Standard*, 27 February 1857, where the Earl of Ellenborough spoke of damage to the profession of a 'religion of mercy, of benevolence, of virtue, of goodwill'. In anti-slavery, the phrase 'religion of mercy' figures in the gold box given to Thomas Clarkson by the City of London, *Morning Advertiser*, 24 November 1838 [p.2].

115 J. Forbes, *Oriental Memoirs* (4 vols: London: for the author, 1813), vol.2, p.134.

116 'Monody', *Asiatic Annual Register; or, a View of the History of Hindustan, and of the Politics, Commerce, and Literature of Asia for the Year 1799* (2nd edn; London: Debrett, 1801), p.193.

117 *Parliamentary Debates from the Year 1803 to the Present Time. Vol. 27. Comprising the Period from the Fourth Day of November to the Sixth Day of June 1813–1814* (London: Longman, Hurst, Rees, Orme, and Brown, 1814), House of Commons, 14 June 1813, cols.1162–1163, East India Company's Affairs; see also J. Prinsep's *Strictures and Observations on the Mocurrery System of Landed Property in Bengal*, in *Critical Review*, October 1794; 'East India Enormities', *Political Review*, June 1808, p.xcv on braving God's attributes of justice and mercy.

118 'Debate at the East-India House', 14 July 1841, in *The Asiatic Journal* 35:140 (August 1841). This was a general court of proprietors of East India Stock, see comments of Burke, p.306, and 15 July, George Thompson, p.359.

119 *Imperial Magazine*, April 1830, p.350.

120 R.M. Martin, *The Progress and Present State of British India* (London: Low, 1862), p.ix.

121 T. Tryon, *A Dialogue between an East-Indian Brackmanny, or Heathen-Philosopher, and a French-Gentleman, Concerning the Present Affairs in Europe* (London: Newman and Baldwin, 1691), p.6.

122 E. Hamilton, *Translation of the Letters of a Hindoo Rajah* (London: Walker, 1811), vol. 1, p.18.

123 E.g. G-B. Depping, *Evening Entertainments, or, Delineations of the Manners and Customs of Various Nations* (London: Hailes, 1829), p.51.

124 W. Howitt, *Colonization and Christianity. A Popular History of the Treatment of the Natives by the Europeans in All Their Colonies* (London: Longman, Orme, Brown, Green, and Longman, 1838), p.502.

125 *Colonization and Christianity*, p.485.

126 G. Young, *Parallel between King David and King George: A Sermon Preached in Cliff-Lane Chapel, Whitby February 16, 1820, Being the Day of The Funeral of His Majesty King George III* (Whitby: Clark, 1820), p.25.

127 [D. Wilson] *A Defence of the Church Missionary Society against the Objections of the Rev. Josiah Thomas, M.A. Archdeacon of Bath* (2nd edn; London: Wilson, 1818), p.33.

128 B.W. Noel, Church Missionary Service sermon (1835) quoted in R. Marley, *Medical Missionaries; Or, Medical Agency Cooperative with Christian Missions to the Heathen* (London: James Blackwood, 1860), p.38.

129 See 'Mitis', 'On the Anniversary of the Missionary Society', *Evangelical Magazine* 20 (August 1812), pp.327–8 [p.328].

130 J. Hunt, *Memoir of the Memoir of the Rev. William Cross, Wesleyan Missionary to the Friendly and Feejee Islands* (London: Mason, 1846), p.159, and p.110 on the merciful act of Namosemalua; 'Fiji and the Fijians', *Baptist Magazine and Literary Review* 51 (February 1859), pp.76–81 [p.81] from a report by the Reverend Joseph

Waterhouse; *The Panoplist and Missionary Herald* 14:6 (June 1818), p.279 after detailing changing practice in warfare in Tahiti in 1815, notes they 'embrace the new religion which is so distinguished by its mildness, goodness and forbearance'; T. Smith, *The History and Origin of the Missionary Societies* (2 vols; London: Kelly and Evans, 1825), vol.2, p.70; T. Smith and J.O. Choules, *The Origin and History of Missions: Containing Faithful Accounts of the Voyages, Travels, Labors and Successes of the Various Missionaries Who Have Been Sent Forth to Evangelize the Heathen* (2 vols; Boston, MA: Walker, and Lincoln and Edmands, 1832), vol.1, p.584.

131 'The Gospel for the World', *First Truths; or, Lessons and Hymns for Christian Children* (new edn; London: SPCK, 1843), p.51.

132 D. Wilson, *Sermons Delivered in India during the Course of the Primary Visitation* (London: Hatchard, 1838), p.167.

133 Reverend H. Woodward, 'Divine Justice and Mercy', a Tamil tract, translated in *English Translations of Select Tracts Published in India: Second Series* (Madras: Laurie, 1870); 'On the Mercy of God', essay by 'C.P.C.' (Kasi Podma Choudree), Serampore College, *Evangelical Christendom* (London: Partridge and Oakey, 1849), pp.316–17; *The First Hindoo Convert: A Memoir of Krishna Pal, a Preacher of the Gospel to His Countrymen More Than Twenty Years* (Philadelphia, PA: American Baptist Publication Society, 1852).

134 *Missionary Papers for the Use of the Weekly and Monthly Contributors to the Church Missionary Society*, No.11, midsummer 1816 [unpaginated, p.2].

135 S.K. Das, *The Shadow of the Cross: Christianity and Hinduism in a Colonial Situation* (Delhi: Munshiram Manoharlal Publishers, 1974), p.29, p.98, on mercy and atonement.

136 *Missionary Intelligencer*, August 1869, p. 236. See 'A Voice from the Himalayas. A Missionary Leaflet written at Simla, September, 1868', reprinted in *Lectures and Tracts: First and Second Series* (London: Strahan, 1870). J. Robson, *Hinduism and Its Relation to Christianity* (Edinburgh: Oliphant, 1870) discusses Hindu and Christian ideas of atonement.

137 S.D. Collet, 'Indian Theism and Its Relation to Christianity', *Contemporary Review*, January–March 1870, pp.230–45; W.H. Fremantle, 'The Brahmo Somaj and the Religious Future of India', *Contemporary Review*, August–November 1870, pp.67–80; 'The Brahmo Somaj of India', *Allen's Indian Mail*, 16 February 1870, p.143.

138 Dr Duff, *Christian Work*, reporting on the Reform Hindu Party in Bengal, reprinted in J. Murdoch, *Indian Year-Book for 1862* (Madras: Graves, Cookson, 1863), pp.202–3. See D. Knopf, *The Brahmo Samaj and the Shaping of the Modern Indian Mind* (Princeton, NJ: Princeton University Press, 1979), p.173, on critique of Christian ideas of divine mercy. Rajah Rammonhum Roy's engagement with Christian, and Unitarian ideas, is a significant moment.

139 See the lecture on redemption by Reverend J. Vaughan, delivered in Saint Paul's Cathedral, Calcutta 10 November 1865, and printed in his *The Christian Scheme of Salvation. A Course of Lectures to Educated Natives of India* (Calcutta: Lepage, 1866), p.68.

140 Lecture by Sen, 23 January 1869, reproduced in appendix to T.E. Slater, ed., *Keshab Chandra Sen and the Brahma Samáj: Being a Brief Review of Indian Theism from 1830 to 1884* (Madras: SPCK, 1884), p.16 (which praised the parable of the prodigal son). Sen's emphasis on God's mercy is discussed in D.H. Bishop, 'Keshub Chunder Sen and the Brahmo Samaj', in D.H. Bishop, ed., *Thinkers of The Indian Renaissance* (1982; New Delhi: New Age International, 1988), pp.46–7; see also M. Borthwick,

Keshub Chunder Sen: A Search for Cultural Synthesis (Calcutta: Minerva, 1979). For Sen's visit to Britain, *Birmingham Daily Post*, 7 June 1870, p.5, quoting Sen on God's 'infinite and all-conquering mercy'.

141 'The Reform Party in Bengal', *Church Missionary Review* 17 (September 1866), pp.270–9 [p.277]: a talk by Sen reprinted from the *Indian Mirror*. See *The Life and Letters of the Right Honourable Friedrich Max Müller* (2 vols; London: Longmans, Green, 1902), vol.2, Appendix A, p.470, discussing responses to Christian missionaries on justice and mercy.

142 D. Prasad, transl., *An English Translation of the Satyarth Prakash; literally, Expose of Right Sense (of Vedic Religions). Of Mahrishi Swami Dayanand Saraswati, 'The Luther of India'* (Lahore: Virjanand Press, 1908), p.465. The *Ocean of Mercy*, translated by Prasad includes a vegetarian treatise, *Caruna Nidhi*. On the Vedic Hindu and founder of the Arya Samaj, Dayananda, see K.W. Jones, 'Swami Dayananda Saraswati's Critique of Christianity', in K.W. Jones, ed., *Religious Controversy in British India: Dialogues in South Asian Languages* (Albany: SUNY Press, 1992), p.60.

143 See P. Chatterjee, 'The Moment of Departure: Culture and Power in the Thought of Bankimchandra', reprinted in P.J. Cain and M. Harrison, eds, *Imperialism: Critical Concepts in Historical Studies* (3 vols; London: Routledge, 2001), vol.3, pp.137–70, where analysis of India and European development by the Calcutta intellectual Bankim Chandra Chattopadhyay includes (in Bengali *Krishna Charitra* of 1886) the place of mercy and force in the respective societies (pp.155–6); and P. Chatterjee, *Nationalist Thought and the Colonial World: A Derivative Discourse* (Minneapolis: University of Minnesota Press, 1993), p.70. For Islamic responses, e.g. U. Ryad, *Islamic Reformism and Christianity: A Critical Reading of the Works of Muhammad Rashīd Ridā and His Associates (1898–1935)* (Leiden: Brill, 2009), p. 267.

144 For useful context for the eighteenth century, see 'Social emotions in eighteenth-century moral philosophy', in ch.3 in Frevert, *Emotions in History – Lost and Found*. For examples of theologians and philosophers commenting on mercy in this period, who are not touched on in this chapter, N. Fiering, *Jonathan Edwards's Moral Thought and Its British Context* (Chapel Hill: University of North Carolina Press, 1981) especially ch.5, 'Hell and the Humanitarians'.

145 Thus *Legal Examiner*, 13 February 1833, pp.485–8 reprinting Professor Christian's law lecture, covering certainty of punishments and crown prerogative.

146 F. Hutcheson, *An Inquiry into the Original of Our Ideas of Beauty and Virtue* (London: Ware, 1753), p.269. For Hutcheson – an influence on Hume – on mercy, G. Pettigrove, 'Passions, Perceptions and Motives: Fault-lines in Account of Moral Sentiment', in H. Kerr, D. Lemmings and R. Phiddian, eds, *Passions, Sympathy and Print Culture: Public Opinion and Emotional Authenticity in Eighteenth-Century Britain* (Houndmills: Routledge, 2016), pp.203–22 [p.206].

147 Thus, 'Reflections on the Harmony of Sensibility and Reason', from the miniature painter John Donaldson's *Elements of Beauty* (Edinburgh: Elliot, 1780), reprinted in *The Universal Magazine of Knowledge and Pleasure* (1780), November 1780, pp.229–31.

148 D. Hartley, *Observations on Man: His Frame, His Duty, and His Expectations, in Two Parts* (London: Richardson, 1749), p.471, p.478.

149 'Of the Affections by which we grieve for the Misery of others', in Hartley, *Observations on Man*, pp.476–7.

150 D. Hume, *An Enquiry Concerning the Principles of Morals* (London: Millar, 1751), p.22. Hume locates it, p.102, among the 'social virtues', with 'humanity, generosity, charity, affability, lenity … and moderation'; and debates the moral attributes of the divine in relation to human virtues, e.g. *Dialogues Concerning Natural Religion* (1779; 2nd edn; London, 1779), p.186, 'In what respect, then, do his benevolence and mercy resemble the benevolence and mercy of men?' Hume's attitude towards mercy is discussed in G. Pettigrove, 'Hume on Forgiveness and the Unforgivable', *Utilitas* 19:4 (December 2007), pp.447–64, where his use of 'forgiveness', 'mercy' and 'pardon' are synonymous (pp.451–2).

151 Hume, *An Enquiry Concerning the Principles of Morals*, p.154.

152 J. Priestley, *Letters to a Philosophical Unbeliever, Part I.* (London: Pearson and Rollason for J. Johnson, 1787), pp.100–1.

153 E. Gibbon, *The History of the Decline and Fall of the Roman Empire* (6 vols, 1776–1789; London: Strahan and Cadell, 1776), vol.1, p.133; on capital punishment reflections, vol.5 (1788), p.68.

154 T. Paine, *A Letter to the Hon. Thomas Erskine on the Prosecution of Thomas Williams, for Publishing the Age of Reason* (Paris: for the author [1798]), p.19.

155 *An Enquiry Concerning Political Justice, and Its Influence on General Virtue and Happiness* (2 vols; London: Robinson, 1793), vol.2, p.797. His diary entry for 15 April 1793 notes, 'J. Hollis calls, talk of justice & mercy', see 'William Godwin's Diary', http://godwindiary.bodleian.ox.ac.uk/diary/1793-04-15.html (accessed 12 August 2018). He noted in his diary in 1828 revisions to lines on 'clemency' in a study of the Commonwealth, Dep. e.223, fol. 21v, and http://godwindiary.bodleian.ox.ac.uk/diary/1828-10-10.html (accessed 12 August 2018). See W. Godwin, *History of the Commonwealth of England, From Its Commencement to the Restoration of Charles II* (4 vols; London: H. Colburn, 1828), vol. 4, p.594.

156 W. Godwin, *Essays by the Late William Godwin, Author of Political Justice* (London: H.S. King, 1873), preface to Essay 1, p.18.

157 M. Wollstonecraft, *A Vindication of the Rights of Woman with Strictures on Political and Moral Subjects* (London: Johnson, 1792), p. 105.

158 See Meyer, *The Justice of Mercy*; Murphy, 'Mercy and Legal Justice', pp.1–14.

159 E. Smith, *Phaedra and Hippolitus: A Tragedy* (1703; 4th edn, Glasgow: Foulis, 1750), p.52.

160 E. Darwin, *The Botanic Garden. A Poem in Two Parts* (London: Johnson, 1791), Part II, p.85.

161 S. Parr, *Characters of the Late Charles James Fox: Selected and in Part Written by Philopatris Varvicensis* (2 vols; London: Mawman, 1809), vol.2, p.773, discussing justice on p.425, line 13. The Duchess of Devonshire's verse for the bust of the Whig statesman, at Woburn, laments (vol.1, p.160), 'Oh! had his voice in Mercy's cause prevail'd'.

162 *Remarks on the Policy of the Allies*, in *The Works of the Right Honourable Edmund Burke* (6 vols; Boston, MA: West, 1807), vol.4, p.121.

163 E. Burke, *Three Memorials of French Affairs* (3rd edn; London: Rivington, 1797), p. xxvii.

164 See H.A. Bedau, *Death Is Different: Studies in the Morality, Law, and Politics of Capital Punishment* (Boston, MA: Northeastern University Press, 1987), ch.3, 'A Utilitarian Critique of the Death Penalty'; A. Tuckness, and J. Parrish, 'Mercy as Cruelty in Bentham and the Utilitarian Tradition', in *The Decline of Mercy in Public Life* (Cambridge: Cambridge University Press, 2014), pp. 201–22.

165 From the editors' outline, *Benthamiana or Select Extracts from the Works of Jeremy Bentham: With an Outline of His Opinions on the Principal Subjects Discussed in His Works* (Edinburgh: W. Tait, 1843), p.388.

166 J. Bentham, *Rationale of Judicial Evidence: Specially Applied to English Practice* (5 vols; London: Hunt and Clarke, 1827), vol.1, p.600.

167 J. Bentham, in *Constitutional Code*, in *The Works of Jeremy Bentham, Now First Collected: Under the Superintendence of His Executor, John Bowring* (Edinburgh: Tait, 1843), vol.9, p.36, in section II. Penal Law: 'To the vocabulary of tyranny belongs the word mercy. The idea expressed by this word is a sort of appendage to, or antagonizes with, the ideas designated by the word justice'.

168 'Radicalism Not Dangerous', *The Works of Jeremy Bentham*, vol.3, p.619.

169 Ibid.

170 'On Locke's Essay on Human Understanding', reprinted in *Literary Remains of the Late William Hazlitt* (2 vols; London: Saunders and Otley, 1836), vol.1, pp.256-7.

171 Moore, *Pardons: Justice, Mercy, and the Public Interest*, p.46 refers to Hegel, *Elements of the Philosophy of Right* (1820), as the 'last furious philosophical blast at pardons in the nineteenth century, before the topic faded away for a hundred years as philosophers turned their attentions to other things'.

172 W. Whewell, *Elements of Morality Including Polity* (2 vols; London: Parker, 1848), vol.1, p.73.

173 J.S. Mill, *An Examination of Sir William Hamilton's Philosophy: And of the Principal Philosophical Questions Discussed in His Writings* (London: Longmans, Green, 1865), p.432.

174 H. Sidgwick, *The Methods of Ethics* (London: Macmillan, 1874), p.219. Sidgwick refers to mercy in passing, p.298. The chapter on benevolence debates distinction between justice and benevolence, p.213. Chapter 5 concerns justice. F.H. Bradley, *Ethical Studies* (London: King, 1876).

175 *Review of Reviews*, February 1906, p.191, summarizing Algar Thorold, in *Independent Review*, on Maeterlinck as moralist.

176 See the allusion to Darwin and moral qualities in a Hospital Sunday sermon by the Reverend Arthur Ingleby, *The Zoophilist*, 1 August 1884, p.84; for references to mercy, H.A.S., *Darwin and His Works: A Biological & Metaphysical Study* (London: Bale, 1888), p. 52; A.R. Wallace, *Darwinism: An Exposition of the Theory of Natural Selection with Some of Its Application* (London: Macmillan, 1889), p.37, p.477; on Darwin, sympathy and pity, see Dixon, *The Invention of Altruism*; C. Darwin, *The Descent of Man, and Selection in Relation to Sex* (2 vols; London: Murray, 1871), vol.1, pp.71-98. Darwin speaks of humanity, including to lower animals as one of the 'latest moral acquisitions', p.101.

177 C. Darwin, *The Expression of the Emotions in Man and Animals* (London: Murray, 1872), p.218; Darwin, *The Descent of Man*, p.77.

178 F. Galton, *Inquiries into Human Faculty and Its Development* (1883; New York: Dent and Dutton, 1907), p.197.

179 F. Galton, 'Hereditary Improvement', *Fraser's Magazine* 7:37 (January 1873), pp.116-30 [p.120].

180 J.A. Lindsay, 'Eugenics and the Doctrine of the Super-Man', *Eugenics Review*, January 1916, pp.247-62 [p.252]. The philosopher L.T. Hobhouse attacks eugenics on the grounds of its treatment of mercy, in *Development and Purpose: An Essay Towards a Philosophy of Evolution* (London: Macmillan, 1913), pp.9-10.

181 H. Spencer, *The Principles of Psychology* (2nd edn; London: Williams and Norgate, 1872), vol.2, p.622.
182 H. Spencer, 'Religion: A Retrospect and Prospect', *The Nineteenth Century* 15:83 (January 1884), pp.1–12 [p.4]. See his 'On Justice', *The Nineteenth Century* 27:157 (March 1890), pp.435–48, on negative and positive beneficence, and *The Principles of Ethics* (2 vols; London: Williams and Norgate, 1893), vol.2, p.18 and part 4.
183 P. Kropotkin, 'The Morality of Nature', *Nineteenth Century* 57:337 (March 1905), pp.407–26.
184 W.E.H. Lecky, *History of European Morals from Augustus to Charlemagne* (2nd edn; 2 vols; London: Longmans, Green, 1869), vol.1, pp.239–41.
185 H.A.L. Fisher, 'Lord Acton's Lectures', *Independent Review* 11 (October–December 1906), pp.225–8 [p.227]. Smith's assertion is in *Lectures on Modern History Delivered in Oxford, 1859–61* (Oxford: Parker, 1861), p.23, p.24.
186 'Prolegomena', in T.H. Huxley, *Evolution and Ethics: and Other Essays* (London: Macmillan, 1894), p.30, p.42.
187 'Prolegomena', pp.82–3.
188 Ibid., pp.83–5, 115.
189 St George Mivart, *On the Genesis of Species* (1871; 2nd edn; London: Macmillan, 1871) in T.H. Huxley, *Critiques and Addresses* (London: Macmillan, 1873), p.288. See also W.W. Smyth, *Evolution Explained and Compared With the Bible* (2nd edn; London: E. Stock, 1883), p.46: 'The ancient Process was strictly one of rigid Law, of firm Justice; but here we reach the *quality of mercy* which rejoices against judgment.'
190 L.T. Hobhouse, *Morals in Evolution: A Study in Comparative Ethics* (London: Chapman, Hall, 1906), Part I, pp.116–17; on mercilessness, e.g. p.256. See also C.M. Williams, *A Review of the Systems of Ethics Founded on the Theory of Evolution* (London: Macmillan, 1893), p.578.
191 J.E. Bicheno, *An Inquiry into the Nature of Benevolence, Chiefly with a View to Elucidate the Principle of the Poor Laws, and to Show Their Immoral Tendency* (2nd edn, London: Hunter, 1824), p.150.
192 On equity, Fortier, *The Culture of Equity in Restoration and Eighteenth-Century Britain and America*.
193 'Anthropology and Social Innovation', *Popular Magazine of Anthropology* 3 (July 1866), pp.93–7 [p.95]. J.W. Burrow, 'Evolution and Anthropology in the 1860s: The Anthropological Society of London, 1863–7', *Victorian Studies* 7:2 (December 1963), pp.137–54, notes the Anthropological Society's 'unsavoury reputation for godlessness', p.150; see also R. Rainger, 'Race, Politics, and Science: The Anthropological Society of London in the 1860s', *Victorian Studies* 22:1 (Autumn 1978), pp.51–70.
194 The barrister and historian L.O. Pike, 'The Psychical Characteristics of the English People', *Memoirs Read before the Anthropological Society of London* 2 (1865–6), pp.153–88 [p.186]; W. Winwood Reade, 'Burton's Mission to Dahome', *Anthropological Review*, November 1864, pp.335–43 [p.342].
195 J. Kaines, 'The Interpretation of Mythology', *Anthropologia* 4 (April 1875), pp.463–75 [p.473].
196 See, in a defence of Spencer, E.L. Linton, 'Professor Henry Drummond's Discovery', *The Fortnightly* 56 (1894), pp.448–57 [p.449]. I have not looked closely at the lexical association between the new word and 'mercy', but see the gloss provided by Robert

Blatchford, *Altruism: Christ's Glorious Gospel of Love against Man's Dismal Science of Greed* (London: 'Clarion', 1898), p.3.

197 The summary F.P. Cobbe provides in her review, 'Darwiniansm in Morals', *Theological Review*, April 1871, reprinted in *Darwinism in Morals, and Other Essays* (London: Williams and Norgate, 1872), pp.1–33 [pp.9–10]. She does not discuss it in terms of mercy, though conceivably this is covered by her reference to Darwinian theory as 'an hypothesis for the origin of relenting Pity' (p.25).

198 D. Hird, *An Easy Outline of Evolution* (London: Watts, 1903), p.125.

199 See, for reference to mercy and compassion as protection against the 'biologic law of evolution' for 'reform Darwinists', opposed to conservative social Darwinists, in M. Zachariah, 'The Impact of Darwin's Theory of Evolution on Theories of Society', *The Social Studies* (February 1971), pp.69–77 [p.75].

Chapter 2

1 J. Wilson Mccutchan, 'Justice and Equity in the English Morality Play', *Journal of the History of Ideas* 19:3 (June 1958), pp.405–10 notes mercy (and truth and justice) in *The Castle of Perseverance* c.1405; W.F. Neff, *Victorian Working Women: An Historical and Literary Study of Women in British Industries and Professions 1832–1850* (New York: Columbia University Press, 1929) refers to justice and mercy enacted in a meeting-house, p.105.

2 The critic in *Female Revenge: Or, the British Amazon: Exemplified in the Life of Boadicia.* (London: Cooper, 1753), p.20.

3 *Encyclopaedia Britannica* (3rd edn; 18 vols; Edinburgh: MacFarquhar, 1797), vol.11, p.403; *Encyclopædia Perthensis* (2nd edn; 23 vols; Edinburgh: Brown, 1816), vol.14, p.459.

4 Murphy, 'Mercy and Legal Justice', p.2.

5 There is extensive scholarship on this: e.g. S. Magedanz, 'Public Justice and Private Mercy in "Measure for Measure"', *Studies in English Literature, 1500–1900* 44:2 (Spring 2004), pp.317–32; E.V. Spencer, 'Scaling the Deputy: Equity and Mercy in *Measure for Measure*', *Philosophy and Literature* 36 (2012), pp.166–82. Portia and Isabella are discussed in A.B. Jameson's *Characteristics of Women, Moral, Poetical and Historical* (2 vols, London: Saunders, Otley, 1832), vol.1, pp.1–60.

6 M.D. Conway, 'The Pound of Flesh', *The Nineteenth Century* (May 1880), pp.828–39 [p.839].

7 'Select passages from Shakespeare', *The Universal Magazine of Knowledge and Pleasure* 92 (1793), p.247.

8 S. Fielding, *The Cry, A New Dramatic Fable* (3 vols; London: Dodsley, 1754). On the novel, C.D. Johnson, *A Political Biography of Sarah Fielding* (Abingdon: Routledge, 2017), ch.7.

9 James Hook's 'The Trial', 17 May 1788, BM 7321, in D. O'Quinn, *Staging Governance: Theatrical Imperialism in London, 1770–1800* (Baltimore, MD: Johns Hopkins University Press, 2005), pp.224–6, commenting on Fox's intervention in Warren Hastings's trial.

10 *The Country Constitutional Guardian* (Bristol), May 1822, p.450.

11 *Morning Post*, 21 March 1836, p.2.

12 J. Campbell, *The Lives of the Lord Chancellors and Keepers of the Great Seal of England* (London: Murray, 1846), 2nd series, vol.5, pp.670–1.
13 'Art.7: Piozziana; or, Recollections of the Late Mrs Piozzi, with Remarks', *Monthly Review*, April 1833, p.550.
14 See *Classical Journal*, September 1824, p.122, for a prize-winning rendition in Greek.
15 'The "Merchant of Venice" at the Prince of Wales's Theatre', *Fraser's Magazine* 12:67 (July 1875), pp.65–71 [p.69].
16 'Mercy', John Heywood's *Fifth Manchester Reader: A New Series for Elementary Schools of All Grades* (Manchester: Heywood, 1871), p.21.
17 H.D. Smith, *Beauties of Penmanship* (London: Relfe, 1852).
18 J. Hankey, 'Victorian Portias: Shakespeare's Borderline Heroine', *Shakespeare Quarterly* 45:4 (Winter 1994), pp.426–48.
19 J.W. Cole, *A Defence of the Stage: Or an Enquiry into the Real Qualities of Theatrical Entertainments, Their Scope and Tendency* (Dublin: Milliken, 1839), p.153.
20 G.W.M. Reynolds, *Ellen Percy* (London: Dicks, 1856), p.58.
21 National Portrait Gallery, Sarah West as Portia after Thomas Charles Wageman, published by John Cumberland; Ellen Terry, *cartes de visite* by Window and Grove.
22 D.E. Baker, *The Companion to The Play-House, Or, an Historical Account of All the Dramatic Writers (and Their Works) That Have Appeared in Great Britain and Ireland* (2 vols; London: Becket and Dehondt, 1764), vol.1, entry for *Merchant of Venice*.
23 *The Theatrical Review; or, New Companion to the Play-house* (2 vols; London: Crowder, 1772, vol.1 p.40.
24 E. Griffith, *The Morality of Shakespeare's Drama Illustrated* (London: Cadell, 1775), p.62.
25 'The Merchant of Venice, written by Shakespeare', *The Dramatic Censor; or, Critical Companion* (2 vols; London: Bell, 1770), vol.1, p.296, for wider assessment of actors, pp.296–8.
26 *Dramatic Censor*, vol.1, p.297; J. Fisher, '"The Quality of Mercy" in the Eighteenth Century; or Kitty Clive's Portia', *Restoration and Eighteenth-Century Theatre* 14 (1999), pp.19–36, and (not studied here), F.J. Ritchie, '"The Merciful Construction of Good Women": Women's Responses to Shakespeare in the Theatre in the Long Eighteenth Century', unpublished PhD, King's College London, 2006.
27 *The English Review*, May 1783, p.441.
28 *Minutes of Evidence. Authentic and Interesting Memoirs of Mrs Clarke from Her Infancy to the Present Time* (London: Chapple, 1809), p.9; and entry in P.H. Highfill, K.A. Burnim, and E.A. Langhans, *A Biographical Dictionary of Actors, Actresses, Musicians, Dancers, Managers and Other Stage Personnel in London, 1660–1800* (Carbondale: Southern Illinois University Press, 1991), vol.14, p.415.
29 *Theatrical Inquisitor*, October 1816, p.317.
30 In depiction of the trial scene, by B. Wesley Rand; and with J.P. Kemble as Shylock in an oil painting, listed in 'Siddons' entry in *A Biographical Dictionary of Actors*, vol.14, p.62.
31 *The Portfolio*, 10 June 1826, p.50.
32 *The Literary Chronicle*, 27 January 1821, p.62.
33 *The Spectator*, 19 June 1858, p.651.
34 [S.M. Threipland], *Letters Respecting the Performances at the Theatre Royal, Edinburgh, Originally Addressed to the Editor of the Scots Chronicle, under the Signature of Timothy Plain, and Published in That Paper during the Years 1797, 1798, 1799, and 1800* (Edinburgh: Gray, 1800), p.57.

35 *Edinburgh Dramatic Review*, 5 January 1824, p.19.
36 *The Boston Lyceum*, 15 October 1827; Federal Street Theatre, 20 October 1827, p.197.
37 J. Boaden, *Memoirs of Sarah Siddons, Interspersed with Anecdotes of Authors and Actors* (2 vols; London: Colburn), vol.1, p.72; see also J. Gamble, *Society and Manners in Early Nineteenth-Century Ireland*, ed. B. Mac Suibhne (Dublin: Field Day, 2011), p.9.
38 'Humble Critic', 'Essay on the Morality of the Stage', *London Magazine*, December 1777, pp.607–9 [p.608].
39 *The Cabinet*, August 1807, p.62.
40 In a review of J.J. Engel's *De Kunst van Nabootzing door Gebaarden*, a Dutch edition of the German text (English title *The Art of Theatrical Imitation*) in *Appendix to the Ninth Volume of the Monthly Review Enlarged*, 1792, pp.520–31 [p.530].
41 'M.S.' '*Measure for Measure* illustrated from the Bible', *Gentleman's Magazine*, August 1795, p.645; and Reverend W.L. Bowles's defence of the speech as appropriate to the pious, *A Word on Cathedral Oratorios, and Clergy-Magistrates, Addressed to Lord Mountcashel* (London: Murray, 1830), pp.19–20.
42 E.C. Porter, 'The Poets in the Temple. IV. Shakespeare a Christian poet', *Church Monthly* (Boston) March 1864, p.142.
43 G. Arbuthnot, *Shakespeare Sermons Preached in the Collegiate Church of Stratford-on-Avon* (London: Longmans, Green, 1900), p.93.
44 'The Siege of Rochelle', *Literary Panorama*, May 1808, cols.281–4 [col. 283]. On Smith in the role, *Monthly Mirror*, April 1808, p.285.
45 [S. Pratt], *Sublime and Beautiful Scripture: Being Essays on Select Passages of Sacred Composition* (2 vols; London: Murray, 1777), vol.1, p.84.
46 V. Ward, *The Stage: A Dangerous and Irreconcilable Enemy to Christianity, Asserted and Proved, in a Letter, Addressed to a Comedian* (2nd edn; Aberdeen, Chalmers, 1819), p.6.
47 *Proceedings of the Sheffield Shakespeare Club* (Sheffield: Crookes, 1829), 5 December 1827, p.119.
48 *Theatrical Times*, 5 June 1847, p.172.
49 *Stamford Mercury*, 26 February 1847 [p.3].
50 *The Heir*, Act 4: scene 1. On justice and injustice in literature, R.C. Sterne, *Dark Mirror: The Sense of Injustice in Modern European and American Literature* (New York: Fordham University Press, 1994).
51 *A Dictionary of Quotations from the British Poets* (London: Whittaker, 1824), p.218.
52 A. Hill, *King Henry the Fifth: Or, The Conquest of France by the English* (3rd edn; London: Lowndes, 1765), p.46.
53 J. Banks, *The Albion Queens; or, the Death of Mary Queen of Scots. A Tragedy* (London: Bell, 1797), p.18.
54 J. Gay, *The Captives: A Tragedy* (Dublin: Grierson, 1724), p.34.
55 W. Thompson, *Poems on Several Occasions, to Which Is Added Gondibert and Birtha, a Tragedy* (Oxford: printed at the Theatre, 1751), p.395.
56 *The Recruiting Serjeant, a Musical Entertainment* (London: Griffin, 1770), p.26.
57 A. Yearsley, *Earl Goodwin, an Historical Play* (London, G.G.J. and J. Robinson, 1791), pp.12–13, p.76, and comment, p.90; L. Kasmer, *Novel Histories: British Women Writing History, 1760–1830* (Lanham, MD: Farleigh Dickinson University, 2012), pp.61–4.

58 G. Colman junior, *The Surrender of Calais. A Play in Three Acts* (Dublin: Byrne, 1792), p.58, p.60. See S. Valladares, *Staging the Peninsular War: English Theatres 1807–1815* (Abingdon: Ashgate, 2015), pp.179–80.
59 *Morning Post*, 31 May 1802, p.1. The work's history is explored in G. Taylor, *The French Revolution and the London Stage, 1789–1805* (Cambridge: Cambridge University, 2002), p.34. See also P. Shaw, *Suffering and Sentiment in Romantic Military Art* (Farnham: Ashgate, 2013).
60 R. Cumberland, *Jew of Mogadore, A Comic Opera, in Three Acts* (New York: Longworth, 1808), p.55.
61 H. Salvin, *Mary Stuart, The Maid of Orleans, from the German, with a Life of the Author* (London: Longman, Hurst, Rees, Orme, Brown, and Green, 1824), p.63.
62 J. Wilson, *The City of the Plague and other Poems* (Edinburgh: Constable, 1816), p.248.
63 Non-British playwrights and librettists dealt with mercy, I. Nagel, *Autonomy and Mercy: Reflections on Mozart's Operas*, transl. M. Faber and I. Nagel (Cambridge, MA: Harvard University Press, 1991).
64 S. Johnson, *The Lives of the Most Eminent English Poets with Critical Observations on their Works* (4 vols; London: Bathurst etc., 1781), vol.1, p.414. Johnson by implication accepted the precepts of mercy in Milton, *Paradise Lost*, as an epic that 'displays the power and the mercy of the Supreme being' (p.241), at p.248 he contrasts ancient epic poets with Milton in relation to moral sentiments and virtues including justice and mercy.
65 An example of sacred poetry on the theme, W. Wells, *Election, A Poem, Comprising the Mercy of God, and the Love of Christ, Etc* (London, for the author, 1772).
66 B.H. Malkin, *A Father's Memoirs of his Child* (London: Longman, Hurst, Rees, Orme, 1806), p.xxxii, and pp.xxxiii, 'The Divine Image'.
67 [W. Allen], *The Philanthropist* 5:20 (1815), pp.342–63 [p.343].
68 'Sacred Poetry', *Blackwood's Edinburgh Magazine* 24:147 (December 1828), pp.917–38 [p.920]. See also 'W.' 'A Few Thoughts upon Sacred Poetry', *The British Magazine* (July 1832), pp.450–7 [p.454].
69 S.F. Williams, 'About Wordsworth's Poetry', *The Rose, the Shamrock, and the Thistle* 4:23 (March 1864), pp.468–80 [p.468].
70 A.B. Grosart, *The Poems of Phineas Fletcher, B.D. Rector of Hilgay, Norfolk: For the First Time Collected and Edited: With Memoir, Essay, and Notes* (4 vols; private, 1869), vol.1, p.98, taking to task Macdonald's 'Antiphon on Justice and Mercy as Personified in "Christ's Victorie"'.
71 A.B. Grosart, *The Complete Works of Joshuah Sylvester: For the First Time Collected and Edited* (Edinburgh: Edinburgh University Press, 1880), vol.1.
72 W. Collins, *Odes on Several Descriptive and Allegorical Subjects* (London: Millar, 1746), pp.20–1; J. Langhorne, *The Poetical Works of Mr William Collins: With Memoirs of the Author; and Observations on His Genius and Writings* (London: Becket and Dehondt, 1765), p.115; H.D. Weinbrot, *Britannia's Issue: The Rise of British Literature from Dryden to Ossian* (Cambridge: Cambridge University Press, 1993), p.378; see D. Griffin, *Patriotism and Poetry in Eighteenth-century Britain* (Cambridge: Cambridge University Press, 2005), p.138. For later odes, Mary Leapor, 'An ode to mercy. In Imitation of Part of the 145th Psalm', *Poems upon Several Occasions* (London: Roberts, 1748), pp.12–15.
73 J. Langhorne, *The County Justice. A Poem by One of His Majesty's Justices of the Peace for the County of Somerset. Part III* (London: Becket, 1777), p.477. His 'A Case where

Mercy should have mitigated Justice' concerns the lack of discretion in sentence for a robber who shared stolen food with a starving baby.

74 I. Watts, *The Psalms of David Imitated in the Language of the New Testament, and Apply'd to the Christian State and Worship* (London: Clark, 1719), pp.257–8.
75 E. Ward, *The Modern World Disrob'd: Or, Both Sexes Stript of Their Pretended Vertue, by the Author of the London-Spy* (London: Bragge, 1708).
76 J.C. Prince, *Autumn Leaves, Original Poems* (Hyde: Booth, 1856), pp.8–10 (p.10).
77 'Angel of Mercy', E.T. Pilgrim, *Hymns, Written Chiefly on the Divine Attributes of the Supreme Being* (1832; Exeter: West of England Institution for the Deaf and Dumb, 1837), p.29; 'Justice, Mercy and Humility'; G. Blyth *In Poems* (Cupar: Westwood, 1874), p.212; G. Eveleigh, *Science Revealed: A Poem, Descriptive of the Works of Creation and the Truth of Scripture Record* (London: Churchill, 1863), pp.55–6, pp.68–9.
78 See 'Caerphilly Eistedfodd', *South Wales Daily News*, 11 June 1878, p.3.
79 P.W. Roose, 'Sweet Mercy', *The Argosy* 65 (September 1898), pp.269–76. Tennyson has the expected exchange on mercy in his play *Queen Mary. A Drama* (London: King, 1875), p.61, with Renard's remark to the queen, 'Yet too much mercy is a want of mercy' and in the poem 'Rizpah' (written 1878, printed in *Ballads and other Poems* (London: Kegan Paul, 1880) a pathetic appeal is made to the Lord, 'Full of compassion and mercy', in a poem about a son hanged in chains.
80 R.W. Dixon, *Songs and Odes* (London: Elkin Mathew, 1896), p.25.
81 H. Orel, *Thomas Hardy's Epic-drama: A Study of The Dynasts* (1963; New York: Greenwood Press, 1969), p.52. Hardy's Great War poetry includes, 'Often when warring' (1915), on enemy-soldier compassion as 'deed of grace', viewed as 'natural midsight'. 'And there was Great Calm', on the Armistice features the Spirit of Pity and mentions 'Heaven distilled ... clemency'. His 'Compassion. An Ode' in celebration of the RSPCA centenary, ends with 'Blessed are the merciful'. His pessimistic 'Thoughts at Midnight' in the posthumous *Winter Words in Various Moods and Metres* (London: Macmillan, 1928), ends, p.5 with the locutor saying: 'God, look he on you, | Have mercy upon you!'
82 'Ode on the Late Success of Admiral Rodney', *Newcastle Courant*, 8 June 1782, reprinted 20 April 1888, p.2.
83 *Eliza Cook's Journal*, 27 September 1851, p.345.
84 Swinburne's oeuvre can be studied through the online Algernon Charles Swinburne Project, see http://webapp1.dlib.indiana.edu/swinburne/
85 *Saturday Review*, 9 June 1900, pp.704–5.
86 L. Morris, *Idylls and Lyrics* (London: Kegan Paul, Trench, Trübner, 1896), p.12.
87 L. Morris, *Harvest-tide: A Book of Verses* (New York: Crowell, 1901), p.153.
88 F.W.O. Ward, *Confessions of a Poet* (London: Hutchinson, 1894).
89 F.W.O. Ward, *English Roses* (London: Simpkin, Marshall, Hamilton, Kent, 1899), p.190.
90 T.W. Crosland, *The Five Notions* (London: Richards, 1903), pp.97–9 [p.98].
91 W. Watson, *The Poems of Sir William Watson: 1878–1935* (London: Harrap, 1936), p.168.
92 'On Being Styled Pro-Boer', *The Poems of William Watson* (2 vols; London: Lane, 1905), vol.2, p.86.
93 G. Barlow, *The Poetical Works of George Barlow* (10 vols; London: Glaisher, 1903), vol.10, p.225.
94 The poem, originally concerning injustice in Egypt, appeared in *In Vinculis* (London: Kegan Paul, Trench, 1889).

95	'T.W.H.C.' 'Mr Masefield's Poetry', *Saturday Review*, 15 June 1912, pp.749–50 [p.749]. In his historic novel *Live and Kicking Ned* (London: Heinemann, 1939), the protagonist ruminates on mercy in relation to sentences for death, p.418.
96	E.g. St John Honeywood, 'On Crimes and Punishments' in *Poems* (New York: Swords, 1801), p.108.
97	'The Punishment of Death. [No. III.]', *Morning Advertiser*, 7 February 1842, p.3.
98	'Be Merciful after thy Power', *Bristol Times*, 15 December 1849, p.6.
99	'The Convict's Appeal', in the anonymous *Trifles; a Collection of Original Poems: Containing High Beach, an Historical and Descriptive Sketch. Market Day Elegies, Odes, Songs, &c* (Little Eastcheap: Plummer, 1815), pp.54–66, about the drawer of a forged bill; also 'Philologus', on the execution of the forger John Vartie, *Lancaster Gazette*, 10 January 1818, p.4.
100	*Westmorland Gazette*, 18 September 1819, p.8.
101	'The Law of Mercy', *Household Words* 14:81, 11 October 1852, p.60.
102	'A Dissertation on Revenge and Cruelty', *Universal Magazine of Knowledge and Pleasure*, 3:16 (July 1748), pp.16–18; 'The Visitor. Number LI', on the first page of *The Public Ledger*, 16 October 1760; ' Clemency', in supplement to vol. 2 of *Oxford Magazine*, 3 July 1769, pp.241–2; 'Prize Essay. On Mercy', *St James's Magazine*, August 1775, pp.355–6; *Westminster Magazine*, December 1777, p.631, using Shakespearian quotations; – 'This passage can never be too often read'; 'Justice and Mercy', *Town and Country Magazine*, May 1788, p.211; 'A Friend to Justice', *Cheltenham Chronicle*, 16 November 1815 [p.3]; *Ladies' Monthly Museum*, 1 November 1821, pp.268–71; *Ladies' Monthly Museum*, 1 December 1821, pp.309–12.
103	*The Ladies Diary; or, the Women's Almanack* (London: Company of Stationers, 1751), p.42. The answer came in the next year's *Almanack*.
104	*The Ladies Library* 1, 1739, p.84.
105	*Kentish Register*, September 1795, p.347.
106	*Blackburn Standard*, 5 January 1895, p.8.
107	*Manchester Courier*, 31 March 1883, p.11, reporting prizes for essays by Liverpool branch of RSPCA.
108	'The Obligation to relieve the distresses of our fellow creatures', Bishop Sherlock, *Canterbury Journal*, 18 March 1837, p.190; 'Hospital Sunday. Newcastle', *Newcastle Journal*, 31 October 1870, p.3; 'Religious Readings. The Strangest Sight of Mercy, An Allegory', *Essex Herald*, 15 April 1882, p.2; 'Religious Readings. Mercies', *Essex Herald*, 6 October 1883, p.2.
109	E.g. J. Davies, 'The Merciful Spirit', *Baptist Magazine*, November 1848, pp.660–6; 'Sunday Errands', *The Churchman's Monthly Penny Magazine and Guide to Christian Truth* 8 (January to June 1854), pp.139–40; R. Glover, 'The Beatitudes. V', *The Sunday at Home* (1887), pp.602–4; *Sunday Magazine*, October 1876, Page's series on 'Errands of Mercy' and verse by Reverend Henry Downton, 'Mercy', *Sunday Magazine*, 1876, p.190.
110	P. Bayne, *The Christian Life, Social and Individual* (1855; London: Hogg, 1859), p.36. A.C. Swinburne, *Notes of an English Republican on the Muscovite Crusade* (London: Chatto and Windus, 1876), p.5 refers to the unlikeliness of Carlyle (writing 28 November, *The Times*) 'as a preacher of philanthropy and mercy'.
111	For instance, on penal-law amelioration, 'Mercy Is Twice Blessed', *Nottingham Review*, 23 January 1846, p.8; 'Justice and Mercy', *Portsmouth Evening News*, 22 November 1880 [p.2].

112 *London Magazine*, October 1827, cited in *Morning Chronicle*, 1 October 1827 [p.2].

113 E.g. letter to editor, 'Petro', *Birmingham Daily Gazette*, 9 October 1877, p.6; '"Mob Mercy." Home Secretary's Protest', *The Scotsman*, 11 February 1928, p.10.

114 On 'private mercy' in *Tom Jones* (1749), L. Bellamy, *Commerce, Morality and the Eighteenth-Century Novel* (Cambridge: Cambridge University Press, 2005).

115 W.P. Scargill, *Usurer's Daughter* (1832; London: Clarke, Beeton, 1854), p.17.

116 A. Stewart, *Justice & Mercy, or, a Tale of All Hallow's Eve* (London: Dolman, 1858).

117 L. Fasick, 'Women's Moral Role in Selected Victorian Religious Novels', Indiana University PhD, 1990, p.191. His novel *What's Mine's Mine* (3 vols; London: Kegan Paul, 1886) features a character named Mercy, mercy figures in sermons in *Alec Forbes of Howglen* (2 vols; Leipzig: Tauchnitz, 1865), vol.2, p.31, p.237. His non-fiction reflections on mercy and justice include one of the beatitude-themed 'organ songs', 'Blessed are the Merciful', in *The Disciple: And Other Poems* (London: Strahan, 1867), pp.228–9; *Unspoken Sermons* (London: Strahan, 1867); and the discussion of Giles Fletcher's poetry, in *In England's Antiphon* (London: Macmillan, 1874), p.150.

118 M. Thormählen, 'Anne Brontë and Her Bible', *Brontë Studies* 37:4 (2013), pp.339–44, explores Brontë's reflections on mercy in her reading of the Bible and *Agnes Grey*; mercy and justice in *Middlemarch* through Dorothea is noted in N.L. Paxton, *George Eliot and Herbert Spencer: Feminism, Evolutionism, and the Reconstruction of Gender* (Princeton, NJ: Princeton University Press, 2014), p.189.

119 A. Trollope, *Phineas Redux* (2 vols; London: Chapman, Hall, 1874), vol.2, ch.55, 'Phineas in Prison'.

120 E.g. 'The Power of Mercy', *Household Words* 1:14 (29 June 1850), pp.323–5.

121 *Pall Mall Gazette*, 28 August 1886, p.4. S.E. O'Dell, *Merciful or Merciless* (London: T. Fisher Unwin, 1886), p.72.

122 See C.J. Barker, *The Way of Life: A Study in Christian Ethics* (London: Lutterworth, 1947).

123 M.C. Nussbaum, *Sex and Social Justice* (Oxford: Oxford University Press, 1999), pp.168–70.

124 On fairy tales, mercy and justice, see T. Crofton Croker, 'The Banshee of the Mac Carthys', in W.B. Yeats, ed., *Fairy and Folk Tales of the Irish Peasantry* (London: Walter Scott, 1888), pp.113–27 [pp.118–19]. J.R.R. Tolkien, 'On Fairy-Stories' in 1938, reprinted in *Tree and Leaf* (1964; London: Unwin Hyman, 1988), p.42 quoting G.K. Chesterton ['On Household Gods and Goddesses', 1922] on children, being innocent, loving justice whilst most adults being wicked prefer mercy.

125 J. Schramm, *Atonement and Self-Sacrifice in Nineteenth-Century Narrative* (Cambridge: Cambridge University Press, 2012), p.31; ch.4, 'Sacrifice and the sufferings of the substitute: Charles Dickens and the Atonement controversy of the 1850s' looks at the theology of mercy.

126 J. Schramm, 'The Bible and the Realist Novel', in M. Knight, ed., *The Routledge Companion to Literature and Religion* (Abingdon: Routledge, 2016), pp.263–73 [p.269]. I would add *Oliver Twist; or, the Parish Boy's Progress*, and penultimate paragraph, 'that Being whose code is mercy, and whose great attribute is benevolence' (serialized 1837–9). E. Gaskell's *Sylvia's Lovers* has mercy and forgiveness in the assize sermon to judges in York Minster, on Zechariah vii, 9 (2 vols, Leipzig: Tauchnitz, 1863), vol.2, p.74, and discussion of mercy and forgiveness between Sylvia and Philip, pp.103–4. For parabilistic elements in Victorian novels,

S.E. Colón, *Victorian Parables* (London: Continuum, 2012). George Eliot's play *The Spanish Gypsy* (completed 1868) has self-critical discourse on mercy from the Prior.

127 J. Schramm, 'The Bible and the Realist Novel', p.268.

128 C. Brontë, *Jane Eyre* (1847; 2nd edn; London: Smith, Elder, 1848), vol.3, p.295.

129 See T. Sparks, 'Sensation Intervention: M.C. Houston's *Recommended to Mercy* (1862) and the Novel of Experience', ch.2 in A. Beller and T. MacDonald, eds, *Rediscovering Victorian Women Sensation Writers: Beyond Braddon* (London: Routledge, 2015). On Mercy Merrick, see G. Watt, *The Fallen Woman in the Nineteenth Century English Novel* (London: Croom Helm, 1984).

130 Dr Bohnstedt, 'The Life and Writings of Charles Dickens', *Jahresvericht der höhern Bürger und Real-Schule su Siegen womit zu der am Freitag den 7 April 1854 abzuhaltenden öffentlichen Prüfung einladet Dr Carl Schnabel* (Siegen: Drud and Papier der Vorlander, 1854), p.20.

131 'A Homily on the Theology of Charles Dickens', *The Homilist; or, The pulpit for the people* 24 (London: Simpkin, Marshall, 1871), pp.193–202; G. Gissing, *Charles Dickens. A Critical Study* (New York: Dodd, Mead, 1898), p.105. On Dickens's relationship to the bible and treatment of mercy, J.L. Larson, *Dickens and the Broken Scripture* (Athens: University of Georgia Press, 2008); see also J.R. Reed, *Dickens and Thackeray: Punishment and Forgiveness* (Athens: Ohio University Press, 1995).

132 E. Berdoe, 'Prevention of Cruelty to Animals. Meeting in Gloucester', *Gloucester Journal* (5 October 1895), p.6.

133 J. Routledge, *Chapters in the History of Popular Progress Chiefly in Relation to the Freedom of the Press and Trial by Jury* (London: Macmillan, 1876), p.172.

134 S.R. Tucker, *The Virtues and Vices in the Arts: A Sourcebook* (Eugene, OR: Cascade, 2015); R. Brown-Grant, B. Ribemont and A.D. Hedeman, eds, *Textual and Visual Representations of Power and Justice in Medieval France* (Farnham: Ashgate, 2015); E. Stafford, *Worshipping Virtues: Personification and the Divine in Ancient Greece* (London: Classical Press of Wales, 2000); S.C. Chew, *The Virtues Reconciled: An Iconographical Study* (Toronto: University of Toronto Press, 1947), ch.4, 'Mercy and Peace'; S. McKeown, 'Configuring Virtue: The Emergence of Abstraction, Allegoresis and Emblem in Swedish Figural Sculpture of the Seventeenth Century', *Baltic Journal of Art History* 9 (Spring 2015), pp.115–48.

135 Quoted in H. Ladd, *The Victorian Morality of Art: An Analysis of Ruskin's Esthetic* (New York: Long and Smith, 1932), p.162.

136 G.F. Teniswood, 'Flaxman as a Designer. No. IV', *Art-Journal*, 1 October 1872, p.257.

137 For sculptural rendering of abstract virtues, J.G. Herder, *Plastik. Einige Wahrnehmungen über Form und Gestalt aus Pygmalions bilendem Traume* (Riga: Hartknoch, 1778), p.135.

138 M. Sbriccoli, 'Le triade, le bandeau, le genou', *Histoire et Societes* 9:1 (February 2005), pp.33–78; including symbol of knee for mercy [p.26]. See S. Boyse, *A New Pantheon* (London: Newbery, 1753), p.198, on this habit in classical culture.

139 See C. Harbison, *The Last Judgment in Sixteenth Century Northern Europe: A Study in Art, Revolution and Change* (New York: Garland, 1976); D. Beauregard, 'Virtue Ethics in Michelangelo's The Last Judgment: Christ as Severity and Mary as Clemency', *Logos* 19:2 (Spring 2016), pp.33–52.

140 On difficulties in representing mercy in statuary and painting, see 'The Statue of Mercy', *Sydney Mail*, 5 April 1879, p.528.

141 Digby, *Mores Catholici*, vol.2, p.338.
142 E.g. E. Burke, *Reflections on the French Revolution, and on the Proceedings in Certain Societies in London Relative to That Event: In a Letter Intended to Have Been Sent to a Gentleman in Paris* (1790; 2nd edn; London: Dosley, 1790), p.199.
143 See Thomas Rowlandson and A.C. Pugin's image of the Old Bailey in *The Microcosm of London*, dated 1 March 1809.
144 See 'The Statuary in Newgate', B. Martin, *Miscellaneous Correspondence, Containing a Variety of Subjects, Relative to Natural and Civil History, Geography, Mathematics, Poetry, Memoirs of Monthly Occurrences, Catalogues of New Books, &c* (London: Owen, 1759), p.46.
145 See *Law Times*, 31 December 1859, p.170; *Illustrated London News*, 4 February 1860, p.105; *Art Journal*, 1 February 1860, p.39; *The Spectator*, 7 January 1860, p.19.
146 *British Quarterly Review*, 1 April 1860, p.537.
147 *The Athenaeum*, 20 January 1844, p.66.
148 *Morning Chronicle*, 1 July 1845, p.5.
149 *Encyclopaedia Londinensis* (24 vols; London: Adlard, 1815), vol.13, p.491.
150 W.C. Oulton, *The Traveller's Guide, or English Itinerary* (2 vols; London: Cundee, 1805), vol.2, p.939. The mottos were 'Cuique suum' and the 'Miseris succurro'.
151 *Lancaster Gazette*, 22 July 1815, p.4; S. Jefferson, *The History and Antiquities of Carlisle* (Carlisle: Jefferson, 1838), p.279.
152 See J. Resnik and D.E. Curtis, *Representing Justice: Invention, Controversy, and Rights in City-states and Democratic Courtrooms* (New Haven, CT: Yale University Press, 2011); C. Graham, *Ordering Law: The Architectural and Social History of the English Law Court to 1914* (Aldershot: Ashgate, 2003).
153 *Illustrated London News*, 26 August 1843, pp.4–5.
154 *Northampton Mercury*, 21 May 1864, p.6.
155 The unsigned 'Truth, Mercy, and Justice, (as seen at the Foor Coorts, Dublin.)' Published by William Lawrence of Dublin, c.1900, it shows an exchange between a rustic and a Q.C. resembling Edward Vaughan Kenealy.
156 A. Waterhouse, 'A Short Description of the Manchester Assize Courts', in *Papers Read at the Royal Institute of British Architects* (London: Parker, 1865), pp.165–76 [p.172].
157 J. Cooke and J. Maule, *A Description of the Royal Hospital for Seamen, at Greenwich* (Greenwich, 1813), p.15.
158 E.A. Gowing, 'Lady Rachel Russell', *Belgravia*, July 1892, pp.247–70 [p.247].
159 'Britannia and the Blacks', *Punch* 12 (1847), p.176.
160 Quoted by Viscount Mahon to Sir Robert Peel, 25 April 1844, *Third Report of The Commissioners on the Fine Arts* (London: Clowes, 1844), p.27.
161 G.F. Teniswood, 'Flaxman as a Designer. No. IV. – The Lord's Prayer, and the Acts of Mercy', *The Art-Journal*, 1 October 1872, pp.257–60. He depicted a knight's acts of mercy for his wife, A. Cunningham, *The Lives of the Most Eminent British Painters, Sculptors and Architects* (6 vols; London: Murray, 1830), vol.3, p.313.
162 It *was* reported that the memorial included justice, temperance, purity and mercy, see *The Art-Journal*, 1 January 1867, p.14 but this is not the case.
163 E.C. Agnew, *Illustrations of the Corporal and Spiritual Works of Mercy, In Sixteen Designs, Engraved in Outline* (London: Dolmain, 1840).
164 G. Wakeling, *The Oxford Church Movement: Sketches and Recollections* (London: Sonnenschein, 1895), p.95. For references to 'corporal acts of mercy'

by the movement, see anti-Tractarian T.H. Horne, *The Identity of Popery and Tractarianism* (privately printed, 1844), pp.11–12.

165 For memorial windows, see *Southend Standard*, 23 May 1879 [p.5], on St Margaret's in Westminster, commemorating Lady Hatherley; *Glasgow Evening Post*, 23 October 1893, p.6 on stained glass as medieval revivalism.

166 *Illustrated London News*, 27 December 1851, p.772.

167 'The Life of An Architect', *Bentley's Miscellany* 32 (1852), pp.291–9 [p.291]. E.F. Finden's series *Royal Gallery of British Art* included an engraving of this work by George Thomas Doo, 1848.

168 *The Athenaeum*, 15 August 1857, p.1037; 'Fine Arts', London *Daily News*, 28 May 1858, p.2; 'Sculpture', *Western Times*, 27 March 1858, p.5.

169 *Globe*, 12 December 1887, p.5.

170 *The Scotsman*, 22 May 1888, p.5.

171 *The Builder*, 9 June 1888, p.407; *The Globe*, 10 August 1888, p.5; E. Manning, *Marble & Bronze: The Art and Life of Hamo Thornycroft* (London: Trefoil, 1982), p.179.

172 G.K. Chesterton, *G.F. Watts* (London: Duckworth, 1904), p.87.

173 The comment on this tradition, from M.J.H. Liversidge, C. Edwards, *Imagining Rome: British Arts and Rome in the Nineteenth Century* (London: Merrell Holberton, 1996), p.144.

174 Jerry Barrett's image of Fry was engraved in 1863. James Edgar's portrait of Guthrie was created 1862, engraved in May 1863 and described when exhibited at the Scottish Royal Academy, as 'very offensive Exeter Hall-ism' for showing as picturesque, a private act of piety, *Daily Review* (Edinburgh), 21 February 1866, p.2. A photograph of Guthrie's image, like Burne-Jones's 'Merciful Knight', and other images concerning mercy such as St Bernard Dogs (1878) and 'A Merciful Man is Merciful to His Beast', was copyrighted at Stationer's Hall.

175 L. Lippincott, 'Murder and the Fine Arts: Or, a Reassessment of Richard Dadd', *J. Paul Getty Museum Journal* 16 (1988), pp.76–94.

176 *London Evening Standard*, 3 February 1872, p.6.

177 *Leeds Mercury*, 14 May 1872, p.7; *The Scotsman*, 30 April 1881, p.6.

178 E. Péteri, *Victorian Approaches to Religion as Reflected in the Art of the Pre-Raphaelites* (Budapest: Akadémiai Kiadó, 2003), p.78.

179 Engraved by Archibald Dick, *Mirror of Literature*, 30 March 1839, p.207.

180 'The Royal Academy', *Fun* 45:1149 (18 May 1887), p.215. See *Pall Mall Budget*, 5 May 1887, pp.16–17 and 'The Royal Academy Exhibition', *Art Journal*, August 1887, pp.277–80. See *The Reminiscences of Frederick Goodall, R.A.* (London: Scott, 1902), p.151, and *The Artist* 8, p.171 reprinted in S. Weintraub, *Bernard Shaw on the London Art Scene, 1885–1950* (University Park: Pennsylvania State University Press, 1989), p.164.

181 For coupling of mercy (with branch) and truth in British iconography, see Angelica Kaufman's painting engraved by Charles Taylor, in a series of *Moral Emblems*, c.1780, British Museum, 1872, 0810.109; and 'See Truth, Love & Mercy descending', Mercy with sword and Truth identified with looking-glass, with Cupid flying above them and etching after Henry Corbould, frontispiece to *The Poetical Works of James Beattie, L.L.D and William Collins* (London: Rivington, 1823).

182 *The Book of Art: Cartoons, Frescoes, Sculpture, and Decorative Art, as Applied to the New Houses of Parliament and to Buildings in General* (London: How, 1846), p.88.

183 Langhorne, *The Poetical Works of Mr William Collins*, p.115. See the critique of the elaborate colour printed version, T.C. Hansard, *Typographia: An Historical Sketch of*

184   the Origin and Progress of the Art of Printing (London: Baldwin, Cradock and Joy, 1825), p.915.
185   Gallery of Poets, Pall-Mall and Fleet-Street, April 2, 1790. Catalogue of the Third Exhibition of Pictures, Painted for Mr Macklin by the Artists of Britain, Illustrative of the British Poets, and the Bible (London: Bensley, 1795), no. v, p.115. See J.C. Watson, 'William Artaud's "The Triumph of Mercy"', Burlington Magazine 123 (April 1981), pp.228–31.

185   Burne-Jones's watercolour was inspired by Kenelm Digby's recounting of the tale of St John Gualberto, see Peteri, Victorian Approaches to Religion as Reflected in the Art of the Pre-Raphaelites, pp.121–2.

186   Advertised in the Kentish Gazette, 8 March 1791 [p.1].
187   Freemason's Monthly Magazine (Boston), 1 December 1841, p.57. See the sermon at Portsmouth by Reverend T.T. Haverfield, Freemasons' Quarterly, 31 December 1842, p.460. In G. Oliver, The Historical Landmarks and Other Evidences of Freemasonry, Explained, a Series of Practical Lectures, with Notes (London: Spencer, 1846), p.166, on the Omniscient and Omnipresent Deity, 'the circle represents his eternity, and the two perpendicular parallel lines, his equal justice and mercy'. Mercy was presented in verse, in The Free-Masons' Melody, Being a General Collection of Masonic Songs (Bury: R. Hellawell, 1818), p.259.
188   The Era, 29 June 1873, p.7.
189   Our Young Folks, April 1871, p.248; and reproduced e.g. Dick's Parlor Exhibitions (New York: Dick and Fitzgerald), p.44.
190   Justice and the navy were the supporters of the tin-plate workers' union iconography.
191   The writer Laman Blanchard penned a humorous song about the habit of assigning the female gender to virtues, 'A Song for "The Sex"', Ainsworth's Magazine 2 (1842), p.72.
192   S.P. Casteras, Images of Victorian Womanhood in English Art (Rutherford, NJ: Fairleigh University Press, 1987), p.53. See also M. Warner, Monuments and Maidens: The Allegory of the Female Form (London: Weidenfeld and Nicolson, 1985).
193   But see The Angel of Mercy: A Little Book of Affection: To Which Is Prefixed an Essay on Heavenly Spirits (London: G. and W.B. Whittaker, 1823).
194   'The Angel of Mercy at Sandringham', Illustrated Police News, 30 December 1871, p.1.
195   The designer, Charlotte Canning, thought it an angel of resurrection; others called it the angel of pity. See S.J. Heathorn, 'Angel of Empire: The Cawnpore Memorial Well as a British Site of Imperial Remembrance', Journal of Colonialism and Colonial History 8:3 (Winter 2007), pp.1–33. For identification with mercy, see E. De Valbezen, The English and India: New Sketches Translated from the French (With The Author's Permission) by a Diplomat (London: Allen, 1883), p.178.
196   A.W.N. Pugin, The True Principles of Pointed or Christian Architecture: Set Forth in Two Lectures Delivered at St. Marie's Iscott (London: Bohn, 1853), p.37.
197   M. Bostridge, Florence Nightingale: The Making of an Icon (New York: Farrar, Strauss and Giroux, 2008), p.267.
198   See The Christian Witness and Congregational Magazine, 1868, pp.303–4.
199   The Lancet, 16 June 1826, p.332.

Chapter 3

1 *Gentleman's Magazine*, January 1787, p.87. *Old Bailey Proceedings Online* (www.oldbaileyonline.org, version 7.0, 23 July 2014), February 1787 (s17870221-1). See C. Koslofsky and D. Rabin, 'The Limits of the State: Suicide, Assassination, and Execution in Early Modern Europe', in A. Bähr and H. Medick, eds, *Sterben von eigener Hand: Selbsttötung als kulturelle Praxis* (Köln: Böhlau Verlag, 2005), pp.45–65 [pp.57–60]; L. MacKay, 'Refusing the Royal Pardon: London Capital Convicts and the Reactions of the Courts and Press, 1789', *London Journal* 28:2 (2003), pp.21–40.
2 *Hereford Journal*, 17 June 1789, p.1; *Ipswich Journal*, 26 September 1789, p.1. The duchess of Cumberland and Mrs Fitzherbert attended the Old Bailey court, as six women had rejected transportation for life.
3 *Gentleman's Magazine*, April 1788, p.360; T. Keneally, *The Commonwealth of Thieves. The Improbable Birth of Australia* (2006; London: Vintage, 2007), p.227; T. Hitchcock and R.B. Shoemaker, *Tales from the Hanging Court* (London: Hodder Arnold, 2006), p.233.
4 *Hampshire Chronicle*, 27 February 1792, p.2.
5 R.W. Emerson, *English Traits* (Boston, MA: Osgood, 1876), p.305.
6 *Punch*, 4 November 1848, p.179; *Exeter and Plymouth Gazette*, 28 October 1848, p.3. *Punch* attacked royal pardon for innocent people, in 'The Dyspeptic of the Home Office', 17 January 1857, p.22, in the case of the wrongfully convicted John Markham.
7 So national virtues are listed as 'righteousness, judgment, mercy, and such like' in H. Knight, *The Natural and Providential Effects of National Virtue and Vice Consider'd in a Sermon [on 1 Sam. Xii. 24, 25] Preach'd in Part, the Last Fast-day November the 25th 1741* (London: Noon, 1742), p.23.
8 In a similar fashion, Cleall, 'From Divine Judgement', p.449, notes 'justice was one of the many concepts through which missionaries could evoke both likeness and alterity'.
9 For English-language accounts of British mercy and justice, see chapters 25 and 26, in A.B.C. Merriman-Labor, *Britons through Negro Spectacles: or, A Negro on Britons with a Description of London Illustrated* (London: Imperial and Foreign Company, 1909).
10 R.M. Baum, 'John Williams's Captivity Narrative: A Consideration of Normative Ethnicity', in F. Shuffelton, ed., *A Mixed Race: Ethnicity in Early America* (Oxford: Oxford University Press, 1993), pp.56–76 [p.62].
11 On this aspect of Fiji, see missionary discourse into the twentieth century, like N. Walker's *Fiji: Their People, History and Commerce* (London: Witherby, 1936), p.63.
12 *Sketches of the African Kingdoms and Peoples* (London: SPCK, 1860), p.154.
13 R.M. Martin, *The British Colonies*, p.114.
14 *Pall Mall Gazette*, review of Suyematsu, *A Fantasy of Far Japan*, 27 December 1905, p.4. The reviewer accepted magnanimity 'has always been in every race and every age the crowning virtue of noble minds'.
15 *Parliamentary Debates*, 2nd series, vol.5, House of Commons, 23 May 1821, col.933.
16 H.B. Stowe, *Sunny Memories of Distant Lands* (2 vols; Boston, MA: Phillips, Sampson, 1854), vol.2, p.65.
17 Review of F.P. Cobbe, *What Has Annexation Done for Italy? National Review* 18 (1864), pp.19–51 [p.24].

18   F.P. Cobbe, 'Ireland and Her Exhibition in 1865', *Fraser's Magazine*, October 1865, pp.403–22 [p.409].
19   'The Priest Lane Tragedy', *Londonderry Sentinel*, 5 August 1876 [p.2].
20   *An Original Collection of the Poems of Ossian, Orrann, Ulin: And Other Bards, Who Flourished in the Same Age* (Montrose: Review Newspaper Office, 1816), p.lxxii; T. Travers Burke, *Fingal: An Epic Poem. Versified from the 'Genuine Remains of Ossian.' With notes* (London: Cowie, Jollond, 1844), p.xv. See Weinbrot, *Britannia's Issue*, p.531 on the merciful Celtic warrior contrasted with the Anglo-Saxon.
21   See P. Sears, *A Pillar of Fire to Follow: American Indian Dramas, 1808–1859* (Bowling Green, OH: Bowling Green University, 1982), pp.36–43.
22   T. Gordon, *The Independent Whig* (2nd edn; London: J. Peele, 1741), vol.3, p.108.
23   See E. Hanson, *God's Mercy Surmounting Man's Cruelty* (Philadelphia, PA: Keimer, 1728); P. Williamson, *French and Indian Cruelty: Exemplified in the Life, and Various Vicissitudes of Fortune, of Peter Williamson* (London: for the author, 1759); *Journal of the Life and Religious Labours of John Comly: Late of Byberry, Pennsylvania* (Philadelphia, PA: Chapman, 1853), p.8; R.I. Dodge, *Our Wild Indians: Thirty-Three Years' Personal Experience among the Red Men of the Great West* (Hartford: Worthington, 1882), p.91; A.R.H. Moncrieff, *The Wigwam and the War-Path: Or Tales of the Red Indians* (London: Blackie, 1884), which begins with white men's cruelty, and lack of mercy, and revenge as 'a religion among savages', pp.9–10. The English Emma Hardinge's *Modern American Spiritualism: Twenty Years' Record of the Communion between Earth and the World of Spirits* (2nd edn; New York: the author, 1870) argued, pp.481–2 vengeance for injuries was exchanged for the 'gentle theories of Christianity … deeds of love and mercy', in explaining the role of Indian spirits as healing mediums. See *Our Wild Indians*, ch.151, for Indian cruelty.
24   J.P. Dunn, *Massacres of the Mountains: A History of the Indian Wars of the Far West* (2 vols; New York: Harper, 1886), vol.2, ch.21, entitled 'Cruelty, Pity and Justice', p.717, cites the argument about Indians not expecting or showing mercy in war, in reports of the Board of Indian Commissioners established in 1869.
25   H.R. Schoolcraft, *Oneóta: Or Characteristics of the Red Race of America from Original Notes and Manuscripts* (New York: Wiley and Putnam, 1845), p.129. See how he describes the ruler Joseph Brant, Thayendanegea, in *The American Indians: Their History, Condition and Prospects, from Original Notes and Manuscripts* (Buffalo, NY: Derby, 1851), pp.149–50 and 'tardiness to execute *purposed* mercy'. The lack of Cherokee mercy is noted in the 'scalping and withholding of mercy' in the Anglo-Cherokee War of 1758-61, L.M. Stevens, '"Spare His Life to Save His Soul"', in T. Bower and T. Chico, eds, *Atlantic Worlds in the Long Eighteenth Century: Seduction and Sentiment* (New York: Palgrave Macmillan, 2012), pp.97–113 [p.103]. On discourse of Native American mercilessness, R. Malhotra, 'American Exceptionalism and the Myth of the Frontiers', in R.K. Kanth, ed., *The Challenge of Eurocentrism: Global Perspectives, Policy, and Prospects* (New York: Palgrave Macmillan, 2009), 171–216 [pp.181–2]; and Eustace, *Passion Is the Gale*, pp.252–3, p.368.
26   See Quint, 'The Culture That Cannot Pardon: "Des Cannibales" in the Larger *Essais*', ch. 3 in *Montaigne and the Quality of Mercy*.
27   J. Martin, *An Account of the Natives of the Tonga Islands, in the South Pacific Ocean: With an Original Grammar and Vocabulary of Their Language* (2 vols; London: Murray, 1818), vol.2, p.139.
28   'Mercy', *The Times*, 14 September 1918, p.9.

29 [W. Baucke], *Where the White Man Treads* (Auckland: Wilson and Horton, 1905), p.23.
30 Suyematsu, *A Fantasy of Far Japan*, p.31 in which Suyematsu is told by a Westerner that she has heard the virtue of pardon or forgiving 'is wanting in oriental ethics, though the notion of pity exists', and he explains that 'mercy and forbearance' are fundamental to Buddhism. K. Suyematsu, *The Ethics of Japan (from the Smithsonian Report for 1905, pp.293–307)* (Washington, DC: Government Printing Office, 1907), originally *Journal of the Society of Arts* (London), 10 March 1905, discusses 'jen' and the 'tenderness of heart of a Japanese warrior', p.303.
31 E.g. S. Spencer, *A System of Synthetic Philosophy. Vol. VI. The Principles of Sociology* (London: Williams and Norgate, 1876) on primitive man and fellow feeling, kindness or altruism, pp.75–8.
32 I owe this insight to Darren Aoki. See I. Nitobe, *Bushido: The Soul of Japan* (1899; Tokyo: Teibi, 1908), p.33, pp.37–8. Relevant to a later chapter is warrior mercy, 'Bushi no nasake', the 'tenderness of a warrior (p.42). For British response, A. Stead, 'Bushido, the Japanese Ethical Code', *The Monthly Review* 14 (1904), pp.52–62; and his *Great Japan: A Study of National Efficiency* (London: Lane, 1905), p.46, and contrasting with the 'religious morality of the West', in teaching 'mercy and patience under insult', p.57. Stead also detects, p.328, 'long before the Geneva Convention was even dreamed of, Bushido had inculcated the principle of valour and mercy hand-in-hand'. The article was reproduced in newspapers, e.g. *Dublin Daily Express*, 26 December 1906, p.8.
33 A. Bain, *An English Grammar* (London: Longman, Green, Longman, Roberts, and Green, 1863), p.77. See R. Von Horrum-Schramm, 'In woman, immutable fundamental principles of humanity find their more distinctive representation, and give inspiration to both plastic and pictorial art, as for instance, in the representation of such qualities as justice, charity, mercy', in 'A Free Lance for Woman Suffrage', *The Woman's Signal*, 15 April 1897, p.229. In other cultures, association between mercy and gender is closer still, the Arabic for 'womb' (*rahim*) shares its etymology with 'mercy' (*rahma*), see V.A.M. Ashrof, *Islam and Gender Justice: Questions at the Interface* (Delhi: Kalpaz, 2005), p.11.
34 On gendering of emotions and modern research on crying as gendered in Western culture, see Frevert, ch.2. 'Gendering Emotions', in *Emotions in History – Lost and Found*. The primary sources are largely German, but this reveals a similar discourse to the Anglophone, of feminine compassion and benevolence.
35 *Mores Catholici*, p.464.
36 Appendix, 'Illustrations of Romish doctrine of invocation still existing from Liguori's Glories of Mary', in E.B. Pusey, *The Articles Treated on in Tract 90 Reconsidered and Their Interpretation Vindicated, in a Letter* (Oxford: Parker, 1841), p.210; 'Mariolatry in the Romish Church', *Christian Guardian and Church of England Magazine* (October 1849), p.435, reprinting M. Hobart Seymour, *Mornings among the Jesuits at Rome* (London: Seeleys, 1849); 'Glories of Mary', *Christian Remembrancer* 30 (1855), pp.417–67 [p.467 for the quote on stern judge].
37 G.A. Cobbold, *Religion in Japan; Shintoism, Buddhism, Christianity* (London: S.P.C.K., 1894), p.65.
38 For example the Quaker Mary Dudley, in a sermon at Epping, 14 June 1812, reprinted in C. Tylor, *Memoirs of Elizabeth Dudley; Consisting Chiefly of Selections from Her Journal and Correspondence* (London: A.W. Bennett, 1861), pp.334–6.

39 *A Diary of the Religious Experience of Mary Waring* (London: W. Phillips, 1809), p.212, p.217; *Portions of the Diary, Letters and Other Remains of Eliza Southall* (Birmingham: White and Pike, 1855), 2 August 1846, p.72.
40 [F.P. Cobbe] 'The Defects of Women, and How to Remedy Them. [From an English Point of View.]', *Putnam's Magazine*, n.s., 4 (August 1869), pp.226–33 [p.231]. Partially reprinted in *The Ladies' Treasury and Treasury of Literature* 8 (London, 1870), pp.12–17.
41 S. Nearing and N.M.S. Nearing, *Woman and Social Progress; a Discussion of the Biologic, Domestic, Industrial and Social Possibilities of American Women* (New York: Macmillan, 1912), p.241.
42 [M.L. de la Ramée], 'The Quality of Mercy', *Nineteenth Century* 40 (August 1896), pp.293–305.
43 C. Kingsley, 'Three Fishers' (1851), 'For men must work – | And women must weep'; Walter Scott, *Marmion* (3rd edn; Edinburgh: Ballantyne, 1808), canto 6, stanza 30, p.362 for 'A ministering angel thou'.
44 See G. Crabbe, 'Woman!' in *Poems* (London: Hatchard, 1807), pp.253–6 [p.255]; J.C. Prince, 'A Plea for Woman', *The Poetical Works of John Critchley Prince* (2 vols: Manchester: Heywood, 1880), vol.2, pp.147–9. Prince also depicts mercy as angel in 'The Three Angels. A Vision', *Poetical Works*, vol.1, pp.223–6.
45 'Mercy; pity; tenderness', S. Johnson, *A Dictionary of the English Language* (3rd edn; Dublin: Jones, 1768) [unpaginated]. Meaning mercy, pity, sorrow, according to W.M. Smith, *A Complete Etymology of the English Language* (New York: Narnes, 1876), p.149.
46 'Das Richterschwert, womit der Mann sich ziert, | Verhaßt ist's in der Frauen Hand', the translation in *The Literary World* (New York) 9, 13 September 1851, p.1.
47 See *Freemason's Magazine and General Miscellany* (Philadelphia), May 1811, p.128; *Saturday Magazine*, 5 November 1836, p.183. T.A. Jankowski, *Women in Power in the Early Modern Drama* (Urbana: University of Illinois Press, 1992), notes presentation of women as merciful in the drama of this period, looking at Thomas Heywood's *If You Know Not Me, You Know Nobody* (1605), p.202.
48 Calidore to Mr Paley, on his 'Principles of Philosophy', *Gentleman's Magazine*, March 1788, p.223.
49 J. Watts Lethbridge, *Woman the Glory of the Man* (London: T. Richardson, 1856), p.159.
50 'The Position of Women', W.E.H. Lecky, *History of European Morals*, vol.2, p.381; H. Spencer, *A Study of Sociology* (New York: Appleton, 1874), p.374; 'An Advanced Frenchman's Views', *Woman's Herald*, 16 November 1893, p.620, on Alfred Fouillé, *Revue des Deux Mondes*, October 1893.
51 E. Berdoe, M.R.C.S., 'Prevention of Cruelty to Animals. Meeting in Gloucester', *Gloucester Journal*, 5 October 1895, p.6.
52 See K. Badger, R. Simpson Craft, L. Jensen, 'Age and Gender Differences in Value Orientation among American Adolescents', *Adolescence* 33: 131 (Fall 1998), pp.591–6.
53 'God's Mercy: A Sermon, preached by the Rev. Reuben Seddon', *Hackney and Kingsland Gazette*, 5 February 1883, pp.3–4.
54 For manly pity, G. Moberly, *Sermons on the Beatitudes: With Others Mostly Preached before the University of Oxford* (Oxford: Parker, 1860), p.91.
55 Mercy combined with 'manly qualities' to raise a man's character, see *The Name of Jehovah* (London: Seeley, Jackson and Halliday, 1863), pp.8–9, for discussion of Hebrew 'merciful'; on Christ combining feminine and masculine virtues, see

Reverend Thomas's lecture, 'Famous Women of Scripture', *East London Observer*, 18 June 1870, p.2.

56   See J.F. Russell, *The Ancient Knight, or Chapter on Chivalry* (London: Cleaver, 1849), p.183. For mercy as 'twin sister with English valour', see C. Kingsley, *Westward Ho!* (2 vols; Leipzig: Tauchnitz, 1855), vol.2, p.197.

57   J. Greig, ed., *The Farington Diary by Joseph Farington* (New York: Doran, 1928), vol.8, pp.24–5 in conversation, 20 July 1815. Cited in P. Langford, *Englishness Identified: Manners and Character 1650–1850* (Oxford: Oxford University Press, 2000), p.154.

58   An extract from S.A. Bradsley's *On the Use and Abuse of Popular Sports and Exercises, Resembling Those of the Greeks and Romans, as a National Object*, in *Cobbett's Political Register* 8 (July to December 1805), col.375; Attwood, House of Commons, 21 July 1834, *Mirror of Parliament for the Second Session of the Eleventh Parliament of Great Britain and Ireland in the Fourth Year of the Reign of King William IV. Appointed to Meet 3rd February 1834. Vol. 4* (1834), p.2842.

59   'The Sympathy of Christ' (4 November 1849), in *Sermons Preached at Trinity Chapel, Brighton by Frederick W. Robertson* (4 vols; Leipzig: Tauchnitz, 1861), vol.1, pp.102–18 [p.115]. See 'E.M.S.' 'Points for Home Thought. Benevolence – Manliness', *Eliza Cook's Journal* (5 June 1852), pp.90–1.

60   Quoted in 'The Deeside Suffragette Wedding', *Aberdeen Press and Journal*, 20 January 1912, p.4.

61   'Portia Unmasked', *Daily Herald*, 14 February 1921, p.4, Gertrude Landa dissects the character as 'heartless minx'. For non-British discourse, see, cited in Frevert, *Emotions in History – Lost and Found*, ch.2, A. Kirchhoff, ed., *Die Akademische Frau* (Berlin: Steinitz, 1897), which surveyed, among other professions, male legal professionals.

62   F. Fenwick Miller, 'Should Women Be Jurors?' *The Woman's Signal* (26 August 1897), p.131.

63   Seeley, *Ecce Homo*, p.248.

64   'N.A.', *Women's Franchise*, 14 June 1909, p.344.

65   On the name, 'a title in which a sweet womanly relation is blended with the name of that Divine attribute so dear to fallen nature', see *Life of Catherine McAuley, Foundress and first Superior of the Institute of Religious Sisters of Mercy* (New York: D. and J. Sadleir, 1866), p.150.

66   'Sisters of Mercy; or, Popery and Poverty' reprinted in *The Bulwark, or, Reformation Journal* 17 (1867–8), pp.128–30 [p.128]. See C.M. Mangion, 'The "Mixed Life": Challenging Understandings of Religious Life in Victorian England', in L. Lux-Sterritt and C.M. Mangion, eds, *Gender, Catholicism and Spirituality: Women and the Roman Catholic Church in Britain and Europe, 1200–1900* (Basingstoke: Palgrave Macmillan, 2011).

67   See F.B. Alberti, *Matters of the Heart: History, Medicine, and Emotion* (Oxford: Oxford University Press, 2010), pp.9–10 on the observation that collective emotions have been less studied than those linked to 'modern subjective and individualistic identities'.

68   W.L. Bowles, *Charity* (Bath and London: 1823), p.5.

69   W.T. Stead, 'The Queen's Empire – A Retrospect of Sixty Years', *Review of Reviews* 15 (January–June 1897), p.692.

70   J. Brownlow, *The History and Design of the Foundling Hospital: With a Memoir of the Founder* (London: W. and H.S. Warr, 1858), 'merciful even to seducers in the midst of horror of their crimes', p.22. On the Highmore painting, see J. Riding, *Basic*

Instincts: Love, Lust and Violence in the Art of Joseph Highmore (London: Holberton, 2017); C. Bugler, 'Angel of Mercy', *Country Life* (22 November 2017), pp.96–7. See A. Levene, *Childcare, Health and Mortality in the London Foundling Hospital, 1741–1800: 'Left to the Mercy of the World'* (Manchester: Manchester University Press, 2007). See D.P. Presciutti, *Visual Cultures of Foundling Care in Renaissance Italy* (Farnham: Ashgate, 2015), p.52 on foundlings in the medieval and early modern 'master frame' of Acts of Mercy.

71 Quoted in *Dublin Evening Post*, 26 October 1815, p.2.
72 On denominations acting in works of mercy, 'An Answer to Dr Dale, on P. Bunting', defending social work by religious organizations, quoted in *Review of Reviews*, vol.7, April 1893, p.405. For acts of mercy as 'freedom from the importunities of opinion', G. Eliot, 'Janet's Repentance', *Scenes from Clerical Life* (2 vols; Edinburgh: Blackwood, 1858), vol.2, p.324, see also p.357.
73 *The Champion*, 7 May 1837, p.266; *Westmorland Gazette*, 27 October 1838, p.1, quoting from the *Leeds Intelligencer*.
74 G. Crewe, *A Word for the Poor, and against the Present Poor Law, Both as to Its Principle and Practice* (Derby: Rowbottom, 1843), p.29; and the anonymous *A Plea for the Aged and Infirm Poor: With a Few Hints to Employers Generally, and to the Guardians of the Poor in Particular* (London: Roake and Varty, 1836), pp.15, 23.
75 G.R.W. Baxter, *The Book of the Bastiles: Or, the History of the Working of the New Poor Law* (London: Stephens, 1841), p.194.
76 J. Kay, *An Appeal to the Benevolent, and to Real Christians. The New Poor Houses Weighed and Found Wanting, in the Balances both of Humane Feeling and of Christianity* (2nd edn; London: Groombridge, 1837), p.13.
77 'The Unrecognised Visitor', *Punch*, 21 July 1866, p.27.
78 William Cobbett, *Parliamentary Debates*, 3rd series, vol.19, House of Commons, 5 July 1833, col.249.
79 H. Morley, 'Ground in the Mill', *Household Words*, 22 April 1854, pp.224–7 [p.225].
80 *Tait's Edinburgh Magazine*, February 1844, p.131. Ebenezer Elliott's 'The Ranter', *Corn Law Rhymes* (3rd edn; London: Steill, 1831), p.11, refers to 'pleading mercy [as] a trampled worm'.
81 M.E. Robinson, ed., *The Wild Wreath* (London: Phillips, 1804), pp.64–6 [p.67]. The poem was used in other contexts than mercy towards the felon, see *Manchester Times*, 8 April 1848, p.7 in the context of working-class political agitation. See, in linking penal reform to mercy, 'Mercy Is Twice Blessed', *Nottingham Review*, 23 January 1846, p.8.
82 See 'An Act of Mercy. II', *All The Year Round* 8: 192 (27 December 1862), pp.372–8 [p.378].
83 B. Waugh, 'The Angel of The Little Ones, or The National Society for the Prevention of Cruelty to Children', *Review of Reviews*, November 1891, pp.521–30 [p.522]. On Barnardo describing his work as an errand of mercy, see S. Barnardo and J. Marchant, *Memoirs of the Late Dr Bernardo* (London: Hodder and Stoughton, 1907), pp.112; on his life as errand of mercy, and the quotation on the 'mercy seat', see J.H. Batt, *Dr Barnardo: The Foster-Father of 'Nobody's Children'* (London: Partridge, 1904), p.5.
84 See S. Ash, *Funding Philanthropy: Dr Barnardo's Metaphors, Narratives and Spectacles* (Liverpool: Liverpool University Press, 2016), p.124.
85 'Juvenile Department', *The British Friend*, May 1850, p.121.

86 E.K. Catterton, *Britain's Record, What She Has Done for the World* (London: Sidgwick and Jackson, 1911), p.268.
87 'Art. IV. – Events of the Month', *The Englishwoman's Review*, 15 July 1876, p.302.
88 *Punch*, 3 December 1887, p.256.
89 Lucy Aikin to William Ellery Channing, 18 April 1838, in *Correspondence of William Ellery Channing DD and Lucy Aikin from 1826–1842* (London: Williams and Norgate, 1874), p.306.
90 *Women's Penny Paper*, 14 December 1889, p.87.
91 *Woman's Signal*, 19 September 1895, p.188.
92 The journal of the movement was the *Band of Mercy Advocate*, established in 1879.
93 H. Primatt, *A Dissertation on the Duty of Mercy and Sin of Cruelty to Brute Animals* (London: Hett, 1776); S. Trimmer, *Fabulous Histories: Designed for the Instruction of Children, Respecting Their Treatment of Animals* (London: Longman, 1786); J. Oswald, *The Cry of Nature; or, an Appeal to Mercy and to Justice on Behalf of the Persecuted Animals* (London: Johnson, 1791); J. Lawrence, *A Philosophical and Practical Treatise on Horses and on the Moral Duties of Man towards the Brute Creation* (2nd edn; London: Symonds, 1802). The description of Oswald is from *Scots Magazine* 54 (January 1792), review, p.22.
94 A. Smith, *A Scriptural and Moral Catechism, Designed Chiefly to Lead the Minds of the Rising Generation to the Love and Practice of Mercy, and to Expose the Horrid Nature of Cruelty to the Dumb Creation* (Birmingham: Peart, 1833).
95 See R. Bosch, *Labyrinth of Digressions: Tristram Shandy as Perceived and Influenced by Sterne's Early Imitators*, transl. P. Verhoeff (Amsterdam: Rodopi, 2007), p.150.
96 'Cruelty to Brutes', in *Divine Hymns Attempted in Easy Language; for the Use of Children* (12th edn; London: Paris, 1812), pp.48–9; and reprinted in J. Campbell, *The Marrow of Modern Hymn-Books* (9th edn; London: J. Snow, 1842), p.10. A lengthy poem on cruelty to animals, S.J. Pratt, *The Lower World, a Poem, in Four Books, with Notes* (London: Sharpe and Hailes, 1810), also referenced mercy.
97 *Coventry Standard*, 6 April 1849, p.4.
98 See H. Kean, *Animal Rights: Political and Social Change in Britain since 1800* (London: Reaktion Books, 1998), pp.18–19.
99 See S. Trimmer, *An Essay on Christian Education* (London: F. and J. Rivington, 1812), p.108 on *mercy* to even the most insignificant, whereas *humanity* was the 'exclusive claim of the human species'.
100 See also 'Of Misquoted Texts', *Christian Guardian and Church of England Magazine*, December 1833, p.477, which described it as often heard, a misquotation of 'A righteous man regardeth the life of his beast'.
101 A Sunday sermon on 'Animals in Relation to God', by J. Sanger Davies, Chapel of Ease, *Kent and Sussex Courier*, 22 January 1886, p.6.
102 'The Dogs of Constantinople', *Tipperary Free Press*, 9 March 1844 [p.4], quoting *Wanderings of a Journeyman Tailor*, *Worcester Journal*, 10 October 1822, p.4, quoting Turner on the Levant and linking this to Martin's animal welfare efforts. Vegetarians referred to the 'merciful Hindoo', see *Vegetarian Messenger* 3:32 (June 1852), p.12. See also, T. Thornton, *The Present State of Turkey* (2nd edn; 2 vols; London: Mawman, 1809), vol. 2, p.160.
103 'Proposita Philanthropica', *Literary Panorama* 5 (March 1809), col.1150.
104 T. Clarkson, *The Diversions of the Field* (London: Harvey and Darton, 1827), p.3 from Clarkson's *Portraiture of Quakerism*.

105 W.H. Drummond, *The Rights of Animals and Man's Obligation to Treat Them with Humanity* (London: Mardon, 1838), p.15.
106 See (competition essay for the SPCA), Sarah Burdett, *The Rights of Animals; or, the Responsibility and Obligation of Man, in the Treatment He Is Bound to Observe towards the Animal Creation* (London: Mortimer, 1839), at pp.55–6; *An Essay on Condemnation of Cruelty to Animals* (Stamford: Sharp, 1851), pp.1–2. See references to mercy in a sermon by the Reverend Thomas Greenwood, in *The Voice of Humanity: For the Communication and Discussion of All Subjects Relative to the Conduct of Man towards the Inferior Animal Creation* (London: Nisbet, 1830), vol.1, p.146.
107 *The London Quarterly Review* 44 (July 1875), p.527.
108 'Kindness Toward Animals, Mercy toward Human Beings', *Advocate of Peace* 57:4 (April 1895), pp.86–7.
109 From a review of W.H. Drummond's *Humanity to Animals*, in *Monthly Repository* 4: 41 (May 1830), p.323.
110 'E.F.M.' 'Cruelty of Children', *Woman's Herald*, 16 January 1892, p.12.
111 K.J. Ready, '"What then, poor Beastie!": Gender, Politics, and Animal Experimentation in Anna Barbauld's "The Mouse's Petition"', *Eighteenth-Century Life* 28:1 (2004), pp.92–114.
112 F. Kemble, *Records of a Girlhood* (New York: Holt, 1879), p.418, 11 June 1831. On Magendie, e.g., 'Charlotte Elizabeth', 'Home Atrocities', *The Christian Lady's Magazine* 17 (January–June 1842), pp.400–8.
113 James Maden Holt, MP, 15 December 1875, *Report of The Royal Commission on the Practice of Subjecting Live Animals to Experiments for Scientific Purposes; With Minutes of Evidence and Appendix* (London: Eyre and Spottiswoode, 1876), p.320; on the vivisector lacking mercy, 'The Vivisector in the Lunatic Asylum. A Shocking Story', *The Zoophilist*, reprinted *Woman's Signal*, 11 November 1897, p.311.
T.H. Huxley's endorsement of mercy in religion is ironically noted, from his essay, 'The Interpreters of Genesis and the Interpreters of Nature', *Nineteenth Century* 18:106 (December 1885), pp.849–1860 [p.860], in *The Zoophilist*, 1 January 1886, p.155.
114 'Woman and Vivisection', an anonymous paper printed from Brighton, *Herald of Health* (London: Nichols, 1881), p.96.
115 *The Zoophilist*, 1 September 1885, p.86.
116 W. Weldon, *A Plea for Mercy to Animals: Being an Argument Briefly Stated against Vivisection* (London: Shaw, 1876), p.7.
117 *The Zoophilist*, 1 August 1885, p.71 (Timmins); *Mercy and Truth v. Cruelty and Contradiction. A Reply of the Bristol and Clifton Anti-Vivisection Society to E.D. Girdlestone, B.A.* (London: Simpkin, Marshall, 1884); *Zoophilist*, 1 May 1884 (Genius of Pity), p.17. The painting, of 1883, has Pity (called 'Mercy' by Hilda Kean, *Animal Rights: Political and Social Change in Britain since 1800*, p.147) with a balance on which the heart outweighs a laurel-garlanded brain, her other arm protecting a muzzled dog. For a contemporary review, *St James's Gazette*, 1 April 1885, p.6; *Ipswich Journal*, 6 November 1883, p.4 notes its reception in Germany.
118 See for the report in the letter by 'Humanitas', *Aris's Birmingham Gazette*, 30 December 1833, p.2; report of seventeenth annual meeting of supporters of the RSPCA, *Morning Post*, 13 May 1841, p.6.
119 See F.S. Milton, 'Taking the Pledge: A Study of Children's Societies for the Prevention of Cruelty to Birds and Animals in Britain, c.1870–1914', Newcastle University PhD, 2008; and entry by Milton in L. Brake and M. Demoor, *Dictionary*

of *Nineteenth-century Journalism in Great Britain and Ireland* (Ghent: Academia Press, 2009), pp.37–8. G. Stringer Rowe, *T.B. Smithies (Editor of 'The British Workman')*. *A Memoir* (London: Woolmer, 1884), pp.62–4. See J.M. Davis, *The Gospel of Kindness: Animal Welfare and the Making of Modern America* (Oxford: Oxford University Press, 2016); and S.J. Pearson, *The Rights of the Defenseless: Protecting Animals and Children in Gilded Age America* (Chicago, IL: University of Chicago Press, 2011) on the American movement. The mercy aspects in iconography and argument are noted by Pearson, p.130, p.168. The journal was renamed *Band of Mercy* in 1883.

120 *Band of Mercy Melodies by Various Composers. Compiled by the Editor of the 'Band of Mercy Advocate'* (London: Partridge, 1881).
121 A.G. Burdett-Coutts, ed., *Woman's Mission: A Series of Congress Papers on the Philanthropic Work of Women by Eminent Writers* (London: Sampson Low, Marston and Company, 1893), pp.331–3; F.K. Prochaska, *Women and Philanthropy in Nineteenth-century England* (Oxford: Clarendon Press, 1980), p.75.
122 E. Saville, 'The Dew of Mercy', *Westminster Review* 173: 1 (January 1910), pp.86–95.
123 H. Rawnsley, 'Ad Misericordiam', *Nature Notes* 12 (January 1901), pp.4–7.
124 *Nature Notes* 4 (1893), p.226.
125 W.H. Hudson, 'An Appeal to the Clergy', *Nature Notes* 7 (1896), pp.26–8.
126 [Barry Pain], 'Murder Hats', *The Chronicle*, reprinted in *Nature Notes* 7 (1896), p.163; Catharine M. Whitehead, 'Inconsistency', *Woman's Herald*, 30 July 1892, p.10; J. Buckland, *Selborne Magazine* 21 (1910), p.106. See also C.N. Foyster, 'The Quality of Mercy', *Herald of the Golden Age*, 15 November 1899, p.129.
127 The poet Sydney Dobell, *The Life and Letters of Sydney Dobell* (London: Smith, Elder, 1878), vol.2, p.58, in an address to medical students in Edinburgh, 1856, discusses this.
128 'Moral Aspect of Vivisection', a sermon on Matt.v.7 reported in *The Zoophilist*, 1 August 1884, p.84.
129 Frances Power Cobbe, *The Zoophilist*, 2 November 1885, p.116.
130 *The Zoophilist*, 1 July 1884, p.46, responding to *Le Soir*, 23 June 1884.
131 The Scandinavian League against Scientific Cruelty, reported in *The Zoophilist*, 1 December 1884, pp.154–5.
132 *Vegetarian Advocate*, 15 January 1849, p.69; *Vegetarian Messenger* 2:15, January 1851, p.1.
133 *Vegetarian Advocate*, 2:9, 1 May 1850, p.111; and *Vegetarian Messenger* 1851, p.8, p.43.
134 J. Allen, 'Look Within', *Herald of the Golden Age*, 15 June 1900, p.63.
135 See *Daily News*, 10 February 1883, on 'merciful death-dealing'.
136 Hardy promoted the pig-sticking scene in the novel, to the editor of *Animals' Friend*, see C. Sumpter, 'On Suffering and Sympathy: Jude the Obscure, Evolution, and Ethics', *Victorian Studies* 53:4 (2011), pp.665–87 (p.666).
137 Pliny, *Naturalis Historia*, see J. Bostock and H.T. Riley, transl., *The Natural History of Pliny* (London: Bohn, 1855), vol.2, Book 8, ch.19, p.267.
138 M. Rowlands, *Can Animals Be Moral?* (New York: Oxford University Press, 2012).
139 'The Higher Morals in Animals', *Our Animal Friends*, 22, April 1895, pp.169–71.
140 H. Innes, *Goldsmith's Natural History, with Notes Collected, with a Life of O. Goldsmith by G.M. Bussey* (London: Lofts, 1853), p.267, reprinting text circulating since the late eighteenth century, via Goldsmith and Buffon's *Natural History*, and drawing on the account by Andrew Battel printed in 1625.

141 J. Couch, *Illustrations of Instinct Deduced from the Habits of British Animals* (London: van Voorst, 1847), p.236.

142 'St Bernards in the snow, on a mission of mercy', from a watercolour by Basil Bradley, *The Graphic*, 3 May 1879; W.C.L. Martin, *The History of the Dog: Its Origin, Physical and Moral Characteristics, and Its Principal Varieties* (London: Knight, 1845), p.88, p.169. Sir Edwin Landseer's painting on the subject was reproduced, e.g. in oil-print by the Baxter process.

143 See J. Mayer, 'The Expression of the Emotions in Man and Laboratory Animals', *Victorian Studies* 50:3 (2008), pp.399–417 (p.407), quoting George Hoggan's widely reprinted letter of 1875, 'as far as eyes, ears, and tail could make a mute appeal for mercy eloquent, they tried it in vain'.

144 [John Heskin?] 'A Passage in Milton Restored', *The Student, or, the Oxford and Cambridge Monthly Miscellany* 2:9 (1751), p.346: here the word 'mercy' is restored to a line in 'Poem on the Death of a fair Infant of his dying of a cough'.

145 J.B. Owen, *Lectures and Sermons* (London: Macintosh, 1873), p.181.

146 'Praise for Birth and Education in a Christian Land', *The Children's Friend*, 1 January 1869, p.13; from Dr Watt's *Divine and Moral Songs*.

147 R. Wells, *Model Sabbath-School Lesson* (Philadelphia, PA: Garrigues, 1864), p.16.

148 J. Fawcett, *Hints on the Education of Children* (Halifax: Holden and Dowson [1807]), pp.16–17; *Early Education; or, the Management of Children Considered with a View to Their Future Character* (London: G. and W.B. Whitaker, 1821), chs.11–16 on mercy. See C. De Rothschild, *Addresses to Young Children; Originally Delivered in the Girl's Free School, Bell Lane* (London: Wertheimer, 1861), ch.27, on mercy and truth in a collection of discourses for the Jewish Girls' School in Spitalfields. For home culture, see 'Justice', *Pleasant Pages. A Journal of Home Education on the Infant-School System* (London: Houston and Stoneman, 1851), vol.2, pp.225–6.

149 G. Chapman, *A Treatise on Education* (4th edn; London: for the author, 1790), p.226.

150 R.M. Macbriar, *Chapters on National Education* (London: Simpkin, Marshall, 1845), p.111; C. Baker, *Contributions to Publications of the Society for the Diffusion of Useful Knowledge, and the Central Society of Education* (n.p., 1842), p.291.

151 W. Ellis, 'Middle Class Education – What to Aim at, as Well as How to Aim', *The Museum, and English Journal of Education*, 1 March 1865, pp.441–8 [p.442].

152 R. Cust, 'Reading for Magistracy: The Mental World of Sir John Newdigate', in J.F. McDiarmid, *The Monarchical Republic of Early Modern England: Essays in Response to Patrick Collinson* (Abingdon: Routledge, 2016), pp.181–99 [p.187].

153 J.B. Laughton, *Christ the Counsellor; or, Practical Teaching for an Age of Progress, An Exposition of our Lord's Sermon on the Mount* (London: Nisbet, 1869), ch.5, 'Blessed Mercy', p.66.

154 J. Straley, 'Of Beasts and Boys: Kingsley, Spencer, and the Theory of Recapitulation', *Victorian Studies* 49:4 (2007), pp.583–609 (p.588).

155 H.M. Thompson, 'Moral Instruction in Schools, concluded', *International Journal of Ethics* 15:1 (October 1904), pp.28–47 [p.45].

156 For its activities in schools after the Education Act in 1870, A. Clapp-Itnyre, *British Hymn Books for Children, 1800–1900: Re-Tuning the History of Childhood* (Farnham: Ashgate, 2012). The Merciful Brigade magazine of that name in 1883 was incorporated in *Our Darlings*.

157 E.F.M., 'Cruelty of Children', *Women's Herald*, 16 January 1892, p.12.

158 *The Zoophilist*, 1 September 1885, p.86, quoting *Our Dumb Animals* (Boston).
159 M. Flegel, '"How does your collar suit me?": The Human Animal in the RSPCA's *Animal World* and *Band of Mercy*', Victorian Literature and Culture 40 (2012), pp.247–62.
160 [J. Mortimer] *Advice to Parents; or, Rules for the Education of Children* (London: Boulter, 1704), p.18.
161 E.W. Whitaker, *Sermons on Education* (London: Rivington, 1788), pp.91–2. Other works of education included reflections on cruelty to animals: C.M. Graham, *Letters on Education. With Observations on Religious and Metaphysical Subjects* (London: Dilly, 1790), p.121, pp.192–4.
162 [Louisa Hoare] *Friendly Advice on the Management and Education of Children; Addressed to Parents of the Middle and Labouring Classes of Society* (2nd edn; London: Hatchard, 1824), pp.21–3; *The Evangelical Magazine and Missionary Chronicle* 14, October 1806, p.480.
163 'M.H.', 'Hints for preventing Cruelty to Brutes', *European Magazine and London Review*, October 1811, pp.273–4.
164 T. Spencer, *Remarks on National Education* (Fifth thousand; London: Green, 1840), p.7.
165 J. Simpson, *Necessity of Popular Education, as a National Object; with Hints on the Treatment of Criminals, and Observations on Homicidal Insanity* (Edinburgh: Adam and Charles Black, 1834), p.370.
166 T. Tate, *The Philosophy of Education; or, the Principles and Practice of Teaching* (2nd edn; London: Longman, Brown, Green, Longmans and Roberts, 1857), pp.238–9.
167 'R.K.', *The Educational Reporter and Science Teachers' Review*, 5 October 1869, pp.2–3.
168 G.T. Angell, 'The New Order of Mercy', *Autobiographical Sketches and Personal Recollections* (Boston, MA: American Humane Education Society, 1882), p.30.
169 'W.B.', 'La Fontaine', *Temple Bar*, August 1870, pp.58–71[p.63]. La Fontaine's words appear in 'Les deux pigeons', Book IX, Fable II; and the phrase appears as the caption to an image by M. Dargelas of boys beating a cat, reproduced in *Le Monde Illustré*, 25 June 1864, p.413. See Sanchez, *Pity in Fin-de-siècle French Culture*, p.13.
170 S. Colvin, 'Some Phases of English Art under George III', *Fortnightly Review* (1 March 1874), pp.342–58 [p.358].
171 G.S. Hall, *Youth, Its Education, Regimen, and Hygiene* (London: Appleton, 1907), p.221.
172 For the role of literature on cruelty, mercy and emotions generally, geared towards children, M. Flegel, *Conceptualizing Cruelty to Children in Nineteenth-Century England: Literature, Representation, and the NSPCC* (Farnham: Ashgate, 2009) on texts for children on cruelty and kindness; U. Frevert, P. Eitler, S. Olsen, U. Jensen, M. Pernau et al., *Learning How to Feel: Children's Literature and Emotional Socialization, 1870–1970* (Oxford: Oxford University Press, 2014).
173 D. Kilner, *First Going to School: Or, the Story of Tom Brown, and His Sisters* (1804; London: Tabart, 1806), p.36, p.113.
174 J. Bowring, *Minor Morals for Young People* (3 vols; London: Whittaker, 1834), vol.1. The work is criticized in *The British Magazine* 8 (September 1835), pp.317–22.
175 L. Watts, *Pretty Little Hymns for Good Little Children* (London: T. Allman, 1850), p.171. See also *Songs of Love and Mercy for the Young* (London: Morgan and Scott, 1875), which concerns God's mercy rather than mercy by children.

176 *Susy's Flowers; or, 'Blessed Are the Merciful for They Shall Obtain Mercy'* (London: Nelson, 1862).
177 W. Chambers and R. Chambers, eds, 'Mercy', *Chambers's Educational Course. The Moral Class-Book* (Edinburgh: Chambers, 1839), p.97.
178 For instance, *Young England*, 1 December 1886; For other visual representation of this trope, see 'On an Errand of Mercy', *Quiver*, 9:421 (January 1874), pp.113–14 (engraving and verse); Ethel Parkinson, 'An Errand of Mercy', Edwardian postcard by C.W. Faulkener of London.
179 See 'Mrs Simpson's Lecture on Education', *Cleave's Gazette of Variety*, 25 May 1839, p.4.
180 'The Preceptor', in S. Johnson, *An Essay on Education. A Poem. In Two Parts. I. The Pedant. II. The Preceptor* (Shrewsbury: Pryse, 1771), p.45. V. Knox, *Liberal Education: Or, A Practical Treatise on the Methods of Acquiring Useful and Polite Learning* (London: Dilly, 1795), p.16.
181 C. Baker, *Contributions to Publications*, p.293. For later reflections, see F.H. Matthews, *A Dialogue on Moral Education* (London: Sonnenschein, 1898), p.186.
182 This comment appears in an article on reform of Secondary Schools, *Western Times*, 4 February 1899, p.2.
183 Or rather, Anglo-Saxons had used 'mildheartedness', see T.B. Shaw, *Outlines of English Literature* (New York: Sheldon, 1866), p.31.
184 A. Clarke, 'The Nature and Practice of Mercy. Part 1', *The Arminian Magazine* (September 1796), pp.423–9 [p.425].
185 *Calmet's Dictionary of the Holy Bible. By the Late Mr Charles Taylor* (London: Holdsworth and Ball, 1832), p.643; W.H. Hutchings, *Some Aspects of the Cross, Seven Discourses Delivered in Substance in S. Andrew's Church, Clewer, during Lent, 1871* (London: Masters, 1872), p.145; J. Miley, *Systematic Theology* (2 vols; New York: Hunt and Eaton, 1895), vol.1, p.210. Its status as an emotion is debated in modern texts, see A. Ben-ze-ev's *The Subtlety of Emotions* (Cambridge, MA: MIT Press, 2000), p.333, which describes it as 'essentially not an emotion but a certain attitude conveyed by action ... is related to emotions by being a partial and discriminative attitude'.
186 It is noted as a fact, in a passage on mercy, by the Puritan George Swinnock, *Men are Gods, or The Dignity of Magistracy and the Duty of the Magistrate* (London: Simmons, 1660), p.251. For Scottish position, W. Steele, *A Summary of the Powers and Duties of Juries in Criminal Trials in Scotland* (Edinburgh: Clark, 1833), p.3. See L. Stevenson, 'On the Supposed Exclusion of Butchers and Surgeons from Jury Duty', *Journal of the History of Medicine* 9 (1954), pp.235–8.
187 See F. Naiden, *Ancient Supplication* (Oxford: Oxford University Press, 2006).
188 'The Philosophy of Gesture – For the Port Folio' *The Port Folio* 2:6(Philadelphia; December 1813), p.624.
189 J. Bunyan, *A Discourse upon The Pharisee and The Publican*, reprinted in H. Stebbing, ed., *The Entire Works of John Bunyan* (4 vols; London: Virtue, 1860), vol.2, p.364.
190 'Have Mercy on Me', *Quiver* 14:681 (January 1879), pp.609–10.
191 See 'Rescued from the Floods', text accompanying engraving in *Religious Emblems: Being a Series of Engravings on Wood, Executed by the First Artists of That Line, from Designs Drawn on the Blocks Themselves* (London: Bensley, 1809), unpaginated, the engraving by A.R. Branston.

192	See E. Atherstone, *Israel in Egypt. A Poem* (London: Longman, Green, Longman and Roberts, 1861), p.315, delineating the altered state of Pharaoh.
193	E.g. sacred poetry, P. Cunningham's 'A Sacred Ode', *Derby Mercury*, 25 December 1788 [p.4]; romantic poetry, 'The Retrospect', *Norfolk Chronicle*, 21 October 1876 [p.4]; and Matthew Lewis's 'The Felon', cited above.
194	H. Siddons, *Practical Illustrations of Rhetorical Gesture and Action; Adapted to the English Drama; from a Work on the Subject by M. Engel* (2nd edn, London: Sherwood, Neely and Jones, 1822), pp.371–2. The original by Johann Engel, *Ideen zu einer Mimik* published in 1785.
195	W. Tooke, *View of the Russian Empire: During the Reign of Catharine, the Second, and to the Close of the Eighteenth Century* (3rd edn, 3 vols; Dublin: Wogan, 1801), vol.2, p.40. See Straight's comments, 'Uniquely Human: Cultural Norms and Private Acts of Mercy in the War Zone', p.502: 'cross-culturally understood gestural grammars pleading for mercy'.
196	T. Browne, *Religio Medici* (1646; 7th edn; London: Crook, 1672), p.49.
197	T. Woolnoth, *The Study of the Human Face* (London: Tweedie, 1865), pp.159–62.
198	See the education of the Rao of Kutch, Rao Delsalji, by Lieutenant Crofton (emphasizing the young man's rule in justice and mercy), *Asiatic Journal*, July 1835, pp.168–9, with the phrase, 'benefitted by the knowledge of European laws and ethics'.

Chapter 4

1	See R. McMahon, '"Let the Law Take Its Course": Punishment and the Exercise of the Prerogative of Mercy in Pre-Famine and Famine Ireland', in S.P. Donlan and Michael Brown, eds, *The Laws and Other Legalities of Ireland, 1689–1850* (Farnham: Ashgate, 2011), pp.133–64 [p.162].
2	Several words are glossed as mercy in *Focaloir Gaoidhilge-Sax-Bhearla or an Irish-English Dictionary* (Paris: Valleyre, 1768) in the Gaelic.
3	P.O. Sullivan, 'Early Irish Prototypes of Some Modern Institutions' before the Skibbereen Branch of the Gaelic League, *Southern Star*, 5 March 1910, p.2, p.7.
4	See 'Sympathy with the Pope. Great Meeting of the Diocese of Elphin', *Freeman's Journal*, 2 January 1868, p.4; *Irish Examiner*, 1 October 1847, p.2 on merciful treatment of Father James Burke (convicted in 1838 of swearing away the life of an innocent man at a trial in 1834) by the Bishop of Cork, arguing against the Protestant *The Constitution*.
5	*Freeman's Journal*, 24 October 1839, p.3.
6	*Newry Telegraph*, 21 September 1848 [p.1].
7	*Kerry Reporter*, 16 August 1924, p.7 quotes the entire verse with no context; the lines were quoted in court by the conman James Stewart, see *Belfast Newsletter*, 23 June 1933, p.9; *Donegal News*, 1 July 1933 p.10. Shakespeare was praised for embodying 'an English pity for the fallen', 'The Ter-centenary of Shakespeare', *Belfast Newsletter*, 29 April 1916, p.8.
8	A point made in A. Gibson, *Misanthropy: The Critique of Humanity* (London: Bloomsbury Academic, 2017), p.127.
9	The Reverend Bell, in *Leinster Express*, 22 June 1850, p.4. On mercy in discourse of the Tenant League, see also *Irish Examiner*, 8 November 1848, p.2. See also M.D.

McDougall, *The Letters of 'Norah' on Her Tour through Ireland* (Montreal, 1882), e.g. p.238.
10   Mr Maguire, *Irish Examiner*, 14 May 1851, p.3.
11   W. Sheridan, *Several Discourses: viz. Of Three Books Which Teach Us the Knowledge of God. Of Justice and Mercy in General. Of Mercy in Relieving the Poor. Of Mercy in Forgiving Enemies, and of Humility* (London, Sawbridge: 1705), 'Of Justice and Mercy in general, Of Mercy in relieving the poor, or Mercy in forgiving enemies'.
12   T. Ken, *A Crown of Glory, the Reward of the Righteous* (London: Bettesworth, 1725), p.67; previously *The Royal Sufferer: A Manual of Meditations and Devotions* (n.p., 1699), p.67.
13   A. Thornburg, 'Women in Sir John Temple's The Irish Rebellion', in M.D. Lee and E. Madden, eds, *Irish Studies: Geographies and Genders* (Cambridge: Cambridge Scholars Press, 2008), pp.135. In response to this interpretation, M. Carey, *Vindiciae Hibernicae; or Ireland Vindicated. An Attempt to Develop and Expose a Few of the Multifarious Errors and Misrepresentations Respecting Ireland, in the Histories of May, Temple, Whitelock ... and Others* (etc.) (1819; 3rd edn; Philadelphia, PA: R.P. Desilver, 1837).
14   D. O'Connell, *A Memoir on Ireland Native and Saxon* (Dublin: Dolman, 1843), vol.1, p.353.
15   See J. Tillotson, *Stories of the Wars, 1574–1658: From the Rise of the Dutch Republic to the Death of Oliver Cromwell* (London: S.O. Beeton, 1865), p.394.
16   Quoted by R. Ansell, 'The 1688 Revolution in Ireland and the Memory of 1641', in M. Williams and S.P. Forrest, eds, *Constructing the Past: Writing Irish History, 1600–1800* (Woodbridge: Boydell and Brewer, 2010), pp.73–93 [p.76].
17   The phrase relating to the king's desire is the new Viceroy's, reported in *The Anti-Jacobin Review*, July 1798, p.246, commenting on the attempt to censure Cornwallis's predecessor by praising a new policy of 'mildness and mercy'.
18   See reflections on mercy, 'Extracts from the Memoirs of Counsellor Sampson', in *The Irish Magazine or Monthly Asylum for Neglected Biography*, May 1810, pp.230–7 [pp.234–5].
19   See M. De Nie, *The Eternal Paddy: Irish Identity and the British Press, 1798–1882* (Madison: University of Wisconsin Press, 2004), p.62, and in general on the response of the British press.
20   J. Barrington, *Historic Memoirs of Ireland: Comprising Secret Records of the National Convention, the Rebellion, and the Union; with Delineations of the Principal Characters Connected with the Transactions* (2 vols; London: Colburn, 1835). For modern study, T. Bartlett, 'Clemency and Compensation: The Treatment of Defeated Rebels and Suffering Loyalists after the 1798 Rebellion', in J. Smyth, ed., *Revolution, Counter-revolution and Union: Ireland in the 1790s* (Cambridge: Cambridge University Press, 2000), pp.99–127, and in the same volume, M. Durey, 'Marquis Cornwallis and the Fate of the Irish Rebel Prisoners in the Aftermath of the 1798 Rebellion', pp.128–45.
21   *Freeman's Journal*, 17 February 1784, p.1.
22   Reprinted in F. Plowden, *Strictures upon An Historical Review of the State of Ireland, or, a Justification of the Conduct of the English Governments in That Country, from the Reign of Henry the Second to the Union of Great-Britain and Ireland* (London: F.C. and J. Rivington, 1804), pp.220–5 [p.225].
23   Anon., *Union, Prosperity, and Aggrandizement* (London: Myers, 1800), p.27 reprints an anecdote about sectarian justice in which a Catholic man condemned to death is shown no mercy by a viceroy ('Lord T -'), although 'disposed to'.

24 W. Drennan, *A Letter to His Excellency Earl FitzWilliam* (London: White: 1795), p.36.
25 *Dublin Evening Post*, 19 November 1796 [p.3].
26 C.H. Teeling, *Personal Narrative of the 'Irish Rebellion' of 1798* (London: Colburn, 1828), p.130.
27 Ibid., p.89.
28 *Extracts from The Press: A Newspaper Published in the Capital of Ireland, during Part of the Years 1797 and 1798* (Philadelphia, PA: W. Duane, 1802). On Orr, see *A Brief Account of the Trial of William Orr: Of Farranshane, in the County of Antrim* (Dublin: Chambers, 1797); and G. Beiner, 'Forgetting to Remember Orr: Death and Ambiguous Remembrance in Modern Ireland', in J. Kelly and M.A. Lyons, eds, *Death and Dying in Ireland, Britain,* and *Europe: Historical Perspectives* (Dublin: Irish Academic Press, 2013), pp.171–202.
29 *Extracts from The Press*, p.67.
30 *Extracts from The Press*, p.208. It was also commented, reprinted in *The Lives and Trials of Archibald Hamilton Rowan, the Rev. William Jackson, the Defenders, William Orr, Peter Finnerty, and Other Eminent Irishmen* (Dublin: Duffy, 1846), p.491, of Orr's conduct 'in the heathen world less heroic magnanimity would have been deified'.
31 *Kilkenny People*, 23 October 1897, p.5; 'Remember Orr', *Flag or Ireland*, 23 October 1897, p.5; *Donegal Independent*, 25 May 1906, p.6.
32 *Extracts from The Press*, p.263.
33 *The Lives and Trials of Archibald Hamilton Rowan, the Rev. William Jackson*, p.504.
34 *The Right Honorable John Philpot Curran Master of The Rolls in Ireland on The Late Very Interesting State Trials Speeches* (2nd edn; Dublin: Stockdale, 1808), p.281.
35 *The Lives and Trials of Archibald Hamilton Rowan, the Rev. William Jackson*, p.502.
36 *Extracts from The Press*, 16 January, p.296.
37 Kingsley, *Westward ho!*, vol.1, p.241.
38 From letter of 'W.H.G.', 3 October 1798, in *An Impartial Narrative of Each Engagement Which Took Place between His Majesty's Forces and the Rebels, during the Irish Rebellion, 1798* (Dublin: J. Jones, 1799), Part II, p.272.
39 *An Impartial Narrative of Each Engagement Which Took Place*, p.276.
40 Ibid., p.276; W.T.W. Tone, ed., *Life of Theobald Wolfe Tone* (2 vols; Washington, DC: Gales and Seaton, 1826) W.E.H. Lecky, *A History of Ireland in the Eighteenth Century* (London: Longmans, Green, 1898), vol. 5, p.63; P. Harwood, *History of the Irish Rebellion of 1798* (London: Chapman, 1848), p.232; A. Seward, *Letters of Anna Seward. Written between the Years 1784 and 1807*, vol.5, p.161. [J. Stock] *A Narrative of What Passed at Killala, in the County of Mayo, and the Parts Adjacent, during the French Invasion in the Summer of 1798* (London: Crutwell, 1809), p.27, partly links lack of bloodshed by peasantry in Connaught with French influence.
41 *Sequel to Personal Narrative*, p.246; *Hull Advertiser*, 29 September 1798 [p.2].
42 *Freeman's Journal*, 25 September 1789, p.3, *Chester Chronicle*, 5 October 1798 [p.2]; *Sequel to Personal Narrative*, p.243.
43 Gordon, *History of the Rebellion in Ireland, in the Year 1798, &c., Containing an Impartial Account of the Proceedings of the Irish Revolutionists, from the Year 1782, till the Suppression of the Rebellion* (London: Hurst, 1808), p.367.
44 *Hampshire Chronicle*, 21 July 1798 [p.3].
45 Gordon, *History of the Rebellion*, p.78. Gordon was a 'moderate Loyalist', see B. Browne, 'Rev. James Gordon – A Loyalist Historian of the 1798 Rebellion', *The Past: The Organ of the Uí Cinsealaigh Historical Society* 29 (2008), pp.5–13.

46 'B. Borohme the Younger', *Ireland, as a Kingdom and a Colony* (Dublin: S. J. Machen, 1843), p.217.
47 H.M. Field, *The Irish Confederates, and the Rebellion of 1798* (New York: Harper, 1851), p.248.
48 Reprinted in *The Irish Shield and Monthly Milesian*, vol.1 (December 1829), pp.451–2. For Ascendancy women's roles in tempering justice see comments of R. Sawyer, *We are But Women: Women in Ireland's History* (London: Routledge, 2002), pp.28–9.
49 *Report of the Proceedings of the Common Council, of the City of Dublin, on the Demands of the Irish Romanists*, March 18, 1807 (Dublin: Lagrange, n.d.), p.17.
50 W.H. Maxwell, *History of the Irish Rebellion in 1798: With Memoirs of the Union, and Emmett's Insurrection in 1803* (9th edn; London: G. Bell, 1871), p.158.
51 G. Taylor, *An Historical Account of the Rise, Progress and Suppression, of the Rebellion in the County of Wexford, in the Year 1798: To Which Is Annexed, the Author's Account of His Captivity, and Merciful Deliverance* (Dublin: John Jones, 1800).
52 R. Musgrave, *Memoirs of the Different Rebellions in Ireland* (3rd edn; 2 vols; Dublin: Marchbank, 1802), vol.1, p.576.
53 Anon., *A History of the Irish Rebellion in the Year, 1798… Collected from the Best Authorities: with Notes, Historical and Explanatory, etc* (Dublin: A. Stewart, 1799), p.28.
54 T. Hancock, *The Principles of Peace, Exemplified in the Conduct of the Society of Friends in Ireland, during the Rebellion of the Year 1798 with Preliminary and Concluding Observations* (Philadelphia, PA: Kite, 1829).
55 'Veritas', *A Vindication of the Roman Catholic Clergy of the Town of Wexford, during the Late Unhappy Rebellion* (2nd edn; Dublin: Fitzpatrick, 1798), p.7.
56 For the 'Walking Gallows', see representation and essay in *The Irish Magazine, and Monthly Asylum for Neglected Biography* (January 1810), pp.1–2 and July 1810, pp.290–2; for the pitch caps, see February 1810, pp.49–50.
57 'Welch Loyalty', *The Press*, 9 December, reprinted in *Extracts from The Press*, p.226; T. Cloney, *A Personal Narrative of Those Transactions in the County Wexford, in Which the Author Was Engaged, during the Awful Period of 1798* (Dublin: McMullen, 1832), on the massacres at Kilkomney.
58 Teeling, *Sequel to Personal Narrative*, p.128.
59 Ibid., p.120.
60 *Monthly Magazine*, October 1798, p.302. For mercy on the part of the rebel leaders, see review of T.C. Croker, *Memoirs of Joseph Holt, General of the Irish Rebels in 1798. Edited from His Original Manuscript*, in *Monthly Magazine, or, British Register*, 25 (February 1838), p.208.
61 *The Oeconomist, or Englishmen's Magazine for 1798*, p.266.
62 W. Bailey, *Records of Patriotism and Love of Country* (Washington, DC: n.p., 1826), p.55.
63 A. O'Connor, *State of Ireland* (privately printed, 1798), p.174 – the closing lines of the tract. See also *The State of Ireland. By Arthur O'Connor: Second Edition. To Which Are Added His Addresses to the Electors of the County of Antrim* (London: n.p., 1798).
64 Teeling, *Sequel to Personal Narrative*, p.195.
65 T. Crofton Croker, ed., *Memoirs of Joseph Holt, General of the Irish Rebels, in 1798* (2 vols; London: Colburn, 1838), vol.1, pp.210–11. E. Hay, *History of the Irish Insurrection of 1798: Giving an Authentic Account: And a Genuine History of Transactions Preceding That Event* (Dublin: Duffy, 1842), p.77 on the Earl of

Donoughmore; on the mercy of Sir James Fowlis, president of the court-martial in Wexford; p.134 on indiscriminate fury; pp.255–6 on 'arraigning benevolence and humanity'; p.319 (report of meeting 28 December 1795, of magistrates of Armagh).
66 *Memoirs of Joseph Holt*, p.14.
67 Ibid., p.116.
68 Gordon, *History of the Rebellion*, p.228.
69 Teeling, *Sequel to Personal Narrative*, p.192.
70 W.H. Curran, *The Life of the Right Honourable John Philpot Curran* (London: Longman, Hurst, Rees, Orme, and Brown, 1819), p.150.
71 Anon., *The History of the Late Grand Insurrection, or, the Struggle for Liberty in Ireland* (Carlisle: Loudon, 1805), p.158.
72 E. Wakefield, *An Account of Ireland, Statistical and Political* (2 vols; London: Longman, Hurst, Rees, Orme, and Brown, 1812), vol.1, p.372 and cited in Gordon, *History of the Rebellion*, p.218. On Cornwallis in Ireland, see F.B. Wickwire and M.B. Wickwire, *Cornwallis: The Imperial Years* (Chapel Hill: University of North Carolina Press, 1980).
73 *Freeman's Journal*, 26 June 1798, p.3; *Dublin Evening Post*, 23 July 1798.
74 38th of Geo. II. cap. 55, *Statutes Passed in the Parliaments Held in Ireland: 1797–1798* (Dublin: Grierson, 1799), pp.572–7.
75 *Morning Post*, 4 August 1798 [p.3].
76 *Freeman's Journal*, 24 July 1798, p.8, and 31 July 1798, p.3. See A. Alison, *Lives of Lord Castlereagh and Sir Charles Stewart, the Second and Third Marquesses of Londonderry* (3 vols; Edinburgh: Blackwood, 1861), vol.1, p.65.
77 'Jacobin Prints, Speeches', *Anti-Jacobin Review*, October 1798, p.496. The Division of the United Irishmen meeting at Red Lion Square, 10 March 1799 condemned 'such a deceitful mockery of mercy' as the amnesty: 'perfidious clemency extolled', *Kentish Gazette*, 26 March 1799 [p.2].
78 W.E.H. Lecky, *A History of Ireland in the Eighteenth Century*, vol.5, p.104.
79 C. Vane, ed., *Memoirs and Correspondence of Viscount Castlereagh, Second Marquess of Londonderry* (4 vols; London: Colburn), vol.4, p.480. On Cornwallis's clemency in the case of John Hevey, a brewer, of Dublin, see *Trial by Nisi Prius in the Court of King's Bench, Ireland, in the Case Wherein Mr John Hevey Was Plaintiff and Charles Henry Sirr, Esq., Was Defendant* (Dublin: Stockdale, 1802).
80 *A Report of the Debate in the House of Commons of Ireland, on Wednesday and Thursday the 15th and 16th of January, 1800. On an Amendment to the Address Moved by Sir Laurence Parsons, Bart. On the Subject of an Union* (Dublin: Moore, 1800), p.95.
81 P. Duigenan, *A Fair Representation of the Present Political State of Ireland: In a Course of Strictures on Two Pamphlets* (Dublin: Milliken, 1800), p.166. For the British press treatment of Cornwallis, see de Nie, *The Eternal Paddy*, p.68.
82 *Freeman's Journal*, 13 February 1800, p.2.
83 National Maritime Museum Collection, AAA4414, creamware jug transfer-printed in black, *c.*1797, https://collections.rmg.co.uk/collections/objects/4138.html. But see, in the case of the rape of a child, W.J. Fitzpatrick, *A Note to the Cornwallis Papers: Embracing, with Other Revelations, a Narrative of the Extraordinary Career of Francis Higgins, Who Received the Government Reward for the Betrayal of Lord Edward Fitzgerald* (Dublin: Kelly, 1859), p.44 – in which verse appears where a statue of Justice is too ashamed to be exhibited.
84 See *Chester Chronicle*, 10 August 1798 [p.2].

85 *The Reign of George III. Being a Continuation of Dr Goldsmith's History of England Down to the Peace of Amiens* (London: Richardson, 1805), p.353.
86 R.R. Madden, *The United Irishmen, Their Lives and Times* (2 vols; London: Madden, 1842), vol.2, p.256.
87 Ibid., pp.369–72.
88 Cloney, *A Personal Narrative of Those Transactions*, p.118.
89 'Sketches of Life and Manners: From the Autobiography of an English Opium Eater', *Tait's Edinburgh Magazine*, May 1834, pp.263–73 [p.265].
90 'Unanswered Arguments and Unnoticed Phenomena of the Repeal Agitation', *Dublin University Magazine* 24:141 (October 1844), pp.431–49 [p.432].
91 H.H. Milman, *Annals of St Paul's* (London: Murray, 1868), p.486.
92 J.A. Froude, *The English in Ireland in the Eighteenth Century* (3 vols; London: Longmans, Green, 1874), vol.3, p.464.
93 On recent interpretations, see H.T. Dickinson, 'The Irish Rebellion of 1798. History and Memory', in U. Broich, H.T. Dickinson, E. Hellmuth and M. Schmidt, eds, *Reactions to Revolutions: the 1790s and Their Aftermath* (Münster: Lit, 2007), pp.31–60.
94 *Freeman's Journal*, 7 June 1847 p.3; the original French, L.-M. de Lahaye, *Livre des Orateurs* (11th edn; Paris: Pagnerre, 1842), p.566.
95 On presenting emancipation as an act of mercy and justice, see eyewitness account, Chief Secretary of Ireland's Office Registered Papers, CSO/RP/CA/1826/33, c.1826, of a Catholic Association meeting, http://www.csorp.nationalarchives.ie (accessed 26 July 2018).
96 *Britannia*, quoted in *Warder and Dublin Weekly Mail*, 21 November 1840, p.6.
97 *Kerry Evening Post*, 14 April 1838, p.2.
98 Mr Everard, quoted in *Sligo Champion*, reprinted in *Freeman's Journal*, 30 August 1836, p.3.
99 See V.A.C. Gatrell, *The Hanging Tree: Execution and the English People 1770–1868* (Oxford: Oxford University Press, 1994), p.526 (footnote 24), citing a letter to Lord Melbourne, 29 January 1839 in L.C. Sanders, ed., *Lord Melbourne's Papers* (London: Longmans, Green, 1889), from which I also quote, p.391.
100 *Freeman's Journal*, 8 March 1837, p.3. On Mulgrave's period, see P. Gray, 'A "People's Viceroyalty"? Popularity, Theatre and Executive Politics 1835–47', ch.8 in P. Grey and O. Purdue, eds, *The Irish Lord Lieutenancy, c.1541–1922* (Dublin: UCD Press, 2012), pp.158–78. McMahon '"Let the Law Take Its Course"', cites, p.143, Patrick and Thomas Dunne's petition to the lord lieutenant, in which he is eulogized as humane, generous, merciful, as his rank is 'exalted in representing royalty' (NAI, CRF/1838/Dunne/68). McMahon, p.156, also cites [NAI, CRF/1838/Dunne/68] Normanby, now home secretary, speaking of having 'lost his situation when lord lieutenant of Ireland for doing good for Irishmen' and wanting to avoid similar attempts at leniency towards Irishmen now.
101 *Morning Chronicle*, 2 July 1838, p.2; reprinted in *Caledonian Mercury*, 7 July 1838, p.4.
102 Quoted in *London Standard*, 7 May 1838, p.3.
103 *Freeman's Journal*, 9 November 1837, p.3; *Connaught Telegraph*, 17 January 1838, p.4.
104 E.N. Hoare, *Letters on Subjects Connected with Ireland: Addressed to an English Clergyman* (Dublin: Milliken, 1839), p.53.

105 'Irish Policy of the Whigs', *The British and Foreign Review* 10 (1840), pp.246–92 [p.288]. See also 'Pacata Hibernia', *Dublin Review*, July 1836, pp.474–99, on the 'stern aspect of justice' mitigated under Mulgrave (p.491), and mercy seasoning justice (p.492).
106 *Drogheada Argus and Leinster Journal*, 21 November 1835, p.2.
107 *Tuam Herald*, 10 June 1837, p.3.
108 *Freeman's Journal*, 3 August 1837, p.2.
109 For his presentation as Fop O'Mulgrave, *Leinster Express*, 23 September 1837, p.4. See defence of his Jamaican career reprinted from *Morning Chronicle* in Irish papers, e.g. *Tuam Herald*, 21 October 1837, p.4.
110 'The Last Days of the Whigs', *Church of England Quarterly* 6 (1839), pp.212–45 [p.217].
111 *Peel Club Papers for Session 1839–40* (Glasgow: Richardson, 1840), p.2.
112 For ascendancy coverage see 'Lord Mulgrave versus the Judges', *Kerry Evening Post*, 18 October 1837, p.2; *Leinster Express*, 12 May 1838, p.5; *Kerry Evening Post*, 7 July 1838, p.2; 'More Normanby Clemency', *Dublin Evening Mail*, 30 November 1838 [p.2]; for critique of Tory press coverage, see *Freeman's Journal*, 30 April 1838, p.2; *Tralee Mercury*, 20 June 1838, p.2.
113 'The Cabinet and the Country', *Blackwood's Edinburgh Magazine*, October 1838, pp.429–38 [p.437].
114 'State of Ireland', *Annual Register* (London: Rivington, Cladwin and Cradock, 1838), p.29. For reports of the opinion of the 'largest body of independent Protestant gentry of Ireland ever known', *Freeman's Journal*, 13 February 1837, p.2; the petition is reprinted in *Belfast Newsletter*, 5 May 1837, p.1.
115 Sir Robert Peel spoke on abuse of clemency by lord lieutenants, in the debate on Municipal Corporations in Ireland, *Parliamentary Debates*, 3rd series, vol. 36, 8 February 1837, col.388–96.
116 W. Hutcheon, ed., *Whigs and Whiggism: Political Writings by Benjamin Disraeli, 1833–1853* (1913; New York: Macmillan, 1914), p.270. See P. Gray, *The Making of the Irish Poor Law, 1815–43* (Manchester: Manchester University Press, 2009), p.148, on the executive strategy of 'Justice to Ireland'. For other critiques, see 'What is the Use of a Lord-Lieutenant of Ireland?' *Fraser's Magazine*, April 1836, pp.475–87. In support, see 'Justice in Ireland', *Tait's Edinburgh Magazine* 4 (December 1837), pp.781–6. See J.H. Murphy, *Abject Loyalty: Nationalism and Monarchy in Ireland during the Reign of Victoria* (Washington, DC: The Catholic University of America Press, 2001), p.24; also K.A. Miller, *Ireland and Irish America: Culture, Class, and Transatlantic Migration* (Dublin: Field Day, 2008), pp.203–4, for some sense of the Protestant response.
117 House of Lords, Monday, 20 November 1837, *The Spectator*, 25 November 1837, p.1131.
118 *Parliamentary Debates*, 3rd series, vol.47, House of Commons, 15 April 1839, col.66, col.70. See J. Grant, *Random Recollections of the Lords and Commons: Second Series* (London: H. Colburn, 1838), vol.1, pp.304–8, for Peel's comic performance. See also pamphlets such as A. Meyler, *Irish Tranquillity under Mr O'Connell, My Lord Mulgrave and the Romish Priesthood* (Dublin: Carson, 1838); anon., *The Merits of the Whigs; or, a Warning to the People of England* (London: James Fraser, 1840), p.110, which condemned the 'fatal lenity of him in whose hands was vested the power of mercy'.

119 *The Mirror of Parliament for the First Session of the Thirteenth Parliament of Great Britain and Ireland in the First and Second Years of the Reign of Queen Victoria* 2nd series, vol.1 (London: Longman, Orme, Brown, Green and Longmans, 1838), 28 November 1838, p.212; for republication in pamphlet, see pro-Mulgrave *Connaught Telegraph*, 1 January 1838, p.1.

120 The Russell Papers in TNA, not studied here, include his thoughts on the royal prerogative of mercy, PRO 30/22/2E.

121 This work, published by Ridgway of London in 1837, had an epigram from Dryden on 'milder beams of mercy' on the title page. For an appreciative review, *Freeman's Journal*, 21 February 1837, p.2.

122 *Drogheda Argus and Leinster Journal*, 6 December 1835, p.2 on meeting in King's County; address to Mulgrave from the county of Mayo, *Freeman's Journal*, 16 January 1836, p.3; Reverend Edward Fitzgerald PP of Cahirciveen, meeting in the Court House, *Drogheada Argus and Leinster Journal*, 21 November 1835, p.2. For a declaration by Liberalism of Down, and a controversy from D.R. Ross of Rosstrevor's qualms, *Freeman's Journal*, 26 November 1839, p.4 and *Freeman's Journal*, 19 December 1839, p.1

123 *Western Times*, 25 May 1839, p.3.

124 *Cabinet Colloquies. No.1. An Imaginary Conversation between Her Majesty and Certain of Her Ministers concerning Divers Weighty Topics* (London: Southgate, 1839), p.10.

125 On addresses to Mulgrave at his departure, all from *Freeman's Journal*, 15 February 1839, p.1; 16 February 1839, p.3; 18 February 1839, p.3; 11 April 1839, p.1. See Francis Du Bourdieu, of Soldierstown, Moira, *Northern Whig*, 17 March 1853 [p.4], 'Impartial Justice' sword to wield, | The oppressed to guard with Mercy's shield', on Edward Eliot the Earl of St Germans.

126 *Cassell's History of England* (London: Cassell, 1909), vol.5, p.397. In John Doyle's cartoon *A Scene from a Popular Farce of Tom Thumb*, dated 20 February 1837, Mulgrave orders Morpeth to release the prisoners now that rebellion is dead, both are dressed in eighteenth-century garb.

127 'The New Home Secretary', *The Times*, reprinted *Westmorland Gazette*, 21 September 1839, p.4; the phrase 'Matilda of the home department', from a critique reprinted in *Manchester Courier*, 11 January 1840, p.3; on sympathizing clemency, *Dorset County Chronicle*, 21 May 1840, p.4; the comments on Jail Delivery in *Dublin Evening Packet*, 16 July 1840, p.3; on gaol-delivery, by the Reverend David Daniel of Bradford upon Avon, reprinted in *Leicester Herald*, 18 July 1840; see also *Wexford Conservative*, 14 September 1839, p.1; 'The Late Home Secretary and the Middlesex Magistrates', *Morning Post*, 14 January 1840, p.5.

128 *Freeman's Journal*, 16 April 1849 [p.3].

129 *Freeman's Journal*, 7 March 1848 [p.2]. See on wider charitable response, C. Kinealy, *Charity and the Great Hunger in Ireland: The Kindness of Strangers* (London: Bloomsbury, 2013), and R.B. Forbes, *The Voyage of the Jamestown on Her Errand of Mercy* (Boston, MA: Eastburn's Press, 1847).

130 'Month's Mind of The Late Very Rev Dr Collins', *Cork Examiner*, 27 August 1847 [p.1]. See Sadler, in the House of Commons, 18 February 1831, in *The Mirror for Parliament Second Portion of the First Session of the Ninth Parliament of Great Britain and Ireland, (Commencing 3d February, 1831) in the First Year of the Reign of King William IV* (London: 1831), vol.1 p.330, discussing Irish famine in those terms, when speaking of a 'wise and graduated system of poor-laws', and landlord

absenteeism and draining of wealth via rentals. See C. Driscoll, *The Duty of Showing Mercy to the Afflicted. A Sermon [on Job. Xxxi. 14] for the Famine in Ireland* (London: Harchard, 1847).

131 A. De Vere, *English Misrule and Irish Misdeed* (London: J. Murray, 1848), p.115; and M. Fagan, *Literature and the Irish Famine 1845–1919* (Oxford: Oxford University Press, 2002).

132 *The Vindicator* [Belfast], 10 April 1847 [p.2]; see also T.F. Meagher, *Speeches on the Legislative Independence of Ireland* (New York: Redfield, 1853). The essay attributed to Isaac Butt, 'The Famine in the Land', *Dublin University Magazine* 29:172 (April 1847), pp.501–40 also includes at the end an appeal to God's mercy, after practical and political commentary (p.540): endorsing proclamation of a day of humiliation and prayer, imploring God's mercy. For a sermon arguing God's vengeance for national sins (and imploring mercy), W. Trollope, *Three Sermons Having Reference to the Prevailing Famine* (Cambridge: Hall, 1847). On British responses, see H. Waters, 'The Great Famine and the Rise of Anti-Irish Racism', *Race & Class* 37:1 (1995), pp.95–108; P. Gray, 'National Humiliation and the Great Hunger: Fast and Famine in 1847', *Irish Historical Studies* 32:126 (November 2000), pp.193–216; see also P. Williamson, 'State Prayers, Fasts and Thanksgivings: Public Worship in Britain 1830–1897', *Past & Present* 200 (August 2008), pp.121–74.

133 *The Pilot* [Dublin], 16 August 1848 [p.4].

134 *Leinster Independent*, quoted from the *Leinster Express* in *St James's Chronicle*, 8 May 1838 [p.4].

135 'Trial by Jury in Ireland', *The Irish Felon*, 8 July 1848, p.34. See also, reprinted from J. Mitchel's *United Irishman*, 27 May 1848: 'Murder by Jury', *The Irish Felon*, 22 July 1848, p.73.

136 *The Nation*, 22 July 1848, p.473.

137 It was written from prison, and read by the trial judge to the court (chief baron), Dublin Commission, sentence of Martin, see *Nenagh Guardian*, 23 August 1848, p.2.

138 'Our Portrait Gallery – No.LI. James W. Whiteside', *Dublin University Magazine* 33 (March 1849), pp.326–39 [p.337]; *Coleraine Chronicle*, 14 October 1848 [p.1].

139 *Freeman's Journal*, 19 October 1848 [p.3].

140 *Cork Examiner*, 13 October 1848 [p.2].

141 Ibid., 11 October 1848 [p.2].

142 Ibid., 8 September 1848 [p.2].

143 'Movement in Ireland', *Tait's Edinburgh Magazine*, August 1848, pp.560–7 [p.562].

144 *Galway Vindicator*, 11 August 1849 [p.2].

145 *Freeman's Journal*, 1 August 1849 [p.2].

146 *Freeman's Journal*, 9 August 1849 [p.2]; *Illustrated London News*, 11 August 1849, p.89.

147 *Cork Examiner*, 28 June 1850 [p.2]. On Irish petitioning effort, C. Kinealy, *Repeal and Revolution: 1848 in Ireland* (Manchester: Manchester University Press, 2009); G.F. Duffy, 'William Smith O'Brien: Petitions of Mercy', *Clogher Record* 15:2 (1995), pp.101–3. See also 'Memorials for Mercy', *Limerick and Clare Examiner*, 25 October 1848 [p.4].

148 So argued James Morgan, in a public meeting, *Cork Examiner*, 28 June 1850 [p.2].

149 *Cork Examiner*, 23 October 1848, p.4 refers to the 'twice blessed virtue' which is 'mightiest in the mightiest'. *Sligo Champion*, 21 October 1848 [p.2] quoted the passage in appealing to the queen.

150 *Cork Examiner*, 11 October 1848 [p.2].
151 *The Examiner*, 14 October 1848, p.657.
152 *Dublin Evening Mail*, 16 October 1848, p.2; *Clare Journal*, 19 October 1848 [p.4].
153 See R. Sloan, *William Smith O'Brien and the Young Irelander Rebellion of 1848* (Dublin, Four Courts, 2000).
154 *Galway Mercury*, 7 April 1849 [p.2].
155 'Ireland under Lord Clarendon', *The Economist*, 18 March 1848, p.312. See also, reporting the journal's views on 'true mercy' for Ireland, 'Ireland's Necessity is England's Opportunity', in *Kerry Evening Post*, 13 September 1848, p.2.
156 *Morning Advertiser*, 18 June 1850, p.3. See 'Bill to provide for Abolition of Office of Lord Lieutenant of Ireland, and for Appointment of fourth Secretary of State' (17 May 1850). It intended to transfer any powers of pardon vested in the lord lieutenant to the monarch.
157 *Anglo-Celt*, 26 August 1848, p.1; J. Savage, *'98 and '48: the Modern Revolutionary History and Literature of Ireland* (New York: Redfield, 1856), p.330.
158 See debates in the Commons on the transportation for treason (Ireland) bill, following Napier's presentation of a petition from O'Brien and others, *Globe*, 19 June 1849 [p.3]. See *Irish Examiner*, 27 October 1848, p.2, on Meagher's fate, 'is it mercy to doom him to pass from the dawn of manhood to the night of age in penal exile'.
159 *Galway Mercury*, 27 April 1850 [p.2].
160 E.g. reporting a memorial from Castlebar, *Nation*, 24 April 1852, p.5.
161 *Cork Examiner*, 5 July 1850, p.3; see *Cork Examiner*, 19 July 1850, p.4, for discussion of this language in the Dublin Town Council; *Cork Examiner*, 24 July 1850, p.4. See J.H. Murphy, *Abject Loyalty*, on the treatment of the Queen by the Young Irelanders.
162 *Cork Examiner*, 3 March 1852, p.3.
163 See T.F. Meagher, 'The Queen Will Visit Ireland This Summer', *The Irish Felon*, 1 July 1848, on her 'fair and tender hand … royalty inspires that high sentiment of chivalry'. The gendering of rebellion is another issue too, see 'Mary', 'To the Women of Ireland', *United Irishman* (13 May 1848), calling on women to drop their horror of bloodshedding, for a righteous war, reprinted in A. Bourke, M. Luddy et al., eds, *The Field Day Anthology of Irish Writing*, vol. 5 (New York: New York University Press), p.903.
164 *Cork Examiner*, 24 July 1850, p.4.
165 *Irish Examiner*, 22 September 1848, p.2.
166 'William Smith O'Brien', *Prisoner's Friend*, December 1848, pp.163–6 [p.166].
167 *Anglo-Celt*, 12 January 1849, p.1; *Northern Star*, 3 February 1849, p.7.
168 Tupto, 'The Purcells – A Memory of '98', *The Shamrock*, 2 May 1868, p.527.
169 *Cork Examiner*, 27 August 1868, p.2.
170 *Nation*, 15 May 1869, p.4.
171 J.J. Gahan, *Ireland's Position Explained and Justified* (Quebec: L'Evenement Press, 1873), p.10.
172 *Ulster Herald*, 12 October 1907, p.3, quoting Davis's *The Nation*.
173 'One who Knew Him', *Davitt's Life: In Sunshine and Shade* (Dublin: W.J. Alley, 1881), p.8.
174 *Dublin Weekly Nation*, 12 September 1885, p.8. The same event, with ironic title on British mercy appeared in *Anglo-Celt*, 25 February 1905, p.11; *Meath Chronicle*, 18 January 1919, p.6.

175 R.M. Henry, *The Evolution of Sinn Fein* (Dublin: Talbot Press, 1920), p.56.
176 *Irish News and Belfast Morning News*, 24 November 1902, p.6.
177 G. Lansbury, *The Miracle of Fleet Street* (London: Victoria House, 1925), p.55.
178 The Bishop of Down, quoted in T. Hennessey, *Dividing Ireland: World War One and Partition* (London: Routledge, 1998), p.80.
179 *Londonderry Sentinel*, 9 May 1916, p.3.
180 'Eight Rebel Leaders Shot but Mercy Extended to Many', *The People*, 7 May 1916, p.3, which refers to the commander in chief, 'the difficult question of punishment, tempers stern military justice with mercy'. See also the photograph 'Wounded rebels in temporary hospital in Dublin Castle', *Manchester Guardian History of the War* (16 August 1916), a serialized history that appeared in book form, the image was reproduced in postcards.
181 *The Nation*, 18 May 1916, p.589. For wider response, M.S. Neiberg, '"I Want Citizens' Clothes": Irish and German-Americans Respond to War, 1914–1917', in G. Barry, E. Dal Lago and R. Healy, eds, *Small Nations and Colonial Peripheries in World War I* (Leiden: Brill, 2016), pp.37–53.
182 *The Sphere*, 17 June 1916, p.262.
183 See *Weekly Freeman's Journal*, 23 December 1916 on the *Independent*, p.3; *Skibbereen Eagle*, 13 May 1916, p.4.
184 For instance, 'Mercy for the Rebels. An English Review's Plea', *Dublin Daily Express*, 1 June 1916, p.8, citing 'Judex'; 'The Sinn Fein Rising: A Plea for Mercy', *Fortnightly Review*, June 1916, pp.989–96; 'Irish Nationalists and the Revolt' (also reprinted *Kerry Evening Post*, 3 June 1916), *Roscommon Messenger*, 20 May 1916, p.2, p.5; 'A Plea for Clemency', *Leitrim Advertiser*, 11 May 1916 [p.2]. See Hennessey, *Dividing Ireland*, pp.140–1, on press positions on treatment of the rebels.
185 *Northern Whig*, 2 August 1916, p.6.
186 E.g. *The Liberator* (Tralee), 22 June 1916, p.4.
187 *The Times*, 16 May 1916, p.9.
188 'Judex', 'The Sinn Fein Rising: A Plea for Mercy', p.995; 'A Plea for Clemency', *Drogheda Independent*, 13 May 1916, p.4.
189 'Judex', 'The Sinn Fein Rising: A Plea for Mercy', p.994.
190 *The Voice of Ireland; Being an Interview with John Redmond, M.P., and Some Messages from Representative Irishmen Regarding the Sinn Fein Rebellion* (London: T. Nelson and sons [1916]), p.20.
191 Urban District Council of Queenstown, *Sheffield Daily Telegraph*, 12 May 1916, p.5.
192 'Government of Ireland', *Parliamentary Debates*, 5th series, House of Commons, vol.86, House of Commons, 18 October 1916, cols.581–696 [col.619; col.638]. For debates in the Lords about 'even handed' justice and 'undue' clemency, see 'The Sinn Fein Rebellion', *Parliamentary Debates*, 5th series, House of Lords, vol.21, 11 May 1916, cols.1002–36.
193 *Milngavie and Bearsden Herald*, 1 January 1915, p.5. The theme of contrast with Boer rebellion is noted in J. Lee, *Ireland, 1912–1985: Politics and Society* (Cambridge: Cambridge University Press, 1989), p.35.
194 *Derry Journal*, 1 September 1916, p.6.
195 *The Scotsman*, 23 May 1916, p.3; *Belfast News-Letter*, 31 July 1916, p.8.
196 S. Brooks, 'The Irish Insurrection', *The North American Review* 204:728 (July 1916), pp.57–69 [p.69].
197 *The People*, 7 May 1916, p.3.
198 *Leeds Mercury*, 4 May 1916 [p.2].

199 Quoted in *Western Gazette*, 5 May 1916, p.8.
200 *Birmingham Daily Post*, 6 May 1916, p.6.
201 'Rebellion and Clemency', *The Spectator*, 13 May 1916, p.5.
202 *Daily Herald*, 27 May 1916, p.4.
203 *Liverpool Echo*, 8 May 1916, p.6.
204 *Kirkintilloch Gazette*, 5 May 1916 [p.3].
205 *Belfast News-Letter*, 4 May 1916, p.4; *Northern Whig*, 27 June 1917, p.4; *Northern Whig*, 31 May 1916, p.6 (on lord lieutenants). The Royal Commission of Inquiry into the rebellion's causes discussed the lord lieutenant's prerogative of mercy, see *Ballymena Observer*, 2 June 1916.
206 *Ballymena Weekly Telegraph*, 6 May 1916, p.4.
207 *Larne Times*, 23 June 1917, p.4. Mercy was also debated on the grounds of political expediency – Irish, imperial and American feeling – in relation to Roger Casement's Execution, see 'A Matter of Policy', *Derry Journal*, 26 July 1916 [p.2]; and the argument reported from the *Manchester Guardian*. See *Weekly Freeman's Journal*, 5 August 1916 [p.6], for English press views against the policy of execution (*Manchester Guardian* and *Daily News*).
208 *Report of the Royal Commission on the Rebellion in Ireland*, Parliamentary Papers, Session 1916, vol. 11, p.171; 'Lord Wimborne's Revelations', *Sinn Fein Rebellion Handbook* (Dublin: Irish Times, 1917), p.161, see also p.196; K.T. Hoppen, 'A Question None Could Answer: 'What Was the Viceroyalty For? 1800–1921' in Gray and Purdue, eds, *The Irish Lord Lieutenancy*. The biographer of Edward Carson describes him as 'cipher', see I.D. Colivin, *The Life of Lord Carson* (New York: Macmillan, 1937), p.154.
209 *Londonderry Sentinel*, 9 September 1916, p.6, citing a *Times* report about the 'profound feeling' stirred in the South East and South West.
210 F.S.L. Lyons, 'The New Nationalism', in W.E. Vaughan, ed., *A New History of Ireland, vol.6 Ireland under the Union, 1871–1921* (1989; Oxford: Oxford University Press, 2012), pp.224–39 [p.225]; see also, on the impact of the executions, K. Lusk and W. Maley, eds, *Scotland and the Easter Rising: Fresh Perspectives on 1916* (Edinburgh: Luath Press, 2016), letter from Margaret Ashton, 1916 quoted in T. Bowden, 'Ireland: Background to Violence', in M. Elliott-Bateman, J. Ellis and T. Bowden, eds, *The Fourth Dimension of Warfare: Revolt to Revolution: Studies in the 19th and 20th Centuries* (Manchester: Manchester University Press, 1974), vol.2, pp.187–210[p.222]. See D.G. Boyce, 'British Opinion, Ireland, and the War, 1916–1918', *Historical Journal* 17 (1974), pp.575–93.
211 P.J. Lally, *Facts of Irish History and English Propaganda* (Cambridge, MA: P. Lally, 1916), p.12.
212 The argument of the Lord Chancellor of Ireland, quoted in M.A. Doherty, 'Kevin Barry and the Anglo-Irish Propaganda War', *Irish Historical Studies* 32:126 (November 2000), pp.217–31 [p.223]; see also D. Foxton, *Revolutionary Lawyers: Sinn Féin and the Crown Courts in Ireland and Britain, 1916–1923* (Dublin: Four Courts, 2008).
213 See D. Paul, 'Forgiveness in the North', *The Furrow* 34:5 (May 1983), pp.287–90. For capital punishment in Eire, see I. O'Donnell, *Justice, Mercy, and Caprice: Clemency and the Death Penalty in Ireland* (Oxford: Oxford University Press, 2017).
214 *Leitrim Advertiser*, 11 May 1916 [p.2].
215 'Manifesto to the Friends of Freedom', June 1791, reprinted in J.X. Regan, *What Made Ireland Sinn Fein* (Boston, MA: the author, 1921), pp.42–3.

Chapter 5

1. See J.V. Douthwaite, 'Le roi pitoyable et ses adversaires: la politique de l'émotion selon J.-J. Regnault, H. M. Williams et les libellistes de Varennes', *Revue D'Histoire Littéraire De La France* 110:4 (2010), pp.917–34; and Douthwaite, 'La Pitié et ses adversaires: La politique de l'émotion dans les écrits révolutionnaires', at the conference 'Emotions et puissance de la littérature', Ecole Normale Supérieure, rue d'Ulm, Paris, 12 June 2009. See also Alessandro De Arcangelis, 'The Politics of Pity: Madame de Staël and the French Revolution', 2015, published at http://passionatepolitics.eu/de-stael-politics-of-pity/ (accessed 28 September 2017).
2. James Gillray's cartoon, published 29 July 1793 by H. Humphrey, No. 18 Old Bond Street, 1793 on Charlotte Corday' trial ironizes justice through the figure of the Tribunal – although blind Justice above the court 'throne' is not particularly ironic. See from the French Political Cartoon Collection, Library of Congress, *Un sans-culotte instrument de crimes dansant au milieu des horreurs, vient outrager l'humanité pleurante auprès d'un cénotaphe* (1793), showing weeping Humanité confronted by a Jacobin, a comment on the king's execution.
3. J.W. Fenno, *Desultory Reflections on the New Political Aspects of Public Affairs in the United States of America since the Commencement of the Year 1799* (New York: Printed for the author, 1800), p.13.
4. E. Burke, *Reflections on the Revolution in France, and on the Proceedings in Certain Societies in London Relative to That Event: In a Letter Intended to Have Been Sent to a Gentleman in Paris* (5th edn; London: Dodsley, 1790), p.222; E. Burke, *A Letter from Mr Burke to a Member of the National Assembly; in Answer to Some Objections to His Book on French Affairs* in *The Works of the Right Honourable Edmund Burke, Collected in Three Volumes* (1791; London: Dodsley, 1792), vol.3, p.337.
5. M.D. Conway, *The Life of Thomas Paine: With a History of His Literary, Political, and Religious Career in America, France, and England* (New York: Putnam, 1892), vol.2, p.8.
6. H. Kett, *History the Interpreter of Prophecy, or, a View of Scriptural Prophecies and Their Accomplishment in the Past and Present Occurrences of the World* (2 vols; 3rd edn; Oxford, 1799), vol.2, p.218.
7. *A Thanksgiving Sermon* (London: Rivington, 1814), p.14.
8. This may echo H.M. William's prefatory remarks in *Letters Containing a Sketch of The Scenes Which Passed in Various Departments of France during the Tyranny of Robespierre, of the Events Which Took Place in Paris on the 28th of July 1794* (London: Robinson, 1795), vol.3, p.1, 'when the laws of mercy are but the echo of the public opinion'.
9. A review of the tenth volume of *Histoire de la Revolution Francaise* (1858), *Westminster Review* (April 1859), p.334. Robespierre's famous statement about mercy, 'Indulgence for the royalists! say some; mercy for villains! no! Mercy for innocence, mercy for the weak, mercy for the unfortunate, mercy for humanity,' appeared in translation later, e.g. G. Long, *France and Its Revolutions: A Pictorial History, 1789–1848* (London: Knight, 1850), p.237.
10. R. Boyd, 'Justice, Beneficence, and Boundaries: Rousseau and the Paradox of Generality', in J. Farr and D.L. Williams, eds, *The General Will* (Cambridge: Cambridge University Press, 2015), pp.147–269.

11 D. Hume, 'The Populousness of Ancient Nations', in D. Hume, *The Philosophical Works of David Hume: Including All the Essays, and Exhibiting the More Important Alterations and Corrections in the Successive Editions Published by the Author* (Edinburgh: Black, 1826), pp.421–508 [p.452].
12 J. M'Queen, *The Campaigns of 1812, 1813, and 1814: Also the Causes and Consequences of the French Revolution, to which Is Added the French Confiscations, Contributions, Requisitions, &c., from 1793, till 1814* (Glasgow: Khull, 1814), p.796. Burke's *Two Letters Addressed to a Member of the Present Parliament on the Proposals for Peace with the Regicide Directory of France* (London: F. and C. Rivington, 1796), p.28, recalls Marie Antoinette's mercy too, interceding for the English prisoner of war in the United States, Asgill, 'did not in vain solicit the mercy of the highest in rank, and the most compassionate of the compassionate sex'.
13 *Letters Written in France, in the Summer 1790, to a Friend in England: Containing Various Anecdotes Relative to the French Revolution; and Memoirs of Mons. and Madame Du F——.* (4th edn; London: Cadell, 1794), p.174.
14 'The Virtues. An ode, May 1794', E. Bentley, *Poems* (Norwich: the author, 1821), p.43.
15 M'Queen, *The Campaigns of...*, p.811. 'Pity is not revolutionary', General François Westermann said, cited in P. McPhee, *The French Revolution, 1789-1799* (Oxford: Oxford University Press, 2002).
16 J.W. Croker, 'Art. IX. The Guillotine', *Quarterly Review* 73:145 (December 1844), pp.235–80 [p.238].
17 Anon., *The First Fruits of the French Revolution* (n.p., 1794?), pp.11–22 [p.14].
18 W. Cobbett, *The Bloody Buoy, Thrown Out as a Warning to the Political Pilots of All Nations* (Philadelphia, PA: Wright, 1797), p.92.
19 L. Du Broca, *Interesting Anecdotes of the Heroic Conduct of Women, during the French Revolution* (London: H.D. Symonds, 1802), p.61. This was the subject of at least one painting: by Claude-Noël Thevenin, 'Elisabeth de Cazotte Sauve la Vie de Son Père à La Prison de L'abbaye. (23 Septembre 1792)'.
20 *An Essay on the True Principles of Executive Power in Great States. Translated from the French of M. Necker* (2 vols; London: G.G.J. and J. Robinson, 1792), vol.1, ch.10.
21 *An Essay on the True Principles of Executive Power*, p.173.
22 Ibid., p.177.
23 Ibid., p.180.
24 Ibid., p.184.
25 Ibid., p.182.
26 Ibid., p.185.
27 Ibid., pp.187–8.
28 Ibid., p.188.
29 National Convention, 5 September 1793, translated in *The Political State of Europe for the Year MDCCXCIII: Containing, an Authentic and Impartial Narrative of Every Military Operation of the Present Belligerent Powers, and a Correct Copy of Every State Paper, Declaration, Manifesto, &c. &c.* (London: Jordan, 1794), vol.5, p.18.
30 J. Gilchrist and W.J. Murray, *Press in the French Revolution: A Selection of Documents Taken from the Press of the Revolution for the Years 1789–1794* (London: Cheshire and Gihn, 1971), p.294; S. Wahnich, *In Defence of the Terror: Liberty or Death in the French Revolution* (2003; translation, London: Verso, 2012), p.54; C. Weber, *Terror and Its Discontents: Suspect Words in Revolutionary France* (London: University of Minnesota Press, 2003), pp.146–61 (and pp.84–5 on Saint-Just on clemency).

31 [J. Courtenay], *A Poetical and Philosophical Essay on The French Revolution* (London: Ridgway, 1793), p.21.
32 H.M. Williams, *Letters Containing a Sketch of the Scenes Which Passed in Various Departments of France during the Tyranny of Robespierre, of the Events Which Took Place in Paris on the 28th of July 1794* (London, G. G. and J. Robinson, 1795), vol.3, p.142; p.145; and quoted in S. Blakemore, *Crisis in Representation: Thomas Paine, Mary Wollstonecraft, Helen Maria Williams* (Madison,WI: Fairleigh Dickinson University Press, 1997), p.168.
33 M.E. Sandford, *Thomas Poole and His Friends* (2 vols; London: Macmillan, 1888), vol.1, p.105. On Southey and Coleridge on Robespierre, see B. Bosserhoff, *Radical Contra-Diction: Coleridge, Revolution, Apostasy* (Newcastle: Cambridge Scholars Press, 2016), p.69.
34 *Star*, 19 August 1795; *A Collection of State Papers, Relative to the War against France Now Carrying on by Great-Britain and the Several Other European Powers Containing Copies of Treaties, Conventions, Proclamations* (11 vols, 1794–1802; London: J. Debrett, 1796), vol.3; *The Register of the Times, or: Political Museum* (London: Whittingham, 1795), vol.6, p.216.
35 *British Critic*, January 1795, p.78.
36 *Oracle and Public Advertiser*, 11 April 1795 [p.3]. G.L. Craik, *The Pictorial History of England: Being a History of the People* (London: C. Knight, 1843), vol.3, p.452 on the Thermidorien party posing as 'angels or ministers of mercy'; 'Madame Tallien: A Biographical Sketch', *St Paul's Magazine* (January 1868), pp.455–75 [p.456]. For Theresa Madame de Fontenay's role in changing him towards mercy, see L. Muhlbach, *The Empress Josephine: An Historical Sketch of the Days of Napoleon* (New York: Appleton, 1867), p.98.
37 [S. Parr] *Remarks on the Statement of Dr Charles Combe. By an Occasional Writer in The British Critic* (London: Bell, 1795), p.84.
38 'Prologue to a Pantomimical Piece. Called the Embarkation. Performed in the Royal Circus, 1793', in G. Turnbull, *Poems* (Dumfries: for the author, 1794), p.8.
39 *European Magazine*, September 1807, p.212.
40 *Gentleman's Magazine*, June 1796, p.508.
41 R.G. Teitel, *Transitional Justice* (Oxford: Oxford University Press, 2001), p.57. Teitel notes the French Revolution's association of the pardoning power as arbitrary and illegitimate, and the critique of arbitrary monarchical clemency by John Locke, and Kant.
42 See the essay on 'The Invasion', *Morning Post*, 13 October 1803, p.2, responding to 'Volunteer'; and *Morning Post*, 10 October 1803. See also *Extermination, or an Appeal to the People of England, on the Present War, with France* (London: Eaton, 1793), p.13 for a pro-French response, which asserted that merciless acts by revolutionaries had never been directed against 'innocent Individuals'.
43 Hay, 'Property, Authority and the Criminal Law', p.37.
44 Thus, as reported in *Universal Magazine*, 91 (1792), p.460: the House of Commons, 20 December 1792, p.460, Sheridan about whether the French nation or leaders possessed 'true valour, justice, magnanimity, and mercy' and exchanges with Burke. Parliamentary debates can be examined, e.g. Earl of Mornington on the regime's 'passionate invective against mercy and justice' and Barrère's views, that justice 'executed in mercy is incompatible with the vigour of a well-ordered state', *Parliamentary Register; or History of the Proceedings and Debates of the House of Commons ... during the Fourth Session of the Seventeenth Parliament of Great*

Britain, vol.37 (London: Debrett, 1794), p.80. Or, also by Mornington during the debate on Grey's motion on reform of parliament in 1794, *Parliamentary History of England from the Earliest Period to the Year 1803. Vol.30. Comprising the Thirteenth of December 1792, to the Tenth of March 1794* (London: Hansard, 1817), col.874, 'in place of the gracious mercy of the Crown the populace have assumed the exercise of a new species of appellate jurisdiction'.

45   See Burke, 'They do not forget that justice and mercy are substantial parts of religion', in *A Comparative Display of the Different Opinions of the Most Distinguished British Writers on the Subject of the French Revolution* (2 vols; London: Debrett, 1793), vol.2, p.6. Burke, *Two Letters Addressed to a Member of the Present Parliament*, p.39.

46   See, for instance, debates over the Traitorous Correspondence Bill, where the legislation proposed in 1793 is referred to by Fox, 15 March 1793, as 'a tyranny which wounded under the garb of mercy', *Parliamentary History of England from the Earliest Period to the Year 1803. Vol. 30. Comprising the Period from the Thirteenth of December 1792, to the Tenth of March 1794* (London: Hansard, 1817), col.638.

47   *Morning Post*, 3 November 1794 [p.1].

48   *The Times*, 24 March 1794 [p.2].

49   *Caledonian Mercury*, 6 December 1794 [p.2]. Erskine in defence, asked just for justice, and referred to the advice given to the jury not to let mercy swallow up justice, *Derby Mercury*, 11 December 1794 [p.2]. On Stone, *The Times*, 30 January 1796 [p.2].

50   *Caledonian Mercury*, 1 November 1798 [p.3].

51   *Caledonian Mercury*, 26 May 1796 [p.4]. See also G.T. Kenyon, *The Life of Lloyd, First Lord Kenyon, Lord Chief Justice of England* (London: Longmans, Green, 1873), p.303, where it is 'every fair leaning to the side of lenity and compassion'.

52   *The Origin & Stability of the French Revolution. A Sermon Preached at St. Paul's Chapel, Norwich, July, 14, 1791, by Mark Wilks, a Norfolk Farmer* (the author, 1791), p.12.

53   *Gentleman's Magazine* 64:2 (August 1794), p.751, quoting petition from Lyons before the Convention. An engraving in the Bibliotheque Nationale has the hand of heaven holding scale of justice, 'Époque de la liberté françoise: Louis XVI conduit par M. Necker sous les médaillons d'Henri IV et Sully, dans le chemin de la gloire, vers les trois ordres réunis et d'accord sous la règle de la Justice', by Joseph Maillet. The Terror was presented by promoters as justice, see D. Andress, 'Sentimental Construction of Martyrdom', in D. Janes and A. Houen, eds, *Martyrdom and Terrorism: Pre-Modern to Contemporary Perspectives* (New York: Oxford University Press, 2014), pp.131–51 [p.147]. See H.G. Brown, *Ending the French Revolution: Violence, Justice, and Repression from the Terror to Napoleon* (Charlottesville: University of Virginia Press, 2006); and M. Walzer, ed., *Regicide and Revolution: Speeches at the Trial of Louis XVI* (London: Cambridge University Press, 1974). See S. Dunn, 'Albert Camus and the Dubious Politics of Mercy', in R. English, ed., *Ideas Matter: Essays in Honour of Conor Cruise O'Brien* (Dublin: Poolbeg Press, 1998), pp.345–56, on Louis XVI's execution and the loss of a moral code of mercy; S. Dunn, *The Deaths of Louis XVI: Regicide and the French Political Imagination* (Princeton, NJ: Princeton University Press, 1994), ch.6.

54   A. Pirie, *The French Revolution Exhibited, in the Light of the Sacred Oracles: Or, a Series of Lectures on the Prophecies now Fulfilling* (Perth: Morison, 1795), p.145.

55   J. Gifford, *The History of France, from the Earliest Times, to the Accession of Louis the Sixteenth* (4 vols; London: C. Lowndes,1793), vol.1.

56 F.B. Goodrich, *The Court of Napoleon; or, Society under the First Empire* (New York: Derby and Jackson, 1857), pp.34–9; on the reality, see P. Friedland, *Seeing Justice Done: The Age of Spectacular Capital Punishment in France* (Oxford: Oxford University Press, 2012), pp.255–6.
57 Hay, 'Property, Authority and the Criminal Law', p.37.
58 *Kentish Register*, October 1793, p.107.
59 Reported in many papers and periodicals, e.g. *The Scots Magazine*, May 1793, p.224. This is derived from the *Convention Nationale, 1793, 370, Rapport de l'execution de Louis Capet, fait à la commune de Paris, le même jour 21 janvier 1793*, where the original is 'Louis Capet a voulu parler de commisération au peuple'. The word ought to be translated as 'sympathy'. Voltaire wrote: 'Nous avons tous deux sentiments qui sont le fondement de la société: la commisération et la justice' in 'VII. Des Sauvages', *Essai sur les Moers et L'Esprit des Nations* (1756) reprinted in *Oeuvres Completes de Voltaire. Tome Seizieme* (Kehl: La Société Littéraire Typographique, 1784), p.35.
60 *London Review*, September 1795, p.204. An interesting letter contrasting the style and practice of mercy of the restored Bourbon, who suffered agonies as result of a 'compassionate breast,' with Napoleon's coldness, appears in 'A Friend of Favras', *Morning Chronicle*, 29 December 1815, p.3.
61 *Morning Post*, 29 August 1814 [p.3].
62 See W. Hazlitt, *The Life of Napoleon Buonaparte* (1828; New York: Wiley and Putnam, 1847), p.201 on the leaders of the Revolution placed in a 'situation above humanity … If they yielded to the amiable infirmities of human nature, they must give up the cause of liberty and independence … It is possible that the feelings of justice and mercy should survive a series of barbarous and cruel acts, sustained by the sacred sense of duty; but it is barely possible – or if in one case not in many.'
63 *Derby Mercury*, 31 May 1798 [p.2].
64 E.g. *Debates in the House of Commons, on the Tenth Day of March, 1794, upon the Motion of Mr Adam, in Behalf of Muir and Palmer* (Edinburgh: Robertson, 1794), p.5.
65 *The World*, 7 March 1794, p.1.
66 *Hampshire Chronicle*, 29 July 1797 [p.4].
67 W. Hales, *The Monstrous Republic: Or, French Atrocities Pourtrayed* (Dublin: Milliken, 1799), p.14.
68 E. Burke, *A Letter from Mr Burke, to a Member of the National Assembly: In Answer to Some Objections to His Book on French Affairs* (London: Dodsley, 1791), p.44.
69 *The Times*, 10 July 1794 [p.3]. See T.B. Macaulay, 'Barère's *Memoirs*', *Edinburgh Review* 79:160 (April 1844), pp.275–351.
70 A. Seward, *Letters of Anna Seward Written between the Years 1784 and 1807*, vol.3, letter LXII, p.204, 17 January 1793. See also her letter to Dr Parr, 17 August 1793, on the loss of mercy and piety among other things, p.303.
71 L. Hawkins, *Letters on the Female Mind* (2 vols; London: Hookham and Carpenter, 1793), vol.2, 2 January 1793, pp.11–112; p.114. She would even extend mercy to those involved in mutilating Lamballe, 'well convinced that vengeance is not mine', p.132.
72 *Kentish Gazette*, 26 November 1799, p.4; *Chester Chronicle*, 4 May 1804 [p.2] on the case of General Moreau, reprinting letters between the Empress and Jean Moreau.
73 E-A-D. Las Casas, *Journal of the Private Life and Conversations of the Emperor Napoleon at Saint Helena* (4 vols; London: H. Colburn, 1823), vol. 2, Pt. 3, p.320.
74 P. Hicks, 'Napoleon as a Politician', in M. Boers, P. Hicks and A. Guimera, eds, *The Napoleonic Empire and the New European Political Culture* (Basingstoke: Palgrave Macmillan, 2012), pp.70–81. On Machiavelli, W.B. Parsons, *Machiavelli's Gospel: The*

Critique of Christianity in the Prince (Woodbridge: Boydell and Brewer, 2016), ch.5, 'Machiavelli's Unchristian Virtue'.

75 *Les clémences de Napoléon: l'image au service du mythe* (Paris: Bibliotheque Marmottan/Somogy, 2004).

76 See R. Rosenblum, *Transformations in Late Eighteenth Century Art* (Princeton, NJ: Princeton University Press 1967), p.100; V. Huet, 'Napoleon: A New Augustus?', in C. Edwards, ed., *Roman Presences: Receptions of Rome in European Culture, 1789–1945* (Cambridge: Cambridge University Press, 1999), pp.53–69 [pp.67–8]. For examples, see Guillaume Colson's *Trait de clémence du General Bonaparte envers une famille arabe lors l'entrée française à Alexandrie*, of 1811, cited by Huet.

77 W.H. Ireland, *The Life of Napoleon Bonaparte* (4 vols; London: Cumberland, 1828), vol.1.

78 'The Caitiff of Corsica', in *Characters, Moral, and Political, of the Principal Personages Throughout the French Revolution, the Consulate, and the Virtuous Imperial Government Which Followed It* (London: Lackington, Allen, 1808), pp.275–6; W. Burdon, *The Life and Character of Bonaparte, from His Birth to the 15th of August* (2nd edn; Newcastle upon Tyne: Anderson, 1805), p.259.

79 On Jaffa there is a large literature, for contemporary discussion, 'Mr Kendall on Buonaparte's Massacre at Jaffa', *The Literary Panorama*, July 1810, cols.519–526.

80 The phrase is Mary Ann Bulmer's. She is described as an 'Amazonian logician' in *The Examiner*, 6 August 1815, p.497.

81 See verse by 'Old Bailey' in *Morning Post*, 5 August 1815, p.3, ironically describing him as the 'mild little merciful man'.

82 *Morning Chronicle*, 3 August 1815, p.3. The letter of 'Alfred', 20 July 1815, in the same paper, p.2, called for rigid justice towards Napoleon and the Bonapartists, 'we do not close the door of our hearts to sympathy, we only turn aside for a time'. 'Lover of Mercy' pled the case of Marshal Ney, *Morning Chronicle*, 17 November 1815, p.2. Ney's case was another where the merits of exercising royal mercy were debated, sometimes with reference to what Britons would tolerate at home, see *Royal Cornwall Gazette*, 2 December 1815, p.2.

83 *Morning Post*, 28 July 1815, p.3; *Durham County Advertiser*, 29 July 1815, p.2 for condemnation of calls for mercy; for imagined trial, 'The Sentence pronounced by the French Minister of Justice upon Napoleon Bonaparte, tried at Paris by a Special Jury of Princes and Marshals, and Convicted of Enormous Crimes', *Morning Post*, 22 July 1815, p.3.

84 W.T. Fitzgerald, 'The Battle of Waterloo', *European Magazine*, 1815, p.55.

85 'Ode for The Regent's Birth-day, 12th August 1815, by an Old Naval officer', *Morning Post*, 11 August 1815, p.3.

86 *Caledonian Mercury*, 6 November 1815, p.4; *Chester Courant*, 1 August 1815, p.4. In his letter to the Prince Regent, Napoleon threw himself 'au foyer du people britannique' – like Themistocles, to seat himself at the hearth of the British people, 14 July 1815, see *Correspondance de Napoléon 1er* (32 vols, Paris: Imprimerie Impériale, 1869), vol.28, p.348.

87 British Museum, 1988, 0502.1. On mercy in English *Bonapartiana*, see for example 'Exercise of Mercy', the page in J.S.C. Abbott, *The Life of Napoleon Bonaparte* (London: Beeton's Historian, 1860), p.180; 'Not Justice, but Mercy', *The Quiver*, 17 May 1862, pp.81–2, on the first consul's mercy to Lazolin after his daughter implored mercy.

88 R. Burnett, *Original Pathetic, Legendary, and Moral Poems, Intended for Young Persons* (London: Scatcherd and Letterman, 1820), p.120.
89 *England's Triumph: Being an Account of the Rejoicings, &c. Which Have Lately Taken Place in London and Elsewhere* (London: Hatchard, 1814), p.80; *Hereford Journal*, 29 June 1814, p.3.
90 In the satirical anthem for Austria imagined in *Morning Post*, 29 August 1815, p.3.
91 See Walter Clark, 'How sadly ended the good BOURBON's reign: | And with them Peace and godlike Mercy fell', *Lancaster Gazette*, 6 May 1815, p.4.
92 C. Vernay, *De la restauration de la Monarchie, ou la clémence de Louis XVIII* (Lyon: Pelzin, 1814); *Un Mot sur la clémence du roi* (Paris: Chanson, 1815). See also Debavay and Roussialle-Tessancourt, *Exposé historique de l'abus que des hommes perfides ont fait; de la clémence de Louis XVIII, et des calamités qui en sont résultées pour la France* (Strasbourg: Levrault, 1815). On mercy in restoration iconography, J.P. Ribner, *Broken Tablets: The Cult of the Law in French Art from David to Delacroix* (Berkeley, CA: University of California Press, 1993), p.60.
93 W.H. Ireland, *The Napoleon Anecdotes* (6 vols; London: Simpkin and Marshall, 1822), vol.1, p.77, referring to a caricature ironically contrasting Louis XVIII's clemency with Napoleon's tyranny. For ironic contrast between Napoleon and Louis XVII, not to the latter's advantage, see 'Napoleon and Louis XVIII. A Friend of Favras', *Examiner* 421 (21 January 1816), p.44; *Niles Weekly Register*, 30 November 1816, p.220, in response to praise of the king's clemency in the *Courier* of London.
94 'French Treatment of Criminals', *North British Review* 27 (August 1857), p.26, on the *ordonnance* and *clemencé royale*: the British reviewer of A. Bonneville's *Traité des diverses institutions complémentaires du Régime Pénitentiare* (Paris: Joubert, 1847), criticising the French for, 'exorbitant and excessive influence given to all sorts of sentiments'.
95 J.B. O'Brien, *A Dissertation and Elegy on the Life and Death of the Immortal Maximilian Robespierre* (London: Holyoake, 1859), p.3; G.H. Lewes, *The Life of Maximilien Robespierre* (London: Chapman, Hall, 1849), p.310.
96 S.T. Coleridge's *The Fall of Robespierre* (1794) in H.N. Coleridge, ed., *The Literary Remains of Samuel Taylor Coleridge* (4 vols; London: W. Pickering, 1836), vol.1, p.9: (Robespierre to Barrère): 'Self-centring Fear! How well thou canst ape *Mercy!*' Robespierre in the play by Henry Bliss, *Robespierre: A Tragedy* (London: Kimpton, 1854), in dialogue with Tallien says, 'Leave colleagues death's detested power, | And grace my breast with mercy, as a flower? | I scorn the gewgaw: nor will grant it them.' Fisk's 'Robespierre Receiving Letters from Friends of his Victims with Assassination Threats', 1863 depicted the leader in his garret gazing at a picture of the guillotine. See C. Haydon and W. Doyle, eds, *Robespierre* (Cambridge: Cambridge University Press, 2006).

Chapter 6

1 W. Cowper, *The Task, a Poem in Six Books* (London: Johnson, 1785), p.47: 'Spread it then, | And let it circulate through every vein | Of all your empire; that where Britain's power | Is felt, mankind may feel her mercy too.' For missionaries' use of these lines, see *Papers Relative to the Wesleyan Missions, and to the State of Heathen Countries*, 9 March 1847, p.124 (on missionaries following British victory in war

in Southern Africa); for quotation in relation to human sacrifice and infanticide among the Khonds, 'The Khonds, Government Measures, Etc', *Calcutta Review* 6 (July–December 1846), p.108. The lines are quoted in James Peggs's *India's Cries to British Humanity, Relative to the Suttee, Infanticide, British Connexion with Idolatry, Ghaut Murders, and Slavery in India* (London: Seely, 1830), p.211; and Peggs's *The Infanticide's Cry to Britain* (4th edn; London: Ward, 1844), p.112.

2. A. Cobley, 'Sarah Ann Gill's Pastor: Hero or Villain? The Reverend William Shrewsbury in Barbados and South Africa', *Journal of the Barbados Museum and Historical Society* LVII (57), pp.77–97 (p.93).

3. See ch.4, 'Staging British India', in J.S. Bratton, R.A. Cave, B. Gregory, M. Pickering, H.J. Holder, *Acts of Supremacy: The British Empire and the Stage, 1790–1930* (Manchester: Manchester University Press, 1991), p.170. 'Love, Mercy and Wisdom' are supposedly India's guiding spirits.

4. R. Frohock, *Heroes of Empire: The British Imperial Protagonist in America, 1596–1764* (Newark: University of Delaware Press, 2004), p.14. On cynical use of a 'gospel of mercy' during the demise of imperialism in the 1930s, see Samuel Beckett's translation of the Paris Surrealist Group's 'Murderous Humanitarianism', in A.W. Friedman, *Beckett in Black and Red: The Translations for Nancy Cunard's Negro* (Lexington: University Press of Kentucky, 2000), p.56.

5. R.M. Martin, *History of the British Possessions in the East Indies* (London: Whittaker, 1837), vol.1, p.61.

6. [H.G. Grey], *Colonial Policy and the State of Our Colonies* (London: Harrison, 1852), p.94; G. Lagden, *The Native Races of the British Empire* (London: Collins, 1924), p.267. Governor George Grey's decision of 9 July 1849 to moderate his enforcing of British laws was known as the 'Mercy, Justice and Prudence' despatch.

7. As noted by A. Jackson, *The British Empire: A Very Short Introduction* (Oxford: Oxford University Press, 2013). See, for example, 'Allegoria sull' impero Inglese' (An allegory of the English Empire) by Augusto Grossi, *Il Papagallo*, issue no. 50 in December 1878.

8. See the work of Caroline Elkins, e.g. *Britain's Gulag: The Brutal End of Empire in Kenya* (London: Cape, 2005). For recent popular treatment of brutal British rule in India, see S. Tharoor, *Inglorious Empire: What the British Did to India* (London: Hurst, 2017).

9. A.B. Forclaz, *Humanitarian Imperialism: The Politics of Anti-Slavery Activism, 1880–1940* (Oxford: Oxford University Press, 2015), p.2, citing M.G. Jeronimo and J.P. Monteiro.

10. See M.I. Swift, *Imperialism and Liberty* (Los Angeles, CA: n.p., 1899), p.14.

11. A.S. Rai, *Rule of Sympathy: Sentiment, Race, and Power 1750–1850* (New York: Palgrave, 2002). M. Pernau, 'Great Britain. The Creation of an Imperial Global Order', in M. Pernau et al., *Civilizing Emotions: Concepts in Nineteenth Century Asia and Europe* (Oxford: Oxford University Press, 2015), pp.46–62, discusses the enlightenment ideas of compassion and sympathy as part of definitions of civilization, against barbarism.

12. See the Dutch contrasted with the Portuguese, 'And now another people appeared on the bloody stage; a race of persevering, industrious merchants, who, by their cautious and humane policy, founded an empire in the East more durable, because more merciful, more kindly, than that of the intolerant Portuguese', in J. Capper, *The Three Presidencies of India* (London: Ingram, Cooke, 1853), p.106, quoted in E.H. Nolan,

The Illustrated History of the British Empire in India and the East (2 vols: London: Virtue, 1859), vol.2, p.375.
13 See C.S. Dawe, *King Edward's Realm. Story of the Making of the Empire* (London: Educational Supply Association, 1901), p.10.
14 See, for instance, the white Jamaican poet Tom Redcam, cited in A.S. Rush, *Bonds of Empire: West Indians and Britishness from Victoria to Decolonization* (Oxford: Oxford University Press, 2011), p.235. A.R.M. Lower, *My First Seventy-five Years* (Toronto: Macmillan, 1967), p.17. Some writers claimed the universality of mercy and other concepts, thus W.G. Palgrave, 'mercy, justice and judgment … belong to no special race or creed; they are the property of all', in *Essays on Eastern Questions* (London: Macmillan, 1872), p.141.
15 J.D. McCabe, *A Tour Around the World by General Grant* (Philadelphia, PA: National Publishing Company, 1879), p.523, 'Mighty, irresponsible, cruel, but with justice, and after safety, mercy'.
16 N.I.D. Buhadoor, *Icbal-e-Furung or British Prosperity: Being a Short Description of the Manners, Customs, Arts and Science of the British* (Calcutta: Medical Press, 1832), p.127.
17 *Homeward Mail from India, China and the East*, 23 June 1902, p.33.
18 E.g. the social reformer and writer from Maharashtra, Mahatma Phule (1827–90), *A Warning* (1885), quoted in H. Singh, *Rise of Reason: Intellectual History of 19th-Century Maharashtra* (Abingdon: Routledge, 2016), p.201.
19 K.N. Mukherjee, *Rabindranath Tagore's Concepts of State, Nation and Nationalism* (Kolkata: Punthi Pustak, 2003), p.149.
20 J.P. Greene, *Evaluating Empire and Confronting Colonialism in Eighteenth-Century Britain* (Cambridge: Cambridge University Press, 2013).
21 E.g. J.M. Mackenzie, ed., *Popular Imperialism and the Military: 1850–1950* (Manchester: Manchester University Press, 1992).
22 On scripture in terms of mercy, see especially, 'What doth the Lord require of thee but to do justly and to love mercy, and to walk humbly with thy God?' Micah 7. 18. For the complexity with which the language of 'justice' was invoked in missionary discourse in nineteenth-century India, see E. Cleall, 'From Divine Judgement to Colonial Courts: Missionary "Justice" in British India, c.1840–1914', *Cultural and Social History* 14:4 (2017), pp.447–61.
23 E.g. P. Peckard, *Justice and Mercy Recommended, Particularly with Reference to the Slave Trade. A Sermon* (Cambridge: Merill, 1788).
24 See 'England's Duty: Vengeance or Mercy', *Cheltenham Examiner*, 23 September 1857, p.4. Canning is described by Baboo Dukhinarunjun Mookerjee Bahadoor, Honorary Secretary and Member for Zillah Roy Bareilly, *Proceedings of the Meetings of the British Indian Association of Oudh 1861–1865* (Calcutta: Thacker, Spink, 1865) as 'the incarnation of Justice and Mercy' in the words of one Brahmin, p.57, and discusses his forbearance in context of 'the duty of charity, forgiveness and mercy' (p.54).
25 Especially in the question of slavery, mercy surfaces: *Letters on the Necessity of a Prompt Extinction of British Colonial Slavery* (London: Hatchard, 1826), p.100; G. Thompson, *The Substance of a Speech* (London: Hatchard, 1832), p.10: 'What! is it mercy to annihilate the slave—is it mercy to keep him in slavery, though you are told, in an accent of mercy, that he has got "four parlours and a saloon?"'

26 A.R. Carman, *The Ethics of Imperialism* (Boston, MA: Turner, 1905), pp.67–9 for discussion of egoism, altruism and mercy, which (p.69) refers to those moments when mercy is wrong when tested by 'racial or national survival' criteria.

27 C. Hodgkins, *Reforming Empire: Protestant Colonialism and Conscience in British Literature* (Columbia: University of Missouri Press, 2002): this cites William Blake on mercy, p.180.

28 G. Troup, *The British Empire and the Christian Faith: Being a Lecture Addressed to the Free Church Literary Union, Etc* (Glasgow: M'Nair, 1852), p.14. For similar assertion of moral influence unparalleled, E. Baylis, 'The British Empire', *The Christian Miscellany and Family Visiter. For the Year* 2nd series: 19 (1873), pp.52–6 (p.54): including the question, 'Ought not those who feel Britain's power to "feel her mercy too?"'.

29 See W.T. Stead, *Her Majesty the Queen: Studies of the Sovereign and the Reign* (London: 'Review of Reviews', 1897), pp.180-90, for childhood response when the work was exhibited at Newcastle.

30 *Missionary Speeches. No. III Right Hon. W.E. Gladstone* (London: S.P.G., n.d., c.1857), p.10. H. Richard, *The Present and Future of India under British Rule* (London: Ward, 1858).

31 Letter to Emily Faithfull, reprinted in *Imperial Federation*, 1 November 1890, p.267.

32 'Civilize and Collapse. Improveable Others, disintegrating English', ch.6 in P.K. Nayar, *The Transnational in English Literature: Shakespeare to the Modern* (Oxford: Routledge, 2015), p.242, citing Elizabeth Bentley's verse, 'On the Abolition of the African Slave Trade, July 1789', which refers to 'sweet mercy's angel form divine'. Cowper's line was uttered in reference to British West Coast of Africa, in the House of Commons, reported in *London Daily News*, 10 June 1871, p.2.

33 E.g. 'Our Colonies', *Evangelical Magazine and Missionary Chronicle*, December 1863, p.789. Newspapers quoted Cowper's lines in other contexts, e.g. against China, 'War with China', *Leicester Guardian*, 17 September 1859, p.5; and *against* aggression towards China, 'The New Quarrel with China', *Leeds Mercury*, 12 January 1860, p.3.

34 M. Tupper, 'A Carmen Saeculare for Christian England On The Pattern and in The Metre of that for Heathen Rome by Horace' in *Sacra Poesis* (London: Nisbet, 1832), pp.66–70 [p.69].

35 Texts presenting British rule as bringing justice and mercy include works for children, see K. Castle, *Britannia's Children: Reading Colonialism through Children's Books and Magazines* (Basingstoke: Palgrave Macmillan, 1996), p.67.

36 'A Christian Monumental Column', *The Ecclesiologist*, February 1857, pp.32–3 [p.33]; *The Builder*, 3 October 1857, p. 564.

37 Alongside justice and wisdom at the Chief Secretary's (originally the Colonial Secretary's) Building, 121 Macquarie Street. *Sydney Morning Herald*, 31 March 1879, p.5. Images of retribution include Edward Armitage's oil painting *Retribution*, for the Indian mutiny (c.1858). Sigismund Goetze's fresco *Britannia Pacificatrix* for the Foreign Office depicts the triumph of the Great War *without* symbols of mercy (the allies, France and Italy, hold fasces and scales).

38 R.L. Boulton of Cheltenham produced colossal statues of mercy and justice for the courts, see *Gloucester Echo*, 9 April 1901, p.3.

39 For mercy and justice in imperial discourse, see 'her sword of mercy rusty and broken at the hilt', *The Jamaica Movement for Promoting the Enforcement of the Slave-Trade Treaties, and the Suppression of the Slave-Trade* (London: Gilpin, 1850), p.304. See H. Douglas and M. Finnane, *Indigenous Crime and Settler Law: White Sovereignty*

40 J. Crawfurd, *An Appeal from the Inhabitants of British India to the Justice of the People of England: A Popular Inquiry into the Operation of the System of Taxation in British India* (London: Hooper, 1839).
41 E. Thornton, *The History of the British Empire in India* (London: W.H. Allen, 1859), p.265.
42 See the letter of Kings Bell and Acqua to Gladstone, reproduced in M.W. Doyle, *Empires* (Ithaca, NY: Cornell University Press, 1986), p.162. Doyle notes (p.42) the 'assailed individual' facing the imperial state, 'cannot even rely on the mercy and justice that sometimes tempers power in the communal domestic order'.
43 D.R. Peterson, 'Introduction', in *Abolitionism and Imperialism in Britain, Africa, and the Atlantic* (Athens: Ohio University Press, 2010), p.26.
44 Anon., *The Progress of Glory, in the Life of Horatio, Lord Nelson of the Nile* (Whitehaven: for the author, 1806), p.42.
45 'The Second Sikh War', *Calcutta Review* 15:30 (January–June 1851), pp.253–98 (p.298).
46 T.L. Buick, *New Zealand's First War: Or, the Rebellion of Hone Heke* (Wellington: Skinner, 1926), p.150.
47 See G. Cory, *The Rise of South Africa* (4 vols; London: Longmans, Green, 1919), vol.3, pp.214–15; and on mercy being viewed as weakness, p.240.
48 Examples of merciless behaviour in response to defeat at Majuba were widely reported in the Boer war, see *Mid-Devon and Newton Times*, 5 May 1900, p.3, quoted in E. Spiers, *Letters from Ladysmith: Eyewitness Accounts from the South African War* (Barnsley: Frontline, 2010): 'We showed them no mercy, but served them all alike.'
49 Justice Gibbs toasting Lord Northbrook at the Byculla Club, 20 November 1872, 'not in the spirit of the Indian conquerors of old', to characterize Canning's tempering of justice with mercy, in G.B. Mullick, *Lord Northbrook and His Mission in India: A Lecture* (Calcutta: Day and Cousin, 1873), p.52. The printed copy of this lecture is prefaced by lines from Thomas Campbell on British misrule, *The Pleasures of Hope with Other Poems* (1799; London: Longman, Hurst, Rees, Orme, and Brown, 1820), invoking Vishnu but also ineffective mercy.
50 T.E.S. Scholes, *The British Empire and Alliances: Or, Britain's Duty to Her Colonies and Subject Races* (London: E. Stock, 1899), p.387.
51 Quoted in 'The Indian National Congress', *Westminster Review* 130 (July–December 1888), p.159.
52 E. Burrows, *Our Eastern Empire: Or, Stories from the History of British India* (London: Griffith and Farran, 1857), p.59.
53 D. Wilson, 'Thoughts on British Colonial Slavery', *The Amulet, or Christian and Literary Remembrancer* (London: Baynes, 1828), pp.291–300 [p.297].
54 Thus 'A Bishop on Modern Mercy', reprinted the sermon of Magee, Bishop of Peterborough, *Indian Mirror*, 20 August 1876, p.4.
55 Reverend Samuel Cox of New York, meeting at Exeter Hall, *Missionary Chronicle*, June 1833, p.279.
56 Charles Montalembert, quoted in J. Kingsmill, *British Rule and British Christianity in India* (London: Longman, Green, Longman and Roberts, 1859), pp.27–8.
57 See D. Short, *Reconciliation and Colonial Power: Indigenous Rights in Australia* (London: Routledge, 2016), p.16, dispensing with mercy from his formula on reconciliation as 'peace making paradigm' (p.178).

58 B. Parsons, *The Greatness of the British Empire Traced to Its Source* (2 vols; London: Cassell, 1851), vol.1, p.16.

59 H.W. Tucker, *The Spiritual Expansion of the Empire: A Sketch of Two Centuries of Work Done for the Church and Nation by the Society for the Propagation of the Gospel* (London: S.P.G., 1900), p.69, referring to funds for Indian famine victims. On benevolence and empire, H. Gilbert and C. Tiffin, eds, *Burden or Benefit? Imperial Benevolence and Its Legacies* (Bloomington and Indianapolis: Indiana University Press, 2008).

60 'J.C.' of Cambridge, 'Critical remarks on Romans, IX, 15–18', *The British Magazine and Monthly Register of Religious and Ecclesiastical Information* 28 (London), 26 August 1845, pp.253–4 [p.254].

61 L.J. Trotter, *The History of the British Empire in India: From the Appointment of Lord Hardinge to the Political Extinction of the East-India Company, 1844 to 1862* (London: W.H. Allen, 1866), p.215.

62 E.g. 'To England, on the Slave Trade', in *The Poetical Works of H. K. W. and J. Grahame. With Memoirs, Critical Dissertations, and Explanatory Notes by G. Gilfillan* (Edinburgh: Nichol, 1856), p.32: 'It is England – merciful and mild! … And English mercy said, Let millions bleed!'

63 Printed in *The Bow in the Cloud: Or, The Negro's Memorial* (London: Jackson and Walford, 1834), p.366. On the poet, see R. Vigne, *Thomas Pringle: South African Pioneer, Poet and Abolitionist* (Woodbridge: Boydell and Brewer, 2012).

64 M. Mukherjee, *India in the Shadows of Empire: A Legal and Political History (1774–1950)* (New Delhi: Oxford University Press, 2010), reflecting on the Royal Proclamation's aftermath and citing H.S. Cunningham, *Earl Canning* (Oxford: Clarendon Press, 1891), p.125, 'prompt to exercise the grand prerogative of mercy'.

65 The 'sloka' by Baboo Sourendro Mohun Tagore, *Hindoo Music from Various Authors. Part 1* (Calcutta: Stanhope Press, 1875); the Victoria-Gîtîka book of Indian music, in *Public Opinion and Official Communications: About the Bengal Music School and Its President* (Calcutta: Stanhope Press, 1876), p.16.

66 R. Temple, *India in 1880* (London: Murray, 1881), p.500.

67 *Manchester Courier*, 26 January 1901, p.17.

68 *Indian Review*, February 1901, p.72.

69 *Indian Review*, January 1903, p.42.

70 H.S. Cunningham, *Chronicles of Dustypore, a Tale of Modern Anglo-Indian Society*, vol. 1 (London: Smith, Elder, 1875), p.95.

71 [Cornwall Bayley], *Canada: A Descriptive Poem, Written at Quebec, 1805. With Satires, Imitations and Sonnets* ([Quebec]: Neilson, n.d., c.1806), 'Thy sons in mercy great, in justice brave, | Fight but to conquer—conquer but to save!'

72 'Politics. Ought The Annexation Policy Pursued In India To Be Adopted Towards China? Affirmative Article.—III'. *British Controversialist, and Literary Magazine* (London: Houlston and Wright, 1859), p.326.

73 *Evangelical Magazine*, June 1853, p.372.

74 *Africa: A Quarterly Journal*, July 1880, p.34. This was a reference to talk of annexing Zululand.

75 See discourse from the peace movement, in which absence of British and European mercy figure, W. Stokes, *British War History during the Present Century* (London: Simpkin, Marshall, 1869), e.g. p.218. For discussion of guilt in India, 'Art. IV – The Marquess Wellesley', *The Prospective Review; a Quarterly Journal of Theology and Literature* 3 (1847), pp.370–95 (p.389).

76 *The Indian News and Chronicle of Eastern Affairs*, 18 October 1851, p.474.
77 John Bristowe, reported in *The Jamaica Movement*, p.192.
78 E.A. De Cosson, 'The Future of the Soudan', *The Fortnightly* 42 (October 1884), pp.516–52 [p.527]; vicar of Malew's sermon, *Isle of Man Times*, 25 June 1887, p.4.
79 The anti-imperialist J.E. Ritchie, *Imperialism in South Africa* (2nd edn; London: J. Clarke, 1881), p.13, quoting verse from the *Kaffrarian Watchman*; H.S.R. St John, *History of the British Conquests in India* (2 vols; London: Colburn, 1852), vol.1, p.93.
80 *Proceedings of the First Anniversary Meeting of the Anti-Slavery Society, Held at the Freemasons' Hall* (London: Society for the Mitigation and Gradual Abolition of Slavery throughout the British Dominions, 1824), pp.70–9 [p.76].
81 V.B. Carroll, 'Recognition of Responsibility in Recent Poetry', *New York Observer* (5 July 1906) pp.13–14 [p.13]: 'The final word is a plea for mercy that rings with the pathos and the earnestness.'
82 W.B. Parker, *The Religion of Mr Kipling* (New York: Mansfield and Wessels, 1899), p.21, notes Kipling's sense of a God 'not … to be wheedled into pity and indulgence', yet justice was tempered with mercy in 'Mulholland's Contract'. See J. Kucich, *Imperial Masochism: British Fiction, Fantasy, and Social Class* (Princeton, NJ: Princeton University Press, 2007), p.8 for characterization of this as posture of 'submissive humility'.
83 See E. Karim, 'Rudyard Kipling's Uncollected Poem on Africa: "The Supplication of Kerr Cross, Missionary"' *Victorian Poetry* 17:4 (Winter 1979), pp.395–8.
84 C. Lyon, *Narrative and Recollections of Van Diemen's Land, during a Three Years' Captivity of Stephen S. Wright* (New York: New World Press, 1844), pp.40–1; on Hintza, Cory, *The Rise of South Africa*, vol.3, ch.7, pp.320–3; on Torrington, J. Forbes, *Recent Disturbances and Military Executions in Ceylon* (Edinburgh: Blackwood, 1850); on Stanley, D.J. Nicoll, 'Stanley's Exploits: or, Civilising Africa', in the Socialist League's *The Commonweal*, 3 May 1890, p.138; on the Bambaata campaign, when mercy came 'quicker than expected – in the shape of a Maxim', *London Daily News*, 16 August 1906, p.7, see L.A. Motler, 'Between Ourselves. Giving Them the Stuff', *Workers' Dreadnought* (17 May 1919), p.1327.
85 W. Walsh, *The Moral Damage of War* (Boston, MA: Ginn, 1906), p.191. For critique of merciless posture, see W.T. Stead on indulgent newspaper treatment of British Lancers' after Majuba defeat, quoted in P.M. Krebs, *Gender, Race, and the Writing of Empire: Public Discourse and the Boer War* (Cambridge: Cambridge University Press, 2004), p.95.
86 'Shady "Imperialism"', *Irish News*, 29 May 1899, p.5; see also *Anglo-Celt*, 11 May 1849, p.1 on a campaign in the Punjab; *Drogheda Argus and Leinster Journal*, 9 April 1904, p.4, 'The Old Game' about Younghusband in Tibet – 'They also speak of the mercy of the British in looking after the wounded. Disgusting!'
87 G.W. Steevens, *Things Seen; Impressions of Men, Cities, and Books* (Edinburgh: Blackwood, 1900), p.14, reprinted from 'The New Humanitarianism', *Blackwood's Edinburgh Magazine* 163 (January 1898).
88 'Darwin and His Influence', *Indian Review*, January 1901, p.48.
89 E.g. *The Scotsman*, 3 July 1901, p.8; 'London Letter', *Western Mail*, 19 November 1901, p.4; 'The Camps of Mercy', *Lichfield Mercury*, 22 November 1901, p.5.
90 In the Upper Scind, see *Indian News*, 18 March 1852, p.121.
91 'Our Colonial Empire, and Our Colonial Policy', *North British Review* 19 (1853), p.367.

92 I owe this reference (quoting S. Zizek, 'Love without Mercy', *Pli* 11 (2001)) to a note in 'The Abject Object. Sovereignty, Sacrifice and the Sacred in Contemporary Australian Politics', ch.8 in J. Clemens and D. Pettman, *Avoiding the Subject. Media, Culture and the Object* (Amsterdam: Amsterdam University Press, 2004), p.203, which denies sympathy, philanthropy can cleanse colonialism, these are the 'sacrificial kernel of the very inequalities they claim to aim at mitigating'.

93 J.A. Hobson, *Imperialism: A Study* (London: Nelson, 1902), p.208.

94 F. Lugard, *Colonial Reports – Annual. No.409. Northern Nigeria Report for 1902* (London: HMSO, 1903), p.26: 'to regenerate this capable race and mould them to ideas of justice and mercy, so that in a future generation, if not in this, they may become worthy instruments of rule'.

95 Colonial Secretary Lord Lloyd, cited in D. David, *Rule Britannia: Women, Empire, and Victorian Writings* (Ithaca, NY: Cornell University Press, 1995), p.35. See *Bulletin of the Imperial Institute* 35 (1937), p.173: 'amongst our members, certain standards of common honesty which all accept, a certain tempering of justice with mercy, a certain tempering of idealism with common-sense'.

96 E. Stokes, *The Political Ideas of English Imperialism: An Inaugural Lecture Given in the University College of Rhodesia and Nyasaland* (London: Oxford University Press, 1960), p.26.

97 E.g. Peggs, *India's Cries to British Humanity*, p.76. Cowper's response to mercy, in restoring his faith, appear in *Memoir of the Early Life of William Cowper, Esq* (London: Edwards, 1816), p.75, 'Still there is mercy'; and in the poem, 'The heart healed and changed by mercy' from *Olney Hymns, in Three Books* (London: Oliver, 1779), Book III, p.385 (and other hymns on mercy).

98 *Christian Observer*, August 1834, p.510.

99 *Acts of the General Assembly of the Church of Scotland, 1638–1842* (Edinburgh: Edinburgh Printing and Publishing Co., 1842), p.909; J. Rippon, *A Sermon Occasioned by the Demise of King George the Third and by the Accession of King George the Fourth* (London: Longman, 1820), p.29. See also, J. Brown, *Memoirs of George the Third, Late King of Great Britain* (Liverpool: Caxton Press, c.1820), p.622, 'The excellent morals of George III renders it almost superfluous to say that in him the Slave trade had neither friend nor patron'.

100 *The Art-Union*, 1 August 1845, p.258.

101 On this point, see Eustace, *Passion Is the Gale*, p.254, on the 'certain degree of autonomy', lacking in the enslaved.

102 See J. Wesley, *Thoughts upon Slavery* (2nd edn; London: Hawes, 1774), p.18.

103 'Philanthropos', 'Slavery Both Unjust and Unmerciful', *The Imperial Magazine*, May 1827, pp.432–8 [p.436, p.435].

104 E. Lewis, *Brief Examination of Scripture Testimony on the Institution of Slavery* (1841); for similar pro-slavery defence, J. Fletcher, *Studies on Slavery, In Easy Lessons* (Natchez: Warner, 1852), and for Godwin, 'Lecture III' in B. Godwin, *The Substance of a Course of Lectures on British Colonial Slavery: Delivered at Bradford, York and Scarborough* (London: Hatchard, 1830). See also 'Sebastian or the Tables Turned', *The Negro's Friend, or, the Sheffield Anti-Slavery Album* (Sheffield: Blackwell, 1826), p.167. But see also the reflections by Harriet Martineau, *Society in America* (3 vols; 2nd edn; London: Saunders and Otley, 1837), vol.2, p.314: 'The good affections of slave-holders like these show themselves in the form of mercy which is as beautiful to witness as mercy made a substitute for justice can ever be.'

105 *Gentleman's Magazine* 61:1, supplement, 31 December 1791, p.1242.

106 See T. Gisborne, *Poems, Sacred and Moral* (London: Cadell, 1798) 'Elegy to the Memory of the Reverend William Mason', p.114: 'While Justice, hand in hand with mercy, led | To Christian Senates cried, and cried in vain.' This was quoted in slave trade context, for example, in *Monthly Review*, August 1797, p.457. See J. Montgomery, *Songs on the Abolition of Negro Slavery*, 'III. Slavery that was', in *A Poet's Portfolio; or, Minor Poems* (London: Longman, Rees, Orme, Brown, Green, and Longman, 1835).

107 *The Commemorative Wreath: In Celebration of the Extinction of Negro Slavery in the British Dominion* (London: E. Fry, 1835), pp.36–7.

108 H. More, 'The Slave Trade', in *The Works of Hannah More, in Eight Volumes: Including Several Pieces Never before Published* (London: Cadell and Davies, 1801), vol.1, pp.113–15. On negotiation between her conception of Liberty and radicals, in this poem, see F.K. Brown, *Fathers of the Victorians: The Age of Wilberforce* (Cambridge: Cambridge University Press, 1961), p.109.

109 H.M. Williams, *A Poem on the Bill Lately Passed for Regulating the Slave Trade* (London: T. Cadell, 1788).

110 R. Mant, *The Slave and Other Poetical Pieces* (Oxford: for the author, 1807), p.29. For Wesleyan ideas about mercy, see T. Taylor, *Britannia's Mercies, and her Duty, considered in Two Discourses, Delivered in the Methodist Chapel, at Halifax, on Thursday, November 29, 1798, Being a General Thanksgiving Day* (Leeds: Binns and Brown, 1799).

111 See J.A. Farrer, *The Monarchy in Politics* (New York: Dodd Mead, 1917), p.87, for Samuel Romilly's outrage at a preacher praising the king for abolition.

112 See 'Dr Johnson's on Grainger's Poem "The Sugar Cane"', *New Monthly Magazine* 11:62 (1 March 1819), p.107, reviewing *The Sugar Cane: A Poem*. See J. Gilmore, ed., *The Poetics of Empire: A Study of James Grainger's The Sugar Cane* (London: Athlone Press, 2000).

113 O. Cugoano, *Thoughts and Sentiments on the Evil and Wicked Traffic of the Slavery and Commerce of the Human Species* (London: n.p., 1787), pp.105–9.

114 E.g. Robert Thorpe, *A View of the Present Increase of the Slave Trade: The Cause of that Increase and Suggesting a Mode for Effecting Its Total Annihilation* (London: Longman, Hurst, Rees, Orme, and Brown, 1818), excerpted in *The Colonial Journal*, March 1818, p.175: quotes a Foulah king 'who knew something of our Abolition Act', asking that George III be told the injustice of this measure from his perspective as monarch.

115 J.A. Rawley and S.D. Behrendt, *The Transatlantic Slave Trade* (1981; revised edn; Lincoln: University of Nebraska Press, 2005), p.272.

116 L. Skousen, 'The Benefits of Mercy: Teaching Law and Exception in the Inquiry-Based Classroom', *Law, Crime and History* 4:1 (2014), pp.82–103 [p.98].

117 'Escheated Slaves, and other Slaves, the Property of the Crown', *Anti-Slavery Reporter* (1 March 1831), p.155.

118 *Anti-Slavery Monthly Reporter*, March 1830, pp.145–6.

119 The letter, 25 August 1783, printed in *American Museum*, February 1787, pp.122–3; see R. Vaux, *Anthony Benezet: From the Original Memoir* (London: A.W. Bennett, 1859), pp.49–50. In 1793 Benezet published *A Letter on the Slave-Trade, Written by Anthony Benezet, to Charlotte, Queen of Great-Britain*.

120 A letter signed 'H', *Public Advertiser*, 20 February 1788, p.1.

121 A letter from the Reverend Charles Farish, fellow of Queen's College, to the king, 1798, TNA, HO42/42/109 (from online catalogue description).

122 *London Review and Literary Journal*, July 1803, p.36.
123 Quoted in T. Burgess, *Considerations on the Abolition of Slavery and the Slave Trade, Upon Grounds of Natural, Religious, and Political Duty* (Oxford: Prince, Cooke, Fletcher, 1789), p.124. On Sharp, P. Hoare, *Memoirs of Granville Sharp* (London: Colburn, 1820), p.31, 'a private and powerless individual standing forth at the divine excitement of Mercy'.
124 In a review of Clarkson's *History*, in *The Critical Review: Or, Annals of Literature* 15:2 (October 1808), p.136.
125 J. Stephen, *England Enslaved by Her Own Slave Colonies. An Address to the Electors and People of the United Kingdom* (2nd edn; London: Hatchard, 1826), p.65.
126 *The Debate on the Motion for the Abolition of the Slave Trade* (n.p., 1792), p.54.
127 J.R. Oldfield, *Transatlantic Abolitionism in the Age of Revolution: An International History of Anti-slavery, c.1787–1820* (Cambridge: Cambridge University Press, 2013), p.192.
128 The watercolour is in the British Museum collection: the figures flanking Britannia are Justice and Religion. See H. Honour, *The Image of the Black in Western Art. From the American Revolution to World War I* (Cambridge, MA: Harvard University Press, 1989), p.321. Stephen Gaisford dedicated *An Essay on the Good Effects Which May Be Derived in the British West Indies in Consequence of the Abolition of the African Slave Trade Including an Inquiry into the Present Insular Policy of Those Colonies* (London: Baldwin, Cradock, 1811) to Gloucester. Buxton in 1831, according to *Antislavery Reporter*, 9 May 1831, p.251, had a letter from Gloucester 'prince of the blood royal of England … lamenting that indisposition and that only should deprive him of the happiness and the honour of assisting on this occasion'. See H. Roscoe, *The Life of William Roscoe* (2 vols; London: Cadell, 1833), vol.1, p.406, p.469, on Gloucester's relationship with this abolitionist.
129 W.C. Oulton, *Authentic and Impartial Memoirs of Her Late Majesty Charlotte, Queen of Great Britain and Ireland* (London: Robins, 1819), p.375.
130 *Flower's Political Review and Monthly Register* 8, January 1810, p.66.
131 *Annual Review and History of Literature; for 1808* (London: Longman, Hurst, Rees, and Orme, 1809), vol.7, p.145. C. Bolton, *Writing the Empire: Robert Southey and Romantic Colonialism* (London: Pickering & Chatto, 2007), p.60, on Southey as the author.
132 *Christian Observer*, May 1843, p.313.
133 *Anti-Slavery Monthly Reporter*, June 1830, p.265, p.268. See *Life of William Allen: With Selections from His Correspondence* (3 vols; London: Gilpin, 1846), vol.1, p.86, on the 'fine young man' agreeing to be president.
134 [H. Brougham], Review Art. VII 'Observations on the Criminal Law of England', *Edinburgh Review*, February 1812, pp.389–415 [p.413].
135 *Colonial Journal* 20 (March 1818), p.180.
136 For the address of the House of Lords, 5 May 1814, see *Parliamentary Debates from The Year 1803 to the Present Time. Vol. 27*, cols.661–2. The prince regent's reply was ordered printed on 9 May.
137 *Journals of the House of Commons from November the 4th, 1813 … to November the 1st, 1814 … Sess. 1813–14*, 69, 27 June 1814, p.389.
138 *Evangelical Magazine*, September 1824, p.410; and reprinted, e.g. T. Willcocks and T. Horton, eds, *Moral and Sacred Poetry* (Devonport: Byers, 1829), pp.232–3. Demerara newspapers reportedly censured ministers and the king for the royal

mercy, T. Rain, *The Life and Labours of John Wray, Pioneer Missionary in British Guiana* (London: Snow, 1892), p.232, quoting *British and Colonial Register*.
139 *Anti-Slavery Monthly Reporter*, 5 October 1830, p.406. Justice and mercy were of course invoked in the address, described as the 'peculiar attributes of your crown' (p.407).
140 *Imperial Magazine*, November 1830, p.1036.
141 *Anti-Slavery Monthly Reporter*, 1 August 1833, p.344.
142 G.N. Wright, *The Life and Reign of William the Fourth* (2 vols; London: Fisher, 1837), vol.2, p.765.
143 Clarkson, *History*, quoted in W. Goodell, *Slavery and Anti-Slavery: A History of The Great Struggle in Both Hemispheres* (New York: Harned, 1852), p.59, which also notes the king's royal assent. The duke, as noted in *Parliamentary Register; or, History of the Proceedings and Debates of the House of Lords ... during the Session of the Seventeenth Parliament of Great Britain vol.36* (London: J. Debrett, 1793), p.162, apologized for comments on Wilberforce.
144 R. Huish, *History of the Life and Reign of William the Fourth, the Reform Monarch of England* (London: Emans, 1837), p.459.
145 *The Parliamentary History of England, from the Earliest period to the Year 1803. Vol. 29. Comprising the Period from the Twenty-Second of March 1791, to the Thirteenth of December 1792* (London: Hansard, 1817), cols.1349–50.
146 *Substance of the Speech of His Royal Highness the Duke of Clarence in the House of Lords, on the Motion for the Recommitment of the Slave Trade Limitation Bill on the Fifth Day of July, 1799* (London: Rivington, 1799): 'I am confident that as hereditary councillors of the crown you will give life and spirit instead of dejection and death to a most numerous and most loyal description of His Majesty's subjects' (p.67). See *Monthly Review*, October 1799, p.230. The Bishop of Llandaff corresponded with the duke about the slave trade, see *Anecdotes of Richard Watson, Bishop of Llandaff* (London: Cadell and Davies, 1817), p.446.
147 R. Bisset, *The History of the Reign of George III to the Termination of the Late War* (4 vols; New York: Inskeep and Bradford, 1811), vol. 3, p.478.
148 J.R. Oldfield, *Popular Politics and British Anti-Slavery: The Mobilisation of Public Opinion against the Slave Trade, 1787–1807* (London: Cass, 1998), p.173.
149 Huish, *History of the Life and Reign of William the Fourth*, p.565 (where Huish focuses on his eloquence rather than examines closely the fact he spoke against abolition).
150 *Hampshire Chronicle*, 9 July 1804, p.2. He 'argued against the Abolition ... on the ground of the injury which must result from the measure to the commerce and naval power of this country ... As for the Slaves in the West Indies he affirmed that they were the happiest set of people in the world', *Substance of the Debates on the Bill for Abolishing the Slave Trade: Which Was Brought into the House of Lords, on the 2d. January, 1807, and into the House of Commons, on the 10th February, 1807, and Which Was Finally Passed into a Law on the 25th March, 1807* (London: Philips, Tard, 1808), p.29. See also, 'postscript', *Christian Observer*, February 1807, p.143 on 'a course worthy of descendant of the House of Brunswick'.
151 *A Letter to His Majesty. The Bandogs; or, Remarks on the Managers against W. Hastings and Lord Melville* (London: Horseman, 1808), p.42
152 *Sheffield Independent*, 2 February 1833, p.4.
153 Thus an inscription bore the legend: 'Jubilee in Commemoration of the Abolition of Slavery in the British colonies in the reign of William IV. Aug. 1, 1834'. His

constitutional role in relation to the approval of legislation is reflected in TNA, CO101/78/10; the report to the King on slavery abolition is CO137/192/91 (online catalogue descriptions consulted).

154 E. Copley, *A History of Slavery and Its Abolition* (1836; London: Houlston, 1839), p.475.

155 P. Brumett, *Mapping the Ottomans. Sovereignty, Territory, and Identity in the Early Modern Mediterranean* (Cambridge: Cambridge University Press, 2015), p.49 on synonyms provided for Turks in the dictionary *English Parnassus* (1654) including 'cruel, unpitying, merciless, unrelenting, inexorable'.

156 For representation of the Turk in early-modern theatre referencing mercy, J. Burton, *Traffic and Turning: Islam and English Drama, 1579–1624* (Newark: University of Delaware Press, 2005), pp.187–8, on Fulke Greville's *Mustapha* (1609), where Camena confronts Soliman her father, and says 'Mercy must hand in hand with Power go'.

157 *Cumberland's British Theatre: With Remarks, Biographical & Critical* (London: Cumberland, 1828), vol.20, p.4.

158 J. Russell, *The Establishment of the Turks in Europe: An Historical Discourse* (London: Murray, 1828), pp.82–3.

159 See note on Saladin's comparative mercy, from biographer Bahadin, glossed by Charles Foster, *Mahometanism Unveiled: An Inquiry in which That Arch-Heresy, Its Diffusion and Continuance, Are Examined on a New Principle, Tending to Confirm the Evidences, and Aid the Propagation, of the Christian Faith* (2 vols; London: Duncan, 1829), vol.2, p.208.

160 See M. Sharafuddin, *Islam and Romantic Orientalism: Literary Encounters with the Orient* (London: I.B Tauris, 1994), pp.205–7 (Moore); and Elizabeth Inchbald's *A Mogul Tale: Or, the Descent of the Balloon*, where the Mughal emperor provides a lesson in mercy against Christian cruelty, see A. Malhotra, *Making British Indian Fictions: 1772–1823* (New York: Palgrave Macmillan, 2012).

161 See J. Salt, *Imperialism, Evangelism and the Ottoman Armenians, 1878–1896* (London: Cass, 1993), p.45, on the 'Merciless' Turk' in Bulgarian atrocities context in 1876; in the Great War see coverage of British prisoners of war, e.g. 'At the Mercy of the Cruel Turk', *Nottingham Evening Post*, 20 November 1918, p.1 after siege of Kut-al-amara; H.H. Johnston, *The Clean Fighting Turk Yesterday, To-Day and To-Morrow* (London: Spottiswoode, Ballantyne, 1918), pp.49–50; post-war, T.P. O'Connor, 'At the Mercy of the Turk', *Daily Telegraph*, 7 September 1922; 'At Turkish Mercy', *Daily Telegraph*, 27 November 1922. Reports of Turkish mercy to children after the conquest of Zettin is framed as rebuttal of reputation for ferocity in *Belfast Newsletter*, 17 September 1790, p.2.

Chapter 7

1 Biography of Major-General Charles Napier by William Napier, reviewed in *The Asiatic Journal and Monthly Miscellany* (November 1844–April 1845), p.255.

2 J.-F Caron, 'An Ethical and Judicial Framework for Mercy Killing on the Battlefield', *Journal of Military Ethics* 13:3 (2014), pp.228–39; S. Deakin, 'Naked Soldiers and the Principle of Discrimination', *Journal of Military Ethics* 13:3 (2014), pp.320–30. See also P. Robinson, *Military Honour and the Conduct of War: From Ancient Greece to*

Iraq (London: Routledge, 2006); T. Meron, *Bloody Constraint: War and Chivalry in Shakespeare: War and Chivalry in Shakespeare* (New York: Oxford University Press, 1998).

3 M. Schellhammer, *George Washington and the Final British Campaign for the Hudson River, 1779* (Jefferson: McFarland, 2012), p.163. For British inhumanity, J. Thacher, *Military Journal of the American Revolution, from the Commencement to the Disbanding of the American Army* (Hartford, CT: Hurlbut, Williams, 1862), p.150, p.177 regarding Colonel Baylor's regiment being massacred.

4 See Digby, *Mores Catholici*, p.357, arguing against the idea that it was a gross abuse to call a warrior merciful according to an unnamed modern writer, and assertion, p.361, that wherever the Catholic code had 'ceased to influence men in military authority ... failed in mercy'.

5 J. Pearn, 'The Quiddity of Mercy', p.604. See G. Best, *Humanity in Warfare: The Modern History of the International Law of Armed Conflicts* (New York: Routledge 1983).

6 See H.G. Adams, *The Peace Reading-Book: Being a Series of Selections from Sacred Scriptures, the Early Christian Fathers, and Historians, Philosophers and Poets, the Wise and Thoughtful of All Ages; Condemnatory of the Principles and Practices of War, and Inculcating Those of True Christianity* (London: Gilpin, 1844), pp.87–90, quotations on mercy and clemency.

7 See A. Starkey, *War in the Age of Enlightenment, 1700–1789* (Westport, CT: Praeger, 2003) for overview of warfare during the American Revolution; W.E. Lee, *Barbarians and Brothers: Anglo-American Warfare, 1500–1865* (Oxford: Oxford University Press, 2011).

8 H. Hoock, *Empire of the Imagination: Politics, War and the Arts in the British World* (London: Profile, 2010), pp.179–80; citing J.G.W. Conlin, 'Benjamin West's *General Johnson* and Representations of British Imperial Identity; 1759–1770, "An Empire of Mercy?"', *British Journal of Eighteenth Century Studies 27* (2004), pp.37–59. See also D.H. Solkin, 'Portraiture in Motion: Edward Penny's "Marquis of Granby" and the Creation of a Public for English Art', *Huntington Library Quarterly* 49:1 (Winter 1986), pp.1–23, on Penny's *Marquis of Granby relieving a Sick Soldier* (1764). Hoock, p.179 notes clemency or compassion in eighteenth-century representations of martial heroes in Westminster Abbey, citing the monument to John André. See also A. McNairn, *Behold the Hero: General Wolfe and the Arts in the Eighteenth Century* (Liverpool: Liverpool University Press, 1997), p.73, p.112, on Wolfe's presentation as merciful conqueror.

9 A.L., 'Universality of the Love of Fame', *Universal Magazine*, January 1795, pp.43–45 [p.45].

10 See S. Schwamenfeld, '"The Foundation of British Strength": National Identity and the British Common Soldier', Florida State University PhD, 2007, pp.135–7.

11 J. Leland, *A Sermon Preached at Eustace-Street, November the 9th, 1760, On Occasion of the Death of His Late Majesty King George II* (Dublin: Bradley, 1760), p.19.

12 See M. Ogborn, *Spaces of Humanity: London's Geographies 1680–1780* (London: Guildford Press, 1998), pp.144–5; and the image by Smirke published in 1811. A description appeared in the papers, see *Leeds Intelligencer*, 16 June 1761, p.2.

13 W.M. Craig, *Memoir of Her Majesty Sophia Charlotte, of Mecklenburg Strelitz, Queen of Great Britain* (Liverpool: Caxton: 1818), pp.117–18, suggested America would not have been lost if the governors and commanders had acted with the king's firmness and moderation, 'who ever wished to temper his justice with mercy and forbearance'.

14   See A.M. Schlesinger, *Prelude to Independence. The Newspaper War on Britain 1764–1776* (New York: Knopf, 1958), p.232, p.250.
15   Eustace, *Passion Is the Gale*, pp.424–5.
16   For overview of the legal position and stance taken by Washington in the conduct of war, see J.F. Witt, *Lincoln's Code: The Laws of War in American History* (New York: Free Press, 2012), ch.1.
17   *Kentish Gazette*, 2 April 1771, p.2. See W. Allen, *The American Crisis. A Letter Addressed by Permission to the Earl Gower* (London: Cadell, 1774), p.55, on the rebels and 'mercy's hope'.
18   *The Parliamentary History of England, from the Earliest Period to the Year 1803: From which Last-mentioned Epoch It Is Continued Downwards in the Work Entitled 'Hansard's Parliamentary Debates'. Vol.18. A.D.1774–1777* (London: Hansard, 1813), col. 595.
19   *London Evening Post*, 29 May 1775 [p.1]; *The Scots Magazine* 37 (1775), p.230.
20   *Scots Magazine*, 1 June 1775, p.328; *Annual Register*, 1776 (3rd edn; London: Dodsley, 1776), p.55. *Leeds Intelligencer* reported in 27 February 1770, p.1, at the time of a conference on America, of a 'great personage': 'Let the dignity of government be supported with firmness but moderation; and for past offences, let justice give place to mercy.'
21   *Public Advertiser*, 18 July 1775, p.2. For criticism of Gage, see *Morning Chronicle and London Advertiser*, 25 August 1775, p.1.
22   *Leeds Intelligencer*, 26 September 1775, p.1; *The London Magazine; or, Gentleman's Monthly* 44 (1775), p.590; J. Sparks, *The Writings of George Washington: Part Second: Comprising Correspondence*, vol.3, part 2 (Boston, MA: Russell, Odiorne and Metcalf, 1834), p.500. Washington's reply, 20 August 1775, p.65.
23   C. Berger, *Broadsides and Bayonets: The Propaganda War of the American Revolution* (Philadelphia: University of Pennsylvania Press, 1961).
24   *Anecdotes of the Life of the Right Hon. William Pitt Earl of Chatham, and of the Principal Events of His Time* (2 vols; London: Jordan, 1792), vol.2, p.130.
25   *Public Advertiser*, 28 March 1776, p.2.
26   W. Gordon, *The History of the Rise, Progress, and Establishment, of the Independence of the United States of America* (London: for the author, 1788), p.245.
27   'Address to the Genius of Britain', reprinted in *The Works of the British Poets: With Prefaces, Biographical and Critical*, vol.11 (Edinburgh: Mundell, 1795), pp.615–16 (p.616). See *Gentleman's Monthly Intelligencer*, November 1775, p.593, for an appreciative review of the address.
28   *Gentleman's Magazine*, Poetical Essays for September 1776, p.427.
29   J. Fletcher, 'American Patriotism', reprinted in *On Evangelical Mysticism and Other Sermons and Essays* (4 vols; New York: Mason and Lane, 1836), vol.4, p.549.
30   W. Belsham, *Memoirs of the Reign of George III* (6th edn; 8 vols; London: Sherwood, Neely and Jones), vol.2, p.300.
31   F. Moore, *Diary of the American Revolution. From Newspapers and Original Documents* (2 vols; New York: Scribner, 1860), vol.1, p.379.
32   *Oxford Journal*, 7 June 1777, p.1.
33   Burgoyne: 29 June 1777; see his address to Indians in Congress, at the camp, River Bouquet: 'The clemency of your father has been abused, the offers of his mercy have been despised'; Moore, *Diary of the American Revolution*, vol.1, p.457.
34   *Gazetteer and New Daily Advertiser*, 7 December 1778, p.1.

35 'Copy of a manifesto of General Washington, Commander in Chief of the Forces of the United States of America, in Answer to General Burgoyne's Proclamation', *Westminster Magazine*, September 1777, p.488; *Caledonian Mercury*, 3 September 1777, p.2.
36 Brigadier Varnum to Colonel Lossberg, in *New York Gazette*, 21 July 1777, reprinted in *The Scots Magazine*, September 1777, p.479. On calls to treat them harshly and controversy when one correspondent in *Pennsylvania Journal* called for the enemy to be 'reduce[d] by clemency, and reform[ed] by mercy', K. Miller, *Dangerous Guests: Enemy Captives and Revolutionary Communities during the War for Independence* (Ithaca, NY: Cornell University Press, 2014), p.111.
37 *Scots Magazine*, 1 August 1778, p.422.
38 J. Thacher, *A Military Journal during the American Revolutionary War: From 1775 to 1783* (Boston, MA: Cottons and Barnard, 1827), p.149; D. Ramsay, *The History of the American Revolution* (2 vols; Trenton, NJ: Wilson, 1811), vol. 2, p.142.
39 *A Narrative of the Life & Travels of John Robert Shaw, the Well-digger, Now Resident in Lexington, Kentucky* (Lexington: Bradford, 1807), pp.20–1.
40 Moore, *Diary of the American Revolution*, vol.2, p.193, derived from *New York Packet and the American Advertiser*, 29 July 1779.
41 *Rivington's Royal Gazette*, 12 July published a letter from Stoney Point, 7 July, see H.B. Dawson, *The Assault on Stony Point: By General Anthony Wayne, July 16, 1779: Prepared for the New York Historical Society, and Read at Its Regular Meeting, April 1, 1862, with Some Illustrative Notes* (New York, 1863), p.99.
42 G.W.P. Custis, *Recollections and Private Memoirs of Washington* (New York: Derby and Jackson, 1860), p.252. See also 'Sir Banastre Tarleton', *Blackwood's Edinburgh Magazine* 116 (October 1874), pp.432–49.
43 *Pasquin or Minute Intelligencer* (near Egg Harbor), 1778, reprinted in Moore, *Diary of the American Revolution*, vol.2, p.34.
44 *Pennsylvania Packet*, 16 March 1780, p.2.
45 *New Jersey Journal*, 7 March 1781, reprinted in Moore, *Diary of the American Revolution*, vol.2, p.389.
46 *Pennsylvania Evening Post*, 1 August 1776, reprinted in Moore, *Diary of the American Revolution*, vol.1, p.276.
47 A.T. Angelis, 'Painting History: John Trumbull and the Battle of Bunker's Hill', *Prospects* 30 (October 2005), pp.73–85; J. Trumbull, *Autobiography, Reminiscences and Letters of John Trumbull, from 1756 to 1841* (New York: Wiley and Putnam, 1841), p.420. Mercy as a possibility from despots is rejected in 'Warren's Address to the American Soldiers, before the Battle of Bunker's Hill', in J. Pierpont, ed. *The National Reader: A Selection of Exercises in Reading and Speaking* (28th edn; New York: Cooledge, 1835), p.250.
48 Paine in *The Crisis*, I, reprinted in M.D. Conway, ed., *Thomas Paine, The Writings of Thomas Paine, Vol. I (1774–1779)* (4 vols; London: Putnam), vol.1, p.177; also *The Crisis*. II. 'To Lord Howe', on mercy as 'specious show of humanity' (p.183); and *The Crisis*. 'VI.: To the Earl of Carlisle, General Clinton, and William Eden, Esq., British Commissioners at New York', in which the offer is really 'an act of mercy' (p.262). On Paine and mercy, see in this volume, rejection of a royal criminal's mercy, by the ghost of General Montgomery, in 'A Dialogue', p.161. In 1776 overtures to peace saw the Howes empowered to pardon, R. Bisset, *The History of the Reign of George III to the Termination of the Late War* (6 vols; London: Longman, Rees, 1803), vol.2, p.353.

49 31 May 1782, reprinted in *The Works of Thomas Paine* (2 vols; Philadelphia, PA: Carey, 1797), vol.1, pp.205–8 [p.206]. Edmund Burke in *Thoughts on the Prospect of a Regicide Peace* (London: Owen, 1796), p.7, contrasted with the French regime, 'the afflicted family of Asgill did not in vain solicit the mercy of the highest in rank, and the most compassionate of the compassionate sex'.

50 C. Gilman, ed., *Letters of Eliza Wilkinson: During the Invasion and Possession of Charleston, S.C., by the British in the Revolutionary War* (New York: S. Colman, 1839), pp.9–10.

51 *Letters of Eliza Wilkinson*, p.65.

52 *Public Ledger*, 12 December 1777, p.1; see also letter from 'Benevolent', *General Evening Post*, 2–4 September 1777, p.4.

53 'Profits of the American War', *Dublin Evening Post*, 10 September 1778, p.3.

54 *The Parliamentary History of England from the Earliest Period to the Year 1803. Vol.19. From the Twenty-Ninth of January 1774, to the Fourth of December 1778* (London: Hansard, 1814), cols.424–5.

55 *A View of the History of Great Britain: During the Administration of Lord North, to the Second Session of the Fifteenth Parliament. In Two Parts. With Statements of the Public Expenditure in That Period* (London: G. Wilkie, 1782), p.283.

56 Ramsay, *History of the American Revolution*, vol. 2, p.41, p.308. In support of the policy, see 'Civis', *Morning Post and Daily Advertiser*, 21 August 1778, p.1.

57 'Indian Warfare', in H. Howe, *Historical Collections of the Great West: Containing Narratives of the Most Important and Interesting Events in Western History* (2 vols; Greenville, TN: Roberts, 1855), vol.1, pp.239–41.

58 Reprinted in R.W. Gibbes, *Documentary History of the American Revolution* (3 vols; Columbia, S.C., Banner Steam-Power Press, 1855), vol. 2, p.177.

59 *Morning Chronicle and London Advertiser*, 17 February 1783, p.3. This was after the Congress resolution 23 April, recommending State legislatures on pardons: 'There is in reality something so divine and christian in the forgiveness of injuries, that it may appear rather invidious to offer any thing in obstruction of the intended clemency.'

60 B.J. Lossing, *The Two Spies, Nathan Hale and John André* (New York: Appleton, 1886), pp.106–8. On Colonel Haynes's execution by the British, *Public Advertiser*, 7 February 1782, p.7.

61 A.H. Kritzer, 'Revolution and After. Heroism and Violence in Early National Plays about the American Revolution', in A.C. Muñoz, R.E. Romero and B.M. Martinez, eds, *Violence in American Drama: Essays on Its Staging, Meanings and Effects* (Jefferson, NC: McFarland, 2011), pp.15–27 [p.24]; W. Dunlap, *André: A Tragedy* (London: Ogilvy, 1799).

62 J.D. Burk, *Bunker-Hill; or, the Death of General Warren: An Historic Tragedy in Five Acts* (New York: Greenleaf, 1797), pp.35–6.

63 M.O. Warren, *History of the Rise, Progress and Termination of the American Revolution* (3 vols; Boston, MA: Larkin, 1805), vol.2, p.158. Warren is actually quoting an unattributed commentator.

64 W. Bailey, *Records of Patriotism and Love of Country* (Washington, DC: n.p., 1822), p.181.

65 Reprinted in *Writings of Levi Woodbury, LL.D. Political, Judicial and Literary* (3 vols; Boston, MA: Little, Brown, 1852), vol.1, p.559.

66 G.J. Hunt, *The Late War, between the United States and Great Britain From June, 1812, to February, 1815* (New York: G.J. Hunt, 1819), p.71.

67 B. Whitehouse, *A Journal of a Young Man of Massachusetts, Late a Surgeon on Board an American Privateer, Who Was Captured at Sea by the British* (Boston, MA: Rowe and Harper, 1816), p.68.
68 W.C. Ford, *Writings of John Quincy Adams. Vol.5 1814–1816* (New York: Macmillan, 1915), p.155, in context of British destruction of Washington and American mercy, 7 October 1814.
69 R. Hughes, *George Washington. The Rebel and the Patriot. 1762–1777* (New York: Morrow, 1927), p.374.
70 'Constitution of Society – Government', *Chambers's Information for the People*, vol.2 (Edinburgh: Chambers, 1849), p.46.
71 See J.F. Kendrick, 'Onward, Christian Soldiers!' in M.W. Van Wienen, ed., *Rendezvous with Death: American Poems of the Great War* (Urbana: University of Illinois Press, 2002), p.118 for a bitter use of the poem's title and the line, 'Mercy is a weakness | All the gods abhor'. On being a Christian and soldier, of tempering bravery with mercy etc., J.A. Sparvel-Bayly, 'Our Citizen Army', *Inverness Courier*, 22 January 1892, p.3.
72 See the verse, extolling mercy, in a Volunteer bazaar, *Cheshire Observer*, 14 April 1877, p.8.
73 M. Cowling, *Victorian Figurative Painting. Domestic Life and the Contemporary Social Scene* (London: Papadakis, 2000), p.43.
74 *Exeter and Plymouth Gazette*, 21 January 1843, p.3.
75 *Illustrated London News*, 22 July 1843, p.55.
76 *Allen's Indian Mail*, 23 May 1846, p.348.
77 *The Battles of the World, or, Cyclopaedia of Battles, Sieges, and Important Military Events* (Montreal: Muir, 1866), p.127.
78 *Gentleman's Magazine*, October 1858, p.395.
79 M. Goodman, *Experiences of an English Sister of Mercy* (London: Smith, Elder, 1862), p.173; p.180.
80 For British coverage, *Daily News*, 22 April 1865; for a call to Britain to do more, 'Help for the Sick and Wounded. No. II', *London Evening Standard*, 27 January 1868, p.5, during Franco-Prussian War; *Red Cross Operations in the North of France, 1870–1872* (London: Spottiswoode, 1872), p.174; 'The Red Cross Knights', *Western Daily Press*, 1 September 1870, p.2; 'The Red Cross Society', *London Evening Standard*, 14 February 1877, p.5. See H. Brackenbury, 'Philanthropy in War', *Blackwood's Magazine* (February 1877), pp.152–74. R. Gill, *Calculating Compassion: Humanity and Relief in War, Britain 1870–1914* (Manchester: Manchester University Press, 2013), pp.5–6 discusses crankish associations of the word 'humanitarian' and speaks of 'theological commitment'.
81 M. Halstead, *Briton and Boer in South Africa; the Story of England's War with the Brave Boers and the Eventful History of South Africa* (Philadelphia, PA: Skull, 1900), p.164.
82 *Gloucester Journal*, 20 July 1901, p.4.
83 *Sussex Express*, 22 November 1901, p.4 (and other British newspapers).
84 *Belfast News-Letter*, 20 December 1901, p.7.
85 *Review of Reviews*, 1 November 1899, p.437.
86 W.T. Stead, 'Lord Kitchener and the End of the War', *The Independent* 54 (New York City, 1902), p.1516.
87 *The Scotsman*, 23 October 1901, p.10.
88 *Black and White Budget*, 19 October 1901, p.124.

89 Marie Mallet, in V. Mallet, ed., *Life with Queen Victoria: Marie Mallet's Letters from Court 1887–1901* (London: Murray, 1968). A review of Sir George Arthur's biography summarizes the impression conveyed, 'Morally he was merciful and he was clean. He was a Christian', 'Literary Supplement', *Cambridge Review*, 1921, p.103.
90 'Rhodesia', *Linlithgowshire Gazette*, 27 September 1901, p.8.
91 E.g. *Globe*, 18 August 1900, p.1.
92 'The Danger of Clemency', *Globe*, 2 December 1902, p.6. Discussion about Britain's exceptional mercy in dealing with rebels in *Pall Mall Gazette*, 2 December 1902, p.2.
93 *London Daily News*, 19 February 1902, p.6. See George Meredith's letter to the editor, published in *Letters: Collected and Edited by His Son* (2 vols; New York: Scribner, 1912), vol.2, p.527.
94 T.J. Lawrence, *Essays on Some Disputed Questions in Modern International Law* (Cambridge: Deighton, Bell, 1884), pp.170–1, and J.S. Risley's *Law of War* (London: Innes, 1897), p.125, on Brussels Convention right of quarter 'now recognised as one of peculiar sanctity'; William George Black, 'No Quarter', *Glasgow Herald*, 4 August 1900, p.5.
95 See, during the siege of Potchefstrom, acts of mercy reported in T.F. Carter, *A Narrative of the Boer War: Its Causes and Results* (London: John MacQueen, 1900), p.411.
96 D. Macdonald, *How We Kept the Flag Flying. The Story of the Siege of Ladysmith* (London: Ward, Lock, 1900), p.23, p.132.
97 Macdonald, *How We Kept the Flag Flying*, p.210; see also E.P. Lowry, *With the Guards' Brigade during the Boer War: On Campaign from Bloemfontein to Koomati Poort and Back* (London: Marshall, 1902).
98 W.F. Regan, *Boer and Uitlander: The True History of the Late Events in South Africa* (London: Digby, Long, 1896), p.87, p.152; on Boer treatment of 'Kaffirs', A.C. Doyle, *The War in South Africa, Its Cause and Conduct* (London: Smith, Elder, 1902), p.137.
99 Colonel John Denny, chairman of Dumbartonshire TA, *Kirkintilloch Herald*, 3 February 1909, p.6. See *Illustrated Naval and Military Magazine* 5 (1886), p.54, on an 'absolute certainty' in war about mistaken mercy leading to unnecessary slaughter.
100 See *The Tatler*, 20 December 1911, p.40, for trophy presented to the 2nd Battalion the Buffs: the figures of loyalty, endurance, courage and mercy surmounted by victory.
101 'The Palace of Peace', *Dundee Evening Telegraph*, 13 December 1911, p.4.
102 *Yorkshire Post*, 6 May 1904, p.7, quoting Bennet Burleigh of *Daily Telegraph*; 'The Red Cross Society in Japan', *Nottingham Evening Post*, 16 September 1904, p.3; surgeon-general T. Ishiguro, 'The Work of the Red Cross Society in Japan', *The Far East* 2:2 (Tokyo; 20 February 1897), p.51. Ishiguro presents a narrative of mercy and chivalry in war linked to *bushido*.
103 Melton Prior the war artist, *Bolton Evening News*, 2 November 1910, p.3.
104 For poetry invoking or debating mercy, 'Reading the Sermon on the Mount', in *Watching the War, Thoughts for the People, Part II* (London: H.R. Allenson, 1915), p.74; C.E. Byles, *Rupert Brooke's Grave, and Other Poems* (London: E. Macdonald, 1919), 'Might and Mercy' (1914), p.33; Vera Brittain, on human mercy turning 'alike to friend or foe', in the German ward of a French hospital, *Verses of a V.A.D.*

(London: E. Macdonald, 1918), 'The German Ward ("Inter Arma Caritas")', p.39; and K. Tynan, 'The Great Mercy' in *Flowers of Youth: Poems in War Time* (London: Sidgwick and Jackson, 1915), pp.51–2. Justice, not clemency, is discussed in Bertram Dobell's 'The Prussian Atrocities', *Sonnets and Lyrics, a Little Book of Verse on the Present War* (London: P.J. and A.E. Dobell, 1915), p.19. See Bombastes's lines, Laurence Binyon's *Bombastes in the Shades: A Play in One Act* (Oxford: Oxford University Press, 1915), p.19, 'But humanitarian sentiments must yield to the necessity of war. There, he who would be truly merciful must show no mercy.'

105 See also B. Russell, *On Justice in War-time. An Appeal to the Intellectuals of Europe* (Manchester and London: National Labour Press, 1915).

106 A.J. Frantzen, *Bloody Good: Chivalry, Sacrifice, and the Great War* (Chicago, IL: University of Chicago Press, 2004). See also S. Goebel, *The Great War and Medieval Memory: War, Remembrance and Medievalism in Britain and Germany, 1914–1940* (Cambridge: Cambridge University Press, 2007). C. Taylor, *Chivalry and the Ideals of Knighthood in France during the Hundred Years War* (Cambridge: Cambridge University Press, 2013), p.178 for chivalry having 'become identified with mercy in the modern imagination. It is this, more than the universal martial values of prowess, courage or loyalty, that is most commonly regarded as the defining, unique essence of chivalry'. For British discussion, C. Mills, *The History of Chivalry Or Knighthood and Its Times* (London: Longman, Hurst, Rees, Orme, Brown, and Green, 1825).

107 W.R. Thayer, *Volleys from a Non-Combatant* (Garden City, NY: Doubleday, Page, 1919), pp.114–15.

108 'Concerning the Love of One's Enemy', *The Scotsman*, 31 July 1915, p.9. See also the ironic 'German "Chivalry"', *Dublin Daily Express*, 22 October 1915, p.4 concerning Edith Cavell.

109 *Volleys from a Non-Combatant*, p.264; *King's Complete History of the World War: Visualizing the Great Conflict in All Theaters of Action, 1914–1918* (Springfield, MA: History Associates, 1922), p.12, p.16; and the Bishop of Down's allusion to the [unnamed] Nietzsche, *Belfast News-Letter*, 7 September 1914, p.4. For wartime discussion of Nietzsche see W.B. Brash, *Peace in Time of War* (London: Kelly, 1914), pp.42–6; C.L. Drawbridge, *Christianity and the War* (London: St Catherine Press, c.1914), p.30; J.N. Figgis, *The Will to Freedom or The Gospel of Nietzsche and the Gospel of Christ* (New York: Scribner, 1917); W.M. Salter, 'The Philosopher of "The Will to Power." Nietzsche on Love and Pity', *Hibbert Journal* 13:1 (October 1914), pp.102–23. On the philosopher in this aspect, G.B. Foster, 'Nietzsche and the Great War', *The Sewanee Review* 28:2 (April 1920), pp.139–51; G. Moore, 'The Super-Hun and the Super-State: Allied Propaganda and German Philosophy during the First World War', *German Life And Letters* 54:4 (October 2001), pp.310–30; on mercy in his thinking, M.C. Nussbaum, 'Pity and Mercy: Nietzsche's stoicism', in R. Schacht, ed., *Nietzsche, Genealogy, Morality; Essays on Nietzsche's 'On the Genealogy of Morals'* (Berkeley: University of California Press, 1994), pp.139–67.

110 'Editorial', *Blast*, July 1915, p.5.

111 'Germans calls for Mercy' *Daily Record*, 20 April 1915, p.6 during the battle of Neuve Chapelle. See J. Munroe, *Mopping Up* (New York: Fly, 1918), p.167, on the 'Hun squeal of fear ... when faced with the steel-points of justice'; E. Parrott, *The Children's Story of the War* (London: Nelson, 1915–19), p.35, on Germans holding up hands and begging for mercy; and poetry, e.g. the Canadians S.B. Fullerton, 'Over the Top. Ypres, July 31st 1917', *Poems* (n.p., 1918) and A.W. Drummond,

Rhymes of a Hut-Dweller (n.p., *c.*1917), 'Kamarad! Kamarad!' p.23; and 'The Word of a German', in Owen Seaman's *Made in England, Verses* (London: Constable, 1916), p.34.

112 'The Abuse of the White Flag: An Incident Showing How Our Men Were Cut Down by an Ambushed Envoy', *The Sphere*, 2 January 1915, pp.16–17; reproduced in other papers, e.g. *Sheffield Daily Telegraph*, 2 January 1915, p.5; and L. Gosling, ed., *Brushes & Bayonets. Cartoons, Sketches and Paintings of World War I* (Oxford: Osprey, 2008), p.48. It was reproduced in L. Marshall, *Horrors and Atrocities of the Great War* (Philadelphia, PA: G.F. Lasher, 1915). For interview with a private in the regiment involved in 'that white flag business', *Coventry Standard*, 1 January 1915, p.7. One coloured postcard had English caption and French translation, 'En Guerre – L'Abus du Drapeau Blanc', another French postcard in monochrome was published by l'At d'Art. For white-flag abuse earlier, 'Germans misuse White Flag', *St Andrews Citizen*, 15 August 1914, p.5. See also, E.C. Crosse, *The God of Battles: A Soldier's Faith. Being an Attempt to Reveal the Power of God in War* (London: Longmans, Green, 1917), p.14.

113 'The Pirates by Night', *Belfast News-Letter*, 24 April 1917, p.8.

114 See 'Immune from Reprisals'. The Kaiser: 'Well, it's been a wonderful protection – so far' reproduced from *Opinion* (London) in *American Review of Reviews* 56 (1917), p.593. The Kaiser is a fox sheltering under an umbrella labelled 'British Forbearance'.

115 *Topical Budget*, 22 July 1916, fifth story, 'Mercy! Kamerade!' in British Film Institute collection.

116 *Blackwood's Magazine*, 1918, p.274; and reprinted 'Klaxon' [J.G. Bower], *H.M.S. –* (Edinburgh: Blackwood, 1918).

117 W.L. Randell, 'Humanity in War', *The Academy*, 21 May 1915, p.325.

118 Citing such texts as *Proclamations Issued by Commanding Generals in Cities of France and Belgium*, e.g. transportation orders for inhabitants in Lille, April 1916, the French 'sera impitoyablement puni'; and proclamation of punishment by Field-Marshal Von der Golt without mercy for inhabitants of places near railways and telegraph lines destroyed by the Allies ('seront punies sans pitié'); *German Proclamations in Belgium and France* (London: Hodder and Stoughton, 1916); *Why Belgium Was Devastated, as Recorded in Proclamations of the German Commanders in Belgium* (1914?). On punishment for signs of mercy, see summary of *German War Practices Part 1. Treatment of Civilians* in catalogue at back of J.S.P. Tatlock, *Why America Fights Germany* (Washington, DC: Committee on Public Information, 1918), p.14.

119 E.g. 'No Mercy on Women', *Dundee People's Journal*, 22 May 1915, special supplement, p.5; and Sergeant-Major Palmer, 'Mercy for the Germans', *Coventry Evening Telegraph*, 3 April 1915, p.2, recounting atrocities from the Front, in writing home. *Evening Despatch* republished John Ruskin's 'For blessing is only for the meek and merciful, and a German cannot be either', 21 September 1914, p.2. On frightfulness as 'sound policy' and mercy as sinful folly, Anon, *The Issues of the War at a Glance* (Washington, D.C.: Committee on Public Information), January 1918, p.6. For atrocities, J. Horne and A. Kramer, *German Atrocities, 1914: A History of Denial* (New Haven, CT: Yale University Press, 2001).

120 *Saturday Review*, 24 October 1914, p.446.

121 Alleged to be translated from 'a song that German school children are singing to-day', with the line, 'Over there in the cowardly trenches lie the enemy, and no one

but a dog will say that mercy should be given to-day', *The Times*, 25 March 1916, p.7; S. Prentice, *The Cloud* (New York: Dutton, 1918), pp.38–9; and quoted in D.T. Curtin, *The Land of Deepening Shadow. Germany-at-War* (New York: Doran, 1917), p.26.

122 L. Raemakers, *Raemakers' Cartoons* (Garden City, NY: Doubleday, Page, 1916), p.133. For comments against the Kaiser at the time, 'No Quarter', *Glasgow Herald*, 4 August 1900, p.5.

123 A.G. Gardiner, 'General von Bernhardi', *The War Lords* (London: Dent, 1915), p.263, quoted in W.L. Grant, *Facts about the War* (London: Heinemann, c.1915), p.28.

124 *Sunday Mirror*, 9 July 1916, p.4.

125 E.g. *The War on Hospital Ships. From the Narratives of Eye-witnesses* (London: T. Fisher Unwin, 1917).

126 'The Quality of Mercy': How British Prisoners of War Were Taken to Germany in 1914 (n.d., c.1918). H.C. Mahoney, *Interned in Germany* (London: Sampson Low, Marston, 1918), p.8, links Prussianism and the quality of mercy by its absence.

127 M. Corelli, *My 'Little' Bit* (New York: Doran, 1919), pp.78–82 [pp.80–1]. Mercy is one of the precepts in F. Colmer, *Shakespeare in Time of War; Excerpts from the Plays Arranged with Topical Allusion* (London: Smith, Elder, 1916), pp.161–2.

128 W. Raleigh, *England and the War Being Sundry Addresses Delivered during the War and First Collected by Walter Raleigh* (Oxford: Clarendon Press, 1918).

129 R. Wilson, *The Post of Honour: Stories of Daring Deeds Done by Men of the British Empire in the Great War* (London: J.M. Dent, 1917), p.97. Cavell's fate occasioned reflections on mercy, pity and the Germans, *Sunderland Daily Echo*, 15 May 1919, p.2.

130 'The Shakespeare Festival of Mercy', *Aberdeen Press and Journal*, 18 February 1916, p.3. A.G. Ferguson, 'Entertaining the Anzacs: Performances for Australian and New Zealand Troops on Leave in London, 1916–1919', in A. Maunder, ed., *British Theatre and the Great War, 1914–1919: New Perspectives* (Basingstoke: Palgrave Macmillan, 2015) notes that the 'quality of mercy' speech in the Shakespeare Hut for the Anzacs reflected the popularity of the speech for suffragists.

131 *The New Crusader* 2:42, 18 October 1918, p.1.

132 Quoted in 'Women and the Empire', *United Empire* 19 (1928), p.151.

133 C. Dawson, *Living Bayonets: A Record of the Last Push* (London: John Lane, 1919), p.158.

134 *The Scotsman*, 12 December 1914, p.12.

135 E.g. Part I so entitled, in *Women War Workers: Accounts Contributed by Representative Workers of the Work Done by Women* (London: Harrap, 1917).

136 'House of Mercy, Baggot St', *Freeman's Journal*, 28 February 1916, p.2.

137 'The Next War', *Saturday Review*, 2 March 1918, p.184; *The Quality of Mercy: How British Prisoners of War Were Taken to Germany in 1914*, p.5.

138 '*The Quality of Mercy*', p.7.

139 See the comic poem, 'R.I.P', 'To My Angel of Mercy', *Cheerbrook Hospital Record*, 9 December 1916, p.2.

140 *Mercy-Workers of the War* (London: Causton, 1916), p.4. For pre-war, M. Mostyn Bird, *The Errand of Mercy: A History of Ambulance Work upon the Battlefield* (London: Hutchinson, 1913), frontispiece by Kenneth Bird.

141 E.g. history of Red Cross in *Dundee Evening Telegraph*, 27 August 1914, p.4; *Daily Express*, quoted in *Lincolnshire Echo*, 11 April 1918, p.2 (on chaplains and

doctors). The conscientious objector willing to carry out non-combatant duties was undertaking 'works of mercy', see P. Snowden, M.P., *Daily Herald*, 18 March 1916, p.7.

142 See *Daily Telegraph* reprinted in *The Vote*, 23 June 1916, p.108; and 'ancient tryst' with mercy with the Red Cross shield, *The Vote*, 25 February 1916.

143 F. Huard, *My Home in the Field of Mercy* (New York: Doran, 1917); A. Von Schrader and P.F. Jones, eds, *Pictorial Library of the World War* (New York and London: Harper and Brothers, 1920), vol.7.

144 *Defenders of Democracy. Contributions from Representative Men and Women of the Letters and Other Arts from Our Allies and Our Own Country* (London: John Lane, 1918), edited by the gift book committee of the 'militia of mercy'.

145 *Belfast News-Letter*, 8 November 1916, p.6.

146 E.g. *Topical Budget*, 26 January 1916, 'In the interests of mercy', representing a procession for Red Cross week. See http://www.screenonline.org.uk/film/id/733420/synopsis.html.

147 On mercy implored by wounded animals, H. Ashton, *First from the Front* (London: A.C. Pearson, 1914), p.103, of horses.

148 'Peace Settlement', *Portsmouth Evening News*, 17 March 1915, p.5.

149 *Birmingham Mail*, 24 March 1917, p.1 advertising a 'picture-song service' with that theme at the Aston Hippodrome.

150 Russell, 'The Philosophy of Pacifism', reprinted in *The Collected Papers of Bertrand Russell. Vol.13. Prophecy and Dissent, 1914–16*, ed. R.A. Rempel (London: Allen and Unwin, 1983), p.148 Russell also spoke, in 'To the Editor of "The Nation"', 15 August 1914, of mercy and reason being deluged by hatred, see *Prophecy and Dissent*, p.7.

151 See 'Cried for Mercy', *Birmingham Daily Gazette*, 5 June 1915, p.8.

152 *West Sussex Gazette*, 14 January 1915, p.5.

153 *Birmingham Mail*, 2 October 1916, p.6.

154 'A Fierce Engagement', *The Scotsman*, 24 November 1914, p.6.

155 A. St John Adcock, *In the Firing Line. Stories of the War by Land and Sea* (London: Hodder and Stoughton, 1914), p.142; E.J. Hardy, *The British Soldier, His Courage and Humour* (London: T. Fisher Unwin, 1915), p.120. For similar tales of mercy withheld due to German lack of pity in the battlefield, 'They Got Mercy!' *Dundee People's Journal*, 28 August 1915, p.11. For the claim British lacked resentment towards the enemy, A.R. Dugmore, *When the Somme Ran Red* (New York: Doran, 1918), p.204.

156 S. Graham, *A Private in the Guards* (London: Macmillan, 1919), pp.220–1. P. Jankowksi, *Verdun: The Longest Battle of the Great War* (Oxford: Oxford University Press, 2014), p.213, refers to 'the official culture ... striving ... to stamp out the quality of mercy from the field'; see testimony in R. Van Emden, *Meeting the Enemy: The Human Face of the Great War* (London: Bloomsbury, 2013), pp.185–6. Works published several decades after the conflict by combatants comment on mercy, e.g. E.L. Spiers, *Prelude to Victory* (London: Cape, 1939), discussing the French at Aisne and obliteration of 'the acquired feelings of civilized man'. On Great War memoirs, B. Bond, *Survivors of a Kind: Memoirs of the Western Front* (London: Continuum, 2008).

157 B. Muse, *Tarheel Tommy Atkins* (New York: Vantage Press, 1963), p.31.

158 F. Flamborough, *War Recollections of 1915* (Alexandria, VA: Alexandria Street Press, 2005), p.5.

159 'The Ethics of Reprisals', *The Spectator*, 23 December 1916, p.796, which looked back via Macaulay to the French revolutionary 'war to the death'.
160 E.g. IWM ref: 85/51/1, Private A.E. Wrench, typescript, Sunday 21, p.89; for German fears of British mercy through rumour from 'women from hell', 28 October 1918, p.258.
161 J.H. Mcilvaine, *Christian Indignation* (n.p., 1918), a Union service, 30 June 1918 at the Presbyterian church, Sewickley, Pennsylvania. See essays such as W. Ward, 'The War Spirit and Christianity', *Fortnightly Review*, December 1914, pp.957–70. A.J. Moore, *God, Germany and Britain in the Great War: A Study in Clerical Nationalism* (New York: Praeger, 1989) references pity, but not mercy.
162 'German Protestant Pastors on the War', *The Scotsman*, 13 January 1916, p.8; 'Recent Utterances of German Religious Teachers', *St Andrews Citizen*, 15 January 1916, p.5. Philippi (1869–1933) is alluded to by V.E. Orlando, 'Heroic Belgium', 10 June 1918, *War Speeches* (Rome: L'Eloquenza Publishing Offices, 1919), pp.217–18.
163 'Inquirer', *Stirling Observer*, 11 August 1917, p.8.
164 W.O. Hart, *Unconditional Surrender and Peace* (New Orleans: W.O. Hart, n.d.), p.32.
165 Quoted in *Review of Reviews*, March 1915, p.240. Gilbert Murray's essay, *Hibbert Journal* (1914) arguing against hating the Germans people, pointing to 'many secret acts of mercy, mercy at risk of life and against orders' they may have done, is reprinted in *Faith, War and Policy. Lectures and Essays* (London: Oxford University Press, 1918), p.9.
166 J.E. Carpenter, *Ethical and Religious Problems of the War, Fourteen Addresses* (London: Lindsay Press, 1916).
167 A. Irvine, *God and Tommy Atkins* (London: Hutchinson, 1918), pp.104–5.
168 Reports of General Fayolle and Mangin in Mainz, *Evening Despatch*, 16 December 1918, p.1; and inscription on the Southport war memorial.
169 *The English Review*, June 1918, pp.492–7. On Great War literature in relation to 'truth', see C. Martin, 'British prose writing of the First World War', *Critical Survey* 2:2 (1990), pp.137–43 [p.137].
170 A. Clutton-Brock, *Thoughts on the War* (4th edn; London: Methuen, 1914), p.76.
171 'Justice Must Be Stern', *Leeds Mercury*, 15 October 1918, p.4; 'No Mercy for the Merciless', *Sheffield Daily Telegraph*, 14 October 1918, p.4. A.E. Carey predicted, with approval, that Germany and her allies would have 'Justice without Mercy', *The Academy* (5 December 1914), p.489; debates on justice, mercy and revenge are throughout the press, e.g. critical of Bishop Frodsham, 'An Argument against Revenge', correspondence in *Saturday Review*, 12 September 1914, p.295.
172 'On false Pacifism', in V.J. McNabb, *Europe's Ewe-lamb, and Other Essays on the Great War* (London: R. & T. Washbourne, 1916), p.171.
173 *Gloucestershire Echo*, 12 October 1918, p.4.
174 Electoral address of a Conservative candidate, for Mile End, *East London Observer*, 14 December 1918, p.7; on New Testament, *Sheffield Daily Telegraph*, 31 July 1919, p.4, the Reverend Elliott, St Paul's Church, Sheffield. For peace treaties from a justice perspective, 'Politicus', 'The Peace Treaty and Mercy', *Fortnightly Review*, August 1919, pp.174–86.
175 C.E. Carter, 'Smuggling Huns', *Daily Express*, 30 May 1919, p.4.
176 E.g. *Western Daily Press*, 3 July 1919, p.8. *League of Nations Journal and Monthly Report* 1 (1919), p.312.

177 Henry Holiday, 'The Birth of a New Spirit', *Review of Reviews* (January 1915), pp.17–19 [p.19].
178 *The Scotsman*, 18 September 1919, p.4.
179 *The Scotsman*, 18 July 1919, p.6.
180 E.g. *The Project of a League of Nations* (Westminster: League of Nations Society, August 1917); Research Committee of League of Nations Union, *The Idea of a League of Nations. Prolegomena to the Study of World-Organization* (London: Humphrey Milford, 1919); F. Pollock, *The League of Nations* (London: Stevens, 1920); 'Humanitarian duties entrusted by it [the Covenant] to the League are evidently also an Anglo-Saxon conception', in *The Aims, Methods and Activity of the League of Nations* (Geneva: Secretariat of the League of Nations, 1935), p.22.

Conclusion

1 'A New Natural Theology', *Saturday Review*, 26 September 1896, p.350.
2 J.H. Dixon, 'Bognor Debating Society', *Bognor Regis Observer*, 1 February 1899, p.2.
3 *Sheffield Daily Telegraph*, 26 August 1880, p.2, in context of anti-Turkish 'Atrocitists'; on capital-punishment abolition, debate between Newdegate and Simon, on the bill, *Parliamentary Debates*, 3rd series, vol.262, House of Commons, 22 June 1881, cols.1067–72; C.H. Hopwood, 'A Plea for Mercy to Offenders' for the Humanitarian League, reprinted in newspapers, e.g. *Todmorden Advertiser*, 8 June 1894, p.8 (and critique, 'The Eclipse of Justice', *Contemporary Review*, March 1891, pp.354–63). 'The Humanitarian Spirit', is discussed by Florence Dixie, *Leamington Spa Courier*, 5 August 1904, p.2, in terms of justice and mercy.
4 C.S. Lewis, *The Problem of Pain* (London: Bles, 1940), p.44.
5 Reverend H. Dudley Lampen, *Islington Gazette*, 14 June 1904, p.4.
6 E.D. Morel, *Red Rubber: The Story of the Rubber Slave Trade Flourishing on the Congo in the year of Grace 1907* (3rd edn; London: T. Fisher Unwin, 1907), p.200.
7 'It was not a time for expressing doubt as to the mercy of God', *Leigh Chronicle*, 26 April 1912, p.3; F.W. Champneys, *Kent and Sussex Courier*, 26 April 1912, p.6.
8 Reverend L.C. Stoddert-Kennedy, 'The Suffragettes and Window Smashing', *Yorkshire Post and Leeds Intelligencer*, 3 March 1912, p.3. For another assertion, John Russell, *Women's Franchise*, 1 July 1909, p.658. Madeleine Lucette Ryley, actor-playwright and suffragette, wrote 'A Visit of Mercy', staged by the Actresses' Franchise League, *Votes for Women*, 21 May 1909, p.690. Ellen Terry delivered Portia's speech in a lecture on 'Some Heroines of Shakespeare', for Pioneer Players, *The Vote*, 3 June 1911, p.69; Marion Terry was Portia in a Pageant of Shakespeare's Heroines, *The Vote*, 10 February 1912, p.188.
9 *Votes for Women*, 30 April 1915, p.251; *The Vote*, 2 December 1911, p.64 (Lloyd George's speech, on altar of mercy). For other assertions of female gentleness, mercy, compassion, *The Vote*, 16 December 1911, p.85.
10 A speech, entitled 'My faith in Woman's Suffrage', reprinted in *Votes for Women*, 14 February 1910, p.319.
11 On prison authorities' unmercy, Elsie Howet, 'Release of the Liverpool Prisoners', *Votes for Women*, 11 February 1910, p.308. On Home Office, *Votes for Women*, 23 July 1908, p.327; for debates in Commons involving Home Secretary Gladstone, 11

November 1908, *Votes for Women*, 19 November 1908, p.125; *Votes for Women*, 16 July 1909, p.345.
12 *The Vote*, 22 April 1911, p.307.
13 See Mrs Charles Hancock, *Daily News*, reprinted *Votes for Women*, 20 June 1913, p.558 on Liberals going back to what Liberalism meant including 'liberty and mercy'.
14 J. Morley, *Recollections* (2 vols: London: Macmillan, 1917), vol.1, p.21, in a chapter, 'Spirit of the Time' prefaced by Blake's words beginning 'For Mercy has a human heart', | Pity a human face'.
15 Thus a 'great money making nation' and her message of relief and mercy, in I. Lee, 'How Red Cross Money Is Handled and Spent', *American Review of Reviews* 56 (1917), pp.615–16 [p.615]. H.S. Canby, 'The American Tradition in Contemporary Literature', *Quarterly Review of the Michigan Alumnus* (Summer 1940), pp.294–302 (p.298), denied a 'superior quality of mercy in the stocks that settle America'.
16 *The War of the Worlds* (London: Heinemann, 1898), p.5; *Mr Britling Sees It Through* (New York: Macmillan, 1916), p.303. In *First Men on the Moon* (1900–1901), Cavor wonders if the aliens 'have ideas of mercy … At any rate of restraint', serialized in *The Strand* 21 (January–June 1901), p.281.
17 *The Shape of Things to Come* (1933; London: Hutchinson, 1935), p.155. Wells said little on justice in *The Salvaging of Civilization. The Probable Future of Mankind* (London: Cassell, 1921) and nothing on mercy.
18 I. Brown, 'The Quantity of Mercy', *Manchester Guardian*, 23 January 1937, p.7.
19 L. Hopkins, *Shakespearean Allusion in Crime Fiction: DCI Shakespeare* (London: Palgrave Macmillan, 2016) on the 'quality of mercy' e.g. p.120; K.T. Hansen, 'Knowing the Unknowable: Detecting Metaphysics and Religion in Crime Fiction', in P. Baker and D. Shaller, eds, *Detecting Detection: International Perspectives on the Uses of a Plot* (London: Continuum, 2012), pp.139–68. Mercy and justice figure or are reflected on, in Christie's *Murder at the Vicarage* (London: Collins, 1930) which refers to the vicar's merciful disposition; *Murder in Mesopotamia* (London: Collins, 1936) where the narrator wonders if she should end with an equivalent of the Bismillah; and *Hallowe'en Party* (London: Collins, 1969), critiques mercy at the expense of justice as leading to further innocent victims. Dorothy L. Sayers dramatized discussion of mercy and justice in *The Just Vengeance: The Lichfield Festival Play for 1946* (London: Gollancz, 1946). On anti-capital punishment novels, S. Hodges, *Gollancz. The Story of a Publishing House 1928–1978* (London: Gollancz, 1978), p.181.
20 J. Goodwin, *Without Mercy, the Story of a Mother's Vengeance* (London: Herbert Jenkins, 1920); interview in *Answers*, 11 October 1919, p.383; *The Bioscope*, 8 April 1926, p.37.
21 'Christian Morals in the Detective Story', *Religion in Life* (New York: Abingdon Press, 1943), p.546. A bishop in Bailey's *The Life Sentence: A Reggie Fortune Novel* (London: Macdonald, 1946) unsurprisingly calls mercy the 'noblest prerogative of power'.
22 H. Belloc, *The Mercy of Allah* (London: Chatto and Windus, 1922). Doblin's work, published by Gollancz, was praised in *Tribune*, 5 March 1937, p.13, the German title judged appropriate for 'individuals and masses in a time of transition'.
23 '"Merciless" Art', *Daily Mirror*, 4 October 1930, p.7.
24 J. Conrad, 'The Heart of Darkness – Conclusion', *Blackwood's Edinburgh Magazine*, April 1899, pp.634–57 [p.649]. Further references to mercy in *The Works of Joseph Conrad, vol.18. Notes on Life and Letters* (London: Heinemann, 1921), p.39, p.93.

25 G.B. Shaw, *John Bull's Other Island, and Major Barbara* (New York: Brentano's, 1907), p.247. T.F. Evans, ed., *George Bernard Shaw. The Critical Heritage* (1976; London: Routledge, 2013), p.380; G.K. Chesterton, *George Bernard Shaw* (New York: Lane, 1909), p.198 discusses Shaw's mercy compared with Nietzsche.
26 E. Waugh, *Vile Bodies* (1930; London: Chapman and Hall, 1965), p.12.
27 L. Strachey, *Eminent Victorians: Cardinal Manning, Florence Nightingale, Dr Arnold, General Gordon* (London: Chatto and Windus, 1918), does not mock Arnold's diary in 1842 with its 'traditional language of religious devotion' including throwing himself on God's mercy, p.209.
28 A. Huxley, *Jesting Pilate: An Intellectual Holyday* (New York: Doran, 1926), p.44.
29 L. Lang-Sims, ed., *Letters to Lalage: The Letters of Charles Williams to Lois Lang-Sims* (Kent, OH: Kent State University, 1989), p.15. Williams' supernatural thriller, *War in Heaven* (1930; London: Faber and Faber, 1947), has repeated utterance of 'God's mercy endureth' by the archdeacon, a Bible belonging to Mrs Hippy has passages relating to God's mercy and compassion underscored, pp.207–8. C.S. Lewis's first novel *Pilgrim's Regress* (1933; London: Bles, 1950), p.180, presents a triolet, 'God in His Mercy', on Hell.
30 G.K. Chesterton, *Fancies versus Fads* (1923; London: Methuen, 1925), pp.86–92; on Shaw, G.K. Chesterton, *Orthodoxy* (London: Lane, 1909), p.50; see also p.179 on Christianity's innovatory 'plan for being merciful and also severe'.
31 W. Holtby, *Mandoa, Mandoa! A Comedy of Irrelevance* (1933; London: Virago, 1982), p.313; V. Brittain, 'Ave Atque Vale. An Epitaph' printed in W. Holtby, *South Riding: An English Landscape* (1936; New York: Macmillan, 1942), p.565.
32 E.M. Forster, *A Passage to India* (London: Arnold, 1924), p.36.
33 G. Cavaliero, *Rural Traditions in the English Novel, 1900–39* (London: Macmillan, 1977), p.89. F. Brett Young's poem *The Island* (London: Heinemann, 1944), p.425, argued the war was about 'those high sanctities – | Truth, Mercy, Justice, that divide mankind | From apes and beasts of prey'.
34 'Moscovitch as Shylock', *Daily Herald*, 30 October 1919, p.4.
35 'What Is to Be Done with the Jews?' *Gloucester Citizen*, 29 November 1938, p.4.
36 'Modern Shakespeare', *Worthing Herald*, 4 September 1926, p.15, Wally Beadle's staging at the New Pier pavilion, Worthing.
37 A. Bryant, *Unfinished Victory* (London: Macmillan, 1940), p.xxix.
38 Bryant, *Unfinished Victory*, pp.41–2, p.81.
39 See C.E. Playne, *Neuroses of the Nations* (London: Unwin, 1925); *Society at War, 1914–1916* (London: Unwin, 1931) and *Britain Holds On, 1917–1918* (London: Unwin, 1936).
40 Playne, *Society at War*, p.373.
41 J.H. Baron, 'Frederick Cayley Robinson's *Acts of Mercy* murals at the Middlesex Hospital, London', *British Medical Journal* 309:6970 (24 December 1994), p.1723.
42 See E. Langmuir, 'Stanley Spencer and the Acts of Mercy – a suggested additional source for the Sandham Memorial Chapel', *Burlington Magazine* 156:1338 (September 2014), pp.590–4. The Scottish National War Memorial included Peace and Mercy (a warrior with child) by George Salvesen, Edinburgh. The assessment about mercy's presence in Christian memorials is derived from keyword and image search in the Imperial War Museum war memorial register, https://www.iwm.org.uk/memorials.
43 A.C. Doyle, 'Work beyond Grave', *Daily Herald*, 23 June 1919, p.5; but on the afterlife's strict justice meaning no need for mercy, R.J. Lees, *Through the Mists; or,*

Leaves from the Autobiography of a Soul in Paradise, Etc. (London: Redway, 1898), p.140.
44 For discussion of mercy and karma, 'C.S.' 'Karma', *Reincarnation* (Chicago), August 1916, pp.251–3; A. Kempster, "Karma', *The Word* (1916), pp.143–56.
45 'The Goddess of Mercy', *Daily Telegraph*, 5 November 1929, a gift of the academic Prince Hopkins.
46 'Kwan-yin: Goddess of Mercy' *English Review*, July 1935, p.49. Chapter 9 of L. Hodous, *Folkways in China* (London: Probsthain, 1929) is devoted to the goddess; J.L. Stewart's *The Goddess of Mercy A Tale of Love and Turmoil in Modern China* (New York: Revell, 1928), reviewed in Britain, featured a lady doctor helping abandoned girl babies.
47 'Mercy', *The Times*, 14 September 1918, p.9; 'Compassion', *The Times*, 26 June 1920, p.19; 'Mercy', *The Times*, 1 April 1922, p.15; 'Mercy. From a Correspondent', *The Times*, 6 April 1935; p.15; 'A Correspondent', 'Mercy and Justice', *The Times*, 6 April 1935, p.15 (and republished, e.g. *Londonderry Sentinel*, 20 July 1935).
48 E.g. 'Our Home Pulpit', *Taunton Courier*, 7 December 1927, p.12; 'Candida', 'The Quality of Justice', *Lichfield Mercury*, 22 January 1937, p.2.
49 John Hawthorn, 'The Wisdom of Mercy', *West Sussex County Times*, 21 February 1931, p.8, taking mercy as in 'common usage … acts of general kindness'.
50 E.g. Aga Khan, 'The King Emperor', reprinted *Nottingham Journal*, 28 January 1936, p.4; *Worthing Herald*, 25 January 1936, p.12: 'Ireland won Home Rule, and in this trouble he showed the kingly quality of mercy'.
51 'King Superior to Dictator. Chichester Dean Makes a Contrast', *Hampshire Telegraph*, 14 May 1937, p.10.
52 'For God's Poor', *Church Times*, 2 June 1933, p.677.
53 C. Tompkinson, 'The Literature of Peace', *The Bookman* 81:483 (December 1931), pp.150–2 [p.150].
54 W.K. Wallace, *The Scientific World View* (London: Simpkin Marshall, 1931), p.213.
55 'Prerogative of Mercy' *Manchester Guardian*, 9 December 1924, p.9; 'The King's Clemency', *The Times*, 10 February 1936; p.14.
56 *The Scotsman*, 31 August 1920, p.5.
57 B. Gillard, 'Reprieved!' *Daily Herald*, 18 August 1928, p.4.
58 A.B. Keith, *The King and the Imperial Crown. The Powers and Duties of His Majesty* (London: Longmans, Green, 1936), p.336.
59 'Magisterial Mercy', *Daily Telegraph*, 1 September 1924; 'Mercy and Justice', *Daily Mirror*, 24 January 1930, p.7; 'Mercy for Two Mothers and a Father', *Daily Mirror*, 10 March 1938, p.2.
60 'Mercy from the Bench. Problems the Magistrate Can't Tackle', *Answers*, 29 October 1932, p.3; 'How Many Chances Should a Man Have? Mercy on the Bench', *Answers*, 1 October 1932, pp.3–4.
61 'Severity of Women Jurors', *Dundee Courier*, 31 July 1926, p.4; also 'Sterner than Men. K.C.s Views on Women Jurors', *Hartlepool Northern Daily Mail*, 22 July 1926, p.3. For stark presentation of its 'unnaturalness', 'Women Jurors', *The Sphere*, 22 January 1921, p.83. See also, 'Portia in Judgment. In an Edinburgh Court', *The Scotsman*, 18 February 1924, p.6.
62 E.g. Canon W.J. Wright's letter, 'Justice or Mercy', *Daily Telegraph*, 17 May 1948, after the House of Lords' debate on capital punishment.
63 V. Van Der Elst, *On the Gallows* (1937; London: Doge, 1939), p.138.

64 J. Douglas, 'Murder and Motherhood', *Sunday Express*, 24 July 1921, p.6; J. Douglas, 'Stop Torturing Those Mothers', *Daily Express*, 30 June 1933, p.10.
65 E. Colpus, *Female Philanthropy in the Interwar World: Between Self and Other* (London: Bloomsbury Academic, 2018) ignores mercy and associated concepts and has few references to justice.
66 *Radio Times*, 163, 12 November 1926, p.15; *Radio Times*, 213, 28 October 1927, p.16.
67 'Benefit Societies and Hospitals. Voluntary System Keeps Alive Mercy and Pity, Says Bishop', *Northampton Mercury*, 1 July 1938, p.13.
68 *The Sketch*, 5 April 1939, p.2.
69 *Leeds Mercury*, 17 April 1935, p.3.
70 See *Daily Telegraph*, 1937.
71 'Have We Improved?' *Daily Mirror*, 17 July 1928, p.9.
72 'Eugenics and Religion. Summary of a Debate Arranged by the Eugenics Society', *Eugenics Review*, July 1933, pp.101–3 [p.103].
73 'Christian Eugenics', *The Spectator*, 14 December 1934, pp.918–19 [p.918].
74 'Navy Not at the Mercy of Air Attack', *Daily Telegraph*, 12 March 1937; on poison gas, *Daily Herald*, 6 July 1934, p.9; '"Merciful" Gas Warfare', *Daily Herald*, 11 December 1934, p.4.
75 'Judge not that ye be not judged', *Saturday Review*, 19 December 1936, p.771.
76 'A Mission of Mercy', appeal for Riff victims, *Saturday Review*, 25 October 1924, p.423; 'A Mission of Mercy', *The Times*, 14 November 1935, p.15.
77 Reprinted in *Is It a New World? A Series of Articles and Letters Contributed by Correspondents to the 'Daily Telegraph', August–September, 1920* (London: Hodder and Stoughton, 1921), p.276.
78 'The Moscow Executions', *Northern Whig*, 26 August 1936, p.6; 'Brotherhood Federation Address', *Portsmouth Evening News*, 19 October 1936, p.5; 'Thanksgiving Service at Belfast Synagogue', *Belfast News-Letter*, 10 May 1937, p.9. On the 'gospel of male harshness' in European totalitarianism, see Frevert, *Emotions in History – Lost and Found*, ch.2.
79 R. Warner, 'The Cult of Power', *Daylight: European Arts and Letters, Yesterday, Today, Tomorrow* 1 (1941), pp.59–71 [p.71]; reprinted in *The Cult of Power* (London: John Lane, 1946), p.20, and cited in A. Rahman, *George Orwell: A Humanistic Perspective* (New Delhi: Atlantic Publishers, 2002), p.22.
80 'Heil, Mercy!' *The Tribune*, 8 April 1938, p.10. Franco's clemency or mercy was disputed in 1939, *Life Returns to 'Normal' in Spain* (report by Parliamentary Committee for Spain), p.4, from University of Warwick Digital Collections.
81 M. Gilbert, *Winston S. Churchill: The Prophet of Truth, 1922–1939. Companion. pt. 3. The Coming of War 1936–1939*, p.583.
82 J. McNair, 'What I Saw in Spain' in McNair, *In Spain Now!* (London: I.L.P., 1937), p.3; F. McCullagh, *In Franco's Spain: Being the Experiences of an Irish War-Correspondent During the Great Civil War Which Began in 1936* (London: Burns, Oates and Washbourne, 1937), p.173.
83 See 'Your Shillings Will Save Lives!' *National Council of Labour* (1937).
84 'Franco Prepares Madrid Assault', *Daily Express*, 17 February 1939, p.1; E.H. Shepard, 'The Highest Cause', *Punch*, 22 February 1939. Franco's reputation for unmercy continued, e.g. Cassandra's 'tender Mercy' on Franco in *Daily Mirror*, 7 December 1940, p.4.
85 T. Ackroyd, 'Deo Gratias. A Moving Story of Red Barbarity in Spain', *Action*, 19 December 1936.

86   F. Voigt, *Unto Caesar* (London: Constable, 1938), p.215.
87   On mercy in Stalinist Russia, M. Raber, *Ministries of Compassion among Russian Evangelicals, 1905–1929* (Eugene, OR: Pickwick, 2016), especially p.6; J.A. Getty, *Practicing Stalinism: Bolsheviks, Boyars, and the Persistence of Tradition* (New Haven, CT: Yale University Press, 2013), pp.31–2; on resilient idea of the merciful ruler, R. Stites, *Revolutionary Dreams: Utopian Vision and Experimental Life in the Russian Revolution* (New York: Oxford University Press, 1991). See also 'Pardons in Russia and the Soviet Union', in *The Modern Encyclopedia of Russian and Soviet History* (Gulf Breeze, FL: Academic International Press, 1982), vol.26, pp.242–5, and on the politics of mercy ('miloserdie'), I.H. Corten, *Vocabulary of Soviet Society and Culture: A Selected Guide to Russian Words, Idioms, and Expressions of the Post-Stalin Era, 1953–1991* (Durham, NC: Duke University Press, 1992), p.82.
88   'Bolshevism without Mercy', *Daily Telegraph*, 8 April 1919 (from whence the Red Army proclamation was also quoted); '"No Mercy" Demand', *Birmingham Daily Gazette*, 17 April 1933, p.1. But see *The Spur* 5:11133, 'such high-strung language is not essentially Bolshevik. We have people over here in England who write like that'.
89   'Soviet Terror and Mercy', *Daily Telegraph*, 19 January 1935; 'The British Appeal for Clemency', *The Times*, 23 April 1923, p.11; 'From Our Correspondent', *The Times*, 26 October 1927, p.14. This related to mutiny and murder on the steamer *Inkerman*.
90   'Soviet Attack on Labour's Plea for Mercy', *Daily Herald*, 24 August 1936, p.2.
91   *Daily Express*, 25 August 1936, p.1.
92   N. Astor, *My Two Countries* (New York: Doubleday, Page, 1923), p.11.
93   *Western Morning News*, 16 October 1937, p.10.
94   D. Collard, *Soviet Justice* (London: Gollancz, 1937).
95   'Germany and France', *The Times*, 1 February 1935, p.15. On rewriting Christ as warrior, L. Berggren, 'Completing the Lutheran Reformation: Ultra-nationalism, Christianity and the Possibility of "Clerical Fascism" in Interwar Sweden', in M. Feldman, M. Turda and T. Georgescu, eds, *Clerical Fascism in Interwar Europe* (2008; London: Routledge, 2013), pp.91–102 [p.96]. For the British situation, N. Watts, *Fascism in the English Church* (London: H.E. Walter, 1938).
96   *Western Daily Press*, 24 March 1941, p.3. See Bishop of Liverpool, 'Mercy Despised', *Liverpool Daily Post*, 13 January 1941, p.3. The American *Jewish Veteran*, March 1943, p.16, alleged the 'Jew primer used in Nazi schools states: "The teaching of mercy and love of one's neighbor is foreign to the German race"'. E.L. Woodward traced schooling in unmercy to before the Great War, *The Origins of the War* (Oxford: Clarendon Press, 1940), p.29.
97   See N. Bentwich, *Judaea Lives Again* (London: Gollancz, 1944), p.180. On Jewish mercy and justice, D. Caesarani, *Justice Delayed: How Britain became a Refuge for Nazi War Criminals* (London: Heinemann, 1992). For pre-war press on Jewish commitment to mercy, 'Jews and Hospitals', *Sheffield Daily Telegraph*, 19 January 1931, p.6.
98   'M. Constantine', *Swastika Night* (1937; London: Gollancz, 1940), p.29; A. Kolnai, *The War against the West* (London: Gollancz, 1938), p.494. See also the talk by Dorothy L. Sayers, *Creed or Chaos?* (London: Hodder and Stoughton, 1940).
99   'Warren Hastings', *Edinburgh Review* 74:149 (October 1841), pp.160–255 [p.166].
100 See 'he has quenched the scruples of mercy, has made cruelty seem kindness', 'Kipling a Barbarian', *San Francisco Call*, reprinted in *The Conservative* (Nebraska),

28 June 1900, p.153. On Kipling's mercy in *The Jungle Books*, P. Mallett, *Rudyard Kipling: A Literary Life* (Basingstoke: Palgrave Macmillan, 2003), p.83. Kipling's *The Ballad of the King's Mercy* (London: Macmillan, 1889) ironically presents an Afghan king's cruelty towards a would-be-assassin.

101 S.S. Kent, *Aftershocks: Politics and Trauma in Britain, 1918–1931* (London: Palgrave Macmillan, 2008), p.87. See N. Lloyd, *The Amritsar Massacre: The Untold Story of One Fateful Day* (London: I.B. Tauris, 2011), endnote 25, p.246. J.R. Raynes, *The Pageant of England, 1900–1920, a Journalist's Log of Twenty Remarkable Years* (London: Swarthmore, 1920), concluded quality of mercy *was* strained, p.268. In the House of Lords debate, 19 July 1920, Viscount Finlay argued for Dyer's use of force as the 'truest mercy', given unrest in the Punjab. The press invoked mercy variously, e.g. 'Justice without Mercy. General Dyer Broken after 34 Years' Service', *Dundee Courier*, 9 July 1920, p.5.

102 Reported widely, e.g. *Yorkshire Post*, 15 December 1919, p.8. On the 'sad imperial logic' of this act, T.H. Parsons, *The Second British Empire: In the Crucible of the Twentieth Century* (New York: Rowman & Littlefield, 2014), p.60.

103 *Daily Herald*, 15 December 1919, p.4.

104 Typescript and speech notes, 28 May 1921, Churchill Archive, CHAR 9/64.

105 *Daily Herald*, 2 January 1920, p.4.

106 *Daily Worker and Morning Star*, 6 December 1932, p.2.

107 'Bombing Most Merciful', *Daily Herald*, 6 November 1935, p.1.

108 J.C. Kerr, *Political Trouble in India* (Calcutta: Superintended Government Printing, 1917), quoting *The Indian Sociologist*, February 1912, at p.111.

109 'World-Citizen', *Sister India. A Critical Examination of and Reasoned reply to Miss Katherine Mayo's Mother India* (Bombay: Sister India Office, 1945), p.ii; J.T. Gwynn, *Indian Politics. A Survey* (London: Nisbet, 1924), p.216.

110 S. Hynd, 'Murder and Mercy: Capital Punishment in Colonial Kenya, c. 1909–1956', *International Journal of African Historical Studies* 45:1 (2012), pp.81–10.

111 P. Hart, *The I.R.A. and Its Enemies: Violence and Community in Cork, 1916–1923* (Oxford: Clarendon Press, 1998), p.130.

112 *Weekly Freeman's Journal*, 9 December 1922, p.5; 'War on the People', *Weekly Freeman's Journal*, 12 August 1922, p.4; 'Leix ambushes', *Weekly Freeman's Journal*, 19 August 1922, p.1.

113 *Freeman's Journal*, 18 January 1923, p.8.

114 See comment in C. Hartnell, *Old Ireland in Pictures: 1916–1922: Two Dublin 'Risings' and Their Consequences* (Dublin: Wilson Hartnell, 1922), p.18: 'Ireland's young army ... its cheerful valour attended by patience and mercy'. On English responses, 'A Time for Mercy', *Daily Herald*, 16 April 1923, p.1; 'A Few Words about Ireland', *The Worker's Dreadnought*, 21 April 1923, p.1.

115 See, on British mercy and Casement, the Bureau of Military History archive, accessed via https://www.militaryarchives.ie/collections/online-collections/bureau-of-military-history-1913-1921, BMH.WS1698 Part 2, Liam de Roiste, 29 July 1916, p.338 of original typescript.

116 G.K. Chesterton, *The New Jerusalem* (London: Nelson, 1920), p.26.

117 *The Anti-slavery Reporter* 19:4 (January 1930), p.165; 'Faith, Mercy, Courage', *The Graphic*, 5 October 1929, p.19, tableau against slave trade by C. Pilkington Jackson.

118 H. Cooper, *How the Empire Grew* (London: RTS, 1920), cited in E. Evans, 'The Victorians at School: The Victorian era in the Twentieth-Century Curriculum', in

M. Taylor and M. Wolff, eds, *The Victorians since 1901: Histories, Representations and Revisions* (Manchester: Manchester University Press, 2004), pp.181–97 [p.185].

119 'Value of Christian Government', *Wells Journal*, 13 August 1926, p.5.

120 A.H. Reid, *Wake up Women of Assam!* (Shillong: Assam Government Press, 1942), p.66.

121 'Hitler Attacks Churchill', *Northern Whig*, 7 November 1938, p.7.

122 'Lord Halifax on War Aims', *The Times*, 8 November 1939, p.9. In interviews before the invasion of Poland, Goering 'displayed drawings of tapestry designs, showing nudes representing Mercy, Goodness, Purity, &c'. 'What We Told Hitler', *Nottingham Evening Post*, 22 September 1939, p.8; quoting *Documents Concerning German-Polish Relations and the Outbreak of Hostilities between Great Britain and Germany on September 3, 1939* (London: HMSO, 1939), p.20 (Neville Henderson to Viscount Halifax, 28 May 1939), these were proposed decorations for Goering's Karinhall.

123 Hitler's Berlin Sports Palace speech, 30 January 1940, *Birmingham Daily Gazette*, 31 January 1940, p.5.

124 S.I. Rosenman, ed., *Public Papers and Addresses of Franklin D. Roosevelt* (13 vols; New York: Harper and Brothers, 1950), vol.12, *The Tide Turns*, p.116 (28 February 1943).

125 Widely reported in the press, see 'Going on to the End', *The Times*, 2 October 1939, p.10; *News Chronicle*, 2 October 1939, p.6. T. Harrisson and C. Madge, eds, *War Begins at Home by Mass Observation* (London: Chatto and Windus, 1940), p.157. See also R. Toye, *The Roar of the Lion: The Untold Story of Churchill's World War II Speeches* (Oxford: Oxford University Press, 2013), p.31. For Churchill's thoughts on mercy in war, see M. Gilbert, *Winston S. Churchill*, vol.6, *Finest Hour, 1939–1941* (London: Heinemann, 1983), p.158, on maintaining mercy at sea, against U-boat crews, reflecting on the behaviour of the *Baralong*.

126 See N. Micklem, *The Theology of Politics* (London: University Press, 1941), and review by D. Morrah, 'Perennial Values', *Times Literary Supplement*, 20 September 1941, p.468.

127 See the question posed to Eugen Spier, by Sir Robert Waley-Cohen, *FOCUS: A Footnote to the History of the Thirties* (London: Oswald Wolff, 1963), p.46.

128 See L. Spence, 'Bushido: Its Rise and Effacement', *Quarterly Review* (July 1942), pp.76–86; A. Ebisawa, 'Relation between the Ethics of Bushido and Christianity', *Cultural Nippon* 8:3, 4 (November–December 1939). *Contemporary Japan: A Review of East Asiatic Affairs* (Tokyo) 12 (1943), p.230, 'the spirit of bushido which prompts us to value righteousness and show mercy, benevolence, compassion and pity to our enemies'.

129 N. Bonavia-Hunt, *Father, in Thy Mercy Hear Us* (1940); Macurdy, *The Quality of Mercy: The Gentler Virtues in Greek Literature* (1940); J. de Liefde, *Errands of Mercy*; E. Bircher and E. Clam, *War without Mercy* (Zürich: Massie, 1940), a translation of Bircher's *Krieg ohne Gnade*.

130 A. Bryant, *Pageant of England. 1840–1940* (New York: Harper and Brothers, 1941), p.175.

131 V. Brittain, *England's Hour* (London: Macmillan, 1941), p.268.

132 V. Brittain, *Testament of Experience: An Autobiographical Story of the Years 1925–1950* (New York: Macmillan, 1957), p.275.

133 H.H. Fyfe, 'The Quality of Mercy', *Times Literary Supplement*, 19 May 1945, p.231.

134 G. Catlin, V. Brittain and S. Hodges, eds, *Above All Nations. Acts of Kindness Done to Enemies, in the War, by Men of Many Nations* (London: Gollancz, 1945). *Testament of Experience*, p.289, reprints 'Europe's Children', *The Friend*, 22 October 1943, calling women to speak 'Lest pity die, and strength betray the weak', and quotes her speech reprinted in *Fellowship* (New York) as 'Has Pity Forsaken Us?'

135 J.C. Powys, *The Pleasures of Literature* (London: Cassell, 1938), p.250, quoted in 'Religious Outlook', *Halifax Courier*, 28 October 1939, p.9.

136 Lewis, *The Problem of Pain*, ch.4, pp.43–4, 'Human Wickedness', argued that for a century the virtue of 'kindness' or mercy had been the focus, so ethics were lopsided, though 'if one virtue must be cultivated at the expense of all the rest, none has a higher claim than mercy'.

137 H.G. Wood, *Christianity and Civilisation* (Cambridge: Cambridge University Press, 1942), pp.2, 5–6, 16, 101. He spoke against the emasculated Jesus reduced to compassion without apocalyptic judgement, 'What I find in the Gospels', *The Spectator*, 16 June 1939, p.9. For British Christianity in 1940s, K. Robbins, *History, Religion and Identity in Modern Britain* (London: Hambledon Press, 1993); A.J. Hoover, *God, Britain, and Hitler in World War II: The View of the British Clergy, 1939–1945* (Westport, CT: Praeger, 1999); S. Parker, *Faith on the Home Front: Aspects of Church Life and Popular Religion in Birmingham, 1939–1945* (Bern: Lang, 2006).

138 T.S. Eliot, *Ash-Wednesday* (London: Faber & Faber, 1930), reprinted in *Collected Poems 1909–1935* (London: Faber & Faber, 1944), p.94; H. Mattingley, 'Personifications', *London Mercury* (1928), pp.159–66 [p.159].

139 Reprinted as 'The Winds of All the World Bring Agonies', *Britain* (New York: British Information Services), February 1943, p.47.

140 J.F. Hendry and H. Treece, eds, *The White Horseman, Prose and Verse of the New Apocalypse* (London: Routledge, 1941).

141 K. Rhys, ed., *More Poems from the Forces. A Collection of Verses by Members of the Navy, Army, and Air Force* (London: Routledge, 1943), exceptions include Francis Scarfe, 'Meditations: The Fear', pp.251–2 [p.252]. Vera Brittain, *Testament of Experience*, p.312, contrasts romantic idealism and realism, remorse and disillusion. See the single invocation of justice and mercy in 'Psalm' by Sergeant H.V.S. Page, *Poems from Italy. Verses Written by Members of the Eighth Army in Sicily and Italy July 1943–March 1944* (London: G. Harrap, 1945), p.73.

142 *Sunday Pictorial*, 17 September 1939, p.3.

143 *Newcastle Journal*, 17 April 1940, p.5; *Daily Herald*, 17 April 1940, p.7.

144 Bishop of Lichfield, 'Bishop and Peace Aims', *Staffordshire Advertiser*, 6 April 1940, p.4; Norman Angell wrote of the Treaty of Versailles in the context of Germany and Britain trying to get the other at their mercy, 'Supreme Grievance of Germany', *Daily Herald*, 7 February 1939, p.8. See Bishop Walter Carey, cited in R. Griffiths, *Fellow Travellers of the Right: British Enthusiasts for Nazi Germany, 1933–1939* (Oxford: Oxford University Press, 1983).

145 Duff Cooper, 'False Foundations of the Nazi Doctrine', *Yorkshire Evening Post*, 9 November 1939, p.8; Reverend S.E. Terry, 'Christianity Entirely Opposed to Nazi Teaching', *Mid Sussex Times*, 24 September 1940, p.7; 'Re-education of Germans', *Newcastle Journal*, 20 November 1943, p.2. For by-election reference to truth, justice and mercy, Mass Observation Archive, University of Sussex Special Collections, Spencer Summers, 'To the Electors of Northampton', Northampton by-election, December 1940, file report 522.6. The problem of a kind god, rather

than mercy, appears in Harrisson's 'What the People Think', article on God and the War, *News Chronicle*, 6 February 1941, p.4, Mass Observation Archive, 556. For theological treatment, G. Farion, 'The National Socialist Heresy', *The Churchman* 55:1 (1941), pp.61–8 [p.66].
146 The headline on a sermon at St Giles Cathedral, *The Scotsman*, 4 September 1939, p.5.
147 'A System of Mercy', *Bellshill Speaker*, 13 October 1939, p.5.
148 Reverend T.A. Angus, 'British Legion Notes', *Wells Journal*, 25 August 1939, p.5.
149 See Patience Strong's 'Mercy and Justice', *Daily Mirror*, 5 June 1940, p.7.
150 See online description, https://www.britishpathe.com, for issue date, 29 January 1945. American newsreel reported British mercy: *News of the Day*, 21 November 1945 covered 'British Mercy Aids Children in Berlin', *Motion Pictures 1940 to 1949* (Library of Congress, Copyright Office, 1953), p.279.
151 Churchill Archive, CHAR 9/153/3-6, notes for broadcast, Washington, 24 December 1941.
152 See 'The Mania of Racial Extermination', *Yorkshire Post*, 8 December 1942, p.2.
153 'No Mercy', *Sunday Express*, 20 April 1941, p.2; 'No Mercy for the Germans Now', *Sunday Express*, 15 September 1940, p.6.
154 S. Spender, *The Thirties and After. Poetry Politics People 1933–75* (London: Fontana, 1978), p.95.
155 H.H. Henson, *Wartime Sermons* (London: Macmillan, 1915), p.8 spoke of 'mercy which has been slowly built up through the Christian centuries'.
156 Brittain, *Testament of Experience*, p.325. 'We British people have never been good haters. We cherish tolerance. We hate hitting those less strong than ourselves, and we loathe brutality', *Daily Express*, 6 June 1943, p.4.
157 'Germans will cry "Mercy"', *Daily Telegraph*, 6 May 1942.
158 On 'right, justice and mercy', see frequently reprinted paragraph, *West London Observer*, 10 January 1941, p.4; sentimental nonsense, *Nelson Leader*, 7 June 1940, p.4; on Nazism knowing no mercy, L.S. Amery MP's letter, reprinted *Evening Despatch* (Birmingham), 8 September 1939, p.4; 'Bishop Henson on Reprisals', *Sunderland Daily Echo*, 28 September 1940, p.3 (from *The Times*, 28 September 1940, p.5); *Yorkshire Post*, 22 October 1940, p.2 for 'winter pants' analogy cited by Reverend G.B. Bentley; 'Layman', 'The Bible and the Social Gospel', *Clitheroe Advertiser and Times*, 19 November 1943, p.6; 'Tasks of 1943', editorial in *Dumfries and Galloway Standard*, 2 January 1943, p.4. On Churchill, Atlantic Charter, and mercy, 'Mussolini's Appeal', *The Times*, 6 July 1943, p.5. On Lord Nathan's comment, 'Post-War Policy towards Germany', *Parliamentary Debates*, House of Lords, 21 May 1942, 5th series, vol.122, col.1150. Henson's letter on reprisals stimulated further debate, e.g. C.H. St J. Hornby, *The Times*, 3 October 1940, p.7. Alexander, first Lord of the Admiralty, emphasized, 'Justice Followed by Mercy', *The Times*, 5 April 1941, p.2. Other invocations of mercy include German execution of hostages, 'Hitler's "Mercy" in France', *The Times*, 25 October 1941, p.4. Other reflections are in 'Christianity and the Crisis. Professor H.G. Wood Stresses Basic Principles', *Leamington Spa Courier*, 20 March 1942, p.6.
159 'A Correspondent', 'Compassion', *The Times*, 14 June 1941, p.6. The British press reported the pope's declarations; see D. Gwynn, *The Vatican and War in Europe* (London: Burns, Oates and Washbourne, 1940).
160 'Unrra's Work of Mercy', *Yorkshire Post*, 8 July 1944, p.4.

161 See T.A. Warren, 'Britain Finds Its Soul', *The Rotarian*, June 1941, p.14, on phrase 'mercy squad'; *Municipal Journal* 52:1 (1944), p.124, on 'mobile mercy squads' and 'Restoring Order from Chaos', *Aberdeen Press*, 12 June 1944, p.2.

162 H. Marchant, 'Must Bombed Women Wait for Hours in Queues?: "Mercy v. Red Tape"', *Daily Express*, 25 September 1940, reported in Mass Observation, 465, 'The Press and the Blitzkrieg', October 1940, p.8.

163 'How Poland Is Meeting the Nazi Terror', *Northern Whig*, 17 January 1942, p.2, reviewing works such as anon., *The New German Order in Poland* (London: Hutchinson, 1942).

164 Excerpts in the press, e.g. *Liverpool Echo*, 24 November 1942, p.4.

165 P. England, 'Thirty Pieces of Tainted Silver', *The People*, 2 August 1942, p.4.

166 'The Jewish New Year', *Ballymena Weekly Telegraph*, 27 September 1941, p.6.

167 '"No Mercy" Order to Germans', *The Times*, 17 January 1942, p.3; 'Goebbels and Jewry. There can be no mercy', *The Times*, 7 May 1943, p.3.

168 C.P. Corrigan, 'Man Who Cannot Forget', *The People*, 7 November 1943, p.4.

169 'We have had a peroration – now for a programme for the Jews', *Daily Herald*, 30 December 1942, p.2; 'Jewish Victims of German Hate. General Smuts Gives a Solemn Warning', *Birmingham Daily Post*, 29 December 1942, p.3; 'Warn Nazi Criminals of Coming Punishment', *Birmingham Daily Gazette*, 15 March 1943, p.2; 'Mr Eden on Peril of Jews in Balkans', *Coventry Evening Telegraph*, 30 March 1944, p.3; 'Puppet Thugs Will Be Made to Pay', *Daily Mirror*, 31 March 1944, p.2.

170 Reverend G.S.B. Knapp, 'What I Saw at Belsen', *Wiltshire Times*, 26 May 1945, p.2; Colonel J.T. Avison's talk to Rotarians at Eastbourne, *Eastbourne Gazette*, 22 July 1953, p.7, on 'works of mercy'; G. Kersh, 'Things We Must Never Forget', *The People*, 17 June 1945, p.3, on mercy in Belsen. Reflections on the camps reinforced wartime understanding about Nazi mercilessness, see 'Tales of Horror', *Dumfries and Galloway Standard*, 21 April 1945, p.4.

171 Sgt E. Parker, 'The Horrors of Belsen', *Derbyshire Times*, 25 May 1945, p.5.

172 C. Morgan, 'The Spirit of Man', *The Spectator*, 14 June 1940, p.11.

173 'The After-the-War Germany', *Dundee Evening Telegraph*, 22 December 1943, p.2.

174 Mass Observation, 1543, 'Germany after the War', December 1942, p.3. On Soviet propaganda of revenge against the Germans, see P.M. Taylor, *Munitions of the Mind: A History of Propaganda* (Manchester: Manchester University Press, 2003), p.233.

175 'What shall we do with the boys of Germany? Kill ... Pity ... Teach ... Them', *Daily Mirror*, 28 October 1944, p.2. On the other hand, 'No Pity, no mercy' was characterized by a correspondent as 'unEnglish as they are unChristian', *Sunday Express*, 13 June 1943, p.3.

176 G. McCarthy, 'Remember – and Be without Pity', *Daily Mirror*, 11 September 1944, p.3.

177 W. Churchill, Guildhall speech, 1 July 1943, reprinted in *Britain Looks Ahead. British Official Statements*, vol.3 (British Information Service), September 1942–September 1943, p.135.

178 *The Times*, 7 August 1945, p.4; Churchill Archive, CHUR 2/3/42-50 (the statement by Churchill was read by Attlee, as prime minister). 'Divine grace' is invoked in correspondence, R.A. Gregory's letter, 'Atomic Bombs', *The Times*, 13 August 1945, p.5; and 'Let's Talk It Over ... the Mighty Atom', *The People* (London) 12 August 1945, p.2. Churchill, 'Fifty Years Hence', republished in *Strand Magazine*, December 1931, referred to science's destructive capacity without mercy and pity. See J.D.

Lyons, 'Strength without Mercy: Winston Churchill on Technology and the Fate of Civilization', *Perspectives on Political Science* 43:2 (2014), pp.102–8.

179 'London Letter', *Western Daily Press*, 9 August 1945, p.3; 'Mighty Atom', *Walsall Observer*, 11 August 1945, p.4, on providence; for God's mercy in its use to hasten the end of the war, 'The Mighty Atom', *The People*, 12 August 1945, p.2. On reducing military casualties, G.C. Durward, *Dundee Courier*, 22 August 1945, p.2. See Mass Observation for file report 2272, 'A Report on Public Reactions to the Atom Bomb', 23 August 1945. There is no mention of mercy in quoted responses; pity and compassion are rejected as meaning 'nothing to the Oriental mind' by one (in 2272.2 'Atom-Bomb') whilst another saw it as requiring nations to become 'more inclined to forbearance and tolerance' (2272.4). See *Peace and the Public. A Study by Mass-Observation* (London: Longmans, Green, 1947).

180 This phrase appears in a New Year's message from the president of the Lancaster Free Church Federal Council, *Lancaster Guardian*, 4 January 1946, p.5.

181 'Treason and Mercy', *Manchester Guardian*, 19 December 1945, p.3, contrasting the fate of Colonel Arthur Lynch during the Boer War with Amery's fate.

182 See British reports such as 'Laval to Die. "I Will Not Ask for Mercy"', *Daily Telegraph*, 10 October 1945; 'Mercy Plea by Petain's Judge', *Daily Telegraph*, 16 August 1945.

183 Cassandra, 'My Blue Heaven', *Daily Mirror*, 14 October 1947, p.4. *Coventry Evening Telegraph*, 21 July 1952, p.2, reported 'Mercy Statues for Japs', with the plan to send 1,000 statues of Guanyin to relatives of executed war criminals, by Masayuki Nakamura.

184 'Goering Told Mercy Plea Turned Down', *Daily Express*, 14 October 1946, p.1; 'Executions at Nuremberg. From Our Special Correspondent', *The Times*, 17 October 1946, p.6; 'Christianity Calling', *Bellshill Speaker* (Lanarkshire), 4 October 1946, p.3.

185 Herbert Thomas, 'Expiation', *Cornishman*, 10 December 1946, p.4. Thomas was an 'ex-American crime reporter'.

186 'Marginal Comment', *The Spectator*, 31 May 1945, p.10.

187 S. Smith, 'Crimes and Punishment. Local Responses to the Trial of Japanese War Criminals in Malaya and Singapore, 1946–48', *South East Asia Research* 5 (March 1997), pp.41–56 [p.46], quoting editorial in *Straits Times*, 6 February 1947; also R.J. Pritchard, 'The Quality of Mercy: The Right of Appeal and the Gift of Clemency Following British War Crimes Trials in the Far East, 1946–1948' in P. Dennis, ed., *1945: War and Peace* (Canberra: Australian War Museum, 1999), pp.167–98.

188 See reviewer's comments on W.A. Robson, *The War and the Planning Outlook*, in *Times Literary Supplement*, 24 January 1942, p.47.

189 W.H. Auden, *For the Time Being. A Christmas Oratorio* (New York: Random House, 1944).

190 Mass Observation, 'Morale in May 1943', M45C on conduct of war in relation to mercy; 49-1-A, in folder 'Victory Celebrations 1945–46, January 1945–December 1946', on mercy to Hitler in the afterlife.

191 'M.R.H.' *Manchester Guardian*, 12 March 1941, p.3.

192 Neave Hobbs, *Worthing Herald*, 25 June 1943, p.3.

193 'Should We Pity the Germans?' *Daily Herald*, 8 February 1945, p.2.

194 '"Realist" Rebuked', *Gloucester Citizen*, 3 December 1946, p.4.

195 'Our Mercy Is Our Glory', *Daily Record*, 2 June 1945, p.5.

196 'Save Europe Now', *Taunton Courier*, 8 December 1945 p.3; *Daily Herald*, 5 November 1945, p.3.

197 For mercy 'train', see *British Zone Review: A Monthly Review of Activities in the British Zone of Germany* 1947, p.22. On Pakenham's policy as a Christian, P. Stanford, *Lord Longford: A Life* (London: Heinemann, 1994), p.210. Konrad Adenauer referenced mercy and justice in relation to treatment due to Germans by victors, in speeches in 1946, J. Herf, *Divided Memory. The Nazi Past in the Two Germanys* (Cambridge, MA: Harvard University Press, 1997), pp.221–2.

198 'Nurses Hear about U.N.R.R.A.' *Worthing Gazette*, 4 September 1946, p.5; W.E. Arnold Forster, *Cornishman*, 9 March 1950, p.8.

199 The lawyer Louis Nizer, *What to Do with Germany* (Bombay: Thacker, 1944), p121.

200 *British Zone Review: A Monthly Review of Activities in the British Zone of Germany* 1946, p.7: 'such treatment was not theirs by right, but was an act of mercy'.

201 'Radio Links Bombed Cities. Coventry Says It with "Forgiveness"', *Coventry Evening Telegraph*, 27 December 1946, p.8.

202 J. Struk, *Photographing the Holocaust: Interpretations of the Evidence* (London: I.B. Tauris, 2004), p.166.

203 'War Aims in Brief', *The Times*, 4 October 1940, p.5. Bertrand Russell's *Education and the Modern World* (New York: Norton, 1932), p.86, referred to education's role in changing boys' 'herd' mentality to something more merciful.

204 'Let there be Mercy', *Birmingham Daily Gazette*, 20 September 1946, p.2.

205 *Aberdeen Press and Journal*, 4 August 1949, p.2. R. Boothby, *I Fight to Live* (London: Gollancz, 1947), p.344 describes communism's rejection of toleration, kindness and mercy.

206 *The Scotsman*, 2 March 1948, p.7 was entitled.

207 *Rochdale Observer*, 17 March 1945, p.4.

208 D.R. Davies, *On to Orthodoxy* (1939; New York: Macmillan, 1949), p.135.

209 'Pre-election Service in St Pauls', *The Sphere*, 13 October 1951, p.10; A. Bryant, 'Our Note Book', *Illustrated London News*, 10 December 1955, p.18.

210 See, via Warwick Digital Collections, the Resolution on system of free hospitals (letter) issued by Rawtenstall Borough Trades Council, 24 March 1943.

211 W.A. Parker, Archdeacon of Stafford, '"Grave Dangers" of Welfare State', *Staffordshire Advertiser*, 30 May 1952, p.3.

212 The League was refounded, as an organization to honour volunteers.

213 'Lesson in Mercy', *Daily Express*, 16 July 1963, p.6.

214 'Quaero', 'The Panel Doctor', *Saturday Review*, 21 February 1931, pp.260–1 [p.260]. H. Spencer, *Social Statics: or, The Conditions Essential to Human Happiness Specified and the First of Them Developed* (London: Chapman, 1851), pp.319–20, warned of 'State-almsgiving' using Portia's speech.

215 M. Aitken, *Success* (Toronto: McClelland, 1921), pp.26–8.

216 'Premier on Moral Values', *The Scotsman*, 10 May 1949, p.4.

217 A conclusion from studying digitized speeches of Conservative, Labour and Liberal/Liberal Democrat Party leaders via http://www.britishpoliticalspeech.org/. On mercy in parliament, see Sir John Hobson, *Parliamentary Debates*, series 5, vol.716, House of Commons, Murder (Abolition of Death Penalty) Bill, 13 July 1965, cols.372–7.

218 A. Koestler, *Darkness at Noon* (translated by Daphne Hardy and first published in English in 1940; New York: Macmillan, 1941), p.149; 'Cassandra', 'This Is Communism', *Daily Mirror*, 25 March 1948, p.2; C.D. Edwards, 'Christmas in the

Jungle', *Hampshire Telegraph*, 23 December 1949, p.13, Malayan and Indo-Chinese soldiers following the Communist 'materialistic creed that allows no time for brotherliness and human mercy'.
219   *Lichfield Mercury*, 7 January 1949, p.5.
220   'Britain's Service to Colonies', *Birmingham Daily Post*, 1 February 1960, p.9 (the rector of Birmingham).
221   'Our Note Book', *Illustrated London News*, 27 January 1968, p.14.
222   R. Vidyārthī, *British Savagery in India* (Agra: S.L. Agarwala, 1946), p.295.
223   A. Campbell-Johnson, *Mission with Mountbatten* (Bombay: Raico, 1951), pp.213–14, see p.205 on 'heroic errand of mercy'.
224   G.N. Perkins, 'Act of Mercy', *Tribune*, 25 March 1955, p.8.
225   'The Gallows in Rodesia', *Illustrated London News*, 9 March 1968, p.1.
226   L. Yutang, *Between Tears and Laughter* (New York: John Day, 1943), p.167. The 'Mencian' common standard of humanity he writes of, concerns the shared sense of mercy, and shame, pp.210–11. His novel *A Leaf in the Storm* was reviewed by R.D. Charques under the title, 'Evil and Mercy', *Times Literary Supplement*, 16 May 1942, p.245.
227   *Carluke and Lanark Gazette*, 15 February 1952, p.3, 'A second requirement of God is mercy. Often it is necessary in the form of sympathy, to soften justice. Sympathy was ever apparent in King George'.
228   'The Neglected Child', *Punch* 208:5431 (21 February 1945).
229   See reprinted essay by American doctor, B.F. Miller, 'Why I Oppose Mercy Killing', *Answers* (London) 118:3048, 30 September 1950, p.3; 'I Was a Mercy Killer', *Daily Mirror*, 5 May 1959, p.1. See mercy claim disputed by the Catholic Archbishop of Westminster, *Daily Mirror*, 4 August 1947, p.4. For mercy killing as theme for television debate, *Paper Talk* (ATV), 18 June 1958, reviewed *Birmingham Daily Post*, 19 June 1958, p.35. The topic was dramatized, *I Thank a Fool* (1962, director Robert Stevens); 'The Defenders: The Quality of Mercy' (BBC, 19 January 1962). For more general study of mercy killing, N.D.A. Kemp, *Merciful Release: The History of the British Euthanasia Movement* (Manchester: Manchester University Press, 2002). Interwar press references include C.K. Millard, 'The Case for Euthanasia', *Fortnightly Review* 130 (December 1931), pp.701–18; Ritchie Calder, 'Mercy Murderer', *Daily Herald*, 30 March 1938, p.1; 'Mercy Murder Theme in Play', *Daily Herald*, 2 September 1936, p.9; '"Kill for Mercy" Campaign', *Daily Herald*, 10 October 1938, p.7; review of Jonathan Stagge's mystery with 'not-too-overworked cover for murder', *Murder or Mercy?* in *Daily Herald*, 20 October 1937, p.8.
230   'The Execution of Ruth Ellis', *The Spectator*, 15 July 1955, p.3; see also 'Cassandra', 'Should Ruth Ellis Hang?' *Daily Mirror*, 30 June 1955, p.9.
231   J. Connell, 'The Quality of Mercy', *The Sphere*, 21 April 1962, p.92.
232   Lord Pakenham quoting 'blessed are the merciful', *Daily Mirror*, 5 December 1957, p.9; see also letter commending courage and 'Christian mercy', *Daily Mirror*, 29 November 1958, p.2. On homosexuals 'at the Mercy of the Blackmailer', *Daily Mirror*, 27 November 1958, p.7. For concern about the impact of 'mercy towards adults' in sentencing, 'Sex Discussed by Doctors and Bishops', *Birmingham Daily Post*, 1 April 1954, p.3.
233   'Free Kirk on mercy and criminals', *Aberdeen Evening Express*, 21 May 1968, p.5 (Moderator of the General Assembly). Clemency and mercy are linked with Roy Jenkins's permissiveness by Arthur Bryant, 'Pitfalls of Permissiveness', *Illustrated London News*, 30 August 1969, p.11.

234 'Of Mercy and Men', *Daily Mirror*, 8 September 1950, p.5, referring to a Fabian Society report on relations between railwaymen and managers.
235 'Mr Churchill Honoured', *The Scotsman*, 11 October 1950, p.7.
236 'Premier on £3600m. Defence Scheme', *The Scotsman*, 13 September 1950, p.7; G. Gale, 'Let's Be Thankful for These Large Mercies', *Daily Mirror*, 31 December 1968, p.6.
237 'On Arab Refugees in Palestine', *Church Times*, 15 January 1954, p.35; 'Hungarians for the Commonwealth', *Church Times*, 22 February 1957, p.3.
238 Reports of the Vatican Radio on public opinion's appeals for human mercy, *Birmingham Daily Gazette*, 19 June 1953, p.1.
239 'Mercy Is Their Business!' *Daily Mirror*, 11 December 1956, p.12 in context of Hungarian refugees.
240 C.S. Lewis, 'The Humanitarian Theory of Punishment', *Twentieth Century: An Australian Quarterly Review* 3:3 (1949), pp.5–12; reprinted in *Res Judicatae* 6 (June 1953), pp.224–30; and *The Churchman* 73:2 (1959), pp.55–60. The essay was triggered by an article on treating homosexuality (not actually explicitly mentioned) as something to be cured rather than crime, in 'one of our Leftist weeklies'.
241 H.R.T. Roberts, 'Mercy'.
242 'Quality of Mercy Is Needed', *Church Times*, 2 December 1977, p.14.
243 C. Strange, *Qualities of Mercy: Justice, Punishment, and Discretion*, p.3.
244 Transcript of 'Speech on *Women in a changing World* (1st Dame Margery Corbett-Ashby speech Lecture)', 26 July 1982, at https://www.margaretthatcher.org/document/105007 (accessed 26 July 2018); 'Speech to General Assembly of the Church of Scotland', 21 May 1988, https://www.margaretthatcher.org/document/107246 (accessed 26 July 2018).
245 See, for example, D. Porter, 'Let the People Sing', *Third Way* 11:7 (July 1988), p.8.
246 She referred to mercy and redemption as the New Testament view, in 29 June 1997, TV Interview for CNN ('Hong Kong reverts to China'), https://www.margaretthatcher.org/document/109211 (accessed 26 July 2018). Her *The Downing Street Years* (London: HarperCollins, 1993) refers to thanking God for small mercies at one point during her fall from power.
247 On post-Christianity, 'A Headmaster', 'The Mental Climate of To-Day', *The Churchman* 66.3 (1952), pp.157–63. In the same journal of British evangelicalism, mercy was asserted as the Christian realization, in M.A.C. Warren, 'The Cataclysm of Our Time', *The Churchman* 66.1 (1952), pp.5–12. On modern journalism and mercy in criminal cases, S. Dew, 'Go and Sin No More': Christian mercy vs. tabloid vengeance', *Criminal Justice Matters* 52:1 (2003), pp.4–5.
248 'Mercy for a Mugger', *Daily Mirror*, 11 January 1978, p.1.
249 So R. Niebuhr, *Discerning the Signs of the Times. Sermons for To-day and Tomorrow* (London: SCM Press, 1946). See T.E. Utley, 'Faith and Politics', *Times Literary Supplement*, 31 August 1946, p.412.
250 W.A. Swallow, *The Quality of Mercy. History of the Humane Movement in the United States* (Boston, MA: Mary Mitchell Humane Fund, 1963).
251 A.D. Menken, *On the Side of Mercy: Problems in Social Readjustment* (New York: Covici Friede, 1933); Sister Rachel, 'The Works of Mercy: Religion in Social Work', *The Living Church*, 22 April 1951, p.23. In the context of Western evangelicalism, M. Tinker, 'Ministries of Mercy, Moral Distance and the Good Samaritan – The Challenge to Evangelical Social Action', *The Churchman* (Spring 2009), pp.53–65.

252 Frevert's definition in *Emotions in History – Lost and Found*, p.12.
253 J.H.F. Schaeffer, G. Den Hertog and S. Paas, eds, *Mercy: Theories, Concepts, Practices (Proceedings from the International Congress TU Apeldoorn/ Kampen, NL June 2014)* (Zurich: LIT Verlag Münster, 2017).
254 B.A. Kautzer, 'The Works of Mercy: Towards a Liturgical Ethics of the Everyday', University of Durham PhD, 2015.
255 W.F. Ransome, '"Above the Sceptered Sway" ...'; A. Sarat, *Mercy on Trial: What It Means to Stop an Execution* (Princeton, NJ: Princeton University Press, 2005); A. Sarat, ed., *Merciful Judgments and Contemporary Society: Legal Problems, Legal Possibilities* (New York: Cambridge University Press, 2011); A.S. Tuckness and J.M. Parrish, *Decline of Mercy in Public Life* (New York: Cambridge University Press, 2014); R.H. Bell, *Rethinking Justice: Restoring Our Humanity* (Lanham, MD: Lexington Books, 2007); R.E. Barkow, 'The Ascent of the Administrative State and the Demise of Mercy', *Harvard Law Review* 121:133 (2008), pp.1333–65. Work on the American legal system compared with European penology discusses comparative mercy, J.Q. Whitman, *Harsh Justice: Criminal Punishment and the Widening Divide between America and Europe* (New York: Oxford University Press, 2003). On migration, see M. Blake, *Justice, Migration & Mercy* (Oxford: Oxford University Press, 2020).
256 C. Herlinger, and P. Jeffrey, *Where Mercy Fails: Darfur's Struggle to Survive* (New York: Seabury Books, 2009), p.ix. S. Chan, 'Can There Be Mercy without the Merciful? A Meditation on Martha Nussbaum's Questions', *Third World Quarterly* 35:9 (2014), pp.1728–47 [p.1747], comments 'what is given and with-held depends upon the arbitration of mercy by those who treat mercy as an instrument. It is not a gentle dew that droppeth from the heavens. It is a self-exoneration, a generosity with a limit – a ceiling'.
257 *Daily Record*, 2 June 1945.
258 *London Magazine*, 1 October 1827, p.204.
259 *The Rising of '98: With an Account of the Volunteers, French Alliances, Invasions, &c* (Dublin: M'Cormick, 1846), p.103.
260 O'Donnell, F.H. *History of the Irish Parliamentary Party* (2 vols; London: Longmans, 1910), vol.1, p.368.
261 'To England on the Slave Trade' in J. Grahame, *Poems* (2 vols; Longman, Hurst, Rees, and Orme, 1807), vol.1, pp.130–1 [p.131]. This was stimulated by the failure of Wilberforce's bill in 1795.
262 R. Whiteing, *No.5 John Street* (London: Grant Richards, 1899), p.65, where this is made an ironic comment on a character's jingoistic identification with the Almighty.
263 A. Lazar and M.M. Lazar, 'The Politics of "Othering" in the New World Order', in F.S. Abdullah, M.H. Abdullah and T.B. Hoon, eds, *Critical Perspectives on Language and Discourse in the New World Order* (Newcastle upon Tyne: Cambridge Scholars, 2008), pp.100–10 [p.104] for mercy and related terms in George Bush's speeches.
264 See Morley, 'Spirit of the Time', p.27, for a Victorian's early-twentieth-century reflections on catchwords like Right, Justice, Equality.
265 Blake, 'The Human Abstract', in A. Gilchrist, *Life of William Blake, 'Pictor ignotus': With Selections from His Poems and other Writings* (2 vols; London: Macmillan, 1863), vol.1, p.64. The argument appears in Sylvia Pankhurst's *Workers' Dreadnought*, 9 June 1928, p.1. Blake's 'To mercy, pity, peace and love' also featured in *Songs for Socialists* (London: Fabian Society, 1912).

266 R. Whytehead, *Claims of Christian Philanthropy* (London: Simpkin, Marshall, 1839), p.197.
267 Thus *Evangelical Magazine and Missionary Chronicle*, August 1839, p.383, on the spirit of Christianity pre-eminently and essentially of mercy. Primatt defined cruelty as atheism, *The Duty of Mercy and the Sin of Cruelty to Brute Animals*, p.288.

Select bibliography

Full bibliographic details including details of primary periodicals, newspapers and official papers (not listed below) are contained in the endnotes.

Digitized primary sources

Websites and databases

Algernon Charles Swinburne Project http://swinburnearchive.indiana.edu/swinburne/archive.org
British Film Institute http://www.screenonline.org.uk/film/id/733420/synopsis.html
British Newspapers Archive https://www.britishnewspaperarchive.co.uk/
British Officers' Diaries from World War 1 (British Online Archives) https://microform.digital/boa/
British Pathé and the Reuters Historical Collection https://www.britishpathe.com
British Periodicals Collections III (ProQuest)
British Political Speech http://www.britishpoliticalspeech.org/
Bureau of Military History https://www.militaryarchives.ie/collections/online-collections/bureau-of-military-history-1913-1921
Chief Secretary of Ireland's Office Registered Papers http://www.csorp.nationalarchives.ie
Churchill Archive (Bloomsbury Publishing Plc) http://www.churchillarchive.com/
Darwin Online http://darwin-online.org.uk/
The Diary of William Godwin, eds. Victoria Myers, David O'Shaughnessy and Mark Philp (Oxford: Oxford Digital Library, 2010) http://godwindiary.bodleian.ox.ac.uk
Google.books
JISC Historical Texts https://historicaltexts.jisc.ac.uk/
Keywords Project (University of Pittsburgh) https://keywords.pitt.edu/
Literature Online (ProQuest)
Margaret Thatcher Foundation https://www.margaretthatcher.org/
Mass Observation Online (Adam Matthew Digital)
National Maritime Museum Greenwich, AAA4414, creamware jug transfer-printed in black, *c.*1797 https://collections.rmg.co.uk/collections/objects/4138.html
Nineteenth Century Collections Online (Gale) https://www.gale.com/intl/primary-sources/nineteenth-century-collections-online
Old Bailey Proceedings Online www.oldbaileyonline.org version 7.0, 23
Trove (National Library of Australia) https://trove.nla.gov.au/newspaper/
UKPressOnline https://ukpressonline.co.uk/
War Memorials Register (Imperial War Museum) https://www.iwm.org.uk/memorials

Primary printed materials

Books

Books and chapters in books published before c.1960

Agnew, E.C. *Illustrations of the Corporal and Spiritual Works of Mercy, in Sixteen Designs, Engraved in Outline* (London: Dolmain, 1840)
Aitken, M. *Success* (Toronto: McClelland, 1921)
Auden, W.H. *For the Time Being. A Christmas Oratorio* (New York: Random House, 1944)
Banks, J. *The Albion Queens; or, the Death of Mary Queen of Scots. A Tragedy* (London: Bell, 1797)
Barnardo, S. and J. Marchant, *Memoirs of the Late Dr Bernardo* (London: Hodder and Stoughton, 1907)
Baxter, G.R.W. *The Book of the Bastiles: Or, the History of the Working of the New Poor Law* (London: Stephens, 1841)
Bentham, J. *Rationale of Judicial Evidence: Specially Applied to English Practice* (5 vols; London: Hunt and Clarke, 1827), vol.1
Bentham, J. *The Works of Jeremy Bentham, Now First Collected: Under the Superintendence of his Executor, John Bowring* (Edinburgh: Tait, 1843), vols 3, 9
Bicheno, J.E. *An Inquiry into the Nature of Benevolence, Chiefly with a View to Elucidate the Principle of the Poor Laws, and to Show Their Immoral Tendency* (2nd edn; London: Hunter, 1824)
Binyon, L. *Bombastes in the Shades: A Play in One Act* (Oxford: Oxford University Press, 1915)
Bowring, J. *Minor Morals for Young People* (3 vols; London: Whittaker, 1834), vol.1
Brett Young, F. *The Island* (London: Heinemann, 1944)
Brittain, V. *England's Hour: An Autobiography 1939-1941* (London: Macmillan, 1941)
Brittain, V. *Verses of a V.A.D.* (London: E. Macdonald, 1918)
Bryant, A. *Pageant of England. 1840-1940* (New York: Harper and Brothers, 1941)
Bryant, A. *Unfinished Victory* (London: Macmillan, 1940)
Burke, E. *Reflections on the Revolution in France, and on the Proceedings in Certain Societies in London Relative to that Event: In a Letter Intended to Have Been Sent to a Gentleman in Paris* (5th edn; London: Dodsley, 1790)
Burke, E. *A Letter from Mr Burke to a Member of the National Assembly; in Answer to Some Objections to His Book on French Affairs* in *The Works of the Right Honorurable Edmunbd Burke, Collected in Three Volumes* (1791; London: Dodsley, 1792), vol.3
Burke, E. *Thoughts on the Prospect of a Regicide Peace* (London: Owen, 1796)
Campbell-Johnson, A. *Mission with Mountbatten* (Bombay: Raico, 1951)
Carlile, R. *Every Man's Book: Or What Is God?* (London: Carlile, 1826)
Catlin, G., V. Brittain and S. Hodges, eds, *Above All Nations. Acts of Kindness Done to Enemies, in the War, by Men of Many Nations* (London: Gollancz, 1945)
Chesterton, G.K. *George Bernard Shaw* (New York: Lane, 1909)
Chesterton, G.K. *Orthodoxy* (London: Lane, 1909)
Cobbe, F.P. *Darwinism in Morals, and Other Essays* (London: Williams and Norgate, 1872)
Cobbett, W. *The Bloody Buoy, Thrown Out as a Warning to the Political Pilots of All Nations* (Philadelphia, PA: Wright, 1797)

Collins, W. *Odes on Several Descriptive and Allegorical Subjects* (London: Millar, 1746)
Conrad, J. *The Works of Joseph Conrad, vol.18. Notes on Life and Letters* (London: Heinemann, 1921)
Conybeare, J. *The Virtue of Being Merciful Stated and Enforc'd* (London: Birt, John and Rivington, 1751)
Cowper, W. *The Task, A Poem in Six Books* (London: Johnson, 1785)
Crabb, G. *English Synonymes Explained with Illustrations and Examples from the Best Writers* (London: Baldwin, 1824)
Crabbe, G. *Poems* (London: Hatchard, 1807)
Crewe, G. *A Word for the Poor, and against the Present Poor Law, Both as to its Principle and Practice* (Derby: Rowbottom, 1843)
Crouch, N. *Wonderful Prodigies of Judgment and Mercy, Discovered in near Three Hundred Memorable Histories* (1682; 8th edn; London: Bettesworth, 1729)
Darwin, C. *The Descent of Man, and Selection in Relation to Sex* (2 vols; London: Murray, 1871), vol.1
Darwin, C. *The Expression of the Emotions in Man and Animals* ((London: Murray, 1872)
Digby, K.H. *Mores Catholici: Or Ages of Faith* (London: Dolman, 1846), vol.2
Dodge, R.I. *Our Wild Indians: Thirty-Three Years' Personal Experience among the Red Men of the Great West* (Hartford: Worthington, 1882)
Doyle, A.C. *The War in South Africa, Its Cause and Conduct* (London: Smith, Elder, 1902)
Driscoll, C. *The Duty of Showing Mercy to the Afflicted. A Sermon [on Job. Xxxi. 14] for the Famine in Ireland* (London: Harchard, 1847)
Drummond, W.H. *The Rights of Animals and Man's Obligation to Treat Them with Humanity* (London: Mardon, 1838)
Dunlap, W. *André: A Tragedy* (London: Ogilvy, 1799)
Eitel, E.J. *Buddhism: Its Historical, Theoretical and Popular Aspects. In Three Lectures* (2nd edn; London: Trübner, 1873)
Eliot, T.S. *Collected Poems 1909–1935* (London: Faber & Faber, 1944)
Ellis, W. *Polynesian Researches, during a Residence of Nearly Six Years, in the South Sea Islands* (London, 1829)
Farrar, F.W. *Mercy and Judgement: A Few Last Words on Christian Eschatology* (London: Macmillan, 1881)
Forster, E.M. *A Passage to India* (London: Arnold, 1924)
Galton, F. *Inquiries into Human Faculty and Its Development* (1883; New York: Dent and Dutton, 1907)
Gaskell, E. *Sylvia's Lovers* (2 vols, Leipzig: Tauchnitz, 1863), vol.2
Godwin, W. *An Enquiry Concerning Political Justice, and Its Influence on General Virtue and Happiness* (2 vols; London: Robinson, 1793), vol.2
Grosart, A.B. *The Poems of Phineas Fletcher, B.D. Rector of Hilgay, Norfolk: For the First Time Collected and Edited: With Memoir, Essay, and Notes* (4 vols; private, 1869), vol.1
Grose, J. *Ethics, Rational and Theological: With Cursory Reflections on the General Principles of Deism* (London: for the author, 1782)
Hanway, J. *An Earnest Appeal for Mercy to the Children of the Poor* (London: Dodsley, 1766)
Harrisson, T. and C. Madge, eds *War Begins at Home by Mass Observation* (London: Chatto and Windus, 1940)

Hoare, L. *Friendly Advice on the Management and Education of Children; Addressed to Parents of the Middle and Labouring Classes of Society* (2nd edn; London: Hatchard, 1824)
Hobhouse, L.T. *Morals in Evolution: A Study in Comparative Ethics* (London: Chapman, Hall, 1906)
Howitt, W. *Colonization and Christianity. A Popular History of the Treatment of the Natives by the Europeans in All Their Colonies* (London: Longman, Orme, Brown, Green, and Longman, 1838)
Hume, D. *An Enquiry Concerning the Principles of Morals* (London: Millar, 1751)
Hutcheson, F. *An Inquiry into the Original of Our Ideas of Beauty and Virtue* (London: Ware, 1753)
Huxley, A. *Jesting Pilate: An Intellectual Holyday* (New York: Doran, 1926)
Huxley, T.H. *Critiques and Addresses* (London: Macmillan, 1873)
Huxley, T.H. *Evolution and Ethics: And Other Essays* (London: Macmillan, 1894)
Ireland, W.H. *The Napoleon Anecdotes* (6 vols; London: Simpkin and Marshall, 1822), vol.1
James, J.A. *Christian Mercy Stated and Enforced* (London: Westley, 1820)
Jameson, A.B. *Characteristics of Women, Moral, Poetical and Historical* (2 vols, London: Saunders, Otley, 1832), vol.1
Johnson, S. *A Dictionary of the English Language* (3rd edn; Dublin: Jones, 1768)
Johnson, S. *The Lives of the Most Eminent English Poets with Critical Observations on their Works* (4 vols; London: Bathurst etc., 1781), vol.1
Kipling, R. *The Ballad of the King's Mercy* (London: Macmillan, 1889)
Knox, V. *Liberal Education: Or, a Practical Treatise on the Methods of Acquiring Useful and Polite Learning* (London: Dilly, 1795)
Kolnai, A. *The War against the West* (London: Gollancz, 1938)
Langhorne, J. *The County Justice. A Poem by One of His Majesty's Justices of the Peace for the County of Somerset. Part III* (London: Becket, 1777)
Lawrence, J. *A Philosophical and Practical Treatise on Horses and on the Moral Duties of Man Towards the Brute Creation* (2nd edn; London: Symonds, 1802)
Lecky, W.E.H. *History of European Morals from Augustus to Charlemagne* (2nd edn; 2 vols; London: Longmans, Green, 1869)
Lewis, C.S. *The Problem of Pain* (London: Bles, 1940)
Lewis, C.S. *Pilgrim's Regress* (1933; London: Bles, 1950)
Madden, R.R. *The United Irishmen, Their Lives and Times* (2 vols; London: Madden, 1842), vol.2
Manners, J. *England's Trust and Other Poems* (London: Rivington, 1841)
Martin, R.M. *The Progress and Present State of British India* (London: Low, 1862)
McCullagh, F. *In Franco's Spain: Being the Experiences of an Irish War-Correspondent during the Great Civil War Which Began in 1936* (London: Burns, Oates and Washbourne, 1937)
Mercy and Truth v. Cruelty and Contradiction. A Reply of the Bristol and Clifton Anti-Vivisection Society to E.D. Girdlestone, B.A. (London: Simpkin, Marshall, 1884)
Moore, F. *Diary of the American Revolution. From Newspapers and Original Documents* (2 vols; New York: Scribner, 1860), vol.1
More, H. *The Works of Hannah More, in Eight Volumes: Including Several Pieces Never before Published* (London: Cadell and Davies, 1801), vol.1
Mostyn Bird, M. *The Errand of Mercy: A History of Ambulance Work upon the Battlefield* (London: Hutchinson, 1913)
Mullens, H.C. *Prsanna and Kamini. The History a Young Hindu* (London: Religious Tract Society, 1885)

Musgrave, R. *Memoirs of the Different Rebellions in Ireland* (3rd edn; 2 vols; Dublin: Marchbank, 1802), vol.1

Necker, J. *An Essay on the True Principles of Executive Power in Great States. Translated from the French of M. Necker* (2 vols; London: G.G.J. and J. Robinson, 1792), vol.1

Newman, F.W. *Theism, Doctrinal and Practical: Or Didactic Religious Utterances* (London: Chapman, 1858)

Nietzsche, F. *On the Genealogy of Morals: A Polemic*, transl. H.B. Samuel (Edinburgh: Foulis, 1910)

Nitobe, I. *Bushido: The Soul of Japan* (1899; Tokyo: Teibi, 1908)

Oswald, J. *The Cry of Nature; or, an Appeal to Mercy and to Justice on Behalf of the Persecuted Animals* (London: Johnson, 1791)

Peckard, P. *Justice and Mercy Recommended, Particularly with Reference to the Slave Trade. A Sermon* (Cambridge: Merill, 1788)

Peggs, J. *India's Cries to British Humanity, Relative to the Suttee, Infanticide, British Connexion with Idolatry, Ghaut Murders, and Slavery in India* (London: Seely, 1830)

Playne, C.E. *Neuroses of the Nations* (London: Unwin, 1925)

Pollock, F. *The League of Nations* (London: Stevens, 1920)

Powys, J.C. *The Pleasures of Literature* (London: Cassell, 1938)

Prasad, D. transl. *An English Translation of the Satyarth Prakash; Literally, Expose of Right Sense (of Vedic Religions). Of Mahrishi Swami Dayanand Saraswati, 'The Luther of India'* (Lahore: Virjanand Press, 1908)

Primatt, H. *A Dissertation on the Duty of Mercy and Sin of Cruelty to Brute Animals* (London: Hett, 1776)

Prince, J.C. *The Poetical Works of John Critchley Prince* (2 vols: Manchester: Heywood, 1880), vols 1–2

Raemakers, L. *Raemakers' Cartoons* (Garden City, NY: Doubleday, Page, 1916)

Ramsay, D. *The History of the American Revolution* (2 vols; Trenton: Wilson, 1811), vol.2

Regan, W.F. *Boer and Uitlander: The True History of The Late Events in South Africa* (London: Digby, Long, 1896)

Rhys, K. *More Poems from the Forces. A Collection of Verses by Members of the Navy, Army, and Air Force* (London: Routledge, 1943)

'The Quality of Mercy': How British Prisoners of War Were Taken to Germany in 1914 (n.d., c.1918)

Robertson, F.W. *Sermons Preached at Trinity Chapel, Brighton by Frederick W. Robertson* (3 vols; Leipzig: Tauchnitz, 1861), vol.1

Savage, J. *'98 and '48: the Modern Revolutionary History and Literature of Ireland* (New York: Redfield, 1856)

Schoolcraft, H.R. *The American Indians: Their History, Condition and Prospects, from Original Notes and Manuscripts* (Buffalo, NY: Derby, 1851)

Seward, A. *Letters of Anna Seward Written between the Years 1784 and 1807* (6 vols; Edinburgh: Constable, 1811), vols 3, 5, 6

Sheridan, W. *Several Discourses: viz. Of Three Books Which Teach Us the Knowledge of God. Of Justice and Mercy in General. Of Mercy in Relieving the Poor. Of Mercy in Forgiving Enemies, and of Humility* (London, Sawbridge: 1705)

Siddons, H. *Practical Illustrations of Rhetorical Gesture and Action; Adapted to the English Drama; from a Work on the Subject by M. Engel* (2nd edn; London: Sherwood, Neely and Jones, 1822)

Sidgwick, H. *The Methods of Ethics* (London: Macmillan, 1874)

Slater, T.E. ed. *Keshab Chandra Sen and the Brahma Samáj: Being a Brief Review of Indian Theism from 1830 to 1884* (Madras: SPCK, 1884)

Smith, T. *The History and Origin of the Missionary Societies* (2 vols; London: Kelly and Evans, 1825), vol.2

Spencer, H. *Social Statics: Or, the Conditions Essential to Human Happiness Specified and the First of Them Developed* (London: Chapman, 1851)

Spencer, H. *A Study of Sociology* (New York: Appleton, 1874)

Suyematsu, K. 'The Ethics of Japan', *Annual report of the Board of Regents of the Smithsonian Institution ... for the Year Ending June 30, 1905* (Washington DC: Government Printing Office, 1906), pp.293–307.

Teeling, C.H. *Personal Narrative of the 'Irish Rebellion' of 1798* (London: Colburn, 1828)

Tennyson, A. *Queen Mary. A Drama* (London: King, 1875)

Thacher, J. *A Military Journal during the American Revolutionary War: From 1775 to 1783* (Boston, MA: Cottons and Barnard, 1827)

Thompson, W. *Poems on Several Occasions, to Which Is Added Gondibert and Birtha, a Tragedy* (Oxford: printed at the Theatre, 1751)

Tonge, E. *Popish Mercy and Justice, Being an Account of Some Later Persecutions of the French Protestants Set Forth [by L. de l'Isle and others] in Their Petition to the French King* (London: Dawks, 1679)

Trimmer, S. *Fabulous Histories: Designed for the Instruction of Children, Respecting Their Treatment of Animals* (London: Longman, 1786)

Tryon, T. *A Dialogue Between an East-Indian Brackmanny, or Heathen-Philosopher, and a French-Gentleman, Concerning the Present Affairs in Europe* (London: Newman and Baldwin, 1691)

Tupper, M.F. *Sacra Poesis* (London: Nisbet, 1832)

Voigt, F. *Unto Caesar* (London: Constable, 1938)

Walker, N. *Fiji: Their People, History and Commerce* (London: Witherby, 1936)

Wallace, A.R. *Darwinism: An Exposition of the Theory of Natural Selection with Some of Its Application* (London: Macmillan, 1889)

Warner, R. *The Cult of Power* (London: John Lane, 1946)

Watson, W. *The Poems of Sir William Watson: 1878–1935* (London: Harrap, 1936)

Weldon, G.W. *A Plea for Mercy to Animals: Being an Argument Briefly Stated against Vivisection* (London: Shaw, 1876)

Wells, H.G. *First and Last Things. A Confession of Faith and Rule of Life* (London: Constable, 1908)

Wells, H.G. *The Undying Fire* (London: Cassell, 1919)

Wells, H.G. *The Salvaging of Civilization. The Probable Future of Mankind* (London: Cassell, 1921)

What One Work of Mercy Can I Do This Lent? A Letter to a Friend (London: Burns, 1847)

Whiteing, R. *No.5 John Street* (London: Grant Richards, 1899)

Why Belgium Was Devastated, as Recorded in Proclamations of the German Commanders in Belgium (1914?)

Whytehead, R. *Claims of Christian Philanthropy, or, the Duty of a Christian Government with Respect to Moral and Religious Education* (London: Simpkin, Marshall, 1839)

Wilberforce, W. *Practical View of the Prevailing Religious System of Professed Christians* (2nd edn; London: Cadell and Davies, 1797)

Williams, C. *War in Heaven* (1930; London: Faber and Faber, 1947)

Williams, H.M. *Letters Containing a Sketch of the Scenes Which Passed in Various Departments of France during the Tyranny of Robespierre, of the Events Which Took Place in Paris on the 28th of July 1794* (London: Robinson, 1795), vol.3

Wilson, D. *Sermons Delivered in India during the Course of the Primary Visitation* (London: Hatchard, 1838)

Wilson, J. *The City of the Plague and Other Poems* (Edinburgh: Constable, 1816)
What One Work of Mercy Can I Do This Lent? A Letter to a Friend (London: Burns, 1847)
Wood, H.G. *Christianity and Civilisation* (Cambridge: Cambridge University Press, 1942)
Yearsley, A. *Earl Goodwin, an Historical Play* (London: G.G.J. and J. Robinson, 1791)
Young, G. *Parallel between King David and King George: A Sermon Preached in Cliff-Lane Chapel, Whitby February 16, 1820, Being the Day of The Funeral of His Majesty King George III* (Whitby: Clark, 1820)
Yutang, L. *Between Tears and Laughter* (New York: John Day, 1943)

Primary articles

'An Act of Mercy. II', *All The Year Round* 8:192 (27 December 1862), pp.372–8
'Adolescens', 'Mercy and Judgment', *Evangelical Magazine* 20 (August 1812), pp.301–3
Binyon, L. 'The Winds of All the World Bring Agonies', *Britain* (New York: British Information Services), February 1943, p.47
Bohnstedt, J.C. 'The Life and Writings of Charles Dickens', *Jahresvericht der höhern Bürger und Real-Schule su Siegen womit zu der am Freitag den 7 April 1854 abzuhaltenden öffentlichen Prüfung einladet Dr Carl Schnabel* (Siegen: Drud and Papier der Vorlander, 1854)
Brackenbury, H. 'Philanthropy in War', *Blackwood's Magazine* (February 1877), pp.152–74
Charques, R.D. 'Evil and Mercy', *Times Literary Supplement*, 16 May 1942, p.245
Clarke, A. 'The Nature and Practice of Mercy. Part 1', *The Arminian Magazine*, September 1796, pp.423–9
Conway, M.D. 'The Pound of Flesh', *The Nineteenth Century* (May 1880), pp.828–39
Croker, J.W. 'Art. IX. The Guillotine', *Quarterly Review* 73:145 (December 1844), pp.235–80
De La Ramée, M.L., 'The Quality of Mercy', *Nineteenth Century* 40 (August 1896), pp.293–305
Ebisawa, A. 'Relation between the Ethics of Bushido and Christianity', *Cultural Nippon* 8:3, 4
'E.M.S.' 'Points for Home Thought. Benevolence – Manliness', *Eliza Cook's Journal*, 5 June 1852, pp.90–1
'Eumenes', 'The Triumph of Mercy', *Evangelical Magazine and Missionary Chronicle* 7 (1799), pp.61–4
Foster, G.B. 'Nietzsche and the Great War', *The Sewanee Review* 28:2 (April 1920), pp.139–51
Gregg, J. 'Misery and Mercy', *Church of England Magazine* 29:840 (24 August 1850), p.135
'Have Mercy on Me', *Quiver* 14:681 (January 1879), pp.609–10
'The Higher Morals in Animals', *Our Animal Friends* 22, April 1895, pp.169–71
Kropotkin, P. 'The Morality of Nature', *Nineteenth Century* 57:337 (March 1905), pp.407–26
Lewis, C.S. 'The Humanitarian Theory of Punishment', *Twentieth Century: An Australian Quarterly Review* 3:3 (1949), pp.5–12
Morrah, D. 'Perennial Values', *Times Literary Supplement*, 20 September 1941, p.468
'The Power of Mercy', *Household Words* 1:14 (29 June 1850), pp.323–5.
Rawnsley, H. 'Ad Misericordiam', *Nature Notes* 12 (January 1901), pp.4–7
Roose, P.W. 'Sweet Mercy', *The Argosy* 65 (September 1898), pp.269–76
Saville, E. 'The Dew of Mercy', *Westminster Review* 173:1 (January 1910), pp.86–95
Sister Rachel, 'The Works of Mercy: Religion in Social Work', *The Living Church*, 22 April 1951, p.23
Spencer, H. 'On Justice', *The Nineteenth Century* 27:157 (March 1890), pp.435–48

Stead, A. 'Bushido, The Japanese Ethical Code', *The Monthly Review* 14 (1904)
Thompson, H.M. 'Moral Instruction in Schools, Concluded', *International Journal of Ethics* 15:1 (October 1904), pp.28–47

Secondary sources

Books

Published in general after 1960.

Ash, S. *Funding Philanthropy: Dr Barnardo's Metaphors, Narratives and Spectacles* (Liverpool: Liverpool University Press, 2016)
Bartlett, T. 'Clemency and Compensation: The Treatment of Defeated Rebels and Suffering Loyalists after the 1798 Rebellion', ch.7 in J. Smyth, ed., *Revolution, Counter-revolution and Union: Ireland in the 1790s* (Cambridge: Cambridge University Press, 2000), pp.99–127
Beiner, G. 'Forgetting to Remember Orr: Death and Ambiguous Remembrance in Modern Ireland', in J. Kelly and M.A. Lyons, eds, *Death and Dying in Ireland, Britain, and Europe: Historical Perspectives* (Dublin: Irish Academic Press, 2013), pp.171–202
Broomhall, S. ed. *Early Modern Emotions: An Introduction* (Abingdon: Routledge, 2017)
Brown, H.G. *Ending the French Revolution: Violence, Justice, and Repression from the Terror to Napoleon* (Charlottesville: University of Virginia Press, 2006)
Burton, J. *Traffic and Turning: Islam and English Drama, 1579–1624* (Newark: University of Delaware Press, 2005)
Chew, S.C. *The Virtues Reconciled: An Iconographical Study* (Toronto: University of Toronto Press, 1947)
Clapp-Itnyre, A. *British Hymn Books for Children, 1800–1900: Re-Tuning the History of Childhood* (Farnham: Ashgate, 2012)
Colpus, E. *Female Philanthropy in the Interwar World: Between Self and Other* (London: Bloomsbury Academic, 2018)
Corten, I.H. *Vocabulary of Soviet Society and Culture: A Selected Guide to Russian Words, Idioms, and Expressions of the Post-Stalin Era, 1953–1991* (Durham, NC: Duke University Press, 1992)
Cowling, M. *Victorian Figurative Painting. Domestic Life and the Contemporary Social Scene* (London: Papadakis, 2000)
Derrida, J. *The Death Penalty* (2 vols; Chicago, IL: University of Chicago Press, 2017) vol.2, eds. G. Bennington and M. Crépon, transl. E. Rottenberg
Dixon, T. *The Invention of Altruism: Making Moral Meanings in Victorian Britain* (Oxford: Oxford University Press for the British Academy, 2008)
Dowling, M.B. *Clemency and Cruelty in the Roman World* (Ann Arbor: Michigan University Press, 2005)
Eustace, N. *Passion is the Gale: Emotion, Power, and the Coming of the American Revolution* (Chapel Hill: University of North Carolina Press, 2008)
Fortier, M. *The Culture of Equity in Restoration and Eighteenth-Century Britain and America* (London: Ashgate, 2015)
Frevert, U. *Emotions in History – Lost and Found* (New York: Central European University Press, 2011)

Frevert, U. et al., *Emotional Lexicons: Continuity and Change in the Vocabulary of Feeling 1700-2000* (Oxford: Oxford University Press, 2014)

Frohock, R. *Heroes of Empire: The British Imperial Protagonist in America, 1596-1764* (Newark: University of Delaware Press, 2004)

Garrett, A. 'Human Nature', in K. Haakonssen, ed., *The Cambridge History of Eighteenth-Century Philosophy* (2 vols; Cambridge: Cambridge University Press, 2006), vol.1, pp.173-7

Goebel, S. *The Great War and Medieval Memory: War, Remembrance and Medievalism in Britain and Germany, 1914-1940* (Cambridge: Cambridge University Press, 2007)

Gray, P. 'A "People's Viceroyalty"? Popularity, Theatre and Executive Politics 1835-47', in P. Grey and O. Purdue, eds, *The Irish Lord Lieutenancy, c.1541-1922* (Dublin: UCD Press, 2012), pp.158-78

Greene, J.P. *Evaluating Empire and Confronting Colonialism in Eighteenth-Century Britain* (Cambridge: Cambridge University Press, 2013)

Griffin, D. *Patriotism and Poetry in Eighteenth-Century Britain* (Cambridge: Cambridge University Press, 2005)

Hall, D.D. *Worlds of Wonder, Days of Judgment: Popular Religious Belief in Early New England* (Cambridge, MA: Harvard University Press, 1989)

Hansen, K.T. 'Knowing the Unknowable: Detecting Metaphysics and Religion in Crime Fiction', in P. Baker and D. Shaller, eds, *Detecting Detection: International Perspectives on the Uses of a Plot* (London: Continuum, 2012), pp.139-68

Hicks, P. 'Napoleon as a Politician', ch.5 in M. Boers, P. Hicks and A. Guimera, eds, *The Napoleonic Empire and the New European Political Culture* (Basingstoke: Palgrave Macmillan, 2012), pp.70-81

Hilton, B. *The Age of Atonement: The Influence of Evangelicalism on Social and Economic Thought, 1785-1865* (Oxford: Clarendon Press, 1988)

Hitchcock, T. and R.B. Shoemaker, *Tales from the Hanging Court* (London: Hodder Arnold, 2006)

Hoock, H. *Empire of the Imagination: Politics, War and the Arts in the British World* (London: Profile, 2010)

Ibbett, K. *Compassion's Edge: Fellow Feeling and Its Limits in Early Modern France* (Philadelphia: University of Pennsylvania Press, 2017)

Kaster, R.A. and M.C. Nussbaum, *Anger, Mercy, Revenge* (Chicago, IL: University of Chicago Press, 2012)

Kemp, N.D.A. *Merciful Release: The History of the British Euthanasia Movement* (Manchester: Manchester University Press, 2002)

Kesselring, K.J. *Mercy and Authority in the Tudor State* (Cambridge: Cambridge University Press, 2003)

Konstan, D. *Pity Transformed* (London: Duckworth, 2001)

Kritzer, A.H. 'Revolution and After. Heroism and Violence in Early National Plays about the American Revolution', in A.C. Muñoz, R.E. Romero and B.M. Martinez, eds, *Violence in American Drama: Essays on Its Staging, Meanings and Effects* (Jefferson, NC: McFarland, 2011), pp.15-27

Lacey, H. *The Royal Pardon: Access to Mercy in Fourteenth-Century England* (York: York Medieval Press, 2009)

McGeary, T. *The Politics of Opera in Handel's Britain* (Cambridge: Cambridge University Press, 2013)

McMahon, R. '"Let the Law Take Its Course": Punishment and the Exercise of the Prerogative of Mercy in Pre-Famine and Famine Ireland', in S.P. Donlan and Michael

Brown, eds, *The Laws and Other Legalities of Ireland, 1689–1850* (Farnham: Ashgate, 2011), pp.133–64

McPhee, P. *The French Revolution, 1789–1799* (Oxford: Oxford University Press, 2002)

Murphy, J.G. and J. Hampton, *Forgiveness and Mercy* (Cambridge: Cambridge University Press, 1988)

Nagel, I. *Autonomy and Mercy: Reflections on Mozart's Operas*, transl. M. Faber and I. Nagel (Cambridge, MA: Harvard University Press, 1991)

Nussbaum, M.C. 'Pity and Mercy: Nietzsche's Stoicism', in R. Schacht, ed., *Nietzsche, Genealogy, Morality; Essays on Nietzsche's 'On the Genealogy of Morals'* (Berkeley: University of California Press, 1994), pp.139–67

O'Donnell, I. *Justice, Mercy, and Caprice: Clemency and the Death Penalty in Ireland* (Oxford: Oxford University Press, 2017)

Oldfield, J.R. *Popular Politics and British Anti-Slavery: The Mobilisation of Public Opinion against the Slave Trade, 1787–1807* (London: Cass, 1998)

Pettigrove, G. 'Passions, Perceptions and Motives: Fault-Lines in Account of Moral Sentiment', in H. Kerr, D. Lemmings and R. Phiddian, eds, *Passions, Sympathy and Print Culture: Public Opinion and Emotional Authenticity in Eighteenth-Century Britain* (Houndmills: Routledge, 2016), pp.203–22

Plamper, J. *The History of Emotions. An Introduction*, transl. K. Tribe (2012; New York: Oxford University Press, 2015)

Punter, D. *The Literature of Pity* (Edinburgh: Edinburgh University Press, 2014)

Quint, D. *Montaigne and the Quality of Mercy: Ethical and Political Themes in the 'Essais'* (Princeton, NJ: Princeton University Press, 1998)

Rahman, A. *George Orwell: A Humanistic Perspective* (New Delhi: Atlantic Publishers, 2002)

Rai, A.S. *Rule of Sympathy: Sentiment, Race, and Power 1750–1850* (New York: Palgrave, 2002)

Rempel, R.A. ed. *The Collected Papers of Bertrand Russell. Vol.13. Prophecy and Dissent, 1914–16* (London: Unwin, 1983)

Resnik, J., and D.E. Curtis, *Representing Justice: Invention, Controversy, and Rights in City-states and Democratic Courtrooms* (New Haven, CT: Yale University Press, 2011)

Sanchez, G. *Pity in Fin-de-Siècle French Culture: 'Liberté, Égalité, Pitié'* (Westport, CT: Praeger, 2004)

Sarat, A. and N. Hussain, eds, *Forgiveness, Mercy and Clemency* (Stanford, CA: Stanford University Press, 2006)

Schramm, J.-M. *Atonement and Self-Sacrifice in Nineteenth-Century Narrative* (Cambridge: Cambridge University Press, 2012)

Schramm, J.-M. 'The Bible and the Realist Novel', in M. Knight, ed., *The Routledge Companion to Literature and Religion* (Abingdon: Routledge, 2016), pp.263–73

Shaw, P. *Suffering and Sentiment in Romantic Military Art* (Farnham: Ashgate, 2013)

Staines, J. 'Compassion in the Public Sphere of Milton and King Charles', in G.K. Paster, K. Rowe and M. Floyd-Wilson, eds, *Reading the Early Modern Passions: Essays in the Cultural History of Emotion* (Philadelphia: University of Pennsylvania Press, 2004), pp.89–110

Strange, C. ed. *Qualities of Mercy: Justice, Punishment and Discretion* (Vancouver: UBC Press, 2001)

Tuckness, A.S. and J.M. Parrish, *Decline of Mercy in Public Life* (New York: Cambridge University Press, 2014)

Warner, M. *Monuments and Maidens: The Allegory of the Female Form* (London: Weidenfeld and Nicolson, 1985)

Wheeler, M. *Heaven, Hell and the Victorians* (Cambridge: Cambridge University Press, 1994)

Secondary articles

Angelis, A.T. 'Painting History: John Trumbull and the Battle of Bunker's Hill', *Prospects* 30 (October 2005), pp.73–85

Baron, J.H. 'Frederick Cayley Robinson's *Acts of Mercy* Murals at the Middlesex Hospital, London', *British Medical Journal* 309:6970 (24 December 1994), p.1723

Cleall, E. 'From Divine Judgement to Colonial Courts: Missionary "Justice" in British India, c.1840 – 1914', *Cultural and Social History* 14:4 (2017), pp.447–61

Conlin, J.G.W. 'Benjamin West's *General Johnson* and Representations of British Imperial Identity; 1759-1770, "An Empire of Mercy?"', *British Journal of Eighteenth Century Studies* 27 (2004), pp.37–59

Dew, S. 'Go and Sin No More': Christian Mercy vs. Tabloid Vengeance', *Criminal Justice Matters* 52:1 (2003), pp.4–5

Duffy, G.F. 'William Smith O'Brien: Petitions of Mercy', *Clogher Record* 15:2 (1995), pp.101–3

Fiering, N.S. 'Irresistible Compassion: An Aspect of Eighteenth-Century Sympathy and Humanitarianism', *Journal of the History of Ideas* 37 (1976), pp.195–218

Fisher, J. '"The Quality of Mercy" in the Eighteenth Century; or Kitty Clive's Portia', *Restoration and Eighteenth-Century Theatre* 14 (1999), pp.19–36

Flegel, M. '"How Does Your Collar Suit Me?": The Human Animal in the RSPCA's *Animal World* and *Band of Mercy*', *Victorian Literature and Culture* 40 (2012), pp.247–62

Foxwell, C. '"Merciful Mother Kannon" and Its Audiences', *Art Bulletin* 92:4 (December 2010), pp. 326–47

Hankey, J. 'Victorian Portias: Shakespeare's Borderline Heroine', *Shakespeare Quarterly* 45:4 (Winter 1994), pp. 426–48

Hestevold, H.S. 'Justice to Mercy', *Philosophy and Phenomenological Research* 46:2 (December 1985), pp.282–91

Hynd, S. 'Murder and Mercy: Capital Punishment in Colonial Kenya, c.1909–1956', *International Journal of African Historical Studies* 45:1 (2012), pp. 81–101

Konstan, D. 'Clemency as a Virtue', *Classical Philology* 100:4 (October 2005), pp.337–46

Langmuir, E. 'Stanley Spencer and the Acts of Mercy – A Suggested Additional Source for the Sandham Memorial Chapel', *Burlington Magazine* 156:1338 (September 2014), pp.590–4

MacKay, L. 'Refusing the Royal Pardon: London Capital Convicts and the Reactions of the Courts and Press, 1789', *London Journal* 28:2 (2003), pp.21–40

Markosian, N. 'Two Puzzles about Mercy', *Philosophical Quarterly* 63:251 (April 2013), pp.169–292

Mohamed, A.S. and R. Ofteringer, '"Rahmatan lil-'alamin" (A Mercy to all Creation): Islamic voices in the debate on humanitarian principles', *International Review of the Red Cross* 97 (2015), pp.371–94

Moore, G. 'The Super-Hun and the Super-State: Allied Propaganda and German Philosophy during the First World War', *German Life And Letters* 54:4 (October 2001), pp.310–30

Murphy, J.G. 'Remorse, Apology, and Mercy', *Ohio State Journal of Criminal Law* 4 (2007), pp.423–53

Nussbaum, M.C. 'Equity and Mercy', *Philosophy and Public Affairs* 22 (1993), pp.83–125

Osanloo, A. 'The Measure of Mercy: Islamic Justice, Sovereign Power, and Human Rights in Iran', *Cultural Anthropology* 21:4 (November 2006), pp.570–602

Pearn, J. 'The Quiddity of Mercy – A Response', *Philosophy* 71 (1996), pp.603–4

Peters, J.D. 'Bowels of Mercy', *BYU Studies Quarterly* 38:4 (1999), pp.27–41

Ransome, W.F. '"Above the Sceptered Sway": Retrieving the Quality of Mercy', *Critica, Revista Hispanoamericana de Filosofia* 40:119 (August 2008), pp.3–27

Ready, K.J. '"What Then, Poor Beastie!": Gender, Politics, and Animal Experimentation in Anna Barbauld's "The Mouse's Petition"', *Eighteenth-Century Life* 28:1 (2004), pp.92–114

Roberts, H.R.T. 'Mercy', *Philosophy* 46:178 (1971), pp.352–3

Sbriccoli, M. 'Le triade, le bandeau, le genou', *Histoire et Sociétés* 9:1 (February 2005), pp.33–78

Smart, A. 'Mercy', *Philosophy* 43 (October 1968), pp.345–59

Spencer, E.V. 'Scaling the Deputy: Equity and Mercy in *Measure for Measure*', *Philosophy and Literature* 36 (2012), pp.166–82

Straight, B. 'Uniquely Human: Cultural Norms and Private Acts of Mercy in the War Zone', *American Anthropologist* 119:3 (September 2017), pp.491–505

Tallbott, T. 'Punishment, Forgiveness, and Divine Justice', *Religious Studies* 29:2 (June 1993), pp.151–68

Tasioulas, J. 'Mercy', *Proceedings of the Aristotelian Society* 103:2 (2003), pp.101–32

van Oyen Witvliet, C. T.E. Ludwig, and D.J. Bauer, 'Please Forgive Me: Transgressors' Emotions and Physiology during Imagery of Seeking Forgiveness and Victim Responses', *Journal of Psychology & Christianity* 21:3 (Fall 2002), pp.219–33

Walker, N. 'The Quiddity of Mercy', *Philosophy* 70 (1995), pp.27–37

Watson, J.C. 'William Artaud's "The Triumph of Mercy"', *Burlington Magazine* 123 (April 1981), pp.228–31

Whitebrook, M. 'Compassion as a Political Virtue', *Political Studies* 50 (2002), pp.529–44

Zachariah, M. 'The Impact of Darwin's Theory of Evolution on Theories of Society', *The Social Studies*, February 1971, pp.69–77

Zyzak, W. 'Mercy as a Theological Term', *The Person and the Challenges* 5:1 (2015), pp.137–53

Index

Above all Nations 144
Acton, Lord 33
actresses, and mercy 38–40
Acts of mercy (artistic representation) 1, 9, 49–50, 53, 138
Afghanistan, British wars with 125
American Revolution 120–5
Americans, Native 59, 123
Amritsar massacre (1919) 142
André, John (executed 1780) 124
Angels 55–6, 61, 130
Anglo-Saxons, and mercy 44, 59, 128, 240 n. 180
animals, and mercy 2, 32, 45, 65–72, 116
Anselm 5
anti-Catholicism 56, 63
anti-Semitism 137, 146
anti-vivisection *See* vivisection
Ascendancy, Protestant (Ireland) 78, 83, 86–7
Asgill, Charles 122, 212 n. 12, 232 n. 49
Asquith, Herbert 92–4
Assize, as metaphor for divine mercy 18
atomic bomb 147, 150–1
atonement 2, 4, 18, 22–3, 26, 29, 46
Augustine 4

Bacon, Francis 1
Band of Mercy Advocate 68
Barnardo, Thomas 64, 66
battlefield, and mercy 2, 50–1, 102, 119, 122–3, 125, 128–9
Beccaria, Cesare 6
Benezet, Anthony 112
Bentham, Jeremy 31–2
Bicheno, James 34
Binyon, Laurence 145, 235 n. 104
biography, and mercy references 8–9, 61–2, 70, 103, 115
Blake, William 18, 153
Boer wars 43–4, 126–7

Botha, Louis (prime minister of South Africa) 93
Bourbon restoration in France, and mercy 100, 103
'bowels' of mercy 72, 130
Bowring, John 72
Bradley, Francis Herbert (philosopher) 32
Brahmo Samaj 29
Brigade, Merciful (branch of Humane Society) 65, 71
Britishness and Englishness, and mercy 41, 59, 120, 135, 137, 143, 147, 150, 153
Brittain, Vera 137, 144, 146
Brontë, Anne 182 n. 118
Bryant, Arthur 138, 144, 149–50
Buddhism, and mercy 26, 29
Bulgarian Atrocities (1876) 117
Burke, Edmund 31, 95, 98–100
Burns, Robert 47
Burton, Robert 17
bushido 26, 60, 144
Buxton, Thomas Fowell 20, 59

Calvinism, and mercy 18, 20
capital punishment 2, 8, 30, 34, 38, 41, 44, 59, 69, 90–2, 107, 114, 117, 135–6, 139, 143, 149
Card, Claudia 5
Carlile, Richard 22
Carlyle, Jane 61
Carlyle, Thomas 45, 95
Catholicism 63, 77, 80–1, 87–8, 93, 95, 106, 119, 130, 137, 140, 143, 151, 153
Cavell, Edith 130
Cawnpore, angel of 55, 107
Cazotte, Elizabeth 96
Celticness 59
Charlotte, Queen of Great Britain (consort of George III) 112, 114
Chesterton, G.K. 52, 137, 143
child welfare 64–5

childhood and mercy 2, 28, 38, 66, 69, 70–2, 125, 130, 142, 149–51
chivalry, and mercy 90, 126, 128, 138
Christianity, claims for mercy 13, 21, 23–4, 26, 28, 67, 117, 135, 142, 144, 154
Church Missionary Society 21, 23
Churchill, Winston 140, 142, 147, 150–1
Clarkson, William 26, 114, 135
Cleall, Esme 9
clemency 1–5, 16, 18, 20, 23–4, 26, 30, 41–5, 48–9, 52, 59, 66, 73, 78–9, 83–4, 88–96, 98–103, 106–7, 116, 119, 120–2, 126–7, 139, 141
Cobbe, Frances Power 59, 61
Cobbett, William 100
Cobden, Richard 64
Coke, Sir Edward 1
Collins, William 43, 54
compassion 1, 3, 5–6, 8–9, 16–17, 26, 30, 32, 38, 41, 43, 59, 61, 70, 119–20, 130, 144, 146, 152–3
concentration camps
    British 110, 126
    Nazis 147
Congo, Belgian 135
Cook, Eliza 43
Cooper, Duff 144
Cornwallis, Charles (1st marquess) 82–4, 122
Cowper, William 105–6
Cox, John Hayter 17
Crabb, George 61
Cromwell, Oliver 8, 78, 94
Cross, Red 126, 130–1, 140, 144–5
cruelty 8–9, 15, 22, 24, 26, 30–1, 32, 44, 59–60, 64–7, 69–72, 80, 82, 102, 120, 123–5, 130, 135–6, 138, 144
Curran, John Philpot 80, 83

Danton, Georges 95
Darwin, Charles and Darwinian ideas 32, 34, 110
Darwin, Erasmus 31
de Gergy, Jean-Joseph Languet 17
de la Fontaine, Jean 72
de La Rochefoucauld, François 157 n. 17
De Quincey, Thomas 46
Derrida, Jacques 2
Desmoulins, Camille 95, 98

detective fiction, and mercy 136
Dickens, Charles 46
Digby, Kenelm Henry 20, 119
Disraeli, Benjamin 87, 90
Duffy, Charles Gavan 89–90
Dyce, William 136
Dyer, General 142

Education, *See* mercy and pedagogy
Egg, Augustus 73
Eichmann, Adolf 150
Elias, Norbert 8
Eliot, George 46
Eliot, T.S. 145
emancipation, female 7, 63, 66
emancipation, West Indies 91, 111, 116
emotions, history of gestures 73
empire and mercy 6, 9, 21, 26, 28, 44, 105–15, 137, 142–3, 150
Enlightenment 1, 6, 29–32, 95
essays, on mercy 44–5, 70, 138
Etty, William 51
Eustace, Nicole 8, 16, 120
eugenics 7, 32, 140
euthanasia 7, 139, 146, 150
evangelicalism 17, 20, 26, 47, 64, 66, 71, 106, 111, 137

factory reform 64
fair play 105, 129
famine, Irish 20, 77, 88
fantasy literature xii, 8
Farrar, Frederic William 19
fascism 2, 140, 145
Febvre, Lucien 7
Fenians 10, 91
Fielding, Henry 45–6
Fiji and mercy 58
Fisher, Herbert 33
Flaxman, John 49
Fletcher, Giles 42–3
Foundling Hospital (London) 64
Frampton, George 51–2
Francis, Pope 153
Franco, Francisco 140–1
Fraser, George 145
freethought 22–3
French Revolution (first) 31, 95–104, 109
fresco 9, 48, 111, 136

Galton, Francis 32
Gay, John 41
gender and mercy 1, 59–63, 73, 89, 136
Geneva Convention 126–7
George III, King of Great Britain 10, 28, 41, 48, 110–12, 121–2
George IV, King of Great Britain 114–15
Gibbon, Edward 30
Gilfillan, Samuel 23–4
Gissing, George 47
Gloucester, Duke of (William Frederick) 113–14
Godwin, William 30
Gollancz, Victor 142, 144
gothic revival 2, 48–9, 54–5, 107
grace 3, 16–18, 43, 60, 63, 70, 72, 83, 120

Halifax, Lord (Edward Fredrick Lindley Wood) 140
Hamilton, Elizabeth 28
Hanway, Jonas 2
Hardy, Thomas 43, 69
Hartley, David 30
Hay, Douglas 7, 99–100
Hazlitt, William 32
Hestevold, H. Scott 5
Hinduism, and mercy 21, 24–5, 29, 137
Hiroshima 147
Hitler, Adolf 143, 145
Hobhouse, Emily 110
Hobhouse, Leonard 34
holocaust, and mercy 146–7, 148
Holt, Joseph 82
Holtby, Winifred 137
homosexuality 150
Howard, John 31
Howells, William Dean 92
humanitarianism 2, 106, 110, 126, 133, 135–6, 138, 146, 149, 151–3
Hume, David 30
Hutcheson, Francis 30
Huxley, Aldous 137
Huxley, Thomas 33, 67
hymns 17, 20, 28, 66, 69, 71–2, 125, 144

India, and mercy 9, 25–9, 44, 105–9, 126, 137, 140–3, 150
India, Empress of 108
Indian mutiny 106, 108, 126

infidelity 21–3
inquisition 20
IRA, and mercy 143
Ireland 38, 44, 54, 59, 63, 77–94, 100, 130, 143, 153
Ireland, young 89
Irishmen, United 79–81, 84, 89, 99
Irving, Edward 18
Isabella, character in Shakespeare's *Measure for Measure* 38, 41
Islam, and mercy 24, 29, 67, 117

Jaffa, poisoning of plague victims by Napoleon's orders at (1799) 102
James, John Angell 23
Jameson, Anna Brownell 38
Jainism, and mercy 26
Japan, and Japanese 26–7, 59–60, 127, 144, 148
Johnson, Samuel 3, 42, 72
Judgement, Last 2, 15
jurisprudence 2, 139, 153
jurors, female 63, 139
juries 59, 79, 87, 89, 99, 138–9
justice 1–9, 15–19, 21–3, 26–33, 35, 37, 41–9, 52, 54, 59–65, 67, 69, 71–2, 77–80, 82–4, 86–101, 103, 105–15, 121–2, 124, 126–8, 130, 132–3, 135–53

Kamerad! 128–9
Kant, Immanuel 1
Karma 138
Kauffman, Angelica 18–19
Kenya 150
Kingsford, Anna 67
Kipling, Rudyard 43, 109, 142
Kitchener, Herbert 126
Krishna 29
Kritzinger, Pieter Hendrik 44, 127
Kroptkin, Piotr 33
Kwannon (Kwanon, Kwanyin) 26–7, 61

Langhorne, John 43
League of Nations 133, 149
Lewis, C.S. 135, 151
Liberalism, and mercy 44, 136
Louis XVI, King of France 96, 98, 100, 122
Louis XVIII, King of France 103
Lubbock, John 69

Macaulay, Thomas 109, 142
Macdonald, George 43
Maeterlinck, Maurice 32
Maori, and mercy 60, 105
Markievic, Constance 94
Martin, Robert 28, 59
Masefield, John 44
Mass Observation xii, 144, 147–8
Measure for Measure 37–8
medicine and mercy 21, 66–7, 125, 152
mercies, small and everyday 9, 148, 153
mercy, and aerial bombardment of civilians 142, 146
mercy, and anthropology 6, 8, 34, 62, 73
mercy, and archives 8–10
mercy, and British constitution 86–7, 99, 139
mercy, and cinema 129, 131, 136, 145
mercy, and classes 57–8, 64, 140
mercy, and Commonwealth 150
mercy, and feminine cruelty 100
mercy, and femininity 3, 48–9, 51, 54, 61–3, 86, 91, 100
mercy, and funerary art, and memorials 9, 49–50, 52, 55, 107, 138, 148
mercy, and infant death (including infanticide) 17, 24, 139
mercy, and Judaism 4, 61, 142
mercy, and male sportsmanship 63
mercy, and manliness 62–3, 95, 119
mercy, and missionaries 9, 21, 26, 28–9, 60, 73, 105, 108–9, 152
mercy, and modernity 5, 137, 151–3
mercy, and pedagogy 70–2
mercy, and physiognomy 73
mercy, and plays 37–42, 136–7
mercy, and poetry 4, 7, 17, 42–4, 59, 61, 72, 102, 107, 111, 117, 121, 125, 127, 145
mercy, and post-war settlement 149–50
mercy, and power 3–5, 8, 26, 31–2, 38, 46, 49, 51, 61–2, 67, 71, 77–8, 80–2, 86, 90–1, 95–6, 101, 103, 105, 108–13, 119–20, 136–7, 140, 142–3, 153–4
mercy, and royal edifices 49
mercy, and royalty 7, 9–10, 31, 41, 86, 88–91, 95–6, 98, 108, 110–16, 119–21, 138–9
mercy, and tableaux 54

mercy, and television 150
mercy, and United Europe 149
mercy, and war criminals 148
mercy, and welfare state 149, 152
mercy, as amateur charity 66
mercy, as discourse 2–4, 8–9, 21, 24, 26, 45, 60, 63, 69, 77, 78, 88, 95, 98–9, 105–9, 111, 116–17, 120–2, 125, 128, 133, 135, 139, 144, 146–8, 150–4
mercy, as emotion (*and as* feeling) 3, 4, 7–9, 16, 23, 29, 32, 34, 39, 70–3, 94–5, 100, 128, 132, 146, 150, 153
mercy, as name 3, 46, 64
mercy, as virtue 1–5, 22–3, 31, 38, 45, 47, 51, 54, 59, 70, 73, 80, 84, 136, 144, 148–9, 153
mercy, Band of 68, 71
mercy, divine (*and* God's mercy) 4, 13, 15–23, 25, 29, 42–3, 46–7, 63, 69–71, 77, 88, 108, 111, 123, 125, 132, 136–8, 147–9, 153
mercy, etymology of word 2–3
mercy, iconography 2, 18–19, 48–9, 107, 114, 138
mercy, in dictionaries and encyclopaedias 3, 15, 38, 41, 73
mercy, in religious paintings 52–4, 138
mercy, individual 4, 6, 46, 59, 119, 126
mercy killings, *See* euthanasia
mercy, League of 65, 130, 139, 149
mercy, medieval 1, 4–5, 7, 18, 37, 47, 61, 87, 119, 128
mercy, to groups 6
Mill, John Stuart 32
Milton, John 18
Mivart, St George 34
Modernism 137
Montaigne, Michel de 1
Montgomery, James 111
More, Hannah 18, 20, 111
Moreau, Madame (wife of General Jean-Victor Moreau) 102
Morley, John 23, 136
Mountbatten, Louis (1st earl) and Edwina, Countess Mountbatten 150
Mulgrave, Lord (Constantine Phipps, 1st Marquess of Normanby) 84–8

Napoleon Bonaparte 8, 101–3
natural disaster 16–17
Necker, Jacques 96–8, 100, 104
New Jerusalem 149
New Poor Law 64
Newman, Francis 23
newspapers and mercy 19, 44–5, 57, 66, 78–9, 90, 93–4, 100, 112, 114, 122, 129, 132, 138–40, 145–7, 151–2
Niebuhr, Reinhold 1
Nietzsche, Friedrich 2, 110, 128
Nightingale, Florence 56
non-English languages and mercy concept *See also* bushido *and* mercy, etymology of word) 60 (Tonga *ofa* and Maori *aroha*), 140 (Russian *miloserdie*), 189 n. 30 (Japanese *jen*), 189 n. 33 (Arabic *rahma*)
novels xii, 16, 21, 38–9, 45–7, 80, 109, 136–7, 142
nursing, and mercy 56, 66, 130–2
Nussbaum, Martha 5, 46

O'Brien, William Smith 88–91
O'Connell, Daniel 84
O'Dell, Stackpool 46
Onward Christian Soldiers (hymn, words by Sabine Baring-Gould) 125
opera and mercy 41–2, 116
oratory 38–40
Orde, Frederick William 44
Ouida (Maria Louise Ramé) 61

pacifism 119, 132, 138, 144
Paine, Thomas 30, 95, 122
peace, and mercy 33, 60, 98–9, 102–3, 107, 109, 111, 119, 127, 130, 132–3, 138, 145, 147, 149, 150, 153
Peel, Sir Robert 87
permissiveness 150
philanthropy 38, 44, 59, 63–5, 108, 138–9, 152
philanthropy, in art 53
philosophy and mercy 5–6, 8, 29–32, 138
pity xii, 3–9, 15–16, 18, 23, 26, 28, 32–4, 59–62, 66–7, 69, 71, 81, 84, 93, 95–6, 98, 117, 124, 128–30, 132–3, 137, 140, 142–8, 152
Pliny, the Elder 69

Pocahontas 58–9
poetry and mercy *See* mercy and poetry
poetry 4, 7, 17, 42–4, 59, 61, 72, 102, 107, 111, 117, 121, 125, 127, 145
of warfare 43–4, 98, 125, 128, 145, 180 n. 81
Portia, character in *The Merchant of Venice* 38–40, 54, 62, 140
pre-Raphaelite art and mercy 54
Priestley, Joseph 30
Primatt, Humphry 66
Prince, John Critchley 61
propaganda, American, on British mercy 121–2, 125
providence 16, 58, 88, 101, 108, 147
Pugin, Augustus 49, 55

Quakerism 81, 112
'Quality of mercy' speech, as Christian text, as set text, as text in court 38, 40, 45, 77
Quran, and mercy 67, 117

race and mercy *See also* anti-Semitism 28, 32, 34, 58–60, 108, 137, 140
rainbow, as metaphor for divine mercy 18, 54
Rawnsley, Hardwicke 69
rebellion, and mercy 9, 77–94, 106–10, 114, 120–1
revenge (and vengefulness, vengeance) 37, 44, 51, 61, 71, 82, 84, 93, 98, 124, 127–9, 132, 136, 144, 146, 149, 153
Reynolds, George 39
Rising, Easter (1916) 92–4
Roberts, Harry R.T. 152
Robespierre, Maximilien François Marie Isidore de 95, 98, 101, 103
Rosenberg, Julius and Ethel Rosenberg 151
Rowe, Nicholas 41
Ruskin, John 47
Russell, Bertrand 132
Russians, and mercy 73, 140–2

Saraswati, Dayanand 29
Sayers, Dorothy L. 241 n. 19
science fiction 8, 136
sculptural mercy 47–52, 55, 107

Seeley, John 63
Sen, Keshub Chunder 29
Seneca 1, 4
sentiment (*and* sentimentalism) 6–8, 29, 33–4, 39, 43–5, 66–7, 69–70, 97, 110, 120, 122, 127, 135–6, 145–6, 153
sermons 15–17, 19, 23, 29, 53, 61, 63, 73, 81–2, 99, 111, 114, 125, 132
Shaw, G.B. 54, 137
Show Trials (Soviet) 141
Schramm, Jan-Melissa 46
Siam (Thailand) 26
Sidgwick, Henry 32
sisters of mercy 56, 63, 130, 140
slavery 42, 106, 109, 110–16
Smart, Alwynne 5, 152
Smithies, Catherine 68, 71
Smuts, Jan 133, 147
soldiers, and mercy 101–2, 119, 125–7, 129, 132, 143, 145
Spanish Civil War 140
Spencer, Herbert 33–4, 60
spiritualism 138
stained glass 50, 127, 148
Stead, W.T. 126
Sterne, Laurence 66
Stone, Marcus 104
Stowe, Harriet Beecher 59
Strange, Carolyn 7
Suffragettes, and mercy 130–1, 136
Swinburne, Algernon 43, 110
sympathy 3, 8–9, 30, 32, 34, 60–1, 69, 71, 88, 105, 108, 132

Tallien, Jean-Lambert 98
Tallbott, Thomas 5
Tasioulas, John 5
Teeling, Charles 79, 82
Teitel, Ruti 99
Teutonic paganism 142
Thatcher, Margaret 152
The Merchant of Venice 1, 38, 100
The Press (Dublin United Irishmen paper, 1797–1798) 79–80, 82
The Task (William Cowper, 1785) 105
The Terror 8, 95–6, 98, 103
theatre and vice 37
theism 23, 29

theology 2–5, 8, 10, 23, 29, 45, 47, 108, 138, 144, 152
Thurlow, Edward 38
Timmins, Thomas 67
Titanic, RMS 136
totalitarianism 140–2, 149
treason, and mercy 28, 41, 80, 90–1, 93, 99
Trimmer, Sarah 20, 67
Trollope, Anthony 46
True Principles of Executive Power in Great States (Jacques Necker, 1792) 96–8
Trumbull, John 122
Turks and cruelty 116–17, 122
Turks and mercy 67

United Nations 2, 148, 152

vegetarianism, and mercy 28–9, 67, 69
Viceroys of Ireland, and mercy 83–9, 94
Victoria, Queen of Great Britain 49, 66, 73, 87, 89, 108
Virgin Mary 61
vivisection 67, 135

war of 1812 125
Washington, George 120, 122, 125
Watts, George Frederic 48
Wells, H.G. 23, 136
Wesley, John 111
Wexford bridge massacre (1798) 81–2
Whewell, William 32
Wilberforce, William 115, 135
William IV, King of Great Britain 114–16
Williams, Helen Maria 96, 98, 101
Williams, Raymond 4
Wilson, Daniel 28, 108
Wilson, John 42
Wollstonecraft, Mary 30
Wood, Herbert 145
Wordsworth, William 44
works of mercy 20, 108, 130, 136, 147, 151–2

Yearsly, Ann 41
Yonge, Charlotte 20
York, Duke of (Prince Frederick) 100

Žižek, Slavoj 110

www.ingramcontent.com/pod-product-compliance
Lightning Source LLC
Chambersburg PA
CBHW052217300426
44115CB00011B/1718